Between the Tracks

Between the Tracks

Musicians on Selected Electronic Music

Miller Puckette and Kerry L. Hagan, editors

The MIT Press
Cambridge, Massachusetts
London, England

This book was set in Stone Serif by Westchester Publishing Services. Printed and bound in the United States of America.

Library of Congress Cataloging-in-Publication Data

Names: Puckette, Miller, 1959– editor. | Hagan, Kerry L., editor.
Title: Between the tracks : musicians on selected electronic music / edited by Miller Puckette and Kerry L. Hagan.
Description: Cambridge : The MIT Press, 2020. | Includes bibliographical references and index.
Identifiers: LCCN 2019055254 | ISBN 9780262539302 (paperback)
Subjects: LCSH: Electronic music—History and criticism. | Computer music—History and criticism.
Classification: LCC ML1380 .B47 2020 | DDC 786.709—dc23
LC record available at https://lccn.loc.gov/2019055254

10 9 8 7 6 5 4 3 2 1

For Pamela Puckette, for her steadfast support and patience

Contents

Preface

We assembled this book to make space for musicians to write about electronic music they feel is undervalued. The European tradition and (doubtless) others obey an inexorable process of sorting and sifting in a process of canonization. We want to look beyond this music. We limited each author to a single piece by their chosen musician in order to put the focus squarely on the music itself. We didn't curate the music at all—only the contributors. The premise of this volume is to grant underrepresented musicians the privilege of in-depth analysis and discussion in a generalized text.

It is traditional in introductions to give a tour of the chapters. Inventing a narrative structure from 12 autonomous choices would be artificial. Nonetheless, in this chaos, we found connecting threads that tied various chapters together.

In chapter 10, Pamela Madsen shows how Anne La Berge shares the responsibility of composing with her performers; in chapter 12, Juliana Snapper details how Cathy Berberian contributed more to Luciano Berio's composition than Berio acknowledged; and in chapter 11, Laura Zattra depicts how Teresa Rampazzi willingly shared credit with the creative collective, but her colleagues are now attributing the work *Taras su tre dimensioni* to her.

Kerry L. Hagan and Marc Battier show how two Asian composers choose to belong (or not) to Western music and to embrace (or not) their Eastern heritage. In chapter 9, Hagan looks at the music of Unsuk Chin, while in chapter 8 Battier does the same for Zhang Xiaofu.

In chapter 3, Leigh Landy studies a soundscape composition by one of the founding composers of the World Soundscape Project, Hildegard Westerkamp, and in chapter 1, Yvette Jackson coins a new phrase, *narrative soundscape composition*, to describe the way Jacqueline George has extended the practice. In chapter 2, Valentina Bertolani describes how Gayle Young makes instruments from the natural soundscape.

David Rosenboom (chapter 6), Jøran Rudi (chapter 5), and Margaret Schedel (chapter 7) show how three composers anticipated algorithmic composition in combinations of analog and digital domains. In many chapters, we hear how the technologies, some new for the time, created the sound of the work. That is most evident in chapter 4, by Miller Puckette.

The diverse backgrounds of our authors result in widely varying terminology. Rather than police definitions between chapters, we embraced the differences between the authors and in their subjects. Nevertheless, the authors tend to use the term *electro-acoustic* consistently to describe the music considered in this text, with minor variations. This usage does not refer to a genre or style but rather to any music mediated by electronic means or speakers. We the editors, however, tend to use the word *electronic* for general purposes, and we had the final say on the book's title.

This book is intended for composers, musicologists, and students of music technology, electronic and computer music, and related fields.

Miller Puckette and Kerry L. Hagan

1 Narrative Soundscape Composition: Approaching Jacqueline George's *Same Sun*

Yvette Janine Jackson

Introduction

This chapter introduces *narrative soundscape composition* as a method for analyzing Jacqueline George's *Same Sun*, a stereo recording released in 2016. I will define and discuss the development of narrative soundscape composition before introducing Jacqueline George, a composer and sound artist who uses field recordings from her Cairo neighborhood to explore and share place with a worldwide audience. Listening to, contextualizing, and reflecting on *Same Sun* are the bases for investigating how the personal experiences of the composer and the listener contribute to a meaningful interpretation of electroacoustic music. Analyses delving into narrative and emotional responses to electroacoustic composition did not find their way into academic discourse until recently (Emmerson and Landy 2016, 15). Narrative soundscape composition is one approach to remedying this oversight.

What Is Narrative Soundscape Composition?

Narrative soundscape composition is a multifaceted term I developed to describe a subgenre of electroacoustic music, a method for pivoting between creative activity and investigative research, and a practice for engaging social issues through sound. It unifies a range of compositional styles that include anecdotal music, concrete melodrama, text-sound composition, and interactive audio games containing narratives that fall anywhere along a spectrum from concrete to abstract. Toward the concrete end, one finds compositions resembling radio drama, wherein voice is used to communicate text related to the plot, sound effects are added to help the listener visualize the location and action, and instrumental music supports the emotional contour of the events that are unfolding. The audience is inclined to have a shared understanding of the story being conveyed. At the abstract end, all elements along the acoustic continuum of speech, music, and soundscape may be manipulated beyond recognition of a coherent story. For example, responding to an abstract composition that shares the same source materials as a radio drama, the listener may be able to identify many of the sounds but be unable to state "This is a story about *x, y, z*" and therefore have to work harder to make sense of the sonic experience. Personal experiences and attributes play a role in how an individual interprets the narrative in works that are situated toward the abstract end of the spectrum.

I use the word *narrative* broadly to mean a series of events that create a story. In soundscape composition, these series of events or facts may receive a linear or nonlinear treatment; the sonic elements may be presented in any order, condensed, expanded, or overlapped. The composer may imply a story via the composition's title and the choice and organization of sonic material, while the listener may be an active participant in the construction of the narrative by engaging their imagination. Jon Appleton uses the term *drama* to explain these narrative accounts as "any series of events having vivid, emotional, conflicting, or striking interest" or "[conveying] a rather specific mood, [giving] rise to laughter or fear" and suggests that the outcome (e.g., change in emotion or mood) is as important as the sequence of events (Appleton 1996, 68). The composer is able to transport the listener from one place or state to another.

R. Murray Schafer brought attention to the concept of the "soundscape" in *The New Soundscape* (1968) and *The Tuning of the World* (1977). Schafer encouraged listening to the world as a macrocosmic composition, and his ideas influenced and developed alongside other participants in the World Soundscape Project (WSP) at Simon Fraser University, including Hildegard Westerkamp and Barry Truax. The WSP, which flourished throughout the late 1960s and 1970s, was established as an interdisciplinary research group, whose combined efforts propelled the field of acoustic ecology. The group's activities and educational goals progressed from archival site-specific documentation to creative recordings and compositions. Schafer spearheaded the group's first major study of locale, *The Vancouver Soundscape* (1973), which focused on source material recorded in 1972 and 1973 around the Vancouver area. This idea was expanded under the direction of Bruce Davis and Peter Huse into a cross-Canada recording endeavor in 1973, and eventually to European villages in Sweden, Germany, Italy, France, and Scotland, resulting in over three hundred tapes for the archive. The 10-part series *Soundscapes of Canada* for the Canadian Broadcasting Corporation aired in 1974, and in 1996 a companion album to *The Vancouver Soundscape* was released (Truax 2016). The World Soundscape Project was initially focused on bringing awareness of the environment and mitigating the negative impacts of our changing world.

At the outset, students were enthusiastic about bringing awareness to the soundscape and environmental issues but were becoming cynical and displaying a "fatalistic attitude that nothing much could be done" (Truax 2012). To counter this mind-set, Truax promoted soundscape composition as an alternative, positive approach to addressing concerns about pollution and the environment. The initial intention of soundscape composition "was to document and re-present recordings of various sonic environments to the listener in order to foster awareness of sounds that are often ignored, and hence to promote the importance of the soundscape in the life of the community" (Truax 2012). Narrative soundscape composition departs from the WSP's objectives by using the process of composing and the resulting composition to create a dialogue between the composer and listener centered on historical events and social issues. It shares the goal of the WSP "to promote the importance of the soundscape in the life of the community" but expands beyond the environmental focus and places greater emphasis on the social aspects of community. The original soundscape composition principles as articulated by Truax (n.d.) appear on the left-hand side of table 1.1.

From its origins as an environmental movement based on listening to the world as a composition, Truax's vision of soundscape composition is a heuristic means of acoustic design that encourages participants to learn from noise and imagine the possibilities of a healthy soundscape. Salomé Voegelin asserts that soundscape composition is based on "poetic intention and educational drive. … [It] evokes a listening somewhere in-between the aesthetic fantasy … and the aesthetico-political demands of sound lobbying for a world heard" (Voegelin 2010, 32). Narrative soundscape composition has the potential to motivate the composer and the listener to learn from one another, engage in dialogue, and become proactive about the possibilities of soundscape as a form of activism.

I have synthesized the World Soundscape Project's tenets with various ideas from composers of programmatic electroacoustic music into the four narrative soundscape composition principles that appear on the right-hand side of table 1.1.

Table 1.1
Principles of soundscape composition (as articulated by Barry Truax) compared to those of narrative soundscape composition

WSP's Soundscape Composition Principles	Narrative Soundscape Composition Principles
• Listener recognizability of the source material is maintained	• Moves freely along all points of the acoustic continuum of speech, music, and soundscape
• Listener's knowledge of the environmental and psychological context is invoked	• Carefully incites the listener's imagination, awakening the theater of the mind
• Composer's knowledge of the environmental and psychological context influences the shape of the composition at every level	• Engages strategies of immersion to help suspend the listener's disbelief within the narrative
• The work enhances our understanding of the world, and its influence carries over into everyday perceptual habits	• Engages strategies of immersion to help suspend the listener's disbelief within the narrative

Kay Kaufman Shelemay applies "soundscapes" to ethnomusicology as a framework by which students examine music in culture by focusing on *sound, setting, and significance* (Shelemay 2015). This method acknowledges sound as the initial sense that informs the listener's understanding of the composition but demands that other information be collected in order to better comprehend the recording. This holistic approach encourages a multisensory interaction with the composition. Through repeated listening, increasing details can be gathered about the sounds or source materials used by the composer and perceived by the listener. Beyond the acoustical properties of the music, Shelemay's concept of setting takes into consideration the performance venue and behavior of the participants. The significance or meaning of the composition is shaped by both the composer's and the listener's personal and cultural backgrounds.

I employ narrative soundscape composition as a pedagogical tool in order to facilitate students' investigation into the ways identity and the intersection of identities can be expressed through sound and music technologies. This approach to ethnographic research uses composition and reflection to develop theses related to class, race, gender, and sexuality. Composition as a means for advancing research is not a new idea. John Levack Drever recommends soundscape composition as ethnography because it can help soundscape practice progress "in a relevant and socially functional way, which reflects the complexities of today's cultures. ... This could mean a greater reflexive mode of operation for the composer, questioning and divulging what he or she may previously have regarded as givens" (Drever 2002, 25). Rather than centering on aesthetic components of analysis, an ethnographic approach to soundscape composition shifts the focus to the "making of representations and consequently power relations" (Drever 2002, 22). This methodology suppresses any aesthetic and artistic tendencies in favor of social and political ones; narrative soundscape composition celebrates the creative act because of its power to be in dialogue with the technical and the political.

Jacqueline George: A New Voice of Egypt

Egypt's position as one of the birthplaces of electroacoustic music traces back to 1944, when the "father of electronic music," Halim El-Dabh, made his wire recorder piece *Ta'abir al-Zaar* (The Expression of Zaar). Four years before Pierre Schaeffer garnered attention for conceptualizing musique concrète in Paris, El-Dabh applied similar techniques using recorded materials as the basis for his compositions. El-Dabh borrowed a portable magnetic wire recorder from an independent local radio station and gained entrance into a women-only healing ceremony known as zaar. His field recordings of women chanting during the exorcism were electronically manipulated into a 25-minute electroacoustic composition that was presented in an art gallery in Cairo.

This landmark composition using recordings from the zaar, which at the time was a ceremony practiced in parts of North Africa and the Middle East, places the listener in a village outside Cairo. The two-minute excerpt of this composition survives as the "Wire Recorder Piece" on which ethereal and reverberant chanting voices can be heard. El-Dabh utilized the studio as an instrument, orchestrating source materials manipulated in an echo chamber and rerecording room with machinery that allowed him to control various parameters, resulting in new timbres (Bradley 2015). His use of the wire recorder technology to capture sounds in and around Cairo for compositional purposes predates the use of the phonograph and magnetic tape in Schaeffer's work. The significance of *Ta'abir al-Zaar* in the context of its place in electroacoustic music history was not recognized at the time and is slowly finding its way into revised, inclusive histories.

El-Dabh was thinking like a narrative soundscape composer, making connections between his creative exploration of sound and the interconnectedness of people, land, and music. This interdisciplinary approach was encouraged by his family's agriculture-related businesses in and around Cairo. In preparing to join his family business, he attended Cairo University and earned a degree in agricultural engineering, which led him to spend time in nearby villages. During this period, he realized the importance and ubiquity of music in the life of the villagers, and his attention to the sounds in relation to his environment began to transform his ways of listening, leading to a career in composition and ethnomusicology. His upbringing, life experiences, and interest in exploring location and culture resonate with the types of socioenvironmental questions raised by narrative soundscape composition. El-Dabh, feeling creatively isolated in Cairo, headed to the United States in 1950, where he eventually held academic positions until his death in 2017.

In this chapter, I do not attempt to draw a direct line in the musical genealogy connecting Halim El-Dabh to Jacqueline George, but I do wish to highlight how the Cairo soundscape is inseparable from George's composing, and I consider her a new voice of electroacoustic music emerging from Egypt. Both composers are listed in Peter Holslin's "A Guide to the Underground Electronic Scene in Cairo, Egypt" (Holslin 2018). Jacqueline George was born in Cairo in 1988; living and working in the region is integral to her creative work, which is focused on identity and social issues. She defines herself as a sound and visual artist, and her music incorporates field recording, creative coding, and a focus on human sounds. Her stylistic influences reflect her academic training and cultural identity. George studied at the Faculty of Art Education in Cairo and received a master's degree in artist's digital games, where she concentrated on digital games as an art medium. Her mentors included Shadi El Noshokaty, with whom she studied early in the new millennium, and Ahmed Basiony, whose life was taken during the revolution in 2011. Basiony introduced her to the concept of the "artist as a researcher," and during this period she began experimenting with visuals, comics, performance art, and the art of sound. He raised her interest in "expression through sound and how to see it" (George, e-mails to the author, 2018–2019). Workshops on human rights studies supplemented George's academic training; her compositions can be read as a social act. The principles of narrative soundscape composition align with George's philosophy and the goals of artist-researchers.

George's prolific output includes improvisation, multichannel and Ambisonic performances and installations, mixed-media composition, visual art, and other solo and collaborative projects. Her live experimental music is programmed in various venues around Cairo, and her live and fixed-media music garner attention in Europe. Works from her repertoire have been presented in workshops, created for radio, and distributed through online platforms. Several of her projects feature girls or women, including the Egyptian Females Experimental Music Sessions (George, e-mails to the author, 2018–2019).

I chose *Same Sun* for this analysis after encountering George's multichannel work at the Borealis Festival in 2017 at the MULTI concert scheduled at Lydgalleriet in the Østre venue in Bergen, Norway. George's *Happening Now* was one of three premieres in an evening of five works heard through the 24-channel speaker rig set up by Trond Lossius, the curator for the event. The fixed-media composition was "inspired by searching for the invisible reality of Cairo" and contained field recordings from Cairo. George diffused an immersive experience for the concert attendees, who were free to seat themselves in any relation to the speakers they desired.[1] Multichannel concerts and sound installations are the ideal venue for being transported by George's narrative works; however, *Same Sun* was selected for this chapter because the recording is available online and easily accessible to readers.

Same Sun

With *Same Sun*, George's usual strategies of immersion, realized through multichannel or multimedia concerts and installations, are distilled into a single stereo track that was released on the Flaming Pines label in 2016 as part of their Tiny Portraits series. The project features sound artists from five continents and was developed by Kate Carr, who hoped "the small personal, story telling [*sic*] nature of these pieces [would bring] a sense of slowness and consideration to thinking about difference and culture, the ways the world connects, and also does not connect, and the different ways we exist and interact with ideas of home, place, and sites of significance" (Ede 2016). Each composer in the Tiny Portraits series was given the same assignment by the label: "to dwell on these connections and disconnections between sound and place, representation and invention by starting somewhere small, somewhere overlooked or obscure, and to interrogate this site using sound." For George, the site of interrogation is Shobra, a Coptic district in Cairo. Listeners with little knowledge of the region might recognize footsteps, car horns, pitch-shifted and muffled voices, machinery, traffic, urban beat-based music, rain, children's voices in recitation, reverberant voices recalling religious chants, low rumbles, rioting in the streets, machine-gun fire, silence, and layers of female voices condensed into an experience lasting 10 minutes 24 seconds. It may be impossible to grasp the form or meaning of the narrative soundscape composition upon initial exposure.

George describes her methods of composition for *Same Sun* as "partly complicated" because of the series of manipulations that take place at the micro and macro levels of manipulating her source materials; therefore, there is no score, official transcription, or Ableton Live session files available for the purpose of study (George, e-mails to the author, 2018–2019). Having knowledge of the composer's tools might make it possible for the listener to reconstruct how the composition was assembled by recognizing certain processing techniques or other means of reverse engineering, but most listeners will only be concerned with the resulting composition as a whole and will not have access to information about the compositional process. Without access to visual representation of the composition, there is a logical incentive to center this analysis on listening, which is congruous with narrative soundscape composition's emphasis on listening. The composer's intent or expectations may be irrelevant to a fruitful analysis. "The intellectual challenges and emotions experienced by the composer are 'independent' from those of the listener" (Roads 2015, 29). We will consider the listener's perspective through macroscopic to microscopic engagements with the soundscape composition.

Analysis

This analysis prioritizes the perspective of the targeted audience, which is presumed to be outside academia. A distinction is frequently made between academic and commercial music. Listeners often regard the former as inaccessible because it challenges expectations of how meter, rhythm, melody, harmony, or instruments should behave. These "plastic" categorizations result in "fixed barriers to appreciation, understanding or learning" (Ramsay 2016, 229). Discogs (2016), a crowdsourced database and marketplace for audio recordings, lists the genre of *Same Sun* as "non-music" and its style as "field recording," exemplifying the difficulty some audiences may have identifying it as a music composition. Flaming Pines promotes and distributes its Tiny Portraits album series primarily through its website, Bandcamp, and Soundcloud, and a wider audience may discover *Same Sun* via social media, blogs, online magazines such as *The Quietus* (Ede 2016), and search engine queries by those seeking information on the composer, label, or Tiny Portraits series.

Listeners wishing to engage *Same Sun* actively as narrative soundscape composition may perceive how the piece is organized more clearly through the process of mapping out the music as I have done. Although the average lay listener may not be motivated to make the effort, producing a visual guide of the recording has the potential to enhance analytical listening; a combination of ears and eyes affords an increasingly nuanced interpretation of the overall meaning of the composition. I have divided *Same Sun* into four sections, A through D, that are characterized by a fundamental sonic layer on top of which other layers are successively added (figure 1.1). The composer's choices are governed by a unique set of rules that shape the arc within each structure. In section A, after the initial sound bed is established, new layers of sonic material fade in, one at a time, until the section ends abruptly. Section B borrows the same formula that governs section A but introduces a new set of sounds. It crossfades into section C, which presents a variation of the same process, but, after it reaches its maximum density, the layers are subtracted until only the initial sound bed of the section remains. A brief silence announces section D, in which three new layers are introduced before reprising sounds from section A. It concludes with the decaying effects of new and reprised materials until they slowly decrescendo.

Section A

The first 90 seconds of *Same Sun* are anchored by a fundamental pulse established by a flanged snare drum pattern that is looped. The two hits of the drum create an off-kilter rhythm that is the harbinger of the rest of the composition. The tempo can be heard

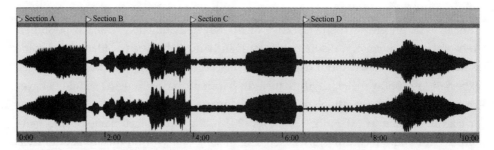

Figure 1.1
A timeline of the sections in *Same Sun*.

as a brisk march at 120 BPM (beats per minute), the default tempo for an Ableton Live session, or as a slow procession at 60 BPM. Read as a march, the snare drum evokes the military, but at the slower tempo, the composition can be felt as a somber procession or protest. Five sonic layers are progressively composed over the drum, each fading in and crescendoing to its peak loudness. A low rumble and footsteps enter promptly, followed by the whine of machinery and intermittent beeping that resembles the timbre of pizzicato strings. About halfway through this opening sequence, a collage of artillery is heard, alternating between single pops and machine-gun spray, and blasts tucked underneath the section. Section A concludes with a rhythmic sequence of honking cars, and in the last six seconds, the passage ends with the guttural sound of a male voice, an unintelligible snippet of speech. The section stops abruptly.

Section B

The next two and a half minutes are unified by a sound bed of machinery. At the start of the section, a female voice can be heard asking in English, "What are you doing?" In Arabic, the male voice responds. For listeners not fluent in the language, the intimacy detected in the tone of the conversation in conjunction with the mechanical sounds stimulates the imagination. One might visualize being inside the workshop of a man who is being visited by a young woman curious about what he is constructing. The sound of the machinery and low-frequency hums increase in loudness, and car horns signal light traffic outside. Voices of young women and music emerging from a sound system move us to an exterior location, the streets of Shobra. The urban rhythms that provide a pulse for this section could be coming from a storefront or a parked car. A thunderstorm triggers emotional tension, and the gradual processing of the rain transforms the sound into something ambiguous that could be interpreted as fire. The voices of children enter and slightly mask the previous sounds. Are the children reciting text in school or playing a game? The listener's imagination and knowledge of the region, landscape, and culture inform this interpretation. The final layer of the section, a chanting male voice, swirls in a reverberant delay. Section B has situated the listener in several spaces, juxtaposing interior and exterior worlds: a workspace, urban streets, a storm, a classroom, and a Coptic church. There is a brief pause in the persistent machinery sounds, and at 3:56 the composition crossfades into section C.

Section C

Section C is sustained by Coptic chanting by a male choir. The voices continue as a low rumble blasts into the soundscape, quickly followed by whistles and cheers from people in the streets of Cairo. The kick and high hats of dance music sneak in, providing a muffled rhythm. The voices in the crowd seem to grow more populous as the reverbera-tion and delay are gradually increased. The last high hat strikes just before 6:19, return-ing the focus to the interior chants from the start of the section, as the outdoor cityscape fades out. The chanting stops, and a few seconds of silence usher in the final section.

Section D

A moment of silence marks the end of all that has come before. The final section of *Same Sun* begins with a heartbeat-like pulse, symbolizing new life. The heartbeat sounds like repurposed microphone breath noise. The first instance is heard as two beats and then continues as an irregular three-beat pattern. The granulation resolution of the first female voice is altered in order to create rhythmic artifacts by shortening the transient envelope to create a gating effect. Additional layers of female voices singing and chanting are added and gradually result in polyrhythms. The pulse of the heartbeat can now be detected oscillating from the left to the right speaker, bringing attention to the stereo field. At 7:43, there is a reprise of sounds from section A—first, the marching footsteps and low rumble. The reverberation and delay times applied to the funda-mental vocal layers begin to increase. The familiar snare returns, followed by honking car horns. The crescendo of the soundscape grows over the next 30 seconds. At 9:01, sibilance in the vocal layers is heightened and creates a rhythmic pattern. Finally, the machine and pizzicato beeping return. The car horns fade out and the mechanical sounds end at 9:27, leaving the delayed voice and footsteps to linger. At this point, we are listening to more of the vocal effect than the original sound source introduced at the start of the section. The listener is left with decaying effects and footsteps, which steadily become quiet until the composition ends.

The timing of the sections and the major events within them are as follows:

Section A (0:00–1:34)

0:00   two flanged snare hits looping and building to a crescendo

0:16   a looped rhythm evocative of marching footsteps accompanied by a low rumble and high hiss

0:40   machinery (bandsaw or table saw) and a two-pitch pizzicato pattern

0:45   gunfire montage

1:06   honking car horns

1:26   male vocal snippet

Section B (1:34–3:56)

1:34   table saw, conversation, outdoor ambiance

2:07   young female voices and music on the streets

2:45	thunder and rain
2:58	children's voices
3:05	male Coptic voices, delayed

Section C (3:56–6:28)

3:56	Coptic chanting, multiple reverberant male voices
5:15	low rumble, chaotic voices, music
6:19	return to Coptic chants only
6:29	silence

Section D (6:31–10:24)

6:31	heartbeat
6:34	voice, gated effect
6:42	second voice
6:58	third voice
7:13	fourth voice
7:19	fifth voice
7:43	reprise of footsteps
7:58	snare fade-in
8:17	honking horns
8:42	machinery, pizzicato pitches
9:01	return to vocal dominance
9:05	snare fade-out
9:27	machinery and pizzicato beeps fade out
9:43	female vocals begin slow fade-out
10:08	slow fade-out of footsteps

Transcribing the sonic events in *Same Sun* creates a visual guide that allows listeners to see the grammar George uses to organize the composition; these rules may be difficult to intuit by listening alone. The composer may not even be cognizant of these rules while composing as she "creates a pattern of acoustic sensations in the form of a code [which] organizes the sensations into meaningful structure" (Roads 2015, 29). Within a composition, the composer's grammar affects the emotional contour of the listener's experience. Across compositions, George's grammar may be used to establish a distinct style that helps the listener distinguish her output from that of other composers. For example, in 2016, George composed *Insect Party* for the "One Minute Symphony" online project for the Spanish label Endogamic. The album, subtitled *Apología de los insectos*, contains 134 contributions of 60-second compositions evoking insects. *Insect Party* begins with a two-chord electric guitar riff with a cymbal crash on the second chord. This repeats as the foundational bed and is layered by a rhythm created out of a buzzing insect seven seconds in. At 0:23, a second, thinner insect-buzzing rhythm is added to the two repeating layers, and the guitar gradually fades out. Around 0:38, a sound evocative of marching slowly fades in. This footstep rhythm is from the same source material that enters at 0:16 in *Same Sun*, although it has been mixed differently. The pace of layering and the choice of source materials are part of George's signature aesthetic. In another example, similar grammatical characteristics are detectable in *Death Proofs Eternity*, George's "multimodal experimental music performance" that was composed for "environmental recordings, cello, oud, violin, and flute with visual and movement interaction about the concept of death in Copts philosophy" (George, e-mails to the author, 2018–2019). She composed a score for the multiple performers, and the work premiered in 2018 at the Goethe Institute, Cairo. The performance exhibits many of the markers common to George's other compositions—the Cairo soundscape, Coptic references, and a social message grounded in cultural philosophy.

Soundscape composition calls for the recognizability of the source material to be maintained. While repeated listening to *Same Sun* allows the structure of the composition to become more apparent, I become less confident in the accuracy of my identification of the source materials; the repetition causes the recognition of some sounds to become increasingly ambiguous. George's use of effects processing and layering is applied to sounds along all points of the acoustic continuum of speech, music, and soundscape, and her techniques sometimes make it difficult to separate sources. As we are exposed to the Shobra soundscape, the voices in private conversations or chanting, punctuated by dance music, coalesce. The listener continues to build and refine a narrative that emerges each time the composition is played back. My personal experiences and imagination bias my perception. Is it possible to listen to *Same Sun* without creating a narrative? When the listener is presented with two sounds, the mind will work to make sense of these sonic events in relation to one another and begin to form a narrative. Curtis Roads states that only one sound is needed, however, for this phenomenon to be realized: "A drone invites internal reflection and meditation. A doorbell alerts a household. An obnoxious noise provokes immediate emotional reaction. Silence invites self reaction. An intense sustained sound commands attention" (Roads 2015, 319). As the narrative is formed in the mind of the listener, *what* is heard may begin to change. For example, in section B of *Same Sun*, what sounds like rain can also be heard as fire, giving new meaning to the composition as a whole. The transformations of sounds take something recognizable and reposition the sound's meaning through reverberation, delay, gating, and other effects. George has shared that *Same Sun* contains "recordings from Cairo streets, a revolution acclaim, Coptic praise and writings recorded by voice" created using Ableton Live (George, e-mails to the author, 2018–2019). The final text in section D is spoken by the author and translates as follows:

> I am the eternal child
> I'll tell him I'm younger than him
> Bigger than, Younger than, Who can be sure?

Listening to *Same Sun* as a narrative soundscape composition requires participation from the audience, who must draw from individual preexisting knowledge, previous experiences, and their imagination in order to engage with the work. The listener may not be able to rely on heuristic knowledge, as with melodic or tonal music, in order to understand and anticipate what will happen next (Huron 2007, 92). Interpretation of *Same Sun* may be further affected by the audience's varying degrees of understanding of the Arab Spring movement and the Egyptian Revolution in 2011 and by exposure to the Tiny Portraits series, Jacqueline George, and her other compositions. A passive listening experience is not likely to convey significant meaning; narrative soundscape composition raises awareness of social issues by leading to discussion and sometimes activism, although that may not always be the explicit goal of the composer. In *Listening to Noise and Silence*, Voegelin points out that "listening is not a receptive mode but a method of exploration, a mode of 'walking' through the soundscape/the sound work. What I hear is discovered not received, and this discovery is generative, a fantasy: always different and subjective and continually, presently now" (Voegelin 2010, 4). For each listener, these combinations of sound sources will generate different images in the theater of the mind. The juxtaposition of source materials in *Same Sun* provokes a specific image of Cairo, suggesting urbanity, violence, and revolution but also humanity and possibility. The sounds of the snare drum, marching, voices speaking, Coptic chants, and machine-gun blasts call to mind the 2011 Egyptian Revolution, which took place just five years before the track was released.

In soundscape composition, the composer presents a series of sonic events that alter the listener's mood from one state to another, and the listener contributes to the experience of the composition by connecting these elements in order to create a story. Jacqueline George is "looking for creative potential inside Cairo's noise, fascinated by how noise carries ideas and mental images" (George, e-mails to the author, 2018–2019). Narrative soundscape composition attempts to activate the theater of the mind, motivating the listener to envision scenes as the sounds play. The potential for creating a vivid spectacle is influenced by the imagination as well as by the way the listening experience is mediated. Listening to *Same Sun* via the Tiny Portraits website will likely direct attention to the text and images on the screen rather than affording a purely acousmatic experience. Some listeners might find that a listening environment devoid of visual stimuli fosters a more conducive setting for igniting the visual imagination.

According to *The Quietus*, "In [an] exploration of sound, space and political, religious and cultural geographies, [George] has composed a piece plotting a journey in the Shobra district of Cairo, which presents the different ways commercial, religious and political agendas compete for sonic space in the streets." For the composer, the exercise of exploring home for the purposes of the Tiny Portraits series forces self-reflection about identity, home, and how and what to convey to a wider audience. George is able to transmit sociopolitical ideas to the listener that prompt dialogue or further action.

Interpreting the Extramusical

The title, program notes, album art, production methods, and events contemporaneous with the time in which *Same Sun* was composed provide contextual information that sways the interpretation of the narrative, in many cases before listening to the recording has taken place. The title is a programmatic clue to the meaning of the composition. The words "same sun" evoke the image of the sun in the sky, daytime. For some, the title might conjure specific thoughts related to humanity, difference, and living together in harmony under a common star. If we have heard the recording or read the program notes, the title places us on the streets of Cairo on a bright day, possibly hot. The title implies unity of people, places, and things under a powerful celestial entity. Our relationship on earth to the sun equalizes our position under its dominion. From the title, we may begin to think about how we are all connected.

Program notes introduce additional text that explicitly reveals the composer's intentions or suggests how the listener should experience the piece, whether read before or after listening. George's notes for *Same Sun* are inserted into the CD-R packaging and are available on the Tiny Portraits website and Bandcamp page:

> Shobra is the largest and most populous neighborhood of Cairo. It is a Coptic word which means "the manor or village." Muhammad Ali Pasha created it in 1809 and it was not originally part of Cairo, but today it is in the heart of the city and replete with people and stories, life and pain, noise … rapid and maybe fickle change, education, action, soul, killing time, presence.
> Jacqueline George, Cairo, Egypt

As we listen with these words in mind, we can see the streets filled with people. We may begin to imagine the faces that accompany the intimate voices in the machine shop in section A or put smiles on the faces of the children heard in section B.

Figure 1.2
Album art for *Same Sun*, released by Flaming Pines in 2016.

The album art functions as an implicit program note. It has the power to set the emotional tone or evoke location or story through the use of color, images, text, and fonts. In figure 1.2, *Same Sun*'s brownish-green shapes atop a black background suggest a Coptic church adjacent to an apartment building with colorful clothes hanging from a balcony. In the upper right, red Arabic text rests at a diagonal. Dark green text displays the album title and the featured country, while the composer's name, district, and city are in white. The text and imagery work together to set expectations that the listener should anticipate an experience related to the urban environment of Cairo. The buildings depicted indicate location, but the people are hidden and only heard in the recording. The album cover's designer, Kate Carr, worked with each composer spotlighted in the Tiny Portraits series, asking them to photograph their neighborhood streetscape. Documenting the streets presented safety concerns for George, so she curated online images of Shobra to send to the designer (Carr, e-mail to the author, 2019). George's agency in choosing the images selected to represent her home are as important as the source materials chosen for the composition. Tiny Portraits exists as an interactive website (see figure 1.3) created by Kate Carr and Arash Akbari exploring "small renderings of place in memory."[2]

Akbari designed and programmed a multimedia experience that features artwork influenced by Google maps. Visitors to the site are greeted by a blue globe floating in a darker celestial blue representing space. The globe can be rotated and magnified to reveal glowing red dots placed around the world. Carr envisioned an interactive platform that would allow users to take a sonic tour by following points along the globe to create a route to explore. Attached to each dot is a blue box with white text displaying the title of a soundscape composition. Using a mouse to hover the cursor over the box, the visitor can see the name of the neighborhood, city, and country where the composition was recorded. Clicking on the title box initiates an animated swipe to a new page, which autoplays the selected track. The eye is drawn to the top of the screen, which has the album art designed by Carr. Below the artwork is the composer's name in a large font, followed by the name of the piece; below that is the location and, in a smaller font, the corresponding latitude and longitude. The composer's notes about the piece are placed at the bottom of the page.

The London-based Flaming Pines label is focused on experimental ambient music. Their distribution outreach is primarily through the social media platforms Facebook and Twitter, supplemented by their website, which links to their releases on Bandcamp. Their discography of 83 releases includes a series of digital albums called Tiny Portraits, featuring artists from Scotland, Japan, Canada, England, Sweden, Russia, Greece, Iran, Latvia, France, Italy, Croatia, Ukraine, Vietnam, Australia, and Hungary. The Tiny Portraits albums are primarily released as a series of single soundscape compositions but are also available in compilations featuring up to four composers on an EP. The packaging

Figure 1.3
Screenshot of interactive Tiny Portraits website designed by Arash Akbari.

of the individual albums as a curated collection provides an incentive for the consumer to discover new composers and to connect fans of one composer to another composer. George receives both a "track by" and "mastered by" credit on the label's Bandcamp page. The project was released as a limited edition batch of one hundred handmade, numbered three-inch CD-Rs with an insert, plus unlimited streaming on Bandcamp of *Tiny Portraits—Jacqueline George*, a "high-quality" download in MP3, FLAC, and other digital formats. The Tiny Portraits website invokes Voegelin's viewpoint of soundscape composition as "occupying a site 'between preservation and invention', an attempt by the composer or field recordist to retain the essence of a site inevitably results via the processes of recording, composition and listening in the creation of somewhere new." The label wants us to consider these very important questions: "In what ways is sound actually able to capture and convey place? Is place something to be captured at all?"

George's field recordings were gathered discreetly using her phone and a portable recorder (George, e-mails to the author, 2018–2019). The recordings, like the images for the album cover, focus on one street from the Shobra neighborhood (Chuter 2017). The source materials were then processed in multiple stages using Ableton Live and then further manipulated during the composition phase of organizing the sounds into a cohesive narrative. Knowledge of the tools used to create a new work might allow listeners who have experience with the same or similar tools to imagine the composer's process, but many active listeners will be satisfied to engage the composition without caring about how it was made. Reflecting on the production tools and processes used to create the piece might lead to a litany of questions. What is lost by *Same Sun* being intended as a two-channel fixed medium rather than a live performance or a multichannel experience diffused to immerse the listener in the soundscape? In what way does private listening, whether through computer speakers, headphones, or beamed to a stereo system via Bluetooth, enhance the meaning of the organized sounds? Does poietic leakage of the composer's intentions interfere with the listener's experience? More importantly, how does the composer transmit her intentions to the listener?

Conclusion

Julian Rhorhuber writes about the exchange of knowledge in networked music, but the ideas translate well to understanding how George's music can impact the listener:

> Sound in general, and voice and music in particular, have often played a key role in cultural techniques of transmission and knowledge exchange, as well as in the reflection about conversation and enquiry. On the one hand, sound is associated with the notion of immediate

connection between phenomena, and the experience of being affected over distance. On the other, it forms a basis for the transmission of signs, and therefore listening is also related to an activity of decoding, to the extraction of meaning that is based on a convention or protocol. Thus the same sound can be perceived in two different ways: as a direct effect of a more or less remote sound source, or as a message encoded into the sound, and left to a listener's interpretation. (Rhorhuber 2017, 138–139)

George fosters an immediate connection with the listener through soundscape composition by imparting her memory and associations of home. The activity of coding and decoding is powered by the reciprocity of imagination from each participant. Although the code carried via the sounds in *Same Sun* remains the same each time it is played, the way the setting and significance of the composition is decoded will shift as the listener becomes more familiar with the recording itself and its related extramusical information.

Jacqueline George represents a new generation of electroacoustic composers emerging from Egypt. Portable recording and production tools make it possible for her to transform her soundscape as she imagines it. "Given the portability of recording and production technology, how will electronic music reflect local and even transient cultures? Does the ease of production imply a healthy democratization of the aesthetic of electronic music or perhaps its corruption" (Schedel 2017, 25)? With a mobile phone, laptop, and digital audio workstation, George is able to experiment with field recordings and text in a way that does not conform to institutional standards. *Same Sun* demonstrates George's effort to use technology to communicate a compositional style that permits her to transform the soundscapes from her Coptic neighborhood in Cairo into an ethnographic investigation. Narrative soundscape composition frames *Same Sun* as a subgenre of electroacoustic music that has the potential to engage the social and invite listeners to contemplate cultural identity and place. Because narrative soundscape composition requires cooperation between the composer and the listener, the potential for the composition to excite the imagination, raise awareness about historical and social issues, and provoke discussion is dependent on the listener's level of participation.

Notes

1. https://jacquelinegeorgen.wixsite.com/jacquelinegeorge/places-s-concepts.

2. http://www.flamingpines.com/tiny-portraits.

References

Appleton, Jon. 1996. "Musical Storytelling." *Contemporary Music Review* 15 (1): 67–71.

Bradley, Fari. 2015. "Halim El Dabh: An Alternative Genealogy of Musique Concrète." *Ibraaz Essays* 9 (5). https://www.ibraaz.org/essays/139/.

Canadian Broadcasting Corporation. 1974. *Soundscapes of Canada*. Vancouver: Canadian Broadcasting Corporation.

Chuter, Jack. 2017. "Attn: Magazine #3—Flaming Pines" (Podcast interview of Kate Carr). *Resonance Extra*, March 28, 2017. https://extra.resonance.fm/episodes/attn-magazine-number-w-slash-kate-carr-2017-03-28.

Discogs. 2016. "Jacqueline George—Same Sun." https://www.discogs.com/Jacqueline-George-Same-Sun/release/10891700.

Drever, John Levack. 2002. "Soundscape Composition: The Convergence of Ethnography and Acousmatic Music." *Organised Sound* 7 (1): 21–27.

Ede, Christian. 2016. "Listen: New Jacqueline George." *The Quietus*. https://thequietus.com/articles/20450-listen-new-jacqueline-george.

Emmerson, Simon, and Leigh Landy, eds. 2016. *Expanding the Horizon of Electroacoustic Music Analysis*. Cambridge: Cambridge University Press.

George, Jacqueline. 2016. *Same Sun* (audio recording). London: Flaming Pines. http://www.flamingpines.com/tiny-portraits/.

Holslin, Peter. 2018. "A Guide to the Underground Electronic Scene in Cairo, Egypt." *Bandcamp Daily*, August 31, 2018. https://daily.bandcamp.com/2018/08/31/cairo-egypt-underground-electronic-guide/.

Huron, David. 2007. *Sweet Anticipation: Music and the Psychology of Expectation*. Cambridge, MA: MIT Press.

Ramsay, Ben. 2016. "Analysis of Foil by Autechre (from Amber (1994))." In *Expanding the Horizon of Electroacoustic Music Analysis*, edited by Simon Emmerson and Leigh Landy, 209–230. Cambridge: Cambridge University Press.

Rhorhuber, Julian. 2017. "Network Music." In *The Cambridge Companion to Electronic Music*, edited by Nick Collins and Julio d'Escriván, 138–139. Cambridge: Cambridge University Press.

Roads, Curtis. 2015. *Composing Electronic Music: A New Aesthetic*. Oxford: Oxford University Press.

Schafer, R. Murray. 1968. *The New Soundscape*. Toronto: Berandol.

Schafer, R. Murray. 1977. *The Tuning of the World*. New York: Knopf.

Schedel, Margaret. 2017. "Electronic Music and the Studio." In *The Cambridge Companion to Electronic Music*, edited by Nick Collins and Julio d'Escriván, 24–37. Cambridge: Cambridge University Press.

Shelemay, Kay Kaufman. 2015. *Soundscapes: Exploring Music in a Changing World*. New York: W. W. Norton.

Truax, Barry. 2012. "From Soundscape Documentation to Soundscape Composition." *Hyper Articles en Ligne*. https://hal.archives-ouvertes.fr/hal-00811391/document.

Truax, Barry. 2016. "World Soundscape Project." https://www.sfu.ca/~truax/wsp.html.

Truax, Barry. n.d. "Soundscape Composition." https://www.sfu.ca/~truax/scomp.html. Accessed August 2019.

Voegelin, Salomé. 2010. *Listening to Noise and Silence: Towards a Philosophy of Sound Art*. New York: Continuum International.

World Soundscape Project. 1973. *The Vancouver Soundscape*. Burnaby, BC: Simon Fraser University.

2 Analysis of Gayle Young's *Ice Creek* (2018)

Valentina Bertolani

There are very few Canadian composers (and composers in general, I daresay) who have been as influential to the international electroacoustic scene as Gayle Young, at least in the last four decades.[1] From 1987 to 2006, she was the editor of *Musicworks*, a publication she collaborated with as far back as 1978. She has also been a member of the editorial board of *Leonardo Music Journal* (Austin 1991). She was secretary of the Canadian Association for Sound Ecology from 1996 to 1999 and a member of the World Forum for Acoustic Ecology. In particular, as the editor of *Musicworks*, she interviewed and reported on dozens of composers, anticipating a very inclusive gaze on the world of experimental music. Her extensive research on Canadian electronic composer and inventor Hugh Le Caine resulted in the book *The Sackbut Blues* (Young 1989).

Since her first compositions in the late 1970s, Young has experimented with a wide variety of sounds and ways of composing and musicking. She has composed dozens of pieces, including music for videos and films; been active with installations and site-specific creations and performances; created her own percussion instruments, the columbine and the amaranth; been a performer of her own compositions and an improviser; performed pieces by Yoko Ono and John Cage, among many others; and was one of the first to earn a Deep Listening® certificate for learning Pauline Oliveros's practice. The list of her achievements could go on. Her work has been presented internationally, and she has participated regularly in festivals and residencies around the world. Her compositions and research have been funded by prestigious Canadian and international organizations, both public and private.

Yet, notwithstanding her undeniable contribution to the contemporary discourse on and in music, almost no secondary literature has been written on her music. The breadth of her work is such that it can barely be encompassed in this book chapter. By focusing on a recent composition, *Ice Creek* (2018), I hope to spark analysis of recurring aspects of her production that are pertinent to the piece at hand and to initiate a discourse on Young's complex and multifaceted sonic world.

Ice Creek (2018)

Young divides her electroacoustic compositions into three groups: "1. Compositions that include synthesized sound, or sound treatment, played live or in pre-recorded format; 2. Compositions that include combinations of pre-recorded sound, such as multi-tracking, but with no changes other than volume envelopes to the sound of the original recording; 3. Compositions in which pre-recorded sound is treated by filtering and resonance" (Young 2019). *Ice Creek* belongs to the second group, as it is written for piano and prerecorded sounds. The piece was composed in 2018 as part of a triptych of compositions for piano and electronics commissioned by pianist and researcher Xenia Pestova with funding from the Canada Council for the Arts. It premiered on June 1, 2018, as part of the New Works Calgary season. The prerecorded sounds are recordings of tuned resonators placed "inside holes in the ice that covered a small waterfall, imparting pitch to the sounds of the water" (Young 2019). The prerecorded sound is not treated other than with volume envelopes. Instead, the piano plays overtones of the bass formed by the resonator recordings. A text describing the setting and the recording process is provided by Young and inserted in the score for use by the performer. *Ice Creek* is about 16 minutes long and is composed of three sections: "Ice Creek" (about eight minutes), "Ice Creek Low" (about four minutes) and "Ice Creek High" (about four minutes). The sections, each of which should be played once, can be played in whatever order the performer prefers. In the performance notes, Young commented that 2018 was the centenary of Debussy's death, and she acknowledges "the influence of his explorations of piano resonance and the harmonies he built based on his observation of higher overtones barely audible in the piano" (Young 2018b).

Resonators

Young has been using long tubes as resonators since the 1990s. These tube-shaped resonators were initially built for site-specific sound installations such as *Les Tuyeaux Sonores* [The Sonic Tubes] (1994), but since 2002 Young has used recordings from these resonators in compositions as well. In 2002, she composed *Fissure*, where, similarly to *Ice Creek*, she used resonators to isolate pitches from a small stream, a waterfall, and the oceanside fissure of the title, a cavelike opening between shoreline rocks with ocean waves slowly washing in and out. For sound in *Tree* (2006), a film by Shelley Niro, she used resonators to isolate pitches in traffic, and in the multichannel installation *Toronto, Hamilton, and Buffalo* (2008), she used resonators to record train sounds. In 2018, the same year *Ice Creek* was released, she premiered *Water Falling* at the Visiones Sonoras Festival in Mexico, combining resonators isolating pitches in waterfalls and the pitches of the strings of the allium, a nine-string instrument she created. Possibly Young finds these resonators so versatile because her experience in building her own instruments leads her to think about them as peculiar musical instruments that need amplification. Without amplification, their use would be impossible because the sound produced would be too feeble (Young quoted in Belair 2019b).

Young discovered resonators to amplify otherwise barely audible environmental sounds in 1994 during an artistic residency in the Lac Saint-Jean area in Quebec, while she and her collaborator, visual artist Reinhard Reitzenstein, were exploring areas for possible outdoor installations:

> As we were watching and listening to the waterfall, it occurred to us that the sound had a resonant low pitch reminiscent of an organ tone. … We tested our perception of the pitch, each quietly humming the note we thought we were hearing, then getting loud enough for the other person to hear: the pitches turned out to be the same, so that we believed the pitch was actually sounding in the environment. This experience became an important influence in the development of *Les Tuyeaux Sonores*: we wanted our installation to bring attention to the sounds of the water. (Young 2002, 123)

This was done using PVC tubing of the kind used in construction and maintenance, cut at half the length of the wavelengths of pitches they wanted to present to people listening through the resonators. In *Les Tuyeaux Sonores*, groups of resonators were assembled at three sites in the area, and at each site people were encouraged to wander from resonator to resonator to explore the amplified frequencies. As Young explained, "This was an installation where people would go up to an assembly of resonators, and actually put their ears against the open ends. There were different lengths of tubing, all in lengths related to just intonation pitch ratios, so you could make your own melody by moving from one opening to another" (Young in Belair 2019b).

The resonators amplify small sounds otherwise inaudible or submerged in louder splashes or roaring sounds of the waterfall. Indeed, Young notices how this type of listening "prompts a sense of intimacy, a personal relationship with the site" (Young 2002, 125). In particular, the need to pause and listen introduced to the spatial and site-specific installation not only a time element but also a direct invitation to slow down, which was appreciated by conservationists. Young recounts that, "The director of the historical site at Val Jalbert expressed appreciation for the role of the installation in slowing people down so that they experienced the place over a period of time instead of rushing up the lift … to the top of the mountain, taking a picture, and immediately coming back down to drive to the next tourist attraction" (Young 2002, 126).

When these resonators are used in compositions, a microphone is placed within the tube to record the sound. The recording is then used to create prerecorded multichannel tracks. Even though this might seem a more composer-centered approach, some of the relational aspects promoted by listening through resonators and explored in the site-specific installation are still recognizable and maintained when used as a compositional technique. For example, the main relational aspect that is preserved in the composition is the invitation to slow down to listen and explore the sonic event in its fullness.

The need for slowing down derives from the need to have a full appreciation of the sonic phenomenon that is happening in a harmonic way rather than from a textural point of view. This need to slow down sonic phenomena, so to speak, was also the main driver that led Young to build her percussion instruments:

> In my last year [1976–1977], in David Rosenboom's composition class, we studied Harry Partch and Iannis Xenakis. I studied their work in quite a bit of detail, and the problem ... was that it is so complex that you can't really hear what's going on. That was my initial impetus to build the metal percussion instrument, Columbine: so I could hear what was going on. At that point I didn't even know if it mattered, or if I could hear the difference. What if you switch from a C major chord where the fifth is perfectly tuned to a D major chord where it's not perfectly tuned? Could you tell the difference? I've concluded that you can't tell the difference if the sound is not sustained long enough. (Young in Belair 2019a)

The pianist interacting with the prerecorded multichannel tracks created with the resonators in *Ice Creek* may respond similarly to the participants in the site-specific installation. It will become clear that the performer is required to do a very similar action, that of listening and picking their melodic path among the gamut of over-tones assigned in relation to the recorded pitches from the resonators—an action that requires time to inquire into and react to (or explore and respond to, as suggested by Young in a personal e-mail exchange with the author in July 2019).

It is interesting to briefly explore the desire to maintain a harmonic sense rather than a textural one. Young is very explicit in her disinterest in traditional Western harmony, or at least in the dichotomies that structure traditional Western musical syntax (major/minor, dissonance/consonance, etc.). She even avoids the term "resolution," as it would suggest the resolution of a tension between dominant and tonic. Instead, she expresses interest in continua and alternative pitch organizations and what "lies in between." As she puts it, "My habits of perception aren't that different from anyone else's. I still hear all the major/minor, V/I that everyone else does. But I like to also elucidate the possibilities of a continuum between extremes rather than go back and forth from one to the other. To hear the less-defined in-between sounds, that might form a connection between the easily-labelled extremes" (Young in Belair 2019a).

Thus, the harmonic structure that one might expect from Young's music in general, and *Ice Creek* in particular, is not a horizontal sense of harmonic resolution but rather a relational exploration of a bass and its overtone formations in ways that resemble melodic investigations rather than clusters. Young argues that we should not even try to listen to pitches qua pitches but just as a property of sound in time: "Frequency unfolds over time, so if I start with one group of frequencies, they would shift to the next group over a period of time. All the vibrations themselves take place in time—440 vibrations a second vs 880 per second—it all happens in time. A lot of the time we're not aware of that. We have ways of describing music like high notes and low notes which are actually fast and slow" (Young in Belair 2019b).

Text Communicating Musical Parameters

Another element displayed in *Ice Creek* that is an original recurring element of Young's work is the creative use of text in her scores. The first fully text-based composition was *Along the Periphery* (1993) for solo violin with electronic treatment. As Young describes it, "Pitches of overtones played on the strings are indicated in the score, but no rhythmic notation is indicated. Instead the musician creates his/her rhythmic playing from a text shown in the score" (Young 2019). In an earlier piece, *Usque Ad Mare* (1981), for four synthesizers, texts describe "changing timbres to be set and then implemented by the performers" (Young 2019).

Young's first food-based ("recipe") piece was *Black Bean Soup* (1994) for any combination of 12-tone and 19-tone instruments, premiered by Critical Band with 19-tone electric guitar (John Gzowski) and violin (Malcolm Goldstein), performed in Toronto and at the Newfoundland Sound Symposium in July 1998. Her recipe pieces are based on written descriptions of methods and variations of food preparation (thus acknowledging that their realization will be a little different every time). She has penned texts that are placed under the staff for the performers to see. These texts provide a varied pool of details.

Texts can be highly evocative of related outdoor experiences and rich with environmental details as in *Ice Creek*, or *As Trees Grow* (2015) for piano and electronics, also premiered by Xenia Pestova. In the latter, the texts describe six food-bearing trees in Umbria, the Italian region where Young was working for six weeks during a composer fellowship with Civitella Ranieri Foundation in fall 2014. Regarding this composition, Young states: "I would use the pitch curve of the spoken text—the intonation—when writing the notes, and that curve would show the phrasing. The scores are not specific about the rhythm, and the overall phrasing is shown in the shape—the melodic contour. The rhythm develops from the way the musician hears the words in the text" (Young in Belair 2019b). Texts can also be about more prosaic actions and highlight more consumerist aspects of our lives, as happens in *Black Bean Soup*, where the text is a recipe for a soup with references to brands such as Kraft and Campbell's (Sutherland and Acord 2007, 130).

Text scores used as frameworks of interaction, similarly to the recipe pieces that Young produced, have a long-standing tradition, and they can also be called "event scores," "verbal notation," and "action scores," among other descriptions. These scores have been widely used by composers whose work is connected to Young's (e.g., Pauline Oliveros, Yoko Ono, Annea Lockwood, and R. Murray Schafer).[2] Also, the very concept of a "recipe" to indicate a framework of interaction is not unusual. The term is often used by dance and theater scholar and dramaturge Pil Hansen in her dance case studies (for example, Hansen and Oxoby 2017). Working on various recipe-like scores, she developed the very useful concept of "performance-generating systems":

> [Performance-generating systems are] rule- and task-based dramaturgies that systematically set in motion a self-organizing process of dance generation. When creating such a system, the focus is not on the completion of a choreographic composition of movements, phrases, series, and interactions with fully set muscle intentionality, tempo, and markers of what takes place where and when in space and time. The choreographer and dramaturg are also not creating frames for improvisation of movement that are based on the dancers' impulses. Rather, when creating a performance generating system, the aim is to arrive at a set of shared tasks and rules that both divides and sharpens the performers' attention, while limiting their options and challenging them to make movement decisions in the moment. (Hansen 2014, 256)

The concept of a performance-generating system will become handy shortly. However, it is important to notice that while some of Young's compositions make partial use of text scores and can be assimilated into recipes or performance-generating systems, her notational use of text is very different from the examples mentioned. Indeed, as well explained by Sutherland and Acord, "What is new here is the use of textual algorithms for musical parameters (rhythm, phrasing, timbre, dynamics, etc.). Within the score, performers find pitch groupings over text—a recipe for black bean soup. The performers create rhythm and phrasing based upon that of the text itself" (Sutherland and Acord 2007, 130).

Analyzing the Score of *Ice Creek*

The notation and indications used are in a fashion that recently has been used consistently by Young, for example in her composition *As Trees Grow* (2015).[3] The score has the piano part in the top four staves, and the bottom two staves notate a four-channel prerecorded track created by using the tube-shaped resonators. The two sets of staves are divided by a text composed of eight verses (see figure 2.1): four for the "Ice Creek" section and two verses each for the sections "Ice Creek Low" and "Ice Creek High."

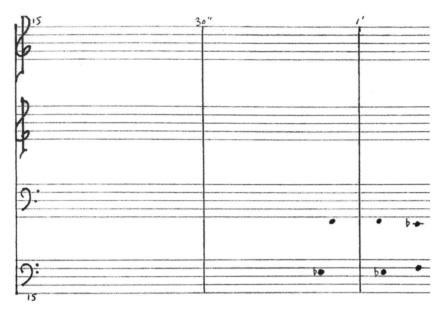

From the trail above the

Figure 2.1
The first 60 seconds of the "Ice Creek" section of *Ice Creek*.

The text describes the environment and the actions of the recording:

"Ice Creek"
From the trail above the waterfall we can barely hear the rushing water,

falling between the steep-stepped rock face and layers of frozen splashes, new drips quickly freezing, ice growing from the edges.

Layers of rippling glittering ice face the morning sun, almost cover the creek, leaving only small dark breathing holes in the centre.

We position one end of a fifteen-foot length of tubing under the ice and listen from the other end to the interior waterfall world.

"Ice Creek Low"

A low hum emerges, louder than the noise of the water, and we gradually notice higher bands of tone, shadows of flickering melodies.

High-pitched splashes tune themselves inside the tubing. In this tiny ice-cave the sounds of the surrounding forest are absent.

"Ice Creek High"

Removing sections of the tube, one at a time, we listen through each shorter length, to a new tone, a higher step in a growing melody,

that carries its own cascading tones and hisses, rhythmic rippling, splashing and dripping, between the ice and the flowing water.

As an additional note to the performer, Young wrote:

Ice Creek (8 minutes): The pre-recorded audio begins on low E-flat and F, later expanding to include A. Repeated shorter-duration E-flat and F tones build in density at four minutes, followed by the introduction of semitones outside the whole-tone pitch set implied by the E-flat, F, and A. An augmented triad on E-natural is established, then expanded by the addition of whole-tone pitches. The piano part at first replicates pitches in the pre-recorded audio, then gradually expands to whole-tone pitch sets throughout the piano register.

Ice Creek High (4 minutes): The pre-recorded audio consists of cross-faded additive sequences of recordings from five tube lengths that form a whole-tone pitch set. Pitches in the piano part are related to overtones of the pre-recorded pitches. Slow pedal tones are combined with the 7th, 9th, and 10th overtones. Paired with these are 14th to 20th overtones notated in higher registers as overlapping groups of four-note and three-note whole-tone clusters.

Ice Creek Low (4 minutes): The pre-recorded audio juxtaposes the three lowest tube sounds, E-flat, E, and F. The piano part shows pairs of pitches in evolving sequences that match the overtones of the pre-recorded audio and those between the piano pitches, shifting among the 14th, 15th, 17th, 18th, and 19th harmonics. Pitches can be played in alternation, in unison pairs, as clusters, and in different octaves. (Young 2018b)

Given all the details described so far, it might seem bizarre that this analysis focuses exclusively on the score for a composition, especially given that the composition has a projected electroacoustic and prerecorded part; the prerecorded part is derived from natural elements that naturally escape writing; and has nonnormative, nonprescriptive notation, so that the written music does not reflect what happens in the performance. Indeed, it might seem that by focusing on the score, I want to erase these elements of uncertainty to inscribe Young's work within the glorious tradition of believing that the score is the sole (or at least the principal) repository of musical knowledge. However, I focus on the score because there is presently no satisfactory audio document that clearly captures the interactions between the prerecorded tracks and the piano part.[4] It is also a choice derived from the very nature of Young's scores, which are places of exploration and dialogue. I therefore hope to identify some decision-making processes, negotiations, and constructed affordances that will make clear how this score is not merely a composition but is instead something between an installation with resonators and a composition. It is indeed a system that generates performance or, quoting Pil Hansen earlier, a shared set of tasks and rules that challenge the performer into making choices in the moment.

For Young, the score is a moment of encounter and attunement among peers. It is indeed a moment of real exchange of information, skills, and even opinions, viewpoints, and experiences. Young's scores reject in a very effective way the traditional hierarchy between the composer and the performer. This becomes clear in a statement by Young cited by Sutherland and Acord: "My recipe pieces provide alternative ways of making use of classical training, on one hand, and alternatives to the usual composer/performer roles, on the other. The concept/method expands the levels of creativity that performers can bring to their playing, and they become co-creators in bringing their versions of the pieces into being. Many different approaches are possible, as so few details (tempo, for example) are pre-established (Sutherland and Acord 2007, 130).

As Sutherland and Acord note, "Young challenges the knowledge of music as embodied in a final product and the relational roles of composer and performer. Musicians approaching these works cannot rely on familiarity with institutionalized symbols and cues. Performers must step outside this, drawing upon wider contexts" (Sutherland and Acord 2007, 130). Indeed, in a personal communication with Young, she expressed to me the need to move on from previously used notational strategies that were very normative toward the performers of her music. Instead, she made explicit her compositional need to introduce performers of her music to the liberating experience of improvising her music and to live her performances in a nonnormative way.

In this context, it is not a surprise that pianist and scholar Xenia Pestova is becoming increasingly involved with Young's music. Pestova has analyzed her approach to the score and score studying at length. In particular, she extensively analyzed what the performer's challenges are in various performance setups, including an electronic part to the performance (Pestova 2018; Pestova 2009). Such an inquisitive approach to the act of reading and exploring the score and its affordances is a huge advantage when it comes to performing pieces such as *Ice Creek*.

Prerecorded tracks   The prerecorded track is projected using four channels and uses pitches recorded at one end of a tube-shaped resonator, the other end being placed inside a hole in the ice that covers an almost-frozen waterfall. The resonator is four inches wide and has been cut at different lengths to isolate different pitches. This is also suggested in the text, where in the "Ice Creek High" part the way to isolate higher pitches is described as follows: "Removing sections of the tube, one at a time, we listen through each shorter length, to a new tone, a higher step in a growing melody" (Young 2018a). The lowest fundamental is a low E-flat, produced when the resonator is 15 feet long. The three sections are differentiated by different sets of fundamentals explored in the prerecorded track (see figure 2.2).

Not only is the range of resonators used very variable, going from the wider range presented in "Ice Creek," to a whole-tone collection of five pitches in "Ice Creek High," to the range of a tone in "Ice Creek Low," but each prerecorded section is also constructed in very different ways. "Ice Creek Low" has a bass line with long, resonant tones presented one at a time. "Ice Creek" presents a richer melodic structure that also has superimposition and pitches presented at the same time. "Ice Creek High" has two intertwined melodic lines. The composer differentiates the two melodic lines through notation: one is written with white notes, the other with crossed white notes. While the two melodic lines use the same collection of pitches and very similar intervallic movements, they are treated differently. The one in white notes has an overall upward trajectory, while the one in crossed notes presents a downward trajectory. This

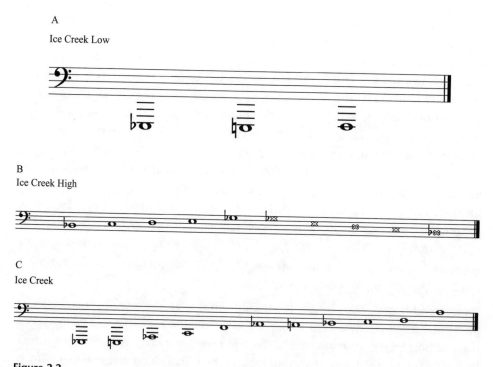

Figure 2.2
Fundamentals of each section of *Ice Creek*: (A) "Ice Creek Low"; (B) "Ice Creek High"; (C) "Ice Creek."

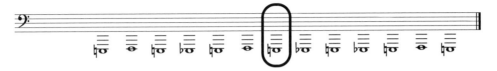

Figure 2.3
Almost perfectly palindromic bass in "Ice Creek Low."

structure of two intertwined different yet related melodies through upward and downward motion resonates with the structure of the resonators' part in "Ice Creek Low." This section is supposed to last around four minutes. Each bar lasts for about 30 seconds. The prerecorded sounds, as noted by Young, explore exclusively the three lowest recorded pitches: E-flat, E, and F. These frequencies are sustained. Except for the last two bars (repeating a final E and then silence), the melodic line these frequencies form is an almost perfect palindrome (see figure 2.3), the only irregularity being the two notes leading to and following the central E, respectively an F and an E-flat.

Notwithstanding the differences among the three sections, the strongest unifying element is the centrality of the E resonator. All three sections have their resonator parts ending in E, even though in "Ice Creek High" it is two octaves above the two others, but E is present in a central position in both "Ice Creek" and "Ice Creek Low." In the latter, the melodic line and its cancrizans structure revolves around E, which is the beginning, the end, and the pivotal element. Similarly, in "Ice Creek," the central bars (at 4:00 and 5:00) are an ostinato alternation of E and F at an interval of a ninth.

Piano Part
As described by Young, the piano pitches are overtones related to the prerecorded bass pitch isolated with resonators from the waterfall recording. While the electroacoustic part of the piece is prerecorded and fixed, the piano part is to be played according to certain indications. For example, in the case of "Ice Creek Low," the piano part includes the fourteenth, fifteenth, seventeenth, eighteenth, and nineteenth overtones of the pitch isolated by the resonator. Among the overtones written in the score, the performer can choose to play the pitches, according to Young, "in alternation, in unison pairs, as clusters, and in different octaves." Even with the freedom granted to the performer, having only five overtones might seem very limiting, especially in "Ice Creek Low," where the bass line is composed of only three pitches and only a semitone apart from each other. Yet the piano material is rather rich. First, the overtones on top of the various bass pitches are rather different. Of the eight different low Es in "Ice Creek Low," each one is given a different set of overtones the pianist can perform with (see table 2.1).

Table 2.1

Some of the sets from "Ice Creek Low"

Bars	Occurrences of E in the bass	Pitches	Overtones
1	E_1 and E_2	D-flat—E—F—G	16th, 17th, 19th [D-flat, not an overtone]
3	E_3	D-flat—D—E-flat—E—F—G-flat	14th, 15th, 16th, 17th, 18th [D-flat, not an overtone]
4	E_4	E-flat—E—F	15th, 16th, 17th
5	E_5	E-flat—F—G-flat	15th, 17th, 18th
6	E_6	E—G-flat—G	16th, 18th, 19th
6	E_7	F—G-flat—G	17th, 18th, 19th
7	E_8	C—E—G-flat	16th, 18th [C not an overtone]

Variations are obtained by changing which overtones are played over the same bass (as table 2.1 shows) or by changing the bass with the same set of overtones as in bar 1. In fact, in the first 30 seconds, the same set of pitches (D-flat—E—F—G) is played over an E (sixteenth, seventeenth, and nineteenth overtones, with D-flat not an overtone) and over an F (fifteenth, sixteenth, and eighteenth overtones, with D-flat not an overtone).

Also, the sixteenth overtone, four octaves above the fundamental, is not listed by Young, but it can be used (maybe considered just as an octave doubling of the fundamental). An interesting element is the use of D-flat in the first 45 seconds of the section. D-flat is not an overtone of E or F but only of E-flat, which appears only in bar 2, after about 45 seconds. Thus, D-flat in the piano part works as a sort of anticipation.

In table 2.1, I treated overtones similarly to pitch classes, following Young's indications that they can be played at any octave. Thus, I played into this freedom suggested in Young's indications. However, there are visual and conceptual cues that if not undermining this suggested freedom at least ask for a moment of reflection before action—a sort of moment of exchange of extra information between the composer and the performer. I would like to call this process a moment of attunement between the different performative and creative experiences between the creator and the performer. These elements that help foster an exchange of experiential knowledge are notational details and the use of the text.

Experiential Attunement between the Composer and the Performer

The way in which the score is written communicates to the performer aspects of the composer's ideas in ways that are not normative and add some personal nuance to the verbal score indications that fall more generally in the tradition of indeterminate music. In fact, the way in which the score is written suggests a closeness to the actual overtone series. For example, G and G-flat are mostly (even though not exclusively) indicated in the central octave, while E and E-flat are mostly (even though not exclusively) indicated in lower octaves.

Moreover, while there are no specific rhythmic indications, there are hints at gestures. For example, while "Ice Creek Low" might suggest a *ribattuto* gesture, "Ice Creek" and "Ice Creek High" suggest at times arpeggios and arabesque gestures. In this sense, the way in which piano pitches are notated is one of the most Debussian aspects of the piece (see figure 2.4). For example, in "Ice Creek" there are groupings suggesting different textures in different registers, a trademark of Debussy's music (see, for example, Parker 2012; Parakilas, Tucker, and Chanan, 2001, 293).

Another aspect that can recall Debussy's style is the whole-tone bass used by Young in "Ice Creek High." It might recall the even-spaced scales used in gamelan ensembles that were appreciated and used by Debussy (Parker 2012).

I call this a moment of attunement between the performer and the composer rather than a direct parameter or indication given by the composer to the performer because it seems to me a more nuanced form of communication. It communicates a different form of knowledge—the experiential knowledge that the composer has of Debussy. This reading of Debussy might or might not be the experiential knowledge that the performer has of Debussy. In deciding how to play the overtones and how to creatively listen and attune the action of the piano produced by the performer to the sound of the prerecorded track fixed by the composer, the performer can also engage in a more intellectual form of attunement by engaging their experiential knowledge to fill the space the hints and prompts provided. This is very similar to what is noted by Sutherland and Acord about Young's *Black Bean Soup*:

> To "know" this piece performers must call upon traditional music conventions such as tuning and pitch notation but must also utilize wider cultural conventions including language, gastronomy and even consumerism (Campbell's and Kraft). Ultimately Young metaphorically highlights the changeability and experiential nature of music itself; as with a recipe, it never turns out the same way twice.
>
> Knowledge is no longer located solely in relations of black notes on a page; it is a wider interaction of varying, individually distinct, socio-cultural contexts. It exists in the interactions of webs of shared meaning and affordance structures, resulting in various configurations, work created together by composers, performers and audiences. [In an email to Sutherland, Young] speculates, "perhaps it is like listening to the poetry of a language you do not understand." (Sutherland and Acord 2007, 131)

These "suggestions" embedded in the notational strategies are paired with another suggestion that works similarly: the text. The text is another element to consider, as it

Figure 2.4

A comparison between (A) register-based motif writing in Debussy (excerpt from Claude Debussy, "La terrasse des audiences du clair de lune," *Préludes* Book 2, 1913) and (B) register-based writing in Young.

provides possibilities to respond to things in two ways: as an idea of what to do (steps) or as rhythms and assonances in the text. The text is partially used to help the performer achieve a more varied and uneven phrasing and rhythm for the piece. However, when Young read the text to me during a Skype call in May 2019 to make me understand how the text could be read, the sounds contained in the text and the meaning contained in the text merged, giving clear cues that the performer could use and work on (literally or creatively) to make their performance decisions. For example, in "Ice Creek Low," Young recited the beginning "a low hum emerges" particularly slowly compared to other parts of the text. "Louder" and "water" were stressed in comparison to "than the noise of," which instead was read calmly, evenly, and more plainly. Similarly, the word "flickering" was said faster, as the meaning also suggests. Yet reading and language pronunciation are forms of a very personal cue. Regional and foreign accents might influence the reading, and certainly, by reading the text to me, Young did not mean to tell me how to read it. She was just sharing how she would read it in that moment. Her personal viewpoint or interpretation is actually offering another possible occasion for a moment of attuning.

Inside, Outside, and the Space of the Performance

A score that can be read as a performance-generating system (i.e., as a sort of recipe that offers clear indications and yet is expected to yield a different result every time) and affords possible moments of attunement between the performer and the composer during the live performance puts on stage a rather intimate situation. That situation is an encounter (and even the possibility of clashes) between different individual and sociocultural contexts and backgrounds, as noted. As we saw at the beginning, resonators were initially used for site-specific installations and were later applied, with little modification, to musical composition. However, the analysis of when and how moments of attunement are created allows us to draw a deeper connection between the initial performative work in installation, in which, as I said earlier, Young was actively trying to create an intimate relation between the listener and the space, and the relationship created between the performer and the composer in her composition.

The installation *Les Tuyeaux Sonores* uses listening as an epistemological and analytical tool to explore the space of possible reactions that listeners could have when invited to spend time with the resonators and their isolated frequencies, by creating their own melodies wandering around from one pitch to the other. *Ice Creek* provides a similar situation for the performer. Rather than having to fulfill a quantitative task—being in time while performing live against a nonflexible prerecorded tape—the relationship to the electronic element in the performance is reversed. Young is asking Pestova or future performers not to rush toward the perfection of the tape and its inflexibility. Rather, she asks them to stop, listen, and make informed decisions on what aspects of what they are hearing they would like to underline with their performance. Similarly to the tourists who stop rushing to the top, taking a picture, and driving away, the result of Young's action is a slowed-down process that allows mindful decision-making and full-body presence in the space and in the time of the present action.

As much as this composition is a hybrid of elements belonging to composition and to site-specific installations, and as much as the score is a meeting place for the composer and the performer, the performance is a meeting place for the audience, which is taken to a place that is neither indoors nor outdoors. In fact, the outside element is brought into the concert hall for people to experience. Yet the piano, with its history and its delicate structure that would be ruined in the outdoor setting from which the recording is taken, invites a commentary and interaction with the outside world. This interaction is deeply rooted in an indoors-only music history (the legacy of Debussy and his indoor rendition of outside elements such as the sea, the wind, architecture, and bucolic landscapes and scenes). The performance practice of this interaction is developed from an outdoor, site-specific form of listening to the natural elements. The result is a personal form of attunement to all these parameters that listeners have to experience and negotiate.

Overall, listening to the microsounds and single frequencies of a waterfall in *Les Tuyeaux Sonores* is a mediated and constructed way of listening to the environment, as those sounds would in normal circumstances be drowned out and made inaudible by the loud noise of the mass of water. Similarly, the experience and space of *Ice Creek* is a fantasy and a cultural construct. It is best met with personal and individual listening as an epistemological tool. This tool informs us about the composition just as much as listening to the composition informs us of our specific modes of listening: How comfortable are we in listening to overtones? Can we connect them to the bass, or do we perceive them as disconnected and not tonal? Are we inside? Are we outside? How was it? What will our next listening action be?

Acknowledgments

I wish to thank Gayle Young for her generosity in offering guidance, help, and time during the writing of this chapter.

Notes

1. Biographical details are available in Colin Eatock and Evan Ware, "Gayle Young." *The Canadian Encyclopedia*, 2006. https://www.thecanadianencyclopedia.ca/en/article/gayle-young-emc. Last accessed May 30, 2019.

2. For anthologies of examples, see, for example, Pauline Oliveros, *Anthology of Text Scores* (Kingston, NY: Deep Listening Institute, 2013). For studies of these scores and techniques to analyze them, see Valentina Bertolani, *Improvising New Consonance: Following the Subterranean Connections between North American and Italian Avant-Garde Collectives (1963–1976)*, PhD diss., University of Calgary, 2018; John Lely and James Saunders, *Word Events: Perspectives on Verbal Notation* (London: Continuum, 2012); Liz Kotz, *Words to Be Looked At: Language in 1960s Art* (Cambridge, MA: MIT Press, 2007).

3. Compare the image with the score excerpt reproduced in Belair (2019b).

4. Even though there is not yet a professional recording, there is a recording available on Soundcloud at https://soundcloud.com/xenia-pestova/gayle-young-ice-creek-version-1.

References

Austin, Larry. 1991. "Introducing the Leonardo Music Journal Editorial Board." *Leonardo Music Journal* 1(1): 2.

Belair, Camille. 2019a. "Generations/Conversations: Gayle Young Part 2." CMC Canadian Music Center—Centre de Musique Canadienne (website), January 10. https://www.musiccentre.ca/node/154861.

Belair, Camille. 2019b. "Generations/Conversations: Gayle Young Part 4." CMC Canadian Music Center—Centre de Musique Canadienne (website), April 3. http://www.musiccentre.ca/node/155292.

Bertolani, Valentina. 2018. *Improvising New Consonance: Following the Subterranean Connections between North American and Italian Avant-Garde Collectives (1963–1976)*. PhD diss., University of Calgary.

Eatock, Colin, and Evan Ware. 2006. "Gayle Young." In *The Canadian Encyclopedia*. https://www.thecanadianencyclopedia.ca/en/article/gayle-young-emc.

Hansen, Pil. 2014. "Dancing Performance Generating Systems." *Theatre Topics* 24 (2): 255–260.

Hansen, Pil, and Robert Oxoby. 2017. "An Earned Presence: Studying the Effect of Multi-task Improvisation Systems on Cognitive and Learning Capacity." *Connection Science* 29, 77–93.

Kotz, Liz. 2007. *Words to Be Looked At: Language in 1960s Art*. Cambridge, MA: MIT Press.

Lely, John, and James Saunders. 2012. *Word Events: Perspectives on Verbal Notation*. London: Continuum.

Oliveros, Pauline. 2013. *Anthology of Text Scores*. Kingston, NY: Deep Listening Institute.

Parakilas, James, Mark Tucker, and Michael Chanan. 2001. "1920s to 2000: New Voices from the Old Impersonator." In *Piano Roles: Three Hundred Years of Life with the Piano*, edited by James Parakilas. , 288–320 New Haven, CT: Yale University Press.

Parker, Sylvya. 2012. "Claude Debussy's Gamelan." *College Music Symposium* 52. http://dx.doi.org /10.18177/sym.2012.52.sr.22.

Pestova, Xenia. 2009. "Models of Interaction: Performance Strategies in Works for Piano and Live Electronics." *Journal of Music, Technology and Education* 2 (2–3): 113–126.

Pestova, Xenia. 2018. "Approaches to Notation in Music for Piano and Live Electronics: The Performer's Perspective." In *Live-Electronic Music: Composition, Performance, Study*, edited by Friedemann Sallis, Valentina Bertolani, Laura Zattra, and Ian Burleigh,131–159. London: Routledge.

Sutherland, Ian, and Sophia Krzys Acord. 2007. "Thinking with Art: From Situated Knowledge to Experiential Knowing." *Journal of Visual Art Practice* 6 (2): 125–140.

Young, Gayle. 1989. *The Sackbut Blues: Hugh Le Caine, Pioneer in Electronic Music*. Ottawa: National Museum of Science and Technology.

Young, Gayle. 2002. "Soundshapes: Public Engagement with Sound." In *Sonic Geography Imagined and Remembered*, edited by Ellen Waterman, 118–129. Newcastle: Penumbra Press.

Young, Gayle. 2018a. *Ice Creek*. Unpublished manuscript, last modified April 5, 2019. PDF files.

Young, Gayle. 2018b. "Ice Creek. For Xenia Pestova. Notes on the Music." Unpublished manuscript, last modified April 5, 2019. Microsoft Word file.

Young, Gayle. 2019. "Gayle Young Electronic Music." Unpublished manuscript, last modified April 5, 2019. Microsoft Word file.

3   Hildegard Westerkamp's *Beneath the Forest Floor* (1992)

Leigh Landy

Setting the Stage

In the introduction to a recent book, Simon Emmerson and I proposed that regarding the analysis of (electroacoustic) music, one should first pose a four-part question (Emmerson and Landy 2016, 11):

- For which users?
- For which works/genres?
- With what intentions?
- With which tools and approaches?

This chapter commences with the answer to this four-part question. The following analysis has been written for a broader readership than many musical analyses because of the very particular nature of soundscape composition. This body of work, although radical in many ways, is accessible to a broad public, given its focus on the known. As appreciation and understanding go hand in hand, broadening this analytical discussion seems a logical step to take. As an example, this chapter examines Hildegard Westerkamp's 1992 composition *Beneath the Forest Floor*. The intention is to investigate relevant aspects of the work in a slightly unconventional manner—as reflected by the unorthodox formatting of this chapter—in particular from the standpoint of the listening experience.[1] However, because we are dealing with a soundscape composition realized by a composer who is committed to having her works act "as a force for ecological engagement with real-world issues" (Westerkamp, personal communication with the author), an analysis excluding those issues would be incomplete. Therefore, the second intention of this chapter is to embed this aspect into the analysis, as clearly many, if not most, electroacoustic works do not engage directly with daily life and certainly do not normally call for social engagement. Other than the straightforward use of the software EAnalysis to assist in making a visualization of this work, no particular tools have been employed. Various approaches are used, reflecting experiencing the work from many angles in order to investigate how one analyzes a soundscape composition. Returning to our book's introduction, we also proposed a "template for analysis" (Emmerson and Landy 2016, 13–18). A selection from this template (e.g., materials, listening behaviors, behavior of materials, ordering, space, intention/reception, and elements specific to a given genre) will be included in the discussion.

ABOUT SOUNDSCAPES: FOR THOSE NEW TO SOUNDSCAPE COMPOSITION, A BRIEF DESCRIPTION OF A SOUNDSCAPE IS IN ORDER, PARAPHRASED FROM THE DEFINITION ON THE ELECTROACOUSTIC RESOURCE SITE (EARS, WWW. EARS.DMU.AC.UK), WHICH IS TAKEN FROM TEXTS WRITTEN BY BARRY TRUAX (TRUAX 1996 AND TRUAX 2000). IT IS A KIND OF ELECTROACOUSTIC WORK IN WHICH ENVIRONMENTAL SOUND RECORDINGS FORM THE SOURCE MATERIAL AND INFORM THE WORK AT ALL ITS STRUCTURAL LEVELS IN THE SENSE THAT THE ORIGINAL CONTEXT AND ASSOCIATIONS OF THE MATERIAL PLAY A SIGNIFICANT ROLE IN ITS CREATION AND RECEPTION. IT IS THUS CONTEXT EMBEDDED, AND EVEN THOUGH IT MAY INCORPORATE SEEMINGLY ABSTRACT MATERIAL FROM TIME TO TIME, THE PIECE NEVER LOSES SIGHT OF WHAT IT IS "ABOUT."

Hildegard Westerkamp puts it this way: "The composer's knowledge of the environment and psychological context of the soundscape material plays an essential and integral part in letting the shape of the composition emerge. … [T]he essence of soundscape composition [is] the free-flowing conversation/relationship between the material/recordings and the composer's musical, creative language, the balance between these and the vast depths of exploration it opens up" (Westerkamp, personal communication with the author). This sentiment is expressed in all her writings closely related to her remark

cited earlier regarding ecological engagement.

TRUAX (1996) ADDS THAT:

LISTENER RECOGNIZABILITY OF THE SOURCE MATERIAL
IS MAINTAINED, EVEN IF IT SUBSEQUENTLY UNDERGOES
TRANSFORMATION.

THE LISTENER'S KNOWLEDGE OF THE ENVIRONMENTAL
AND PSYCHOLOGICAL CONTEXT OF THE SOUNDSCAPE
MATERIAL IS INVOKED AND ENCOURAGED TO COMPLETE
THE NETWORK OF MEANINGS ASCRIBED TO THE MUSIC.

THE WORK ENHANCES OUR UNDERSTANDING OF THE
WORLD, AND ITS INFLUENCE CARRIES OVER INTO EVERY-
DAY PERCEPTUAL HABITS.

THUS, THE REAL GOAL OF SOUNDSCAPE COMPOSITION
IS THE REINTEGRATION OF THE LISTENER WITH THE ENVI-
RONMENT IN A BALANCED ECOLOGICAL RELATIONSHIP.[2]

Writing about what electroacoustic music analysis might entail in a book dedicated to it seems a bit superfluous. Suffice to say that, to me, the main difference is that, other than those analyses studying music of oral traditions, most note-based music analysis is focused on the score and thus on the means of production and notation. A large percentage of electroacoustic music analyses (and of nonnotated forms of music, for obvious reasons) focuses primarily on the listening experience. Naturally, electro-acoustic composers can be asked about how works have been made and, where relevant, performed. Still, only a few use a score as the basis of a work. Those studying music from the standpoint of the listening experience may create a postscriptive score, such as a sonogram, or a more sophisticated representation, using software such as the Acousmographe and EAnalysis, but these are there to offer support, not to dictate the analysis.

There are inevitable and valuable overlaps between note-based and sound-based music analysis, such as structure, pitch, use of sound quality (e.g., timbre and texture), time-related elements, and so on. However, given the distinctive nature of the breadth of electroacoustic composition, including soundscape composition, a host of other aspects need to be taken into account, as is already evident in the description of soundscape composition given earlier. In fact, this description offers an immediate link to what I have called the "something to hold on to factor" in such types of music (Landy 1994). There is an inevitable connection with the sonic material in soundscape composition that offers an access tool to listeners inexperienced with respect to this musical corpus as well as, in the case of Westerkamp's *Beneath the Forest Floor*, the ecological issue being presented. There are thus a number of options for things to hold on to, as will be exemplified in the discussion that follows.

SO HOW DOES ONE APPROACH AN ANALYSIS OF A SOUNDSCAPE PIECE? GOING BACK TO THE FOUR-PART QUESTION, MOST OF THE ANSWER HAS ALREADY BEEN SHARED. IT IS, AMONG OTHER THINGS, THE CONCLUDING SENTENCE OF THE SOUNDSCAPE DESCRIPTION GIVEN EARLIER THAT MAKES THIS ANALYSIS DIFFERENT FROM MOST OTHERS, WHERE ONE SPEAKS OF ESTABLISHING "A BALANCED ECOLOGICAL RELATIONSHIP," SOMETHING WITH WHICH MOST MUSICOLOGISTS ARE NOT INVOLVED. TO BE FAIR, IT IS ALSO RATHER DEMANDING FOR A SINGLE INDIVIDUAL ANALYZING THE WORK TO ESTABLISH. THERE-FORE, ONE CHALLENGE IN THIS CHAPTER WILL BE TO FIND A DISCOURSE THAT ENABLES THIS SUBJECT TO BE INCLUDED WITHIN THE ANALYSIS.

ANOTHER, PERHAPS AWKWARD, QUESTION THAT DESERVES TO BE ASKED AT THIS POINT IS, IS SOUNDSCAPE COMPO-SITION MUSIC? IT IS NOT MY INTENTION TO OPEN A CAN OF WORMS HERE, BUT ONE CAN SIMPLY CITE THE RECEP-TION OF LUC FERRARI'S *PRESQUE RIEN NO. 1: LE LEVER DU JOUR AU BORD DE LA MER*, COMPOSED IN 1970, HIS FIRST SO-CALLED ANECDOTAL COMPOSITION. (ACCORDING TO FERRARI, IT IS NOT SOUNDSCAPE, STRICTLY SPEAKING,

AS HE DOES NOT HAVE SUCH A STRONG PHILOSOPHICAL
STANDPOINT ABOUT ECOLOGY IN SUCH WORKS. NEVER-
THELESS, IT IS STILL OFTEN DISCUSSED ALONGSIDE THE
WORK OF SOUNDSCAPE ARTISTS—SEE, FOR EXAMPLE,
CAUX 2012.) THIS WORK, WHICH WAS RECORDED ON A
BEACH IN WHAT IS NOW CROATIA, COVERS THE EARLY
HOURS OF A DAY WITH VERY SUBTLE EDITS. FIRST
PERFORMED AT THE WARSAW AUTUMN FESTIVAL AND
AROUND THE WORLD EVER SINCE, THE WORK CREATED
ENORMOUS REACTIONS, ESPECIALLY EARLY ON, FOCUSED
ON THE SIMPLE QUESTION, "WHAT IS MUSIC?" I FIRMLY
BELIEVE THAT THE NOTION OF "ORGANIZED SOUND" IS A
GOOD DESCRIPTION OF MUSIC. ARTICULATED IN A DIF-
FERENT MANNER, BOTH THIS WORK AND SOUNDSCAPE
COMPOSITION IN GENERAL *CAN* BE MUSIC IN THE EARS
OF THE BEHOLDER, AND SUCH WORKS DEFINITELY ARE
IN MINE.

Soundscape composition is always based on sampling. One normally thinks of samples in two ways: 44,100 samples per second, as one finds on a CD, or short snippets of sound used in, for example, hip-hop. But samples can be as long as you like (although issues of legal use may become relevant in certain cases). Therefore, it might be said that soundscape composition falls within today's sampling culture regardless of whether some of the samples are subsequently manipulated.[3]

Let's talk about listening. There exist ways of expressing different modes of listening, whether we subscribe to the *quatre écoutes* of Pierre Schaeffer (1977) or terminology emanating from people such as Denis Smalley (1992) or Katharine Norman (1996). I like the term *conduits d'écoute* (listening behaviors) from François Delalande (1998). All this terminology concerns the combination of how attentively we are listening and what we are focused on. Because the following discussion forefronts the listening experience, and the listening experience is the primary conduit of the musical experience, that's what analysis should consider, isn't it?

We normally do not actually focus that much on controlling our listening behavior. Think, for example, of the many people who use background music or television to allow them to tune out. Are they aware of what they are listening to? And, of course, different listeners do not necessarily listen to works in the same way. Extenuating circumstances (e.g., thoughts that have nothing to do with the music "jamming" one's focus, catching one's breath after cycling when arriving late at a concert, and so on) can influence concentration and reception. Still, the composer is often aware of how one is likely to listen in an attentive environment, whether a concert hall or close listening by way of a recording. In such cases, the composer is playing with, and possibly leading, these behaviors.

So what are the listening behaviors relevant to soundscape composition? Using a selection of existing terminology, I would suggest that there are three main active listening behaviors. In this case, I will use my own terminology, including one term borrowed from Schaeffer. Having spoken with many composers of soundscape compositions, I believe the most evident terms are: heightened listening, attentive listening focused on the source and cause of sounds heard and their combination; reduced listening (Schaeffer's *écoute réduite*), almost the opposite of heightened listening, focusing on the quality of the (musical) sounds as opposed to their source and context; and technological or recipe listening, listening to how sounds have been recorded and/or manipulated. There is also a fourth option, "just listening," with less focus on detail and a greater experience of the general flow of things.

However, we cannot overemphasize the importance of these listening behaviors, as we have already concluded that the experience of meaning is important to soundscape. Therefore, another aspect is of great importance here: dramaturgy. This word, when used in a musical context, is mainly restricted to grand forms of Western art music, such as opera and ballet; that is, works involving the stage, performance, and narrative. However, I believe that dramaturgy need not be restricted to such works. I have defined it as follows (from the EARS site): "a term borrowed from theatre which involves the verbal contextualisation of a work or an interpretation or performance thereof. In a sense, the dramaturgy of music is more involved with the question of 'why' something takes place than the 'what' or 'how' of the endeavor. Dramaturgy has always been used to allow someone appreciating art to obtain a greater insight into artists' intention." This last sentence is key. Given that in my opinion the intention/reception loop is more fundamental to soundscape composition than in most other forms of (electroacoustic) music composition, knowledge of the dramaturgy of a soundscape work is of fundamental importance, not least when the audience may include listeners unfamiliar with this method of organizing sounds.

Related to this notion of dramaturgy is another artistic element worthy of mention. Many of the most important pieces I have experienced or been involved in creating have been those that create what I call their own universe. Leaving the universe means entering another reality, which, upon entry, may seem strange even though it's the reality that's part of one's daily life most of the time. Thus, the power of a great work of art is to envelop people in its universe. Most soundscape works are not site specific, meaning that the universe is imagined, which is the case with those works just described. However, soundscapes can be immersive; they can attempt to represent movement in nature (which is very difficult to capture, even using sophisticated recording techniques; for example, the sound of a bird flying from one point in a listening space to another). These are excellent techniques for creating an artistic universe.

Two words deserve to be added to this discussion, albeit with care: *narrative* and *discourse*. John Blacking dealt with the latter in a remarkable manner, stating: "'Musical discourse' can be discourse about music, or the discourse of music. My argument belongs to the first, but is chiefly about the second. It is musical discourse about the discourse of music. It uses the language of words to discuss the language of music" (Blacking 1982, 15). However, discourse is not restricted to language. For example, Simon Emmerson (1986) spoke of the dimension ranging from aural to mimetic discourse in electroacoustic music, where aural had to do with musical attributes such as patterns of pitches and rhythms and mimetic had to do with the signifying potential of referential or extrinsic attributes of sound, which is particularly pertinent to electroacoustic music in general and, more specifically, to soundscape composition.

Is there narrative in a soundscape work? Perhaps not as in a story, but there is a verbal narrative behind each work and, most likely, a less linear one in the composition itself. The handling of discourse in any sense of the term is relevant, and both form part of the work's dramaturgy.

WRITERS ON SOUNDSCAPE (COMPOSITION) TEND NOT TO SPEAK SOLELY ABOUT MUSIC, WHICH SHOULD COME AS NO SURPRISE. THEY ARE NOT ONLY INTERESTED IN SOUNDSCAPES SONICALLY WHEREVER THEY ARE. (AS JOHN CAGE OFTEN SAID, JUST OPEN YOUR WINDOW AND LISTEN; THAT IS, THERE'S MUSIC EVERYWHERE, ALL THE TIME.) THEY ARE ALSO NORMALLY EQUALLY INTERESTED IN SOCIAL ASPECTS RELATED TO SOUNDSCAPE AS WELL AS ARTISTIC ONES, SUCH AS NOISE POLLUTION. THE FIELD OF ACOUSTIC ECOLOGY WAS BORN OF SOUNDSCAPE

SPECIALISTS. AGAIN, TRUAX IS AN EXCELLENT SPOKES-
PERSON FOR THIS EVOLVING FIELD, WHICH TODAY HAS
SPECIALISTS AROUND THE GLOBE (SEE, FOR EXAMPLE,
TRUAX 1984; TRUAX 1999). HIS WRITINGS COMPLEMENT
THOSE OF WESTERKAMP CITED THROUGHOUT THIS TEXT.

Hildegard Westerkamp speaks and writes eloquently regarding her work and the field that fascinates her. In recent years, she has been a frequent keynote speaker on subjects related to acoustic ecology, listening, and her works. One text that pulls important thoughts together is her article "Linking Soundscape Composition and Acoustic Ecology" (Westerkamp 2002), which offers a personal account of many of the issues raised earlier in this chapter.[4]

Westerkamp's writings about her own work are normally focused on dramaturgy. She is fully aware of an intention/reception loop regarding her work and yet, at the same time, she offers her listeners a huge amount of freedom to drift from one mode of listening to another. We will discover shortly how this works in Beneath the Forest Floor. Clearly, ecology, a desire to be in harmony with nature, and a desire to take a soundscape and transform, embellish, and celebrate it artistically are being treated in a single form of artistic expression. But Westerkamp's work goes beyond that—it is about something (e.g., the ecological issue at stake)—and yet we are invited to appreciate parts of her works both in terms of what they are and abstractly, as sound.

... and then there are others who have written about Westerkamp and her work. Of these, I highly recommend Andra McCartney's doctoral dissertation, Sounding Places:

Situated Conversations through the Soundscape Compositions of Hildegard Westerkamp (1999), and Katharine Norman's book chapter "The Same Trail Twice: *Talking Rain* with Hildegard Westerkamp" (2004). *Beneath the Forest Floor* is clearly relevant in both cases, but these texts also focus largely on discussing Westerkamp and her work holistically, not least because of their spending time with her and through their discussions. Both McCartney and Norman investigate Westerkamp's compositions in detail. Both discuss her musical and ecological concerns in equal depth, connecting them with the composer and her ideas. Norman's chapter (along with many of John Cage's writings) also inspired the unusually formatted presentation of the current chapter. Some of the issues that they have discovered in other works by Westerkamp will inevitably be reflected in the following discussion.

Beneath the Forest Floor (1992)

Beneath the Forest Floor was commissioned by CBC radio and produced in their Advanced Audio Production Facility in Toronto. This is important, as it was originally intended as a work of radio art and received a mention at the Prix Italia in 1994. It was recorded on a CD, *Transformations*, in 1996, and, of course, has been presented in concert format. What is relevant here is that, having been commissioned by a radio broadcaster, it had to be a stereo piece. This had implications regarding its use of space that will come up in the following discussion.

Hildegard Westerkamp wrote the following about this piece
(the first three paragraphs from her website/CD text):

"Beneath the Forest Floor" is composed from sounds recorded in the
old-growth forests on British Columbia's west coast. It moves us
through the visible forest, into its shadow world, its spirit; into that
which affects our body, heart and mind when we experience forest.

Most of the sounds for this composition were recorded in one specific
location, the Carmanah Valley on Vancouver Island. This old-growth
rainforest contains some of the tallest known Sitka spruce in the
world and cedar trees that are well over one thousand years old.

Its stillness is enormous, punctuated only occasionally by the sounds
of small songbirds, ravens and jays, squirrels, flies and mosquitoes.
Although the Carmanah Creek is a constant acoustic presence it never
disturbs the peace. Its sound moves in and out of the forest silence as
the trail meanders in and out of clearings near the creek. A few days
in the Carmanah creates deep inner peace—transmitted, surely, by the
trees who have been standing in the same place for hundreds of years.

"Beneath the Forest Floor" is attempting to provide a space in time
for the experience of such peace. Better still, it hopes to encourage
listeners to visit a place like the Carmanah, half of which has already
been destroyed by clear-cut logging. Aside from experiencing its huge
stillness a visit will also transmit a very real knowledge of what is
lost if the forests disappear: not only the trees but also an inner space
that they transmit to us; a sense of balance and focus, on new energy
and life. The inner forest, the forest in us.

In her "Notes on the Compositional Process" (Westerkamp 1992) she
summarizes: "The aim was to re-compose the forest environment with
its own recognizable, unchanged sounds on the one hand and to explore
its acoustic/musical depths by processing some of its sounds on the
other hand." There are times, she continues, where "the listener can get
lost in his or her own acoustic imagination." The work's sociopolitical
focus, already alluded to in the program note, is that she sees the work
as "a mythical confrontation between the ancient forces of the forest
and the destructive forces of modern-day economic 'progress.'"

This dramaturgical description is invaluable and an integral part of the experience
of *Beneath the Forest Floor*, in my opinion. I find that listening to the piece is like taking

a walk, perhaps even a soundwalk,[5] albeit with the added dimension that this work is not one long sample but instead a complex of a huge number of samples, including manipulated ones. The walk is not a normal one for two reasons: because nature has been recomposed and because the work is in a sense episodic, whereas a walk tends to feature gradual changes throughout. The walk is therefore the result of composition.

The fact that *Beneath the Forest Floor* is not a normal soundwalk is made clear immediately. The opening sound of the work is quite low, eerie, and slightly surreal. It sets the tone but does not immediately give away where it was recorded. This sound will become important throughout the work, so we will return to it, as it is too early in this discussion to focus on specific details. Let's first reflect on the listening experience in general and triangulate it with the definition of soundscape as well as Westerkamp's program note, her other notes, and her correspondence with me (in May, June, and October 2016). *Beneath the Forest Floor* is an intimate encounter with a forest, its fauna, and its flora, including a particular interest in water sounds that will be presented later. Much of this work can be listened to specifically in terms of heightened (also called contextual) listening; that is, involving the sources of the sounds that you hear. Much of it can be listened to in terms of more sonic/musical (reduced) listening as well. And, yes, experienced listeners may find themselves involved in technological listening from time to time, focusing on how sounds have been captured, manipulated, and placed spatially. Our mood, the environment in which it is being heard, and, of course, to an extent, the composer's will to have certain parts focused on in different ways all inform the listening experience and consequently the listening behaviors throughout this 17 minute and 23 second composition. In the following discussion, remarks regarding reception will be interwoven with Westerkamp's words.

Let's start with what I consider the most salient elements of the piece, beyond the dramaturgy itself and how it has led the work to be what it is. In general terms, these have to do with the real and the abstracted[6] (at times surreal?), the continuous and the discrete, source recognition—and within this, sources that play a major role in sections of the work, manipulated sounds either playing a role on their own (e.g., that initial sound) or heard in combination, creating "musical" combinations, many related to chromatic pitch combinations, the perception of space and sonic movement, of rhythm, and of structure. Every one of these offers the listener something to hold on to. In the case of the manipulated sounds, as noted, technological or recipe listening can come into play. However, to best appreciate the piece, focusing on how sounds have been transformed can lead one to miss the piece and focus on filter settings, the amount of pitch shifting, the creation of space using reverberation, the composition of the loops, and so on. Although all these and more have clearly been used, this discussion will focus on the sonic result backed up by Westerkamp's own remarks. We will now look at these elements discovered through repeated listenings of the work in a bit more detail before analyzing the piece from beginning to end.

The real and the abstracted: For me as a listener, the most remarkable aspect of *Beneath the Forest Floor* is the challenge—and enjoyment—that arises through the interplay between "as is" samples used as musical material and manipulated ones. Westerkamp courageously starts the work with a manipulated sound, for which she offers an important dramaturgical description, adding an extra dimension to the work's program.

> *Westerkamp considers the initial transposed sound of a raven a "drumbeat," which is indeed quite audible. She wrote: "Its timbre is reminiscent of the native Indian drum on B.C.'s westcoast. The raven itself is one of the totem animals in the native Indian culture and can be seen in the totem poles of various tribes. Totem poles are made from the trees of these old-growth forests and tell the tales and legends of native life within them. The drumbeat, then, became the sonic/musical symbol or totem for the piece, representing the deeply ecological co-existence between forest life and human cultural activities that once existed between native Indians and their environment" (Westerkamp 1992).*

This remark demonstrates that the composer has simultaneously discovered a sound of fundamental importance within her work and realized an important link that this sound has with both tradition and the forest's essence. Soundscape music is music about something, and the program here is quite strong from the very beginning of the work.

The real and abstracted are at times offered in sequence and at times combined. It is fascinating to note how the ambient sounds evolve when moving from one to the other as both the musical and the contextual spaces are continuously evolving. One can listen to the entire composition via either listening strategy, but one would miss a great deal to limit an audition to either important element.

The continuous and the discrete: Although not nearly as prominent as most of the other elements discussed, Westerkamp punctuates sonic continuities with clear, discrete sounds throughout the work. There are very few moments of perceived silence. This interplay can play a significant role in terms of "locating" or focusing on specific sounds.

Recognizable source material: Almost all the recognizable sources represent the flora, and especially fauna, of the forest that inspired *Beneath the Forest Floor*. In terms of animals, it is clear that there are different types of birds and insects to be heard. Westerkamp's information also mentioned the sound of a squirrel that I, for one, would not otherwise have been able to identify (nor did it hinder the listening experience). Beyond this, the most salient feature consists of various water sounds, a creaking tree, and one manmade sound—a chain saw (see the structure section that follows). As previously stated, the sound of the general ambience, whether it has to do with wind or other factors, plays an important role here, as it is one of the most immersive sonic aspects in the work.

Manipulated sounds/musical listening: Most (or possibly all) of the sonic material in *Beneath the Forest Floor* also appears in manipulated form. In terms of salience, the most audible treatments have to do with establishing a clear pitch (normally related to animals), sound quality (especially water and ambience), and rhythm (often, though not solely, by using loops). A few examples will be cited in the discussion of the work's structure that follows.

The perception of space and movement, of rhythm and structure: These aspects all come to the fore in different ways throughout the work. Space is perhaps the trickiest subject. The work as we know it is in stereo. Although radio is evolving—for example, there have been some quadraphonic broadcasts over two broadcasters—stereo is a given. Having made works for radio in the past, I have asked broadcasters whether they would consider asking their listeners to put on headphones in order to hear a binaural (i.e., immersive) recording. None has thus far agreed, so binaural versions have never been broadcast. This is a shame. Nonetheless, Westerkamp has made the most of the circumstances, offering a sense of two-to-three-dimensional space without one hearing anything beyond a linear stereo field. All movement is from left to right or vice versa, yet one perceives being "in" or moving "throughout" space during the composition. One wonders what this work would be like if performed in a more immersive setting.[7]

Rhythm manifests itself through repetition of sounds, such as birdcalls, and through natural patterns. The most rhythmical passages in this piece are constructed, thus heightening the reality of rhythm through (another form of abstracted) composition. Westerkamp's use of loops, in particular with water sounds, establishes the opportunity for familiarization or, as she mentioned in our correspondence, to allow listeners to discover and enter into the "inner complexity" of sounds. What is interesting here is the composer's awareness of when she is placing the forest in the forefront and when she allows its musicality to take over.

Structure did not need to play a key role in this work and, as Westerkamp herself wrote during our correspondence, there was "no preconceived structure." Nonetheless, the recorded and manipulated material led to a work that, when compared with many other soundscape works, electroacoustic works, or contemporary works in general, has a very clearly defined structure. Jean-Jacques Nattiez and others (e.g., Nattiez 1990) speak of the poietic (construction), aesthesic (reception), and neutral (e.g., score) levels when discussing semiotics. I had already plotted out a rough overview of the work before talking to Westerkamp about this subject and before using the EAnalysis software's basic sonogram function, plotting the image in figure 3.1. In all cases, it appears that the work is in four distinct sections. At some points, there is a bridge or (cross)fade between sections. Each section has its distinctive characteristics, although inevitably, as the work is about the soundscape of a particular forest, there are elements in common, some because they are always there and others because the composer wanted them in her composition. The structure offers the same type of "something to hold on to" support as any item listed earlier, as it helps the listener follow the piece at both the local and general levels.

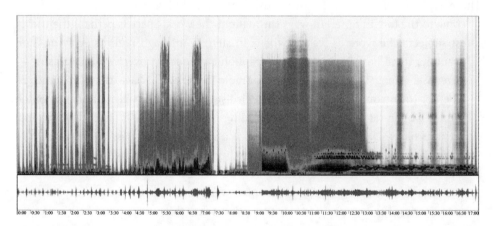

Figure 3.1
EAnalysis sonogram image of *Beneath the Forest Floor.*

Let's look at the four sections in some detail.

I. Section I acts very much like an introduction, presenting much, although not all, the material one item at a time. But this introduction is upside down in a sense because, as we already know, the piece commences in the world of the abstract. In fact, the slowed-down raven sound, which appears in a manner similar to an ostinato, is there throughout the section as well as in the bridge that introduces section II. This sound is interrupted or complemented by unmodified sounds from the forest, the first of which (at 0:26) is also a raven recording, thus exhibiting the source of the foundational sound of the section. This is followed by water flowing from left to right as if one were moving slowly past a stream (at 0:37–0:46; water will feature in section III), after which one hears the raven's second appearance (here the cry is heard twice), other birds, a creaky tree (which features in section II), a more rapid movement of water, a sequence of more or less isolated bird sounds, the squirrel mentioned earlier,[8] insects, water (again repeated twice), insects with birds, and finally the water sound. The order appears to be chosen as a way of introducing the "characters" and the forest space.

Another layer of sound evolves during this passage, which lasts until 3:53, when the bridge at the beginning of section II commences. From 0:57, pitched material is introduced that is not immediately recognizable, creating a slightly surreal ambience. The first tone is on C in different octaves, complemented by a sound a minor third higher. At 1:30, the individual sounds converge as if a chord. I assume that all these are birds. This pitched reverberant material offers a layer of sound, a forest choir, moderate in pace, meditative in character, and independent of both the unmanipulated sound sources and the repeating raven or "drum." The listener has three layers and many specific sources to hold on to and is clearly experiencing an introductory passage in a very special forest. From 2:04, a C-sharp is added, and there is slight dissonance in the choir sounds, but this is simply an example of accumulation, a technique Westerkamp will use occasionally, adding new elements to ones that were repeated earlier. Although some of the pitched material offers the impression of sliding tones early on, they more prominently begin to slide downward from around 3:13, adding another abstracted, perhaps surreal layer to this soundscape.[9] From 3:37, there is a bit of near silence, and all we hear are two successive low raven sounds. The sound that follows those two sounds forms part of the bridge into section II.

The way Westerkamp sees section I is that we are taken to "various specific locations in the forest, e.g. where the raven flies, where the squirrel lives, where the creek flows, where the thrush feeds, where the [S]teller's jay flies, and so on" (Westerkamp 1992), thus offering the listener "different soundscape[s] along with different vegetation and animal life." On the chord, she adds that this foreshadows the

musical treatment that will feature in section IV. She claimed that
"the slowed down bird song calls 'gave' me a musical atmosphere, a
'tone,' perhaps even harmonic structure, for the piece and created the
desire to let the ear descend into these beautiful sounds and explore
their musicality."[10]

In our correspondence, Westerkamp mentioned her preference for the
German word Urwald (primeval forest). This first section excellently
offers a composed Urwald for listeners to enter and experience.

II. The bridge to section II is actually the second accumulation that one finds in this work. Along with the low raven call, we hear a single slowed-down sound. In its next appearance, it merges with a second such sound, and so on until the sixth iteration of the accumulation continues, launching the main part of section II at 4:31.

Section II contrasts greatly with section I. As it begins, the low raven sound finally departs and is replaced by a loud, stormlike general ambience, with rain, rapidly passing birds, the creaking tree sound, and a general sense of eeriness. Again, slowed-down, highly reverberated animals cohabit with natural ones, but the feeling is more claustrophobic and the pitch material seems to be abstracted from a noisy chain saw. Sometimes the ambience is without detail, whereas at other times it becomes dense with activity, until the chain saw seems to shift rapidly downward in pitch, leading to a final sound that reverberates into relative silence.

There is no need to identify which specific sounds are heard when and where as, in my opinion, this would contradict the natural setting of the piece. Clearly, Westerkamp composed this dark, scary ambience, but I believe that this passage from 4:31 until that final sound at 7:15 is one "event" or "sequence" that changes in both detail and density. This final sound decrescendos until 7:22, where it is overcome by a bird flying past, after which the decrescendo moves to real silence at 7:32, ending this section.

Westerkamp (1992) mentions that the slowed-down sounds focus
on squirrels and jays that fly by and, beyond the above-mentioned
confrontation with the real world symbolized by the chain saw,
that the leitmotif here is "the dark side of the forest … a mythical

place full of powerful natural forces and potential dangers." In our correspondence, she added that "the slowed down squirrel seemed to connect to the darker side of the forest and naturally aligned itself with the creaking trees and the storm sounds."

III. After the dark section II, there is a bridging section or interlude that doesn't at all provide a sense of what comes next in section III. Its content simply evolves from that brief silence from 7:35 to 8:42 and then continues in the background of the water-based section III. This bridge commences with two isolated slow sounds, which Westerkamp identified in our correspondence as the slowed-down "phuit" bird's "solo." Each utterance has its own highly reverberated internal melody. This is followed by the slowed-down raven leitmotif, and then bird glissandi appear in the pattern of a rise of a major second and a response a minor third higher, with the same major second glide oddly reminiscent of the blues. These glissando sounds are complemented by occasional raven sounds at normal pitch, all of which are repeated at seemingly independent intervals until 8:42 (and beyond, without the raven, which is replaced by other birds introduced at natural pitch). The presence of birds acts as a layer of sound from this point onward. The introduction of the section's main water sounds comes to the foreground through a rapid movement of the creek sound from right to left, which again fades into the background as a foretaste of what's to come while the birds continue. At 9:10, a bird flies quickly in the opposite direction, and at 9:15 the water rapidly sweeps across again and then envelops us, with all birds singing at their specific pitch. A new bird appears, apparently a baby raven (per Westerkamp's correspondence), at 9:21, representing the sound of a different generation. (It will return between 10:20 and 11:00.) At first, the water sounds like the continuous flow of water, but suddenly (at 9:31) a clear loop of what might be bubbles or droplets is heard within the flow. This sets the scene for a counterpoint of flowing water, water loops, and birds, which apparently are no longer all singing at their own single pitch, for as time goes on, the individual birds start responding to each other in the form of simple melodies, in a sense similar to the loops of water sounds that appear. At around 10:15, the water flow again disappears into the background and there seems to be a "loop solo" focused on more discrete water sounds. The birds also seem to be singing in that same background, their melodies becoming increasingly diverse with time. They move further into the background through the addition of reverberation, while natural sounds appear "above" the water as the flow finally returns in the middle of section III, at around 11:15.

Before moving on, how does one listen to this? What was just described could not have been transcribed during a single audition. Although there is never a high density of sounds, or sounds that are totally abstract or unidentifiable (why would there be?), these layers of sound can be focused on one at a time or in combination, identified with their sources or heard as melodies, sound qualities, and the like. Their rhythmical interplay may become the sonic focus. The listener who is aware of listening behaviors has an inner conflict of choice or, dare one write, goes with the flow of the sounds. One can be there with the sense of birds and water, immersed in sound, or both. Does one think of an endangered forest at this time? Perhaps not, but when one remembers what the piece is about, the thought of this beautiful soundscape disappearing or being radically altered is rather painful.

The remainder of section III is in a sense similar, but it allows the imagination to rove further, as the bird melodies now include long-held pitches that create countermelodies and a sense of space. But what kind of space is this? This is not only the real forest but also an abstracted one, with pitches as its contours. As one dreams within this new sonic universe, the water recedes again into silence (at around 13:12). During one audition, I had the sense of a hymnlike chant evolving from the shorter pitched bird sounds and the longer resonant ones. This interpretation became another the next time I listened. Westerkamp has composed an interplay between real and abstracted soundscapes, although one never forgets the real one and awaits its reappearance. What follows is the road to that reappearance, a long crossfade between sections III and IV.

> *Westerkamp speaks of spending time at the creek, attempting "to lead the listener into the rich microcosm of creekwater timbres and rhythms" (Westerkamp 1992). In our correspondence, she explains that her dramaturgy includes the desire "to immerse the listener into the powerful presence of the Carmanah River and the dripping wetness—heard from the many little creeks and rivulets—that is characteristic for the west coast rainforest with moss everywhere, on the ground, on tree trunks and hanging from tree branches." She emphasizes the importance of the loops that she fades in and out of the general creek ambience. She sees the creek as a place where*

"the listener can get lost in his or her own acoustic imagination;
where it is never clear whether the sounds that one hears are real
or an acoustic illusion" (Westerkamp 1992). She notes in our
correspondence that she had "recorded a small trickle of water that
had a very distinct 'drippy' flow down some tree roots in the forest ...
editing out different sections of the flow and making loops with
different rhythmical structures," adding that she was also fascinated
by a "tiny clicking sound ... created by the stem of a dry leaf that
had fallen into the water in such a way that it obstructed the water
flow in a very subtle way." In this way, she was able to contrast the
more flowing sounds with this more discreet click. On a more poetic
note, she added that "a moving microphone reveals the 'architecture'
of a creek and the fact that it is precisely its structure (the rocks,
branches, sand shoreline, etc., meaning its obstructions) that makes
out the specific character of the creek sounds," concluding that the
sounds of the water are simply the acoustic expression of the water's
relationship to the land formations it meets. This remark underlines
the importance of field recording as part of composition.

IV. The crossfade moves forward without the water but with the reverberant pitched birds singing within the ambience of the long-held pitches. Where are we? At 13:40, our leitmotif of the entire work (low-pitched raven "drum") reappears. It will start and end this section as it starts and ends the entire work. This time it is there with the slowed-down baby raven singing calls and response in a descending fifth. Again, one would have to know one's birdcalls and how they sound octaves lower to discover this. Our correspondence was helpful in identifying their proximity.

This continuing dream world is interrupted by a reminiscence of a recent sound, a water loop from 14:14 to 14:42. As this is fading out, there is a peep sound, starting at 14:31, the sound of a wren (Westerkamp told me in our correspondence), which we have only known in its slowed-down form.

Westerkamp speaks of the contrast between the continuous and the discrete here. In this case, it involves a tiny, low "peep" sound of one of the songbirds. It appears "purposely in the foreground of the grander musical chords in this section" because of "the difference in proportion between the smallness of this little sound and its (and other birdcalls') slowed-down versions. The peep's deep inner beauty, its purity and clarity are revealed when it is slowed down" (Westerkamp 1992). The same holds true for all manipulated sounds. The complex pitch pattern heard in the slowed-down version of this birdcall is indeed undecipherable. In fact, Westerkamp purposefully added no reverb (despite a request from her technician in Toronto). She kept this dry sound to hide the "inner subtleties" that emerged when the pitch was shifted downward.

These peeps certainly form a contrast from the rest in terms of duration and pitch. It knows no time. Amplitude changes. Some pitches or musical voices come to the fore and then recede. The loop returns, as do the glissando calls. This is like a reprise. Nothing is presented in its original recorded form, yet all is familiar. This could go on forever. About a minute before the end, particular sounds come to the forefront, a last breath, and then recede. Our low raven returns, announcing the end of the piece. It was there at the beginning. It occurs to me that there is no beginning, and despite no sound at 17:23, there is no end. There should be no end to the forest.

Thus ...

Beneath the Forest Floor is a soundscape composition. Sometimes, we are in the recorded forest, sometimes in an abstracted, composed soundscape, and at other times in both. The real forest is always there in one form or another. Our focus changes—or is being changed by the composer.

Many people I meet tell me that they do not like or need program notes. A soundscape work represents, or is based on, a program. It is about something (the place), and sometimes this something is *also* about something else, such as the disappearance of the forest in *Beneath the Forest Floor* and forests in general. It is very much about an intention/reception loop in combination with an individual's listening experience. You hear beauty, but this beauty is possibly ephemeral, not in the sense of your going to the forest and leaving it but rather of the forest's leaving after centuries of existence: the *Urwald*—the *nicht mehr Wald* (the no longer forest). Is beauty a reason for survival? No, that's not the right question. Does humankind have to dictate what stays and goes in this world, what flora and fauna have to be killed? Now we're getting close. But who am I, and who is Hildegard Westerkamp, to raise such issues? Answer: if we don't and, more poignantly, if she hadn't, who would?

In the conclusion of a music analysis, one would normally review the work's salient characteristics; for example, the presence/foregrounding or absence/not paying attention to chromatic pitch or the real versus abstract. This summary is not that important here; it is hoped that the items were sufficiently presented earlier in this chapter. The discourse of analysis has been an attempt to discover those elements, how they were composed into a narrative that is open to individual interpretation, and how these elements are fundamentally connected with the work's dramaturgy. I have written an analysis of an electroacoustic soundscape composition in which I have just concluded that we need to talk about how people should care for their world. Is this analysis? In the case of soundscape composition, indeed it is. Westerkamp's dramaturgy is very powerful. Her piece is profound. The combination is vital.

> **Postscript:** *Westerkamp has written (Westerkamp, personal communication with the author): "The trail building was a very smart move and made a lot more people aware of this remote treasure. Around the time or shortly after I was there the Carmanah Pacific Provincial Park was established (or what remained of it, half of the Carmanah area had already been clear cut), which later became the Carmanah Walbran Provincial Park. The Walbran area was a neighboring area that was under a fierce dispute then between the logging company and the environmentalists. Eventually both areas [not all of the Walbran] became protected into one Provincial Park."*[11]

Notes

1. There haven't been many in-depth discussions of this work, Duhautpas, Freychet, and Solomos (2015) being an exception. Fortunately, a book written by the TIAALS team in Huddersfield and Durham, United Kingdom (Michael Clarke, Frédéric Dufeu, and Peter Manning), on their project, which includes a chapter on this work, is expected to offer a text complementary to this one, investigating the composition process of the work via the use of interactive software. Their book is expected to appear around the time this chapter is published.

2. Beyond the writings of Westerkamp and Truax, readers who are unfamiliar with the work of founding pioneer of soundscape R. Murray Schafer are recommended to become familiar with his soundscape-informed music and his writings (such as Schafer 1994) as well as information regarding the World Soundscape Project based at Simon Fraser University in Burnaby, British Columbia, where both Truax and Westerkamp have worked.

3. There are two terms in this paragraph that deserve further attention. Many soundscape composers do not speak of using *samples* in their work; however, given the ubiquity of sampling in today's world, in music and far beyond, this notion in musical contexts is related to recording something (whether from note-based music or any sound) and reusing it in a new work. Therefore, in my view, the term sampling can also be applied to this type of work. Many leave samples as is in their works, regardless of genre. Others happily use tools to *manipulate* sounds, as Hildegard Westerkamp does from time to time in her work; for example, her lowering the pitch and extending the duration of the birdcall at the very start of this work. Sound manipulation here relates to a composition technique used in much electroacoustic composition. Manipulation is therefore not used here in any pejorative sense.

4. Her personal website can be found at www.sfu.ca/~westerka and, within this site, the page listing her writings and including some of her publications is at www.sfu.ca/~westerka/writings. html.

5. A soundwalk is a walk in which the listener's attention is more focused on the sonic environment than usual. These can be led, or any individual can set his or her own soundwalk route.

6. Here I am borrowing a term from Simon Emmerson (1986) that refers to manipulating sounds from real life, eventually making them more abstract. In such cases, those who do recognize the original source may involve that knowledge in their interpretation.

7. In my correspondence with Westerkamp, she made it clear that the 16-channel studio digital recording was mixed to stereo, as she did not believe that digital multichannel playback was an option at the time. She has diffused the stereo recording through multiple loudspeakers in concert performance, however, which does create a live-performed immersive environment.

8. In our correspondence, Westerkamp claimed that the squirrel sounds were their "defence call when you tread on their territory."

9. In our correspondence, Westerkamp informed me that she did not know the name of this particular bird but that she had named it the "phuit" bird, which is "an onomatopoeic expression

for its whistle." She indicated that this was the bird with the glissando sound and that this bird had a "solo" in section II at 7:35.

10. In our correspondence, she added that there were adult and child raven sounds (of which two recordings were made by Norbert Ruebsaat in the Queen Charlotte Islands, also known as Haida Gwaii, not in the forest itself, and thus she inserted them into the soundscape) as well as manipulated recordings of a thrush, a winter wren, and the "phuit" bird mentioned in the previous note. She stated that there were other untreated birds as well.

11. The decision was made in 1990, and the Provincial Park opened in 1991. Further information can be found on its Wikipedia site (https://en.wikipedia.org/wiki/Carmanah_Walbran_Provincial_Park) and the park's own site (http://www.env.gov.bc.ca/bcparks/explore/parkpgs/carmanah/).

References

Blacking, J. 1982. "The Structure of Musical Discourse: The Problem of the Song Text." *Yearbook for Traditional Music* 14:15–23 (published by the International Council for Traditional Music).

Caux, J. 2012. *Almost Nothing with Luc Ferrari*. Berlin: Errant Bodies Press. (Original edition, *Presque rien avec Luc Ferrari*. Nice: Éditions Main-d'œuvre, 2002.)

Clarke, M., F. Dufeu, and P. Manning. Forthcoming. *Inside Computer Music*. New York: Oxford University Press.

Delalande, F. 1998. "Music Analysis and Reception Behaviours: *Someil* by Pierre Henry." *Journal of New Music Research* 27 (1–2): 13–66.

Duhautpas, F., A. Freychet, and M. Solomos. 2015. "Beneath the Forest Floor de Hildegard Westerkamp: Analyse d'une composition à base de paysages sonores." *Analyse Musicale* 76. (See also https://hal.archives-ouvertes.fr/hal-01202407/document. The English version by Duhautpas and Solomos is available at https://hal.archives-ouvertes.fr/hal-01202890/document and in *Soundscape, the Journal of Acoustic Ecology* 13 (1) (2014)" 6–10.)

Emmerson, S. 1986. "The Relation of Language to Materials." In *The Language of Electroacoustic Music*, edited by S. Emmerson, 17–39. Basingstoke: Macmillan Press.

Emmerson, S., and L. Landy, eds. 2016. *Expanding the Horizon of Electroacoustic Music Analysis*. Cambridge: Cambridge University Press.

Landy, L. 1994. "The 'Something to Hold On to Factor' in Timbral Composition." *Contemporary Music Review* 10 (2): 49–60.

McCartney, A. 1999. *Sounding Places: Situated Conversations through the Soundscape Compositions of Hildegard Westerkamp*. PhD diss., York University, Toronto. Available at beatrouteproductions.com/Andradiss.pdf.

Nattiez, J.-J. 1990. *Music and Discourse: Toward a Semiology of Music*. Princeton, NJ: Princeton University Press.

Norman, K. 1996. "Real-World Music as Composed Listening." *Contemporary Music Review* 15 (1): 1–27.

Norman, K. 2004. "The Same Trail Twice: *Talking Rain* with Hildegard Westerkamp." In *Sounding Art: Eight Literary Excursions through Electronic Music*, 75–99. Aldershot: Ashgate.

Schaeffer, P. 1977. *Traité des objets musicaux: Essai interdisciplines*. 2nd ed. Paris: Seuil. (Originally published in 1966.)

Schafer, R. M. 1994. *Our Sonic Environment and the Soundscape: The Tuning of the World*. Rochester, VT: Destiny Books. (Originally published in 1977 as *The Tuning of the World*.)

Smalley, D. 1992. "Listening Imagination: Listening in the Electroacoustic Era." In *Contemporary Musical Thought*, vol. 1, edited by John Paynter, Tim Howell, Richard Orton, and Peter Seymour, 514–554. London: Routledge.

Truax, B. 1984. *Acoustic Communication*. Norwood, NJ: Ablex. (2nd ed., Westport, CT: Greenwood Press, 2001.)

Truax, B. 1996. "Soundscape, Acoustic Communication and Environmental Sound Composition." *Contemporary Music Review* 15 (1): 49–65.

Truax, B. 1999. *Handbook for Acoustic Ecology*. CD-ROM edition. Burnaby: Cambridge Street Publishing. CSR-CDR 9901. Available at http://www.sfu.ca/sonic-studio/handbook/.

Truax, B. 2000. "The Aesthetics of Computer Music: A Questionable Concept Reconsidered." *Organised Sound* 5 (3): 119–126.

Westerkamp, H. 1992. "Notes on the Compositional Process" [of *Beneath the Forest Floor*]. Unpublished.

Westerkamp, H. 1996. *Transformations*. CD, IMED 9631. Montréal: Empreintes DIGITales.

Westerkamp, H. 2002. "Linking Soundscape Composition and Acoustic Ecology." *Organised Sound* 7 (1): 51–56.

4   The Contributions of Charles Dodge's *Speech Songs* to Computer Music Practice

Miller Puckette

Introduction

As one of the composers whom Max Mathews invited to work at Bell Laboratories, Charles Dodge belongs to a select group of musical pioneers. Although this group is quite diverse in technical approach and in musical style, Dodge can still be regarded as something of an outlier, whose work can be much better assessed in long hindsight than might have been possible earlier. The sensibility that he brought to the task of making music, and the way he set about realizing his compositions, set him apart. In this study, I analyze what is perhaps the most radical piece Dodge has written, both in the context of other work done at Bell Labs at the time and in its own internal workings.

When Charles Dodge wrote *Speech Songs* (1972), the use of computer-generated voices in music was nothing new. Max Mathews and Joan Miller's famous arrangement of Harry Dacre's corny *Daisy Bell* 11 years earlier featured a synthetic singing voice whose kick-me affect and buzzy, congested-nose timbre could easily be confused with those of the voice we hear in *Speech Songs*. But while Mathews and Miller's *Daisy Bell* is now best understood as a historical curiosity, *Speech Songs* has an urgent presence, as if it had been written yesterday. What changed was not the sonic palette but rather Dodge's insightful new way of putting the new technology to artistic use.

Mathews himself must have seen clearly that the future of what was then called computer music[1] depended not only on its technological development (in which Mathews himself played a leading role) but, crucially, also on the active participation of a vanguard of composers Mathews brought to Bell Laboratories over the early years (say, 1960–1975) of the new medium's development.

Four of these composers—James Tenney, Jean-Claude Risset, Charles Dodge, and Laurie Spiegel—can each be taken as emblematic of particular directions in which the new practice of computer music pushed the musical language of the day. Of these, the first two are most closely associated with the earliest days of computer music, during which Mathews was implementing the series of computer music rendering languages now collectively referred to as "MUSIC N" (Mathews et al. 1969). Tenney encouraged the development of new unit generators in MUSIC 3 to experiment with randomness and noise (Tenney 1969). Risset (discussed in more detail later) seized on the computer's ability to analyze and reconstruct musical sounds (Roads 1985). Spiegel is closely associated with Mathews's later work on real-time interactive electronic music, creating seminal pieces using the GROOVE system (Mathews and Moore 1970).

Dodge's main contribution, made during his residencies at Bell Labs in the early 1970s, was to uncover the musical potential of vocal synthesis. Synthetic speech had long been an area of intense research interest at Bell Labs, where it was put to use in the design and testing of voice line telephone systems. Dodge's achievement was in part a technical one: he saw and articulated that one could use the ability to separately specify pitch, timing, and other aspects of the voice as musical values and in so doing create an entirely new vocal sound world (Dodge 1989).

Dodge's contribution was also significant in a second respect, in that he saw and took advantage of the poetics of using a clearly synthetic machine voice as the singer of a recorded art song. By the 1970s, the listening public was well accustomed to hearing human voices emerge from loudspeakers, and a listener could identify the sound of a reproduced, prerecorded voice as "real." But replacing this voice with a clearly artificial one put the question of liveness, and of naturalness, back into conscious play in an act of "making it strange." This impression was enhanced by the crudeness of the sounds available at the time. The most important measure of speech quality to researchers at Bell Labs was intelligibility (as opposed to audio quality or classically defined beauty), and the hyperintelligible but metallic machine voice of *Speech Songs* places the listener in an unfamiliar relationship with the music. In exploiting the poetics of this situation, Dodge presages, for instance, Laurie Anderson's *O Superman* and, arguably, the widespread use of synthetic and "autotuned" singing voices in popular music at present.

Dodge's third achievement in *Speech Songs* was to initiate a movement in computer music away from the discrete, symbolic approach of the MUSIC N languages toward the use of manually edited subaudio-rate sampled functions of time—used to control time-varying pitch and timbres—as musical objects on which to compose a piece. Although widely practiced in noncomputer electronic music through real-time inputs of various sorts, the direct use of gestural human input in computer music practice was rare before *Speech Songs*. Dodge's work has encouraged subsequent computer music research aimed at supporting fluid, continuous controls that were not easy to work with in the MUSIC N languages. I can gratefully acknowledge that hearing *Speech Songs*, and hearing Dodge speak about them, has influenced the development of Max/MSP and

Pure Data, two widely used software environments for real-time interactive electronic music. Although widely practiced in noncomputer electronic music, this use of continua in computer music practice is in sharp contrast to works of computer music before *Speech Songs*. Dodge's work helped encourage computer music research aimed at creating human-sounding musical shapes that were not readily achieved using the original MUSIC N programs written by Mathews.

Computer Music Research at Bell Laboratories

Before Dodge realized *Speech Songs*, his experience at Bell Labs consisted mostly of converting sound files he created at the Columbia-Princeton Electronic Music Center. Although he was not resident at Bell Labs as such, he would have been familiar with researchers there since at least around 1969, when his first computer-rendered piece, *Changes*, appeared. Both inside and outside Bell Labs, Dodge met and was potentially influenced by many other active composers in the early days of computer music. His own recollections mention James Tenney, Jean-Claude Risset, Hubert Howe, Godfrey Winham, Paul Lansky, and several others.

The character and atmosphere of Bell Labs has been well documented (Gertner 2012). Although researchers there did not have freedom to investigate whatever they wished,[2] the range of research topics that could be justified as potentially relevant to telephony was vast. It was reportedly at the suggestion of his supervisor, John Pierce, that Max Mathews first wrote a computer program to make musical sounds (Park 2009). Both Pierce and Mathews listened to classical music, and Mathews was also an amateur violinist. At the time, it may have seemed strange to think that making music with a computer would yield insights of use to Bell Labs's mission, but given Pierce's reputation for highly imaginative thinking, it seems possible that he guessed there would be something to learn by doing it. In retrospect, it seems quite visionary on his part. Computer music has since proved to be a fertile area of research, with applications both within and well outside the field of music, with widespread commercial impact.

Mathews was able to continue doing computer music research at Bell Labs from 1957 (the year he wrote MUSIC) until he left in 1985.[3] He also had access to researchers working in related fields and to the composers he was able to invite to work there. During this period, most of the style and practice of "computer music" (considered as a musical genre) came into its present form. Work done at Bell Labs, especially early on, before many other centers were up and running, set important examples.

Using MUSIC N programs in the 1960s, Risset and Tenney (and slightly later, Dodge and probably many others) were able to put into practice a vision of the new computer music that emphasized the relevance of the computer's unique affordances to late serialist compositional techniques in which set operations were used to manipulate pitches, durations, and dynamics. It is easy to imagine why composers taking such a mathematically driven approach would be attracted to the computer, as it allowed them to precisely, numerically specify not only those three qualities of a musical note but also aspects of the note's timbre. Using the computer, one could specify many properties of each note with precision—for example, the frequencies and amplitudes of all the partials of a periodic waveform.

Risset's *Suite from Little Boy* (1968) is an early example of the use of a MUSIC N language to make musical connections between the external properties of notes (in this case, their pitches) and their internal properties (their sinusoidal components). It was apparently Risset's insight that a collection of sinusoids that could be heard together as a single, perhaps inharmonic, tone could also, with appropriate changes of timing or amplitude, be heard as a chord or arpeggio. This "timbre as chord" idea was immensely influential and can be considered central to the composition of such diverse pieces as John Chowning's *Stria*, Jonathan Harvey's *Mortuos Plango, Vivos Voco*, and Philippe Manoury's *Jupiter*.

Little Boy was quintessential MUSIC N music in the sense that the musical objects that were being treated were separated as discrete notes specified by "note cards," whose numerical fields specified the musical values that were to be heard. In effect, all the music sprang from the ten digits and the decimal point. As Trevor Wishart writes, this is in keeping with the Western written music tradition that reduces the continuity of possible sounds into ensembles of separate notes described using discrete alphabets specifying pitches and durations chosen from finite sets of possibilities (Wishart and Emmerson 1996). This is a great convenience, but also a great limitation that prevents describing many kinds of possible musical gestures that cannot be written using Western common practice notation. Far from achieving aesthetic neutrality, the MUSIC N series of languages encoded not only a numerically driven approach to describing musical sounds but also a preference for the discrete over the continuous.

By 1970, a clear understanding of how to make "computer music" using the MUSIC N programs had emerged, with Dodge as one of its practitioners. Between 1971 and early 1973, Dodge began to work with a real-time speech synthesis system being developed by John Olive (Thieberger and Dodge 1995). Dodge recounts that Olive, like Mathews, was interested in music (and particularly in new music), and Dodge was warmly encouraged to use the equipment and to interact with its inventors. Although Dodge had also used MUSIC N software in his earlier computer music compositions, he used only Olive's system, which was not designed for music at all, to realize *Speech Songs*. In this respect, Dodge is an outlier. All the other composers working at Bell Labs apparently used only Mathews's software and hardware systems that were explicitly designed to make music. This may explain in part the sheer radicalism of *Speech Songs*: its realization required abandoning all previous computer music technology.

Music and Vocal Synthesis

Electronic synthesis of spoken or sung voice had been known both inside and outside the context of the MUSIC N programs as early as the late 1960s. As a tool for telephonic research, electronic speech synthesis had been carried out at Bell Labs using a succession of ingenious devices at least since H. W. Dudley's Voder was demonstrated in 1939. Various mechanical vocal synthesizers had been proposed since the late 1700s (Olive 1998).

The 1960s saw an important technological advance: the automatic analysis of recorded speech samples to extract their formants, pitch (when present), pitched or unpitched quality, and amplitude, all as sampled functions of time (Olive 1971). These analyses could then be studied in their own right or, most interestingly for musicians, manipulated and then resynthesized as transformed speech. Olive's speech synthesis system used a general-purpose computer to do the analysis and specialized hardware (Rabiner, Jackson, Schafer, and Coker 1971) to resynthesize speech in real time. The system also had a CRT display and light pen that allowed graphical editing of the analysis data before resynthesis.

Olive's system underwent at least one radical change during the six months in 1972–1973 over which Dodge realized *Speech Songs*. The older two of the four songs ("When I Am with You" and "He Destroyed Her Image") were realized using a synthesis algorithm that could be used to explicitly control several speech formants by using resonant filters. The two others were realized using linear predictive coding (LPC), a newer technique that, while it offered a higher quality of audio output, functioned as a black box in which the individual formants could no longer be individually manipulated. That such radical technological changes could take place over such a short time span is no longer common in computer music research.

In the first known example of computer-synthesized singing, Mathews and Miller's 1962 rendition of *Daisy Bell*, the vocal part was apparently provided by a speech researcher, John L. Kelly. The MUSIC N series of programs (one of which was used to provide a piano-like accompaniment to the synthetic singing voice) were built on a very different model, combining a static "patch" of synthesis modules, called unit generators, with the aforementioned "note cards." Vocal synthesis was later incorporated in MUSIC N series languages as well, in roughly the form it takes in the one surviving such language, Barry Vercoe's Csound. In this language, the relevant unit generators, "lpread" and "lpreson," allow the user independent control of timing and pitch (more generally, source signal) but no handles on the internal structure of the vocal resonance, which appears as a black box. Dodge and many others have since used Csound and its predecessors to synthesize voice in this way, often getting results that sound quite like the later, LPC-realized part of *Speech Songs*. But Olive's system, which predates most speech synthesis using MUSIC N programs, was paradoxically much more flexible in its provisions for editing the analyses before resynthesis.

Musical Antecedents

The voice has been an active subject of exploration by composers of electronic music since its earliest days, having been for instance the sound source in Halim El-Dabh's *The Expression of Zaar* (1944), the earliest known piece of music realized using recording equipment. Pieces such as Stockhausen's *Gesang der Jünglinge* (1956) and Berio's *Thema (Omaggio a Joyce)* (1958) already showed a high level of virtuosity, using tape splicing techniques to break up vocal sounds into short, nonverbal utterances. The other affordances of the day—spatialization, speed change, and, in Stockhausen's case, the addition of purely electronic sounds—made for an expressive musical language of displacement and disembodiment, probably novel to many listeners but musically and logically consistent.

Gesang der Jünglinge can be heard as an attempt to extend serial organization from pitch and time structures (as in Stockhausen's earlier etudes) to the much larger and more unruly realm of timbre. In his combination of vocal samples with electronic sounds, Stockhausen attempts to make a closer union of voice and instrument than that of a singer and accompanist. The unification ultimately fails (the contrast between the vocal sounds and the synthetic ones is simply too great, despite the atomization of the recorded voice into sublinguistic units, for us to hear them as a unified sound palette), but, because of Stockhausen's articulate explanations of the piece, the principles he was working toward were comprehensible, and attractive, to other composers. It would eventually take a computer to make this vision a reality.

The relationship between *Thema* and *Speech Songs* is more direct. Both present a musical surface that veers back and forth between presenting comprehensible poetic language and detached, sometimes onomatopoeic utterances with no clear linguistic meaning. Both take a succession of short, poetic, enigmatic phrases and spin them out in a repetitive, almost oratorio-like manner, except much more finely atomized.

Tape techniques, such as those used in these earlier pieces, were impractical to emulate on computers in the 1960s or even the 1970s, since the computer's capacity for sound storage was exceedingly limited and the equipment needed to enter a sound into a computer in the first place (the analog to digital converter, or ADC) was much more expensive and rare than that needed to output the sound again (the digital to analog converter, or DAC, itself then still a rarity). It is not surprising that echoes of these ideas did not appear in the first decade of computer music at Bell Labs. In contrast, *Speech Songs* shows a clearly audible influence from the tape music tradition and especially from its early engagement with the human voice.

On the other hand, *Speech Songs* can be heard almost as a rebuff to the prettiness of these earlier pieces. There is no use at all of spatialization or of production gloss such as added reverberation. All we hear is a monaural, dry, electronic voice. The listener is made to confront the raw sound of the artificial voice, up close, dissected as if on an operating table. The disembodied quality of the voices in *Thema* or *Gesang* may have been disturbing to some listeners at first, but in this respect *Speech Songs*, in its raw presentation of dissected entrails of the mechanism of human vocal production, goes full technicolor.

Technological Developments

The decade preceding *Speech Songs* saw the end of what is often called the Classical Studio period (Schrader 1982) and the emergence of two new technologies, seemingly quite distinct but in some respects closely related. The previously mentioned MUSIC N languages were under development at Bell Labs and Princeton (but only being made available—and anyway perhaps only of interest—to a very small group of primarily art music composers). Meanwhile, the first commercial voltage-controlled synthesizers were being developed by instrument builders such as Robert Moog and Donald Buchla. Although the first adopters of these synthesizers were art music composers as well, the new voltage-controlled synthesizers of the second half of the 1960s were quickly taken up by popular musicians in various genres.

The most important common thread in these two developments was a rise in the level of automation in the creation of sound. Whereas the tape pieces of the 1950s were painstakingly assembled using razor blades and splicing tape, both the MUSIC N languages and the analog synthesizer allowed the automatic generation of time-varying signals controlled by (in the case of the computer) relatively small numbers of typed parameters or (in the case of the analog synthesizer) knobs on an envelope generator or step sequencer.

The two technologies are also similar in that their model of production is based on the interconnection of collections of standardized modules that can pass audio or control information among themselves. In the MUSIC N languages, this takes the form of unit generators (introduced by Max Mathews in MUSIC 3 around 1961), and in the modular synthesizer, these are the voltage-controlled modules.

The same decade also saw the development (once more at Bell Labs) of a computer system that could generate digital control signals for modular analog synthesizers in real time. This eventually became the GROOVE system (Mathews and Moore 1970). Here, the possibility of modular audio synthesis was retained (via the analog synthesizer), but the full generality of the computer was made available for the creation of the control signals, which could be computed in real time at lower than audio sample rates.

The early 1970s saw another development: real-time digital processing of audio signals. Special-purpose digital hardware was needed to synthesize or process sound digitally in real time. These digital audio processors were not programmable in the way that computers are and could not offer the flexibility of a MUSIC N or modular synthesizer. The real-time speech synthesizer on which Dodge realized *Speech Songs* was one of these.

These last two developments privileged continuous-time controls, which could be stored, edited, and manipulated digitally. This possibility, which was just emerging during Dodge's time at Bell Labs, is crucial to the construction and musical style of *Speech Songs*.

The Musical Language of *Speech Songs*

Speech Songs is a musical setting of four very short poems by Mark Strand. In at least one early collection, the four songs appear in the order they were composed, but we should probably order them as in what is likely the definitive publication (Dodge 1992). In this document, the last two songs to be composed ("A Man Sitting in the Cafeteria" and "The Days Are Ahead") appear as songs 1 and 2, followed by the earlier compositions ("When I Am with You" and "He Destroyed Her Image") as songs 3 and 4. In this ordering, the songs progress from most naturalistic to most highly distorted.

The defining building material of the songs, both musically and technologically, is the analysis and resynthesis of vocal sound, with several possible types of modifications. The analyzed voice is Charles Dodge's own spoken readings of the four Strand poems. The resynthesized voice is perceived as spoken, sung, or (at times in songs 3 and 4) as distorted outside the sonic range of either speech or singing. No other sound source is heard, and, except in the last song to be realized (song 2, "The Days Are Ahead"), the music is strictly monophonic: no two sounds are ever presented simultaneously.

The utterances in the songs are exceedingly short. By Dodge's account, the maximum length of a synthesized sound that Olive's system could generate (before a technical advance appeared in time for song 2) was about four seconds. This seems to have been more an inspiration than a constraint for Dodge: one utterance toward the end of song 1 lasts only 1/7 second.

The utterances were put together in the manner of a classical studio piece, by splicing together a large number of short segments of tape, each containing one real-time utterance from Olive's machine. (Here again, song 2 is an exception, as described later.)

In its earlier version (as used in songs 3 and 4), Olive's speech synthesis system was organized as shown in figure 4.1. The digital signal processing chain (the right-hand side of the diagram) consisted of two signal generators, one for pulse trains and one for noise; a crossfader that could be used to select which of the two sources to use; and a bank of resonant filters. The signal sources modeled the production of vocal sound by the glottis and/or regions of air turbulence, and the filter bank modeled the resonances of the vocal tract.

The left-hand side of figure 4.1 shows the organization of the control inputs of the signal generators. These were realized as stored function tables that supplied time-varying values of pitch (for the pulse generator), a crossfade value to switch between the two signal generators, and, for each of a series of resonant filters arranged in series,

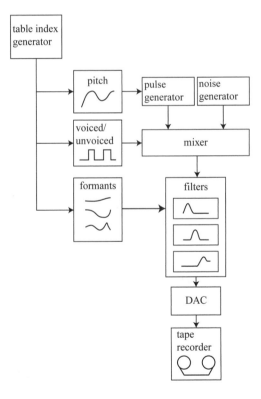

Figure 4.1
Block diagram of the speech synthesis system used by Dodge, showing (right) the signal chain and (left) control sources for the various stages of signal processing. For songs 1 and 2, the series of three resonant filters was replaced by a single higher-order recursive filter whose coefficients were computed using LPC analysis.

controls for gain, bandwidth, and resonant frequency. (Although in analog practice such filter banks would be arranged in parallel, it was common practice in modeling systems digitally to arrange them in series.) To judge from the sonogram of figure 4.2, five resonant filters were used, of which the resonant frequencies of the first three appear to be significant; a fourth resonant frequency around 3,500 Hz was essentially fixed, and the fifth, wavering in a narrow range above 4,000 Hz, probably had little audible effect.

A shared speed control allowed all these control inputs to be read at specified speeds from the various stored tables that held them. This not only permitted time stretching or compression but also was used to select which portion of an analyzed utterance would be used—either an entire phrase, a single phoneme, or sometimes only a portion of a phoneme.

The pitch, crossfade, and filter control values were all initially derived from analyses of Dodge's readings of the poems. If the speed control was set to unity and the various wavetables were left unchanged, the system would then resynthesize the spoken poems.

Dodge could speed up the speech or slow it down via the centralized speed control. Also, he could edit the wavetables holding the various controls (most often, and probably exclusively, pitch and the resonant frequencies of formants) or could simply replace any of them with a constant value independent of time (although he only used that possibility for pitch or for the pulse/noise crossfade value). These alterations were made through a graphical editing interface, using the CRT and the light pen that was integrated into the speech synthesizer software.

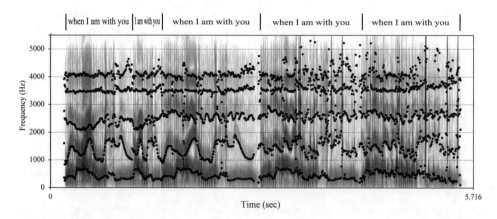

Figure 4.2

An analysis, using the Praat software package, of five repetitions of the phrase "when I am with you," showing five analyzed formant center frequencies.

In songs 1 and 2, the filter section was replaced by a single, probably tenth-order, recursive filter whose coefficients were calculated using LPC. This made for a more natural-sounding (and much less glitchy) sonic output but came at a considerable price: it was no longer possible to edit the resonant frequencies directly. Manipulating the coefficients of the recursive filter would have changed the result unrecognizably or, more likely and even more unfortunately, rendered the filter unstable.[4]

The affordances were thus as follows. First, by changing the speed of synthesis and/or adding splicing tape between utterances, the composer could impose rhythms (musical or speech-like) on the resynthesized speech. For example, at the beginning of song 3, the opening "sung" phrase is metrically timed. A speech-like example occurs at the end of song 2, as the word *later* is repeated at various speed changes (but otherwise naturally); the results are speech-like and nonmetrical.

Second, the pitch could be replaced with another one, either constant or in a series of steps, tuned to one or more musical pitches. This, often in combination with the imposition of metrical timing, is used to produce "singing," again as in the opening phrase of song 3 and also that of song 1. In the opening of song 2, the pitch is set syllablewise into musical pitches, but the timing is that of the analyzed speech (variously normal, accelerated, or decelerated). Throughout *Speech Songs*, the Western tempered pitch scale is used.

Third, the pitch could be replaced by another wavetable, entered by the composer as a curve on the CRT screen. This was done in an editor that initially showed the analyzed pitch trace of the speech, so that the curve the composer entered could be guided by the original or not, as desired. This is used in several repetitions of the word *I* in song 3, in which it is rendered in the form of a question, an emphatic assertion, and a quizzical half-assertion. In song 1, this is used once, to produce a surprising and humorous glissando at the end of a sung phrase.

Fourth, voiced speech could be replaced by unvoiced resynthesis by altering the crossfade value between pulses and noise. (One could presumably do the opposite as well, but Dodge does not, having perhaps discovered that the sonic results were much less interesting.) This appears also on the word *I* in song 3.

Fifth, in songs 3 and 4 (before the LPC filter was introduced), the wavetables setting the resonant frequencies of the three formants could be redrawn in the same way as the pitch wavetables. By raising or lowering the first or second formant a few half-tones (tens of percent in frequency), the perceived size of the vocal tract could be changed, making a throttled sound. More drastic changes could be used to suggest hideous disfigurement. In general, the intelligibility of the text would be greatly reduced, but in *Speech Songs* the setting of the text ensures that the source always remains identifiable.

This is accomplished by juxtaposing the distorted speech with undistorted speech with the same pitch contour and timing.

These transformations are used quite liberally throughout songs 3 and 4. The first two songs rely exclusively on control over pitch and timing, leaving timbre untouched.

The Musical Treatment of Text in *Speech Songs*

Song 3, reportedly the first one Dodge composed, provides the best introduction to his approach and way of using the possibilities of Olive's system. The most fundamental musical transformation is that from speech to "singing." Song 3 can be heard as a sort of exposition-and-variations of a skeletal setting, shown in figure 4.3, folded inward so that the exposition frames the entire piece, the first sentence introducing it and the second one concluding it. This entire "exposition" lasts 15 seconds, about one-sixth of the piece.

The times and pitches shown in the transcription are not exactly as they appear in the song. The time durations were probably guided in part by the length of the analyzed syllables. In transcribing them, an attempt was made to find reasonable quantizations, but timings shown as eighth notes, for instance, vary all the way from about 300 to 450 milliseconds. Most pitches (analyzed using the sigmund~ object in Pure Data) were fairly close to the 12-tone tempered ones shown, except for one note that was 0.6 half-tones sharp (and could therefore have been notated at the next higher half-step, except that the audible interval from the previous note would then have sounded wrong). These deviations likely are not intentional (and they largely disappear in songs 1 and 2), but rather they probably reflect the difficulty of entering exact pitches given the presumably limited resolution of the light pen used to enter them. Software designers might wish to note that graphical entry is not always the best way to specify a pitch.

The transcription in figure 4.3 shows time markings above the staves at five points, where the exposition continues after each of five interruptions that form the remainder of the piece. The first such interruption lasts about 70 of the song's 94 seconds, and not only develops the phrase it follows ("when I am with you") but also connects it with the phrase "when you are with me," which mirrors the earlier phrase.

The first interruption begins by repeating the first phrase, in spoken form, in five variations. The first two can be heard as "spoken" resyntheses of Dodge's original utterance, the first at normal speed (perhaps), the second one truncated to "I am with you" and sped up by a factor of about 2. In the remaining three, the entire phrase is resynthesized, at about two-thirds the original speed, with progressively more distorted formants.

Figure 4.2 shows a formant analysis, made using the Praat software package (Boersma and Van Heuven 2001), of these five repetitions, superimposed onto a sonogram. Although

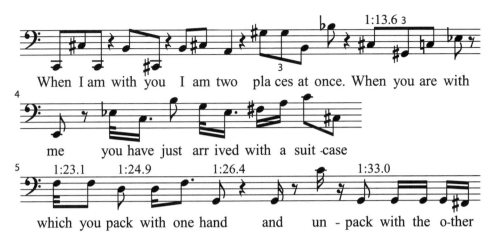

Figure 4.3
Exposition of song 3, as pitches and rhythms extracted from the first sung occurrence of each syllable of the poem. Annotations above notes show where the syllables were found in the piece. Notated rhythms are approximate.

this analysis cannot be taken as a faithful restoration of the formants as functions of time that were edited by Dodge, they show the progression qualitatively. If Praat's analysis algorithm can be trusted (as it probably can, since it is being used to analyze synthetic speech whose production closely agrees with Praat's own modeling assumptions), we find that Dodge redrew the third formant for the first of the three modified resyntheses, then the second, then the first, so that at the final repetition the first three formants have all been denatured. The changes can be roughly described as the addition of synthetic vibrato with no particular effort to "vibrate" coherently in the three formants. All these repetitions maintain the (presumed) original pitch contour of the spoken phrase and are heard as spoken, not sung.

Starting with the second repetition, but especially prominently in the fourth and fifth, we can see the propensity of the filter bank to introduce glitches or clicks into the signal. These glitches momentarily confuse Praat's formant analysis, but they are clearly visible in the sonogram. They are probably caused by numerical overflow in the filters, and they seem to occur at points where the formant evolution is greatly sped up or, especially, when the formants are edited by hand to change quickly in time. They are numerous in song 3, less so in song 4, and do not appear at all in songs 1 and 2. (The LPC implementation was apparently more robust than the discrete filter bank.)

Over the following 40 seconds (from 0:15 to 0:55), the five monosyllabic words are explored in three new ways: as detached units, out of the context of the phrase, and with artificially imposed pitch traces. These three explorations leave the formant structure unchanged. In the first, the syllable "when" is "sung" at four different pitches, then "spoken," much more slowly, at a pitch that sweeps upward over a huge interval (an eleventh)—a prosody that is at once histrionic and deeply ambiguous.

The second such exploration is to repeat one syllable ("I") at varying transpositions and repetition rates. This treatment hearkens all the way back to Pierre Schaeffer in 1949 (the year in which his studio acquired a tape recorder), but with the crucial difference that here the transpositions don't denature the phonemes as they would have in a tape-speed change.

The third exploration develops the first phrase, in spoken form, in three ways. The different syllables are presented out of order, first isolated and then in pairs ("I am," which are consecutive in the poem, but also "I you," which are not). They are given a variety of pseudospoken prosodies; for example, the "I" at 0:30 starts at A4 (440 Hz), dives down three octaves, then settles at E-flat midway between the two As, all in 0.3 seconds.

Increasingly, from 0:15 until about 0:40, the utterances are separated, first into groups and then into unitary or binary sounds, by long, awkward pauses. The effect is of a progressively extreme zooming in. This is then reversed as density builds in preparation for the resumption of the melodic statement at 1:13.6.

Dodge pulls us out of this microscopic examination, and back into the flow of the poem, by exploiting the mirror relationship between the opening phrase and the beginning of the second sentence, "When you are with me." A turning point occurs between 1:00 and 1:05, where the first phrase is "sung" in a series of widening glissandi (alternately upward and downward), followed by a narrowing series on the answering phrase, all symmetrically around the fixed (unheard) pitch C3 (131 Hz). These glissandi sound "sung" and not "spoken" because the pitch track for each syllable spends at least a moment at rest on both the beginning and ending pitches.

After the poem resumes, for the remaining 20 seconds of the piece, the poem sets the pace and the four remaining interruptions act as reminders of the long development section, focusing on different behaviors: first, the word *suitcase* is repeated in a way similar to the five repetitions of the opening phrase (but with the addition of "spoken" prosodic changes, and whispers, that had been introduced later). Then the words *you* and *one* are very briefly adorned with sequences of glissandi, and finally the "un" of *unpack* is repeated at different pitches, Schaeffer-like, as were the words *I* at 0:23 and *you* at 0:52.

Some observations can be made about the song overall. About the piece, Dodge writes that, "The computer-synthesized voice seemed to me an ideal medium for representing the ambivalence indicated in the line ["When I am with you, I am two places at once"].

I could do so directly in sound, I thought, by making a voice that, literally, would do two things at once: articulate the poetry and delineate a pitched musical line" (Dodge 1989).

This is borne out by the transcription of figure 4.3. The melodic contour and rhythm can be heard as a highly theatrical reading of the poem. The opening line, jumping up and down by intervals close to an octave, seems to maintain two voices at once. The setting of "you have just arrived in a suitcase" skitters up and down in thirds in a camp frenzy. The last phrase is recited in a baffled monotone. Throughout, the rhythms and pitches are those of natural (if histrionic) speech, not those that we could reasonably ask a singer to perform. The tessitura, the intervallic reaches, and the timing, while all perfectly reachable in spoken language, would resist being sung by anything but a machine.

The song reinforces the poetics of the phrase "two places at once" in other ways as well. The extreme zooming in of the song's first half can be heard as a gradual change in point of view but alternatively can be understood as a sort of nude-descending-a-staircase effect, offering several points of view on the same speech that can be comprehended simultaneously. And the mirroring in both pitch and time by which the song binds the poem to itself can be seen as another way of keeping multiple reflections of the same object simultaneously in view, in much the same way as real mirrors can.

The song's overall tone of bemused humor is intentional (Dodge 1976). It is maintained in part by the repetitions, which might suggest the way phrases are sometimes repeated in classical musical settings of texts, except that they are often pronouns ("I," "me") or mere syllables that are rendered nonsensical by the repetition ("un"). The timing is that of a joke, with internal repetition leading to an unexpected and precipitous punch-line ending. The prosody contributes as well; for instance, by one syllable "I" stretched over three octaves (at 0:30) and by the heated discussion (as if between two parties) of the word *suitcase* (1:18).

This willing exploitation of the latent humor in Strand's poetry is a departure from the earlier pieces cited here as antecedents. Schaeffer's musique concrète and Stockhausen's early vocal work project ponderous seriousness, seemingly to the point of defensiveness. And Berio, starting from an explosively funny text from Joyce, as voiced by the wildly, jovially charismatic Cathy Berberian, somehow achieves a work of high-art seriousness that elides all the situation's humorous possibilities. I'm thankful to Dodge for not following these antecedents too closely.

Taking song 3 as a point of departure, the remaining songs can be heard as deeper and more focused explorations of ideas that are proposed (or first discovered) in this earliest one. In song 4 ("He Destroyed Her Image"), the technique of repeating "spoken" phrases with progressively distorted formants (while maintaining pitch and timing) allows us to "hear" the phrases even though they are mangled beyond intelligibility.

The comedy here becomes grotesque, even horrible. Dodge also calls attention here to a change in point of view in the poem (Gross 2000). In this case, it is a contrast between the first lines—whose externality calls to mind Shirley Jackson's story "The Lottery"—and the interior narrator of the remainder, which Dodge echoes in his use of contrast between intelligibility and unintelligibility.

As in song 3, there is an underlying setting of the poem, lasting about 10 seconds, which is revealed phrase by phrase as the song unfolds. Also as before, the text is presented in three modes: "sung" (with stable pitches for each syllable, except for occasional connecting glissandi), "spoken" (with the original spoken pitch contour), or on an arc that was presumably drawn using the graphical editor. The rhythms appear to be taken from the original spoken text, in which each phrase proceeds at a nearly steady clip (0.2 seconds per syllable) with a prolonged last syllable. The exception is the four syllables "knew he'd seen her," whose durations are dotted (300 milliseconds), perhaps to make room for the higher density of consonants there. The unsyncopated reading makes room for the listener to hear the timing as musical.

Unlike song 3, with only one exception, all the "sung" synthesis hews to the underlying setting; there is no oratorio-style setting. The exception is that, in the setting of the word *before* at 1:08, the word is repeated three times, the first and third borrowing pitches from immediately neighboring syllables. (*Before* is the last word of the penultimate phrase, before the punch line is revealed.)

In contrast with song 3, in which the punch line cuts off the song in the space of 1.4 seconds, here it is revealed only about three-fifths of the way into the song (missing the golden section by two seconds, which one hopes is just a coincidence). Instead, this song can be heard as an almost serialistic exercise, in which the choices of pitched, spoken, or arched, normal, rapid, or slow speed, and normal or denatured formants create the form.

In song 1 ("A Man Sitting in the Cafeteria"), the use of repetition, variation, and comic rhythmic clashes is further developed. Here there is no longer any timbral manipulation. (If indeed this was done using LPC, as I suspect, the formants could no longer be touched in any case.) No changes are made to the voiced or unvoiced selection either. The entire song relies on manipulation of pitch and rhythm. Dodge further develops the prolongation process used in "When I Am with You," deriving the first 25 seconds of song 1 from only the two syllables "a man." Slightly later, over a period of eight seconds, Dodge races straight to the end of the poem, pausing only to repeat the last three words ("which was fake?") in retrograde (as if alternately weighing each ear choice against the other), before returning to regale the listener with repetitions of "a man" for another eternity (both of which Dodge somehow fits into the 90-second duration of the song).

There is no "spoken" or "arched" text, only "sung." But here the sung text has free range, without any single once-through setting as in songs 3 and 4. The rhythms are even freer than the pitches, not appearing to hew even to any grid or scale, as if the tape montage were done entirely by ear.

The lack of formant manipulation, and the strict adherence to monophonic, pitched synthesis, makes for an interesting affordance: it is a fairly easy exercise to regenerate the entire song using modern, reproducible technology (Puckette 2006). Figure 4.4 shows a representation of one phrase out of the song as I regenerated it using Pure Data. Gray rectangles mark periods of sibilance, and black marks below them mark the beginnings of vocal fragments, each of which extends in time up to the following one. The last marker, whose fragment is represented by a hyphen, finishes the phrase. Pitch (vertical) and time (horizontal) are proportionally spaced, with bass and treble "staves" spaced to respect semitone distances.

While songs 3 and 4 will most likely be available only as tape pieces, song 1 and perhaps song 2 can also be considered open to interpretation by future musicians. As the technology became more sophisticated, in this instance at least, the controls became more abstract and more akin to the specifications found in a traditional musical score, thus inviting reinterpretation.

Song 2, "The Days Are Ahead," the last in order of realization, takes advantage of an apparent advance in the technology that permitted storing sounds with far greater durations than the earlier four-second limit. Also, a hard-disk-based mixing program

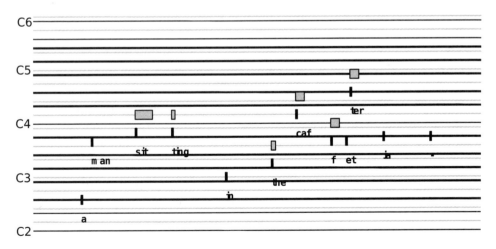

Figure 4.4
Rendition in Pure Data of the phrase "A man, sitting in the cafeteria," from song 1, 0:25–0:30.

had become available that afforded polyphony. (Tape-based multitracking and overdub-
bing were already practiced in analog studios, but they probably were not possible at
Bell Labs for lack of a research justification.) Song 2 revisits the rapid-fire, monophonic
oratorio-style setting of song 1 ("ahead," with the syllable "head" repeated to the point
of exhaustion) but adds contiguous segments, up to 24 seconds long, that are mixtures of
up to four layers. These take the form of canons, "sung" (at the outset), spoken, or finally,
in the longest segment, consisting of phrase-long, crisscrossing glissandi that make a
spider-web pattern of contrapuntally falling and rising pitches (from 0:41 to 1:05).

Here again, timing and prosody are turned to humorous effect. Of the poem's 47
syllables, 34 consist of reciting two seven-digit numbers that differ by exactly one. The
jokey tedium of this exercise is cast in high relief by the musical setting, in somewhat
the same way as in the numerical canon that appears in *Watt* by Samuel Beckett.

As in songs 1 and 4, once the poem has been revealed, it is revisited in a different
light. The reprise starts with a second number recitation, taken up in monophonic
"sung" mode as in song 1 but straight through with no repetition, until the last three
digits burst anew in a polyphonic (but this time synchronous) falling web of glissandi.
The song ends in a spoken, canonical treatment of the ending phrase that echoes an
earlier treatment of the first phrase at the beginning of the song.

Conclusions

Max Mathews's success in attracting a formidable group of composers to work at Bell Labs
during the formative years of computer music might be partly the result of self-selection
on their parts but probably also Mathews's own good judgment. In any case, in the work
of each of the composers who spent large chunks of time there, we can see the formation
of directions of musical inquiry that have had enormous implications for the subsequent
development of computer music and, by extension, electronic music in general.

Charles Dodge's contribution was to apply computer speech synthesis technology
to the production of electronic vocal music, which had earlier been limited to the
manipulation of recorded speech by using tape techniques. Rather than merely adjoin
the new possibilities of the computer to the existing repertory of tape manipulation
techniques (of which he was very well aware from his earlier work at the Columbia-
Princeton Electronic Music Studio), Dodge presented his new world of sound in its
rawest form, as a pure blast from what was then the future of vocal electronic music.

Other composers quickly took note. As early as 1979, Paul Lansky completed *Six
Fantasies on a Poem by Thomas Campion*, in which LPC was used to synthesize a lush,
enveloping world of electronic song. For his part, Dodge, ever the radical, went on to
write *Any Resemblance Is Purely Coincidental* (1978), in which he pushed the poetics of

ambiguity and dislocation, already a major concern in *Speech Songs*, to even further extremes. The roots of computer music lie deep in what might be called high modernism, but *Any Resemblance*, in its breakage of the contract between composer, performer, and listener, is a work of postmodernism.

The four *Speech Songs* give us a record of a year of feverishly fast progress in speech synthesis technology at Bell Labs and its application to computer music. Over this time, the analysis/synthesis technique evolved from a highly cranky discrete-filter method to the much cleaner LPC analysis/synthesis, and, judging from the improvements in accuracy (particularly as to intonation) over the span of the four songs, the techniques for specifying and editing synthesis parameters were also improving rapidly. Polyphony, as well as sounds lasting more than four seconds each, appeared suddenly in the last of the songs.

At the same time, a new paradigm for making music out of vocal sounds was emerging out of Dodge's experiments. A striking and vivid musical vocabulary, essentially a redefinition of song form itself, appeared, almost out of nowhere. In this vocabulary, song and speech, pitch, rhythm, and timbre could all be taken apart and recombined into new sonic forms. In Dodge's words, "It was making music out of the nature of speech itself" (Gross 2000).

Notes

1. Although the term *computer music* originally meant "music made using a computer," this meaning is now obsolete, since almost no published music is made without incorporating one. Today the term is best used to describe a musical genre, dating roughly between 1957 and 1990, during which composers explored new technical possibilities only available in locations, such as Bell Labs, where computers could be used to make musical sounds.

2. Dodge recounts that he was welcomed to Bell Labs under the guise of a research project; simply composing a piece of music would not earn him his visitor's badge (Thieberger 1995).

3. The 1984 breakup of the AT&T corporation resulted in Bell Labs being spun off as an independent (and therefore profit-driven) company. Mathews saw the writing on the wall.

4. Dodge recalls that LPC only became available in time to be used in song 2, but both the overall timbre and consideration of the lack of formant manipulation heard in song 1 suggest that Dodge's recollection is in error and that song 1 was also synthesized using LPC. In this account, I'll go by the evidence of my own ears and posit that songs 1 and 2 were both realized using LPC.

References

Boersma, Paul, and Vincent Van Heuven. 2001. "Speak and unSpeak with PRAAT." *Glot International* 5 (9–10): 341–347.

Dodge, Charles. 1976. *Synthesized Speech Music* (liner notes). Brooklyn, NY: CRI Records.

Dodge, Charles. 1989. "On Speech Songs." In *Current Directions in Computer Music Research*, edited by Max Mathews and John Pierce, 9–18. Cambridge, MA: MIT Press.

Dodge, Charles. 1992. *Any Resemblance Is Purely Coincidental*. CD. San Francisco: New Albion Records.

Gertner, Jon. 2012. *The Idea Factory: Bell Labs and the Great Age of American Innovation*. New York: Penguin.

Gross, Jason. 2000. "Charles Dodge Talks About His *Speech Songs*." Online notes for *OHM: The Early Gurus of Electronic Music*. Roslyn, NY: Ellipsis Arts. http://www.furious.com/perfect/ohm/dodge.html.

Mathews, Max V., with Joan E. Miller, F. Richard. Moore, John R. Pierce and Jean-Claude Risset. 1969. *The Technology of Computer Music*. Cambridge, MA: MIT Press.

Mathews, Max V., and F. Richard Moore. 1970. "GROOVE—a Program to Compose, Store, and Edit Functions of Time." *Communications of the ACM* 13(12): 715–721.

Olive, Joseph P. 1971. "Automatic Formant Tracking by a Newton-Raphson Technique." *Journal of the Acoustical Society of America* 50: 661.

Olive, Joseph P. 1998. "The Talking Computer: Text to Speech Synthesis." In *HAL's Legacy: 2001's Computer as Dream and Reality*, edited by David Stork, 101–129. Cambridge, MA: MIT Press.

Park, Tae Hong. 2009. "An Interview with Max Mathews." *Computer Music Journal* 33(3): 9–22.

Puckette, Miller. 2006. "Phase-Bashed Packet Synthesis: A Musical Test." In *Proceedings of the International Computer Music Conference, International Computer Music Association*. http://msp.ucsd.edu/pdrp/latest/files/dodge-song/doc/icmc06.pdf.

Rabiner, Lawrence R, Leland B. Jackson, Ronald W. Schafer, and Cecil H. Coker. 1971. "A Hardware Realization of a Digital Formant Speech Synthesizer." *IEEE Transactions on Communication Technology* 19(6): 1016–1020.

Roads, Curtis, ed. 1985. *Composers and the Computer*. Los Altos, CA: W. Kaufmann.

Schrader, Barry. 1982. *Introduction to Electro-acoustic Music*. Englewood Cliffs, NJ: Prentice-Hall.

Tenney, James. 1969. "Computer Music Experiences, 1961–1964." *Electronic Music Reports* 1(1): 23.

Thieberger, Ed M., and Charles Dodge. 1995. "An Interview with Charles Dodge." *Computer Music Journal* 19(1): 11–24.

Wishart, Trevor, and Simon Emmerson. 1996. *On Sonic Art*. New York: Psychology Press.

5 The Musical Imagination of Knut Wiggen

Jøran Rudi

Introduction

Several musical genres have their origin in the intersection between technology and art, and thus electronic technologies have left large footprints in the musical landscape. Technology-based music first developed from analog recording technologies and signal processing, and the subsequent incorporation of digital techniques for composition and performance brought qualitatively new aspects to bear in the music. Complexity, accuracy, and control became more easily managed, and adaption of data from arbitrary sources often became part of the musical logic.

This chapter will discuss the musical advances made by Knut Wiggen at the Electronic Music Studio (EMS) in Stockholm during the early 1970s, and in particular *Sommarmorgon* (Summer Morning), which was the first piece he made using his groundbreaking software, MusicBox. From computer printouts of his scores, it is clear that the same approach was used for composing all five of his published studies, and the analysis of *Sommarmorgon* reveals the new compositional method that he believed was necessary for the full exploitation of the new technologies.

Wiggen's personal achievements and technical development at EMS have been described by Hartenstein (2011), Groth (2010), and Rudi (2018) and have also been discussed in Broman's (2007) book on the Swedish history of "music of the future." A degree of repetition from these secondary sources has been deemed necessary for contextualization purposes.

Background and Context

Knut Wiggen (1927–2016) was born in a small Norwegian town near Trondheim, and, like many of his generation, he lived through the musical turbulence that followed in the wake of World War II. After the war, composers sought to make qualitatively new music untainted by the neoclassical tradition and nationalist ideologies that had played a part in the war effort on all sides. In Norway, as well as in other countries, young composers and musicians were turning to international trends, namely the incorporation of technology and modernism's demands for an absolute music unconnected to any agenda other than its own.

Wiggen originally wanted to become a pianist, and his desire for better work opportunities lay behind his move to Stockholm in 1950. At that time, the music community in Norway was not nearly as developed as in Sweden; the economy was better there, and the future seemed brighter for an aspiring musician. Wiggen had studied piano with Robert Riefling in Norway, and in Stockholm he went to study with Gottfried Boon and Hans Leygraf. Leygraf brought Wiggen to the Darmstadt summer courses, which since their initiation in 1946 (by Wilhelm Steinecke) had quickly become a waterhole for modernism in music. Wiggen thrived in that environment to such a degree that he took up residence there from 1952 to 1955, and he became acquainted with the works and ideas of key modernist composers, many of whom would remain in his network throughout his professional career. Pierre Schaeffer, Karlheinz Stockhausen, Bruno Maderna, Gottfried Wilhelm Koenig, Luigi Nono, Luciano Berio, Pierre Boulez, Iannis Xenakis, and Jozef Patkowski, among others, were part of Wiggen's European network. Several of them would visit Stockholm for meetings and conferences, and as teachers in courses that Wiggen produced both before and after he began building EMS. In North America, Wiggen communicated with Max Mathews, Jean-Claude Risset, Lejaren Hiller, Gustav Ciamaga, John Chowning, and others. Wiggen's scores from the 1950s for piano and other acoustic instruments clearly show the serial influence from Darmstadt, but also a romantic sensitivity to the personal expression of both composer and performing musician. It seems clear that the Darmstadt years set Wiggen on the musical path he would follow in the years to come.

As Martin Iddon (2013) has described, although the Darmstadt summer courses were clearly dominated by serialism, they also allowed for many other types of aesthetics and compositional approaches. Electronic music captured Wiggen's attention, with clear constructions that resembled serial music's paradigm of mathematics and strict rules. At the same time, electronic music provided opportunities for "new, unheard sounds," and Wiggen felt that electronic means provided the best opportunities to create a new music that did not draw on the interval-based paradigm.

In Europe, musique concrète with recorded sounds on tape competed with synthesized music, while North America was further along in implementing computers in the compositional process and in the development of digital synthesis.[1] The earliest use of computers in music was in algorithmic composition of computer-generated scores for performance on acoustic instruments. This limitation to interval-based acoustic music did not suit Wiggen's vision of a "music of the future,"[2] since it remained too close to the music traditions of the past. It should be mentioned that he had nonetheless tried his hand at this type of algorithmic composition as well. He made at least two compositions during 1963–1964, *Wiggen-1* and *Wiggen-2*, and discussed them with Lejaren Hiller in Illinois when visiting in 1965.[3] Yet Wiggen had come to see computer-controlled synthesis as the best way forward for musical use of the new computer technology, as he saw that the formalization used in computer organization of pitches could also be used in organizing any synthesized timbre. This approach became important in Wiggen's compositional method.

The modernist credo of art for art's sake regarding music, perhaps most strongly promoted by Princeton professor Milton Babbitt (1958) in his famous article "Who Cares If You Listen?,"[4] did not ring true with Wiggen. In Scandinavia, the political atmosphere was one of constructing and expanding the welfare state. In Sweden, *folkhemmet*[5] and contemporary music enjoyed strong support from the social democrats, who were the dominant political force at the time. In Stockholm, composer Karl-Birger Blomdahl had already established the influential social democratic think tank "The Monday Group" during World War II. This group discussed the role of modern art culture in the new society that was being developed.

In Sweden, centralization of the population in larger cities, coupled with rapid industrialization and technical advances, resulted in new social structures, where distribution of information and increased competence were essential to the success of the large changes taking place. It was expected that the new everyday life would result in, and also depend on, a growing demand for cultural *participation*, not only consumption. To develop such relatively egalitarian societies, it was necessary to make resources available for broad groups, with new music occupying a significant place in the social fabric rather than becoming an elitist expression. Cultural activities needed to incorporate technology to avoid becoming marginalized expressions of the past. Wiggen and others felt that with the development of radio and (the relatively recent) television, the new mediascape *required* a new music that was built for it. Furthermore, it was important to avoid a disjuncture between industry, economy, and culture, a concern held not only by musicians but also by prominent representatives from the scientific and technological communities. An expression of this concern was apparent in a chronicle written by 15 scientists that was published on the front page of one of the largest newspapers in Sweden, *Dagens Nyheter*, in conjunction with the exhibition "Visioner av nuet" (Visions of the Contemporary) in 1966.[6] Wiggen understood this chronicle as a solid support for his efforts in making technology that would change the musical paradigm and increase availability and participation. Music could not remain in the interval-based bourgeois salon or orchestra culture but should be supported by studios for public access to be built across the country.

EMS Tools for Composition

EMS was established in 1964 as part of the Swedish Broadcasting Corporation (SR), and Knut Wiggen was appointed as the founding director. At that time, Wiggen had already established a strong international network and had traveled extensively to studios in Europe and the United States. He had already built a studio for electronic music in Stockholm at Arbetarnas Bildningsförbund (the cultural arm of a labor organization) and had been chairman of the concert presenter Fylkingen since 1959. The Norwegian immigrant was the obvious candidate for this key position.

The project of developing a full-scale hybrid studio for composers was an ambitious one. First, the studio had to be automatic and simple to use in order to reduce the long production times known from analog studios. This would make it possible to facilitate a larger number of composers.[7] Second, the sound quality had to be improved from the low signal-to-noise ratios typical of tape music composition of the time, with its bounces and remixes. Third, the studio had to produce sound in nearly real time when the composer changed parameters, and finally, the studio had to make new compositional methods possible.[8] Today, it is difficult to understand how radical those goals were in the mid-1960s, and as an example, only a few years later, in the early 1970s, it could take 24 hours from input to synthesized result from the famous RCA Mark II machine of Columbia University.[9]

As discussed in Rudi (2018), it is fair to say that these goals were reached, and the large number of productions in the computer studio indicates that the digital/analog system was successful.[10] However, Wiggen's early departure from EMS in 1975 severely reduced the impact of these advancements, since the next studio director, Jon Appleton, and his successor, Lars Gunnar Bodin, prioritized more conventional tape composition techniques.[11] Their focus on the tape studio in turn contributed significantly to extending the EMS reputation that Wiggen had built.

Software development was essential in order to turn computers into useful musical tools, and the coding environment EMS-0 was programmed in Fortran, while EMS-1 was programmed in assembler, for quicker execution.[12] It might seem odd that Wiggen decided to write new programs for EMS, but the MUSIC N family of languages (starting with MUSIC I in 1957) was not written for control of external hardware, which was what EMS needed for its hybrid approach. So instead of modifying, for example,

MUSIC V, new software was made that could be optimized for the EMS hardware. In 1973, James Beauchamp wrote in his unpublished study of hybrid studio development that the EMS studio had "probably the most powerful system in the world to be placed for the exclusive use of composers." (Beauchamp 1973, 18). Once the equipment could be controlled from a computer, the goals of automation and a time-efficient composition process were met. Wiggen has relayed a conversation he had with James Tenney, who at the time worked at Bell Labs in New Jersey, where he explained that it would take him one week to do the same things at Bell Labs that it took him one hour to do at EMS (Wiggen 2004, 34).

The efficiency issue was also addressed through the development of the EMS control console (figure 5.1) that displayed parameter values from the computer and allowed composers to make nearly real-time alterations to their scores. The values, however, could not be generated in real time but instead were stored on and played back from digital tape. When a new compression/expansion method was launched at EMS in 1965, the sound quality was radically improved to a 100 dB signal-to-noise ratio.[13]

Wiggen often described the need for a new compositional method, and he was critical of the less structured approaches of acousmatic composition. He wanted rule-based

Figure 5.1
The EMS control console. Photo source unknown.

approaches that would put distance between the composer and the resulting sound, allowing the composer to focus on structure and logic. Although it is easy to see kinship between this idea and the Darmstadt school, Wiggen felt that the Darmstadt serial approach did not address the new technological reality and that it was not a radical enough break with the musical past.

For Wiggen, the languages EMS-0 and EMS-1 were only steps along the way, and in parallel with the development of EMS-1, he guided the development of a more radical approach, which took shape in the hands of programmer David Fahrland. Fahrland had just completed his master's thesis on the combination of discrete and continuous parameter variations, and he moved from California to Sweden at Wiggen's invitation to work on the proposed new software. At Fahrland's suggestion, the software was named MusicBox.

MusicBox

EMS-0 and EMS-1, which Wiggen described as programs limited to "editing, education, improvisation and timbral exploration" (Wiggen 1972, 141–143), were procedural programs working in much the same manner as the MUSIC N family. Wiggen was critical of MUSIC V's model of separate instructions for instrument and score, and he questioned whether this allowed enough freedom for composers to go beyond interval-based conventions. He praised Xenakis's closer integration of sound and compositional structure and his explicit use of mathematics and modeling in the music. This pointed to a development beyond EMS-1.

MusicBox was the crowning achievement of Wiggen's development work at EMS. It can be described as an object-based domain-specific language for composition, and to my knowledge it was the first of its kind. Other languages that were being developed around hybrid technologies at the time, such as GROOVE (Bell Labs), The Piper (Toronto), and Zinovieff's system from the Electronic Music Studios in London, were oriented more toward real-time control of sound equipment than composition and remained on a research scale rather than being developed for full-scale studio use.

A composition in MusicBox was a network of interconnected boxes that produced control signals for the analog electronic equipment at EMS. Each box contained a mathematical function that would operate on its input and provide an output, and the output message would be the input message for the next box in the network flow. The originality of his approach was that the software produced a data model of the composition and that this model was "simulated" through activation of the components. (Today, we would speak of instantiation of classes.) This idea of models is fundamental to object-oriented programming. The process of connecting boxes in MusicBox was quite different from the procedural EMS-1, where the composer had to describe each event line by line. The efficiency of the software may also be seen in the size of the printouts from Wiggen's compositions; they are just a few pages, while a printout of a seven-minute piece realized in EMS-1 could easily have measured more than 1 cm in thickness.

MusicBox was first realized in Fortran, a programming language used at the time by EMS programmers David Fahrland, Kaj Beskow, Zaid Holmin, and Robert Strömberg. It consisted of predefined micro boxes with defined inputs and outputs, and macro boxes that could be built by arbitrarily combining micro boxes. A set of macro boxes were predefined and thus part of the language, while other macro boxes could be defined for a certain composition. Macro boxes made it easy to manage complexity, and, when composing, they could be changed without the need for reinterpreting the composition. (See appendix A for a full list of the boxes dated January 1973.) In 1976, programmer Kaj Beskow reported that MusicBox consisted of 115 different micro and macro boxes. The boxes sent and received numbers, and the output boxes to the studio controls were precalibrated for appropriate control voltages to make more detailed specification from the composer unnecessary. The user interface of MusicBox was text based.

Spatialization has always been an interesting possibility in electronic music; loudspeakers can be placed around audiences in various formats, and signal processing can enhance both placement and the movement of sounds. Wiggen wrote about how these new possibilities could expand concert hall experiences, as sounds no longer needed to be bound by the fixed placement of ensembles and orchestras. The formalization of these possibilities had not been finished when work on the software began, but John Chowning's (1971) article about the simulation of moving sound sources provided the solution. The methods proposed by Chowning were implemented in MusicBox, and Wiggen became able to control spatialization algorithmically in the same manner as the other musical parameters. A Doppler shift was used to indicate velocity, while reverberation and frequency rolloff were used to indicate the distance to the point of origin of the sounds.

The loudspeakers used for spatialization at EMS were made by Stig Carlsson according to his idea of acoustical correctness, which meant that it was not only the speakers but the total sound in the concert space that needed to be as neutral as possible. Carlsson's speakers came in several models, and the recommended placement was close to the walls of the concert space to optimize room resonances. Several of the speaker types included filters that could be adjusted for typical room types.

MusicBox Development Post-EMS

When he left EMS, Wiggen took the MusicBox code with him, and in the early 1990s he made serious efforts to make the software approach relevant for simulating sound movement in augmented and virtual-reality applications. Later, he also proposed implementing a small part of MusicBox in cell-phone hardware to manufacturer Nokia, particularly a Gabor oscillator that would make a twitter sound very similar to bird-song. Nothing came of these initiatives, and when cell phones became smartphones and portable MP3 players, the demand for custom ringtones evaporated quite quickly.

Wiggen also tried to have MusicBox ported to Windows and Silicon Graphics machines. However, MusicBox was not successfully ported and given a graphical user interface until 2003, when students Håvard Wigtil, Harald Stendal, Nils Tesdal, and Sigurd Stendal at the Norwegian University of Science and Technology (NTNU), under the supervision of Dag Svanæs, rewrote the program in Java. This process involved rewriting the software for computer synthesis instead of addressing the EMS hardware. Since then, Zaid Holmin, one of the original EMS programmers from the 1970s, has added reverberation control and spatialization routines using the libraries of the gaming technology EAX, as well as a number of new micro and macro boxes. The original EMS macro boxes for spatial movement have been replaced with new micro boxes, as has the reverberation control. A synthesis engine in software has replaced the EMS analog sound generators from the 1970s.

During this porting process, the capacity of the software was increased to be able to handle hundreds of boxes and generate hundreds of sine waves simultaneously. At the time of this writing, however, it appears that Windows updates since Windows Vista no longer support EAX, making editing in the program impossible. Running a complete program with the spatialization technology can still be done under Windows XP, but it is clear that MusicBox now will serve more as a program of historical interest than as a current composition tool.

Music

In the early years of his career, Wiggen composed interval-based music. Judging from a survey of his available scores, it seems that he started off writing for voice and piano during his pre-Darmstadt years in Fredrikstad and Stockholm and that he continued to develop his writing for acoustic instruments while in Darmstadt. He wrote mainly for piano and small groups of instruments, and although his works have not been performed often, he was represented at arenas that were important for contemporary music at the time. His *Quartet for Piano, Violin, Clarinet, and Bassoon* (1955) was performed at the International Society for Contemporary Music's World Music Days in 1956, and his piano works were performed at a concert by Ny Musikk in Oslo in 1959.[14] Electronic music soon became his principal interest, and he explained that he considered music for instruments to be a thing of the past—not to be discarded, but preserved as the very valuable resource it was (Bækkelund 1972).[15]

After his return to Stockholm from Darmstadt, Wiggen spent the remainder of his professional years mainly as an organizer. He was elected chairman of Fylkingen in 1959 and quickly changed the agenda of the institution, which had featured conventional chamber music, in particular important works from the previous 50 years. The new focus was on electronic music and radical musical experimentation. Wiggen organized working groups around music analysis, philosophy, pedagogy, and cross-media trends to build vocabulary and reflections about new aesthetics. He organized concerts and seminars, traveled, and gathered information that he needed for building up studio resources for composers, and he built the first studio at Arbetarnas Bildningsförbund (ABF) in Stockholm in 1961. He was director of EMS starting in 1964, and it was only during the last four years of his tenure that he wrote music again, completing five studies that explored whether MusicBox could live up to its promise.

Musikmaskin I

Momentum for electronic music grew in Sweden, and Wiggen went beyond the established tape music paradigm in his promotion of electronic aesthetics wherever possible. His first work using digital means was produced in 1961, when he constructed the sound installation *Musikmaskin I*. It was designed by Öyvind Fahlström, built by Per-Olov Strömberg (who would later construct most of EMS's electronic equipment), and aimed at exploring randomness in music. Wiggen was interested in randomly generated musical structures and how these random processes could be relevant to listeners' meaning-making processes. In a text about the installation, he described the chance operations in John Cage's *Concert for Piano and Orchestra* and Karlheinz Stockhausen's *Klavierstück XI* as being guided more by the musicians' choices and conventions than pure chance; Wiggen wanted the chance operations to be freed from human intentions.[16]

Strangely enough, *Musikmaskin I* was designed as a kind of counterpoint for an exhibition of kinetic art, and according to Hartenstein (2011, 254), it was part of the exhibition aspect 61 at Liljevalchs konsthall (1961). The installation consisted only of a number of immobile and exposed circuit boards (figure 5.2) mounted in a vertical column. The white noise generated by the circuit boards was filtered and distributed in the exhibition space via 19 loudspeakers and given different durations and locations according to a preprogrammed logic in which chance operations played a part.

Figure 5.2
Musikmaskin I: an exposed, vertical column of circuit boards. Photo by Pressens Bild.

Unfortunately, the installation no longer exists; it was destroyed when EMS moved from its first location at Kungsgatan in Stockholm.[17] From the sparse notes and newspaper material, it is difficult to be sure exactly how the installation worked, but some general ideas can be identified. The basis for both sound and control was white noise generated by the boards, and Wiggen wrote that each card stored a "sound element" that would play when a random process produced an amplitude above a certain threshold. The sounds were filtered, and the filters could vary in bandwidth from a full octave to only 2 percent of an octave. The sound was also "cut up," producing a result that could oscillate between mere pulses and stable frequencies in a range up to 10 kHz. The bandwidth of the filter and the cut-up ratios could in part also be controlled manually. In this way, *Musikmaskin I* could produce pulses, tones, percussive sounds, or crackling, and Wiggen described it as a "discovery machine" for exploring transitions between pulse and frequency and between frequency and colored noise. This would explain why the filter was designed so that it could be set to as narrow as 2 percent of an octave.

It is interesting to note that Wiggen was experimenting with the perception of digital aesthetics as early as 1961. He was interested in investigating aspects of absolute music and random processes, and in the previously mentioned German text about the installation, he claims that "the music machines could be just as good a tool for these types of explorations as the symphony orchestras had ever been" (my translation).[18]

On a more pragmatic note, Wiggen wrote that the noise that was used as both sounding and structuring material could be exchanged with other types of sound, and he quipped that clips from radio programs of entertainment music could easily result in a better-sounding installation if used as material. It is clear that processing and logic were important to Wiggen and not the actual sound. Wiggen's experiments had significance for his future compositions—he later said that it was during his work with *Musikmaskin I* that he experienced pure chance operations as being "totally uninteresting" (Wiggen 2004, 89–90) and that he could get more interesting results by using restrained randomness.[19]

Wiggen-1 and Wiggen-2

Wiggen's next works in computer music were realized in 1963 on a Saab computer in Stockholm. Documentation of these pieces has not been found in Wiggen's texts or materials, but when Wiggen visited Lejaren Hiller in Urbana in 1965, he described *Wiggen-1* "as a technical exercise for piano, and not considered to be an authentic composition" (Hiller 1970, 87). Hiller wrote that the ambitions were higher for *Wiggen-2* and that Wiggen conceived the piece as the first of a suite of 10 computer music works. Hiller goes on to describe how Wiggen planned to develop the piece by using relatively independent rule-based and growth-decay patterns. Selection of pitches in one layer would depend on pitches that had already been chosen in the process, and this layer would correspond with another layer that could support, interrupt, or otherwise alter the first layer. The two pieces were programmed in Algol-Genius by Gunnar Hellström, who also named the works.[20] *Wiggen-1* was developed from an instruction set of six pages, and the rules defined how pitches, amplitudes, and durations were chosen. Randomness was essential but became increasingly restricted over the composition's duration, and the random numbers were "filtered" by previous events. Wiggen also described how the composition rules could be stored in the software to be useful as material for other composers at a later time.

Wiggen-1 and *Wiggen-2* are examples of algorithmic compositions to be performed by musicians. From Hiller's description of the compositional ideas, it is possible to recognize Wiggen's focus on processes rather than on specific timbres or melodic contours, much like his processes in *Musikmaskin I*. However, since Wiggen makes no mention of these pieces in his texts, they are best considered as evidence of the interest and direction he would explore later on.

Wiggen's Compositions in the Hybrid Studio

MusicBox was programmed to control the analog equipment at EMS. The digital control gave higher precision than could be achieved in the fully analog studios, but even at EMS, there were small inaccuracies. When listening through old master tapes, the sine tones used for calibration between the pieces are audibly (and visibly) out of phase between the four tracks. The signal-to-noise ratio, however, is excellent.

Wiggen's works using MusicBox were created during three years in the early 1970s, when computer music was still in its infancy, and they are typical examples of a new musical language displaying an interest in using extramusical data for creating structures. Wiggen wrote about this approach in his notes for the unpublished piece *Big Bang*: "The speed of the cluster movement is determined by the value of the module cluster width, measured by the speed of light, plus the small clusters' constant speeds, which are set to randomly chosen galaxy speeds" (my translation).[21] In combination with his descriptions of different density sound clouds, different number ranges for pitches, and so on, it becomes clear that the music was highly constructed, utilizing principles derived from areas other than music. Wiggen's written notes describe how pitch structures repeated more than a set number of times would terminate the composition, and it seems reasonable to believe that he combined serial working methods with principles appropriated from other disciplines.

Other computer music works from the same period, such as James Tenney's *Phases* (1963) and *Fabric for Che* (1967), Herbert Brün's *Sawdust* (1976), Charles Dodge's early compositions, and Lejaren Hiller's and Iannis Xenakis's works, appear to be forcefully driven by a strong compositional logic. The sounds are simpler than the processed sounds of today, and because timbral refinement rarely gets in the way, this simplicity emphasizes the structure. Electronic music's origins in serial composition are easily noticed. Perhaps paradoxically, the recordings of Wiggen's works seem more expressive, in the romantic meaning of the term, something that is difficult to notice when looking at his computer scores and notes. It is possible that some of this may be attributed to the specific sound of the analog sound equipment at EMS.

In the early 1970s, this type of logic-based composition in computer music was in itself an activity critical of other current compositional methods in the sense that it differed from both interval-based techniques and conventional tape music techniques. Computer music opened up new timbres, data from extramusical sources, and advanced levels of precision and complexity. Knut Wiggen's music was composed during this period, and he brought a broader, social orientation into contemporaneous explorations of technical aspects. This interest appears repeatedly in his texts and is particularly well explained in his unpublished *Guidelines for Composing*.[22] The guidelines take perception as their starting point, culturally contextualized in terms of a "worldview" that varied at the individual level. Wiggen believed that one's worldview essentially determined perception, suggesting that he did not consider psychoacoustics an objective science.

Interestingly, Iannis Xenakis described similar ideas when structuring his thoughts on music composition, as seen in his step-by-step description of *Fundamental Phases of a Musical Work* (1992, 22). An important difference is that Xenakis did not include social and philosophical aspects in his understanding of individual variance. The chapters of Xenakis's theoretical work *Formalized Music* were published separately from 1963 to 1971, and it is not unreasonable to expect that this book influenced Wiggen's thinking about new compositional methods and tools.

As described in Rudi (2018), Wiggen developed complex ideas on psychoacoustic testing of synthetic sounds, and, in discussions with Pierre Schaeffer, he planned to systematically test synthetic timbres on large panels of listeners. The listeners would be asked for common language descriptions of the sounds presented to them, expressing reactions that could be analyzed in psychological terms. The descriptions from the panel were to be linked with the numeric control and synthesis parameters in a database, and the database could later be queried by composers by way of these common-language terms, such as dark, happy, friendly, and so on. Composers would then be able to create music directly from established psychological responses evoked by the sounds. Wiggen seems to have aimed for a more thorough exploration of a composer's traditional decision-making processes, and he may have viewed such explicit steps as necessary for his development of new compositional methods. However, these testing and categorization efforts never came to fruition, because of Wiggen's abrupt resignation from EMS in 1975.

Wiggen wrote that his music expressed different "atmospheres" and that these served as proof of the success of his software, in that it could be used to make music and not only appealing sounds. The focus on atmospheres is an interesting contrast to how Wiggen argued for MusicBox, and, for example, he described his piece *Massa* as "something large and dark, but friendly."[23] Wiggen was trying to build a difficult bridge between a compositional method that detached composers from their own taste and a repertoire of shared emotional responses on the part of composers and listeners alike. On the one hand, he was a proponent of the serial approach to absolute music, and on the other hand he insisted that music had little value if it did not communicate with the listener. His composition processes may thus be viewed as experimental, and as the measure of success was emotional response in the listener, it is fair to say that his studies may also be considered psychoacoustic experiments. It is not known whether Wiggen actually conducted research on listener experiences, but because the attempts at realization happened close to his abrupt departure from EMS, it is unlikely that this research was done.

The five electronic works discussed, performed, and released by Wiggen are *Sommarmorgon* (1972), *Etyd* (1972), *Resa* (1972), *Massa* (1974), and *EMS för sig själv* (1975). Computer printouts also include scores for *Kromosom, Double, Cyb, Angels I, Funda, Hannes, Aether, Etude 3, Filt, L3, Mass3, Mass4, Mass7, Microb, REs5,* and *Rymd.* Some of these were separate studies or early versions of the five works he released, and some of the pieces have multiple printed scores. As a whole, his scores evidence extensive experimentation.[24]

Like many other composers, Wiggen reused quite similar timbres and structures in several works. (This also points to the fact that the oscillators at EMS could only generate four different waveform types.) Although identifying overlaps between the works is a demanding task, it is easy to hear that *Resa* contains elements from his first two studies, *Sommarmorgon* and *Etyd*. Wiggen's electronic pieces have not been performed very often, but some were performed in December 1975, the year he left EMS. *Resa* was performed at the Massachusetts Institute of Technology (MIT) in October 1976 as part of the first conference on computer music. This conference was produced as part of the ISCM World Music Days, and a recording from the concert was later broadcast on Swedish radio. In 1976, Wiggen had works performed at a conference for European radio stations, where he also gave a lecture on synthesized music in studios. In 1977, Wiggen was invited by Luciano Berio to submit material to be exhibited in conjunction with the opening of Institut de Recherche et Coordination Acoustique/Musique (IRCAM), but it is unclear whether any of his music was performed in the exhibition. In 1984, his study *EX14C* was performed at Fylkingen,[25] and *Resa* was performed in Amsterdam by the Gaudeamus Foundation in 1985. Four of his electronic works were performed during the 30-year jubilee for EMS in 1994, and all five studies were performed by Norwegian Center for Technology in Music and the Arts (Notam) in Oslo at the Ultima festival on October 8, 2003. The Bergen International Festival included a lecture and concert performances in 2009, and pieces were performed in Trondheim in 2005 and more recently in January 2017. The pieces were released in DTS format as a supplement to one of Wiggen's books (Wiggen 2004), and a stereo reduction of his five studies was released on vinyl in 2018 by O. Gudmundsen Minde (Wiggen 2018).

Sommarmorgon

Wiggen's works are valuable examples of early computer music, and the technical aspects of his compositions can be described with a good level of precision. Zaid Holmin, one of the original programmers of MusicBox, has decoded the 1972 original score for *Sommarmorgon* and reconstructed it in a new graphic interface for the performance in Bergen. This reconstruction is described and analyzed in the following discussion.

Wiggen's intention with *Sommarmorgon* was not complicated. He explained that he was looking to make a very simple structure that could be used in EMS outreach efforts to children and elementary schools in Sweden. The idea of outreach to children might seem surprising coming from a radical thinker with a Darmstadt background. However, for several years, Wiggen had developed distinct ideas on a didactic method for children based on a combination of listening exercises in the Schaefferian tradition combined with simple technological means (see Bodin and Johnson 1966). Wiggen has explained several times that *Sommarmorgon* was given its name by a child who visited the studio one day and told him what it sounded like to her. Wiggen must have taken that as a nod to his ambition of creating atmospheres, and he adopted the title. *Sommarmorgon* is sparse in its use of sound and spacious in its expression. Recently, the piece has been published in a stereo reduction, but in the original quadraphonic version, elements move across the room in more or less complex trajectories, and although this is additional information that the listener needs to process, it does not disturb the sense of quiet. The quietness of the piece is essential as underpinning for a soundscape of small sounds that form a layer of communication, occasionally overshadowed by longer sounds in a lower register. The envelopes and amplitudes of these sounds further indicate a larger sound source, and Wiggen has described them as the sounds of "large birds flying by."[26] The magnitude of the Doppler shift Wiggen used speaks of speed and distance, and consequently of the size of the space in which the piece unfolds. The use of a quite high level of reverberation also reflects this attention to size. In terms of particular acoustics, the reverberation is quite nonspecific, typical for reverberation use at the time. Although many of the shorter sounds are clearly pitched, they often appear in a register too high for a precise identification of pitch by ear. Consequently, the piece does not appear interval oriented or having a tonal center; it is dominated by glistening, short sounds with a harmonic spectrum. Despite its clearly pitched sounds, the attention of the listener is directed toward the continually changing timbre, where the density and balance in the sound itself remain in focus. The piece can be heard as a still image, where amplitude and spectral envelopes are shaped to support a situation rather than a movement.

When MusicBox was migrated to Java and computer synthesis in 2003, some of the original boxes became obsolete and the score had to be rewritten. The Java score used for this analysis is an exact reprogramming of the computer printout from 1972, which was purposed for the EMS sound-processing equipment. However, the new version of the piece sounds different from the EMS version, and there are three possible explanations for this. First, there may have been changes in how some of the objects work. Second, the seed value generated in the Java version of MusicBox is not the same as the one that was generated at EMS. And third, the previously recorded version may have been realized from a slightly different score. In the 1972 score, the duration of the piece is set to exactly three minutes, which with an added reverberation time of approximately four seconds, should render the piece to be no longer than 3:05. The recorded version from that time, however, ends at 3:32, suggesting that a variation of the score was used for realization. What consequences this has had for the pitch and timbral content of the piece are more difficult to evaluate, since just a slight change in seed value for one of the random functions could change the outcome significantly on the micro level. However, the recorded version from 1972 and a recording made from the score migrated to Java in 2008 share a very clear overall form and character, so the differences in duration are of small consequence. Together, these two recordings and the score make it possible to gain a good understanding of how Wiggen composed *Sommarmorgon*, and it is the Java version from 2008 that will be discussed here.

Compositional Method   Wiggen's compositions in MusicBox were networks of boxes that were used to "simulate" the composition as sound. Wiggen specified functions, probabilities, and ranges, and his method had striking similarities with the approach described in Xenakis's book *Formalized Music* (1992). Xenakis modeled natural systems such as gases and particle clouds, and Wiggen used the same mathematical functions.

But whereas Xenakis developed a graphical interface with lines and curves translated into mathematical formulas, Wiggen wanted parameter access by way of boxes.

Like Xenakis, Wiggen worked with restrained aleatoric principles to control the overall stochastic form of the compositions, but he seems to have paid little attention to the individual sounds. There is no indication that spectromorphological qualities played any part in Wiggen's compositional processes, and thus a conventional analysis of emergent timbral aspects in the music might seem irrelevant. This is not to say that he was uninterested in the timbral qualities, and it is reason to believe that Wiggen ran his scores several times and selected the outcomes that he liked the best when fixing versions for performance. With the abstractions that Wiggen used in MusicBox, he could not possibly have had any accurate idea of what the music would sound like before hearing it, and experimentation must have been key in his process.

In sonogram representations, one can certainly identify singular events and patterns of density and intensity, but attempting to construct meaning in the music in this manner seems to be only an "after the fact" approach as applied to Wiggen's compositional method, given that the pieces are programmed with high abstraction and not developed from different aspects of concrete, timbral material. Nonetheless, an analysis based on emergent characteristics can yield insights that cannot easily be identified in a focus on *method*. Lasse Thoresen has developed a graphic notation (Thoresen 2015) based on Pierre Schaeffer's taxonomies and Denis Smalley's further development and extensions, and an interesting analysis of *Sommarmorgon* using his notation is found in Balkir (2018, 216–221).

Wiggen's compositional method must have been difficult in the sense that tweaking a simulation in order to deliberately adjust details in individual elements must have been almost impossible. One can say that the overall conceptual control served to dematerialize the conventional composition process, while rematerialization took place when the composer listened and accepted or rejected the experiments. Wiggen's success criteria were based on audiences' emotional response, recognition, and resonance, and it seems as though he steadfastly asked whether machines could make *music*—if a truly new music was actually *possible*. This type of questioning set him apart from contemporaries such as John Chowning, who in one of his most famous works, *Stria* (1977), controlled pitches, frequencies, and the spectral content of his synthesis in detail, all within the clearly articulated intention of using the golden mean as a structuring principle.[27] Chowning seemingly had a clear structural aim, whereas Wiggen's aim seemed to have been integrated into the composition process itself.

In Wiggen's compositions, decisions about pitch, waveform, and envelopes for amplitude and spatialization were made late in the process, in contrast to works composed in the MUSIC N languages, where instruments and orchestras are precisely defined early in the score. The compositional method in MusicBox was far removed from the sounding object, and the analysis that follows shows how the composer steered the flow of numbers to shape the composition rather than describing and placing the individual events.

The Coding of *Sommarmorgon*

The box structure in figure 5.3 is a graphical representation of the signal flow in the piece and shows the compositional logic.

Sommarmorgon starts with four **Event** boxes that send values (figure 5.3A). The first **Event** box (figure 5.4) starts three **Poisson** boxes and an **OnOff** box (figure 5.3C), the second **Event** box starts two global **Envelope** boxes that set the duration of the piece in milliseconds, and the third **Event** box starts a third **Envelope** box that in turn provides list values for a **Chance** box (figure 5.3B). The fourth **Event** box, at the bottom left of the screen, starts a fourth **Envelope** box that in turn sends values to a four-channel spatialization object (figure 5.3D).

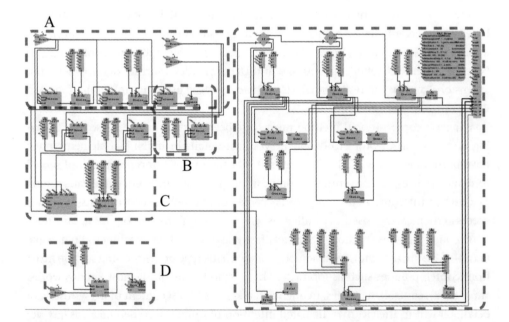

Figure 5.3
This screenshot shows the entire score for *Sommarmorgon* as it appears in the current version of MusicBox. The section on the left is where the raw material is shaped, and the single events are created in the section on the right.

When activated, the first **Poisson** box (figure 5.3A) outputs the received value (0) with a time interval between 2,000 and 5,000 milliseconds, with an average value of 3,000 milliseconds. The seed for the randomization of the time interval is 12,345. The stream of 0s triggers a **Choice** box that selects between values 500, 700, 1,000, 1,400, and 2,000, with corresponding percentage probabilities of 10, 15, 20, 25, and 30 percent. These values change the average time interval for the output from the second **Poisson** box. Thus, the second **Poisson** box outputs 0 with time intervals between 500 and 2,000 milliseconds, with an average starting value of 1,000 milliseconds, but continually varying between 500, 700, 1,000, 1,400, and 2,000, with higher probabilities for 2,000 and 1,400.

The outputs from the second **Poisson** box are "sped up" by the small time intervals determined by the second **Choice** box, varying between 50 and 90 milliseconds, with equal probability. These values constantly change the average time intervals between the 0s that are sent from the third **Poisson** box to a **Chance** box (figure 5.3A). The **Chance** box passes the value 0 through with a probability of 100 percent at the start of the piece but varying with numbers received from the **Envelope** box directly below. The envelope duration is 180,000 milliseconds, and the numerical values of this envelope define the chance for numbers from the entire Poisson processing to make it to the **OnOff** box (figure 5.3C) until the envelope reaches 0 and the piece stops. The Poisson processing as a whole produces a string of 0s that are sent at irregular intervals.

The **OnOff** box is described in the documentation as an "Aleatoric Pulse Shower Train with Independently Chosen Shower and Pulse Average Lengths." It is activated by the first **Event** box and receives trigger signals (0s) from the **Chance** box, as discussed in the previous paragraph, while the density of the pulse train is a product of the values from the first two **Envelope** boxes (figure 5.3C). The durations of these two envelopes define the length of the piece and at the same time are crucial for the development of the dynamics along the timeline. This must be the section where Wiggen composed the overall intensity of the piece.

The first **Envelope** box calculates values from the list of breakpoints (87.5, 75, 50, 100, 100) and the list of proportional durations (50, 20, 1, 29), and the second **Envelope** box does the same from the list of breakpoints (90, 30, 0, 60, 60) and the corresponding list of durations (50, 20, 1, 29). The values they send out change the average durations of two Poisson generators inside the **OnOff** box that control, respectively, the time interval between pulses and their durations. The output of the **OnOff** box is a sequence of alternating 0s and 1s that define an uneven pulse train with varying densities.

The pulse train is sent to a **MULG1** (Multiple Gauss Random Generator) box, which is a macro encapsulation of several micro boxes. In addition to the stream of triggers from the **OnOff** box, **MULG1** takes input from three lists and outputs values between the minimum (35) and maximum (14,000). The result is a sampled mixture of nine Gaussian distributions with outputs ranging from 35 to 14,000. This stream of numbers is sent on to an **If** box at the top right and a **Deter** box at the bottom right and is used in two different ways to generate the sounds in the composition (figure 5.4).

The first **If** box sends values lower than 200 to a **Choice** box (figure 5.4A). The remainder of the values are sent on to the next **If** box, where the stream is separated further, passing numbers lower or higher than 1,600 to two different choice boxes. This first group of three **Choice** boxes is used for several purposes. The numbers they receive are first used to trigger set values: The first **Choice** box selects values from the list (7,000, 10,000, 15,000), the second one values from the list (100, 500, 1,000, 2,000, 4,000, 7,000), and the third from the list (50, 80, 100, 200, 500, 1,000), all with set probabilities. The probabilities in the first **Choice** box are weighted toward the higher numbers, the second **Choice** box toward 100, 500, and 2,000, and the third toward 100, 80, and 200. These numbers are used directly to define tone durations (dur) in the

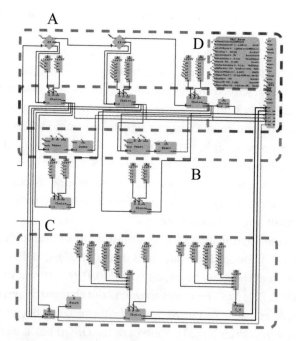

Figure 5.4
The pulse train is routed to an **If** box at the top and to a **Deter** box at the bottom left of this portion of the score. Screenshot from the current version of MusicBox.

MSG (Multiple Segment Generator), 15 different durations in all, but most of them will be 100, 80, and 200 milliseconds, since the last of the three Choice boxes receives more numbers than the two others.

The numbers from this first group of Choice boxes are used also as triggers for the group of Gauss and Choice boxes below (figure 5.4B). The actual values are unimportant; the numbers are just used as triggers for selecting intensity (int) in the MSG box (figure 5.4D). The first Gauss box sends out numbers between 80 and 105 and the second sends out numbers between 55 and 100. The numbers are quantized in Quans boxes, the first with a step of 1, the second with a step of 2, which means that, for example, a value of 97.18 is rounded down to either 97 or 96. The integer output describes the amplitudes of the sounds and is bound to instantiations of pitches.

The Choice boxes in the second group are interesting because this is where Wiggen chose the waveforms, thus, to some extent, controlling details in the sound quality. The first Choice box is triggered only by numbers lower than 200, and with the emphasis from the lists that feed into the MULG1 box, these numbers are few. The box gives an equal chance to each of four waveforms, and there is a 50 percent chance that waveform 1 (sine) is selected, since waveform 1 appears in two of the four slots. In the second Choice box, which determines the waveform for all numbers between 200 and 1,600, the chance of selecting a sine wave is 75 percent, and the second box determines the waveform for all numbers between 200 and 1,600. In addition to sending triggers, the third in the first group of Choice boxes selects a waveform by way of a Deter (i.e., deterministic) box (figure 5.4A) that sends out the value of 1 (sine) each time it gets triggered, and because of the large range of numbers this box receives (all values between 1,600 and 14,000), it gets triggered very often. In this section, it is clear that Wiggen strongly steered the waveform content toward sine tones and left only a small chance for contrasting timbres, and they were only the longer sounds. The first of the Choice boxes is where he selected durations for the previously mentioned long, low-frequency tones in *Sommarmorgon* that he referred to as "big birds passing by." In sum, the waveform, tone duration, and amplitude in the MSG box were controlled by the same pulse train, by triggering sets of values according to arbitrarily set probabilities.

The pitches in the piece are identical to the values from the pulse train MULG1. As the diagram of the entire patch shows (figure 5.3), the values are sent to the If box discussed earlier and to the Deter box at the bottom of the diagram. The Deter box (figure 5.4A) lets a number through each time a duration value is sent from the group of choice boxes on the top right in the diagram. The numbers are sent to frequency (frq) in the MSG box and also used as triggers for selecting envelope values for each pitch, by way of a **Choice** box and an **I_d** box. The breakpoint values are sent to (vli) and the proportions to (pli) in the **MSG** box for synthesis.

In addition to determining pitches, amplitudes, and waveforms, there are parameters for reverberation and spatialization. The Java version of MusicBox uses the EAX reverberation developed by Creative Labs for computer gaming.[28] The reverberation parameters are listed in the **EAX_Room** box and are global values that, in this composition, do not change during the simulation of the piece (figure 5.4D).

The spatialization parameters from the original quadraphonic setup have been migrated to the **Movs_EMS** object, which creates panning envelopes that are sent to the **MSG** box (outrad) and (outang) (figure 5.4D). Spatialization starts at the beginning of the piece and is controlled by an envelope with the same duration as the other envelopes: 180,000 milliseconds. The list values sent from the envelope change the size of the room (2*rad) continually, and the sounds bounce back and forth, with the distance to the center of the room defined by the value in (deva). A Doppler shift is calculated from the size of the room with some modifications and emphasizes the sensation of movement. A little surprisingly, the spatialization is controlled separately and is not integrated into the number flow of the rest of the composition.

Numbers for pitch, duration, waveform, and amplitude envelopes are sent to **MSG** for synthesis, modified by reverberation and spatialization, and Wiggen used a global limiter function (cap) in order to keep amplitudes within bounds.

Summary

Knut Wiggen came from a background of conventional music and was exposed to modernism, serialism and electronic and concrete music after his migration to Sweden and during his subsequent residence in Darmstadt. The summer schools in Darmstadt were magnets for the main composers who developed new contemporary music in the period following World War II. Wiggen developed a deep understanding of the challenges and techniques of this music and built a network of important composers and studio directors across Europe and in the United States. The sonic qualities of electronic means and the expansion of musical opportunities were of particular interest to Wiggen, and he saw that technical challenges such as accuracy, production speed, and efficiency in the use of studio resources could be addressed by automation and the integration of computers. He also believed that analog techniques had exhausted their possibilities and that computers could open up new ways of composing (Wiggen 1972, 104–105).

Upon Wiggen's return to Stockholm, he quickly became an influential organizer, both as head of the concert organization Fylkingen and as founding director of EMS.

As part of his efforts at EMS, he built a functioning hybrid studio with a 9 m controller for real-time work and the EMS-1 software that allowed both offline and online programming of compositions with the analog sound-processing equipment. These efforts, however, were in many ways only extensions of the existing deterministic paradigm of composition. Wiggen saw that algorithmic composition in combination with stochastic processes could be realized with relative ease in computer music, and he pioneered implementation of object-oriented principles in his software MusicBox. As can be gathered from the signal flow in *Sommarmorgon*, complex covariation was an essential element in Wiggen's thinking (figure 5.5).

To verify that an object-oriented approach could have artistic value, Wiggen experimented with composing music and produced five works that he felt successfully presented different atmospheres. One of these works, *Sommarmorgon*, has been analyzed in this chapter, and when comparing the score for this piece with scores for his other pieces, the compositional methodology appears to be the same. Wiggen used constrained random processes to generate number streams, and these streams were exploited for several purposes in his compositions. In *Sommarmorgon*, he controlled an elaborate pulse train using internal variation with three envelopes and used the pulse train to generate pitches and select waveforms, densities, amplitudes, and envelopes. The same numbers affected several immediately audible musical parameters.

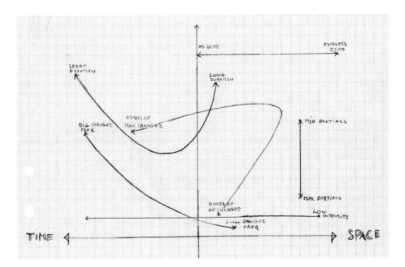

Figure 5.5
A document from Wiggen's archives that illustrates his ideas for covariation. Author's scan from the National Library of Norway.

From this perspective, the underlying structure comprises the essence of the work, and although random numbers produced differences on the surface level from simulation to simulation, more structural changes would only be available through parameter and box changes. This is arguably at the center of what Wiggen often discussed as a new compositional method, removed from individual notes and specific spectral content. His approach has clear similarities to Xenakis's descriptions of his compositional principles, and a drawing found in Wiggen's notes, shown in figure 5.5, clearly shows the type of complex covariation he imagined for his compositions. Managing such complexity was hardly within reach before digital computation became available, and Wiggen's works are early examples of computer music's expansion of the musical paradigm.

Acknowledgments

I thank Knut Wiggen's widow, Carol van Nuys, for taking time for interviews and allowing access to private files; Ingrid Romarheim Haugen at the National Library of Norway for granting access to their Wiggen archive; programmer Zaid Holmin for his patient explanations of the intricacies of MusicBox; and programmer Jarle Stabell for a glance into Wiggen's development efforts during the early 1990s. In the process of finalizing the manuscript, Leigh Landy's numerous and insightful suggestions for improvement were of great importance.

Notes

1. Max Mathews's program MUSIC 1 was used to generate a 17-second piece that was first performed in New York City in 1957.

2. This term was often used by Wiggen in his contributions to public discussions, and it was also adopted as the title for Per Broman's (2007) insightful book about the pioneering years of electroacoustic music in Sweden.

3. Hiller writes about Wiggen's visit and the works *Wiggen-1* and *Wiggen-2* in Lincoln (1970), but no trace of the scores has been found among Wiggen's music and other manuscripts.

4. In his article, Babbitt defended contemporary music as a research field that required the concentration and commitment of specialization, and without this type of musical research, music would cease to develop.

5. *Folkhemmet* literally means "the home of the people" and was a term used to describe the Swedish welfare state with its different programs to reduce inequality between its citizens.

6. Folke Hähnel (1966), "Fylkingen (1933–1966)," Reprinted in Hultberg, 26. The text from the call can be retrieved at http://www.knut-wiggen.com/opprop.php. Visited February 28, 2017.

7. In an unpublished lecture manuscript, Wiggen stated that it would have only taken a few hours in the Stockholm studio to realize Stockhausen's *Studie II*, and that the original production at the Cologne studio probably took several months to complete. Copy in the author's archive.

8. Wiggen described these goals in his *Interface* article (Wiggen 1972).

9. Previous Columbia student Leigh Landy in an e-mail to the author, July 16, 2019.

10. Groth (2010, 192) presents a list of 108 works that were produced in the large studio during the early 1970s.

11. The reader is referred to Groth (2010), Hartenstein (2011), and Rudi (2018), in addition to Wiggen (1971, 1972), for more detailed descriptions and discussions about the development of EMS.

12. The first Norwegian computer music composition was written in EMS-1: *The Emperor's New Tie* (1973), by Kåre Kolberg.

13. A seemingly identical method was patented by David Blackmer in 1971 under the name of *dbx*.

14. Advertisement in the newspaper *VG*, October 20, 1959.

15. Wiggen's position on interval-based music was often misunderstood, but he cleared up this misunderstanding in this newspaper interview.

16. Wiggen has described *Musikmaskin I* in two available documents—one in Swedish and one in German. The more technical description is in German. Both documents are located at the National Library of Norway. Copies in the author's archive.

17. Zaid Holmin in an e-mail to the author, March 6, 2017.

18. The German text reads (p. 4): "Die Musikmaschinen können ein ebenso guten Werkzeug für diese Aufgabe sein wie die Symphonieorchester je gewesen sind."

19. Wiggen restated this position in an interview with Tilman Hartenstein at the Bergen International Festival in May 2009. The video recording of the interview is divided in two parts and can be found at https://www.youtube.com/watch?v=fuQ-HP0nQAs and https://www.youtube.com/watch?v=mOqiP2dEvV0 (in Norwegian only).

20. The journalist "Paus" in a newspaper clipping from Sweden, probably Dagens Nyheter. The clipping is not dated, but since it describes an early stage in the composition process, it is most likely from 1963. Copy at the National Library of Norway.

21. The Swedish text reads: "Clusterets rörelseshastighet bestäms av en uppskattning av modulclusterets bredd mätt i ljushastighet samt småclustrarnas konstanta hastighet lika med fyra randomvalgta galaxhastigheter." Unpublished notes, located at the National Library of Norway.

22. The document *Guidelines for Composing* is found in binder No. 10—Composition rules. Located at the National Library of Norway.

23. "Something large and powerful" was actually also the working title of the piece that ended up as *Massa* and noted on the boxes of his early recordings of this material. An ADAT tape with transfers of the material is located at the National Library of Norway.

24. Box number 5 of the Wiggen archived material at the National Library of Norway contains all the preserved printouts of his computer scores.

25. There is no other reference to this piece in his archive, and *EX14C* might just be another name for one of his five published works.

26. He mentions this also during his last interview, given May 30, 2009, at the Bergen International Festival. A two-part video recording of the interview can be found at https://www.youtube.com/watch ?v=fuQ-HP0nQAs and https://www.youtube.com/watch?v=mOqiP2dEvV0 (in Norwegian only).

27. The interested reader is referred to Menghini (2007) and several other articles in that issue of *Computer Music Journal* .

28. EAX reverb is an extension to Microsoft DirectSound that was launched in 1996. DirectSound has not been supported past Windows XP.

References

Babbitt, Milton. 1958. "Who Cares If You Listen?" *High Fidelity* 8 (2): 38–40. Reprinted in *The Collected Essays of Milton Babbitt*, edited by Stephen Peles, with the new title "The Composer as Specialist," 48–54. Princeton, NJ: Princeton University Press.

Balkir, Elif. 2018. *Étude comparative des approaches créatrices et technologiques au Groupe de Recherches Musicales à Paris et à l'Elektronmusikstudion à Stockholm 1965–1980*. Stockholm: Stockholm University.

Beauchamp, James. 1973. "A Comparison of Electronic Sound (Music) Synthesis Systems for Musical Composition in the United States and Europe." Manuscript at the National Library of Norway, Oslo.

Beskow, Kaj. 1976. "Studio Report" (February 2). Wiggen collection, National Library of Norway, cardboard box no. 4.

Bækkelund, Kjell. 1972. "Provo-musiker slår til." *Dagbladet*, May 18.

Bodin, Lars Gunnar, and Bengt Emil Johnson. 1966. "Teknologier och värderingar—intervju med Knut Wiggen." *Ord och Bild* 75(2).

Broman, Per. 2007. *Kort Historik Över Framtidens Musik: Elektronmusiken och Framtidstanken i Svenskt 50- och 60-tal*. Stockholm: Gidlunds Förlag.

Chowning, John M. 1971. "The Simulation of Moving Sound Sources." *Journal of the Audio Engineering Society* 19 (1): 2–6.

Fahrland, David. 1973. "General Description of MusicBox" (January 3). Wiggen collection, National Library of Norway.

Groth, Sanne Krogh. 2010. *To Musikkulturer—én Institution. Forskningsstrategier og Text-Ljudkom positioner ved det Svenske Elektronmusikstudie EMS i 1960erne og 1970ere*. PhD thesis, University of Copenhagen.

Hartenstein, Tilman. 2011. "Maskinsång från Världens Största Instrument." In *Norsk Avantgarde*, edited by Per Bäckström and Bodil Børset, 247–262. Oslo: Novus.

Hiller, Lejaren. 1970. "Music Composed with Computers—a Historical Survey." In *The Computer and Music*, edited by Harry B. Lincoln, 42–96. Ithaca, NY: Cornell University Press.

Hultberg, Teddy. 1994. *Fylkingen—Ny Musik & Intermediakonst*. Stockholm: Fylkingen.

Iddon, Martin. 2013. *New Music at Darmstadt: Nono, Stockhausen, Cage, and Boulez*. Cambridge: Cambridge University Press.

Menghini, Matteo. 2007. "An Analysis of the Compositional Techniques in John Chowning's *Stria*." *Computer Music Journal* 31 (3): 26–37.

Rudi, Jøran. 2018. "Unpacking the Musical and Technical Innovation of Knut Wiggen." *Organised Sound* 23 (2): 195–207.

Thoresen, Lasse. 2015. *Emergent Musical Forms, Aural Explorations*. London, ON: University of Western Ontario.

Wiggen, Knut. 1971. *De två musikkulturerna*. Stockholm: Sveriges Radios Förlag.

Wiggen, Knut. 1972. "The Electronic Music Studio at Stockholm: Its Development and Construction." *Interface* 1 (2): 127–165.

Wiggen, Knut. 2004. *Musikkens psykiske fundament*. Fredrikstad: Paradigma Forlag.

Wiggen, Knut. 2018. *Electronic Works 1972–1975*. Vinyl LP, OGM005. Oslo: O. Gudmundsen Minde.

Xenakis, Iannis. 1992. *Formalized Music*. Revised edition. Hillsdale, NY: Pendragon Press.

Appendix A: Overview of MusicBox Components

In Kaj Beskow's summary of boxes from January 15, 1973, he lists the boxes in eight categories (Fahrland 1973):

1. Event boxes:
   1.1. Event Generators: Clock, Poisson
   1.2. Event filters: Birth, Chance, Delay, Del1, Synch
2. Value boxes:
   2.1. Value Generators
      2.1.1. Random: Choice, Cyclic, Expran, Gauss, Random, Repell
      2.1.2. Deterministic: Deter, Gener, Seque
   2.2. Value Filters: Cycacc, Repacc, Integ
   2.3. Value Quantizers: Quano, Quans, Quan%

2.4. Value Converters

    2.4.1. Function Converters: Inter, Limit, Linear

    2.4.2. List Converters: I%D, C%I%D

    2.4.3. Special Converters: DB%V, Doppler, Hz%Oct, Loud, Oct%Hz, RA%XY, V%DB, XY%RA

3. Envelope Boxes: Durat, Envel, Ramp

4. Algebraic Boxes: Add, Divid, Multi, Subtr

5. Structuring Boxes: Branch, Selbox, If, Selinp

6. Distributing Boxes: Distr, Quadr, Space

7. Studio Boxes: Alesam, Atod, Collect, Connect, Discon, Fil1, Fil2, Frequ, Inten, Level, Print, Revtime, Tempo, Wave

8. Studio connections: Outputs to the different hardware units, tape controls.

Appendix B: Descriptions of the Boxes Used in *Sommarmorgon*

Chance—Random event deletion.

Choice—When activated on input 0 (val), it delivers a value from (valist) on output 0, chosen with a probability % taken from (prclist). The initial value (Seed) is in the starting value for the pseudorandom choice process.

Deter—Transforms any activating message on input 0 (val) to the value con on output 0.

EAX Room—A reprogramming of the original spatialization from the EMS version of MusicBox, connecting Java-based MusicBox to the spatialization algorithms of the EAX system.

Envel—When activated on input 0 (val), it initiates an envelope on output 0. The form is determined by the %-list pair "valist" (amplitude) and "prclist" (duration). When the envelope time is out, (dur) is transmitted to output 1.

Event—Outputs the value or list of values at (val) at time (time).

Gauss—When activated on input 0 (val), its output delivers a pseudorandom number in the range min to max on output 0, normally distributed with the average (av) and standard deviation (dev). The starting value is set by (seed).

I-d—This box is used for selecting the duration of envelope line segments.

If—Selects one of three outputs as a result of a comparison with a reference value (<, =, >).

ListV—List of values.

Movs_EMS—No description available, but it is clear that the box computes trajectories of sound between Wiggen's four speakers.

MSG—Multiple signal generator connecting MusicBox to the EAX soundcard.

Mulg1—Multiple Gauss-Peak Random Generator.

OnOff—Aleatoric pulse shower train with independently chosen shower and pulse average lengths.

Poisson—The Poisson Event Generator is a discrete probability distribution used to describe events that occur independently of each other.

Quans—When activated on input 0 (val), it delivers the closest step below (val) in the series on output 0.

Appendix C: Wiggen's Acoustic Compositions

Kjærlighet, song II—to Louise. October 10, 1950.

Song I. September 28, 1950.

Preludes, Fugue in E. For piano. Not dated.

For Piano. Not dated.

For Piano. April 1951.

Music for Five Instruments (flute, oboe, clarinet, bassoon, piano). August 13, 1953.

3 Pieces for Piano. Not dated.

Small Suite (clarinet, violin, violoncello, percussion, and piano). Stockholm, January 1954.

Sonata for Solo Violin, Op. 4a. Darmstadt, November 17, 1954.

Study (piano, xylophone, metallophone, and percussion). Stockholm, September 1954.

Study (flute, bassoon, clarinet, violin, violoncello, piano). Stockholm, September 4–11, 1954.

3 Studies for Instrument and Piano. Darmstadt, March 8, 1955, March 13, 1955; Darmstadt and Stockholm, April 14, 1955.

For Piano. Stockholm, August 14–17, probably 1955.

3 Pieces for Piano, Study no. 5 (prepared piano with matches, rubber wedges, and coins). July–August 1957.

6 Exploring Compositional Choice in the SalMar Construction and Related Early Works by Salvatore Martirano

David Rosenboom

Introduction

Salvatore Martirano (1927–1995) was an American composer of extraordinary significance, whose influence on a generation of younger composers has reached far beyond the scope of his own public recognition. Central to his practice was the building of unique compositional systems. Some were applied to particular pieces, while some contributed to an ever-growing toolkit with which he built not only musical works but also singularly powerful, customized electronic music instruments and software. As access to both the material goods of electronic media and a pool of talented engineering collaborators at his home institution, the University of Illinois at Urbana-Champaign (UIUC), expanded during his lifetime, Martirano turned to embodying his compositional systems in circuitry. Central to his electronic oeuvre was the famed SalMar Construction.

Figure 6.1 is a photograph from a concert with the SalMar Construction. Note that the 291 switches and lights on the control panel were not labeled. This meant that only Martirano, a few close mentees, and certain project engineers really knew how they functioned. The control panel remained this way until labels were added when the instrument was restored and then displayed in the Sousa Archives and Center for American Music at UIUC.

I first met Salvatore Martirano during summer 1965, when I was playing in a resident string quartet for UIUC's summer youth music programs. My contact was through extraordinary percussionist William Parsons, who was working with Martirano on the development of extended percussion techniques for his composition *Underworld* (1964–1965). My experience clearly underscored the fact that UIUC was at that time a vital world center of new developments in contemporary music (Rosenboom 2017). I enrolled there as a composition student in the following fall. I was able to study with Martirano soon thereafter, and we remained close friends, colleagues, and occasional collaborators until his death in 1995. During that time, I was privileged to perform

Figure 6.1
The SalMar Construction setup for a concert at the State University of New York at Stony Brook. Martirano gave this picture to the author. The photographer is unknown.

together with Martirano on many occasions, produce various performances of his work, and conduct some of his large ensemble pieces.

It is tempting to launch into dissecting the architecture of the SalMar Construction in great technical detail, for it was a truly innovative instrument for its time. However, another approach, possibly one that could bear new fruit, might be to approach the instrument from the perspective of Martirano's compositional systems and creative predilections. This is because, in my view, the SalMar Construction is an individualized personal instrument, an embodiment of elements in a particular composer's practice. It was not meant to be an object for instrumental standardization. In the design of personal electronic music instruments, composer-designers strike a considered balance between system standardization and customization to serve the objectives of individual artistic visions. Indeed, all electronic instrument design proceeds from some point of view about making music. Achieving idealized universality is not only impractical but also probably impossible and possibly even undesirable.

One of the attractions of electronic media to artists is their very pliability. They are like clay, materials to be molded to serve particular visions and inspirations. It is true that, to do the molding, artists must acquire a necessary degree of technical expertise. Truly innovative artists and musicians have not found this obstacle difficult to overcome. Martirano was such an artist.

This chapter will examine the architecture of the SalMar Construction with the intention of delineating design decisions that were made as *compositional choices*. Where compositional choice in the SalMar Construction's construction lies it is hoped will become clear if we explore its design while always being mindful of how the domains of system design and compositional actions can indeed merge and overlap. The internal technical design specifications of the SalMar have been documented, and it is not my intention to duplicate that effort here. Readers who wish to delve deeper into the SalMar's circuit design details and architecture should refer to other sources, the most clear and thorough of which is by Sergio Franco (1974). Martirano's own *Progress Report #1* (1971) is informative and will be discussed in some detail later.[1] Michael Robinson (1978) provided a more general overview later,[2] and finally, Ron Pellegrino (1982) also offered a brief, but very helpful, system description. (Readers are cautioned about many cursory references to the SalMar Construction that have appeared in various secondary publications over time that I have found often contain errors regarding its technical construction. The sources just mentioned are primary.)

Brief Description and General Principles of the SalMar Construction

At the risk of redundancy, I will attempt to provide the reader with another very brief description of the SalMar Construction, just so it can be kept in mind as we explore a broader musical landscape. The hot time period for Martirano's activities in electronics—into which he threw himself with his typical gusto—that led to developing the SalMar spanned approximately from 1969 to 1972. The evolution of his relevant thinking about compositional systems, however, both predated and postdated this time window.

The SalMar Construction is a hybrid, digital-analog electronic music system. The design team attempted to optimize the balance of digital control mechanisms with analog sound-generating circuitry, matching the time frames within which compositional and performance actions must unfold to the capabilities of digital and analog circuitry at the time as well as possible. No general-purpose, programmable computer, as we think of them now, was involved. However, the actions of the digital circuitry could certainly be thought of as being *programmed*, in this case by the composer-performer, whose actions emphasize improvising on the timescales of emerging compositional form over one-to-one actions that initiate and shape individual sounds. This is an instrument in which the composer-performer can put their hands directly onto circuitry created to embody the designer's personal, individual compositional schemata.

Three major system divisions could be thought of as comprising the SalMar Construction: (1) a system interface consisting of a large panel with 291 touch-sensitive switches and corresponding lights with metal rings that are used to set individual digital bits in programmable digital control systems and display those system states; (2) a complex array of digital logic circuits that generate controls for analog circuits emphasizing subtle, manual control of pseudorandom sequence generators to create data specifying elements of musical form, certain components of sound generation, and spatial diffusion; and (3) a collection of analog circuit modules implementing the microstructural components of the instrument's sonic emanations.

In Martirano's original conception, the analog circuits were arranged to implement what were thought of as four "orchestras" of electronic sound, each with a "soloist" and a specific number of "players." Their circuits were identical, except for two in which special-purpose "percussion" circuits were added. The outputs of these orchestras could either be distributed among four basic system outputs or diffused across a spatial array of 24 loudspeakers typically installed to complement the architectural features of a performance space. Figure 6.2 depicts Martirano's initial system design for the SalMar Construction. Though some things were altered in the final realization, this drawing reflects his thinking about the instrument as a composition.

It is critically important to understand how the terms "instrument" and "composition" are regarded in this context. They are not differentiated in the traditional manner. One might think of the SalMar Construction as a "macrocomposition" because it is a *generative system*, from which an infinite stream of "microcompositions" could emanate, all related, because they are generated by the macrostructure of the instrument, and only differentiated by when they begin and end in time. The SalMar Construction is an instrument in the sense that it was intended for its composer-designer to activate and operationally influence performances in real time. It was not meant to become a performance medium in the sense of a traditional instrument, to be mastered by a culture of musicians who might perform compositions written by a culture of composers

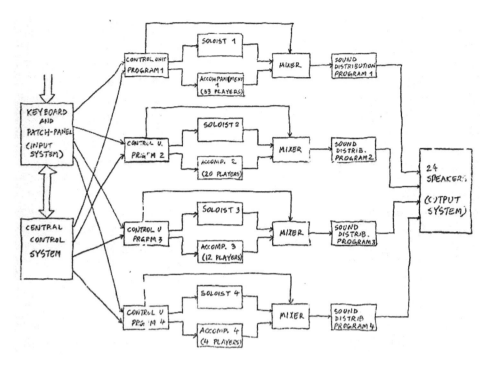

Figure 6.2
Martirano's hand-drawn initial conception of the overall system design for the SalMar Construction (from Martirano 1971).

for performance on the SalMar Construction. Martirano was also a composer-performer with the SalMar Construction, which means that in this context his composing practice and performing practice were inextricably merged. So, as with the terms *composer* and *designer*, the terms *instrument* and *composition* cannot be meaningfully separated when considering the SalMar Construction.

Principles of Design
Several basic principles of design, which could also be thought of as compositional principles, are also important to keep in mind at this stage. The first involves how to work with hierarchies of musical form in real time, from the broadest macrostructural components to the minutest aspects of sonic microstructure. The SalMar Construction was designed so that the composer-performer could have some range of choice about where on a continuum from the micro to the macro their performing actions would be directed. Uniquely, the SalMar's design was weighted toward the macro, leaving much of the micro to automatic operation. The composer-performer could also make

decisions about how much of the system would be put under manual control and how much would be relegated to automatic unfolding. Another way that structural musical hierarchies could be set up was by putting some aspects of the system under control of other aspects. For example, the four orchestras could be driven by a hierarchical system of duration clocks. These could run independently, or some could be put under the control of others. Similarly, both the digital and analog circuits could be interconnected to control each other in hierarchical arrangements.

Pitch System

Martirano's use of pitch relationships in all his music, scales, harmony, interval collections, and the like was highly developed, and no less in the SalMar Construction than in his instrumental and vocal music. Over time, he migrated from complex chromaticism, to dodecaphonic constructions, to equal temperament with multiple divisions of the octave, and back to rich arrays of harmonic permutations, with a sensibility for jazz formulations always in the background. It will therefore be important to keep in mind the pitch systems of the SalMar Construction when we later explore selected examples of Martirano's works composed over several decades.

Pitches in the SalMar were specified with seven-bit binary words, resulting in the possibility of 128 equally spaced pitches within each octave. SHIFT and SHIFT-ENABLE inputs enabled octave shifting, while MOD and MOD-ENABLE inputs could activate modulation at audio frequency rates, both achieved by means of analog circuitry. Two additional control bits, giving four possible combinations of zeros and ones, were available to specify the number of equal pitch divisions per octave, derived from the maximum 128: 12, 16, or 20 tones per octave, and a fourth state that allowed the number of divisions to be continuously varied between 16 and 20. These digitally specified modes were also actualized via voltage-controlled analog circuitry. The lowest base frequency that could be produced was 19.44545 Hz. The frequencies of successive equal-interval scale steps were related via standard multiplicative factors: twelfth root of 2 (for 12-tone equal), sixteenth root of 2 (for 16-tone equal), and twentieth root of 2 (for 20-tone equal). Around the time of the SalMar's restoration in 2004, someone made a tuning chart showing frequencies of tones for the 12-, 16-, and 20-tone equal-tempered modes available in the SalMar ("Sal-Mar Construction Tuning Chart, 2004, March 29," author's personal archive). To my knowledge, Martirano never utilized rational, just tuning systems to any significant degree. His music remained rooted in some version of equal temperament, even though the 20-tone-per-octave system of the SalMar could produce musical intervals as small as 60 cents, slightly wider than one quarter-tone scale step. I believe the choices about what kinds of scales to implement in the SalMar resulted from a combination of the possibilities and limitations of the hybrid circuitry available and from purely subjective musical judgments. In a section about pitch in his *Progress Report #1*, Martirano wrote, "In other words the options available at this time are a reasonable beginning but can be quite easily changed if an opinion resulting from feedback dictates that the rules of the game be changed" (Martirano 1971).

Playing with Pseudorandom Data Structures and Compositional Schemata

Controlled pseudorandomness was a through-principle in the digital circuits' designs and a fundamental technique for controlling sonic complexes and for performing and composing the important musical elements of repetition and surprise. Pseudorandomness is a surprisingly involved and rich theoretical subject. It is also one that can benefit from the sonification of data, through which the integrative capacities of auditory senses can often distinguish qualities that would otherwise require laborious mathematical analyses. In his previous music, Martirano had shown particular interest in combinatorics, manipulating deterministic combinations and permutations of musical elements with hierarchical collections, and in transformations. Working with pseudorandom data generators meshed very well with this.

It also led to a particular overlapping of Martirano's compositional methods with his improvisational practices; he was a master improviser on piano as well as with electronic circuits. Uniquely, these practices emphasized improvising with data structures and compositional schemata. With the SalMar Construction, Martirano found that he could embody these structures and schemata in the hardware of digital and analog circuitry. Thus, playing the SalMar Construction involved improvising, but improvising with known systems for building musical forms. One did not play the SalMar Construction in the manner of traditional instruments, in which a one-to-one relationship is usually established between a performer's physical actions and the resultant sound. Rather, with the SalMar Construction, the performer's physical actions—mainly turning on and off groups of 291 touch-sensitive switches, none of which were labeled on the original instrument—usually involved setting up a scheme for generating musical forms, which could often take some time to unfold. Essentially, the performer's actions involved establishing and directing the macrocontrol elements of musical forms and routing these elements to the microstructural components of sound synthesis and diffusion.

SalMar Construction as a Composition

Martirano regarded the SalMar Construction itself as a composition or a compositional world. He considered all the emanations of this instrument, from its first sonic outpourings to when it went out of use, as representing the unified composition.

Consequently, although he would periodically turn on a tape recorder to capture its sonic output, some concerts were recorded, and a few examples have now been distributed, he did not privilege any single snapshot recording as being a separately identifiable composition. Only the total output from the instrument—and one could never live long enough to hear all its output—comprised the composition.

The title Martirano often used for SalMar Construction performances, "Look at the Back of My Head for Awhile," expresses his sentiment that what is to be seen by the audience is a view of the instrument and the composer-performer's back, and what is to be heard is what happens in the concert venue between the time the power is turned on and the first sound is made and when the power is turned off—nothing more, nothing less.

Aspects of Martirano's Compositional Thinking and Sensibilities

Martirano had a superlative musical ear. He listened deeply and quickly absorbed stylistic elements. Though Martirano's music is deeply imbued with systematic content and sometimes daunting musical formalisms, it also always radiates an arrestingly engaging human quality and an unmistakably characteristic personal stamp in its phrasing. He had a keen flair for elegant and graceful lyricism. Some have speculated that his having studied with Luigi Dallapiccola might have enhanced it (Melby 1996). I recall one evening in Martirano's studio when he brought out a tape of Dallapiccola speaking, expressing his deeply felt opinions about music. It was notable how Martirano was energetically enamored of the sound and syllabic intonation of Dallapiccola's phrasing. Martirano's fondness for Verdi and jazz might also have illuminated his sense of resplendent drama. He was also a good bebop player, who often remarked about how hard it was to achieve the ever-elusive, truly great left hand on the piano. All this was probably ingrained, and it all began with listening.

In writing about Martirano, Roger Reynolds points out, "Over time, one realizes how deeply the *sensibility* of an individual composer defines his or her work. This is more the case for us than for our predecessors because there are so many choices that *can* be made now, so many options for action that did not previously exist. ... A contemporary individual's sense of taste, boundaries, relevance, purpose, risk—these among other factors determine whether a creative life is to be attempted within conventional limits or one is to be driven outside them, requiring engagements with the unknown" (Reynolds 1996).

In the many long discussions about compositional methods I enjoyed with Martirano, starting in the 1960s, clear pathways to compositional decision-making were repeatedly articulated. A particularly important principle was to always go back to a place of beginning when contemplating a new piece and ask: what items are included in the set of the things to which compositional attention will be directed, and what things will be consciously left outside that set? This always brought one back to an initial point of inspiration and conception at which anything could be considered a candidate to reside inside that primary set or not. These would become the parameters that would carry information necessary for articulating the forms of new musical works. They could be conventional or unconventional. Examples relevant to works discussed in this chapter include "sound traffic" (sounds moving along spatial pathways), waveshaping controls, simultaneity and nonsimultaneity, degrees of predictability and surprise, automatic versus human-initiated pattern generation, scales of sound density, number of equal pitch intervals in an octave, degrees of specificity in improvised structures, harmonicity or nonharmonicity, and more. These kinds of elements may be heard shaping musical structures, especially in the electronic music examples discussed in this chapter and also in some involving instrumental resources.

Next, one would consider how comparisons among elements inside the set are to be made and how those comparisons will be quantified. Then, what would be the subsets or subgroupings of elements inside the master set, and how would these be compared? How would they be ordered, permuted, or combined? What minimum significant differences would be necessary to differentiate elements in the set from one another? On what scales would differences be measured? With this practice of questioning and choosing answers, both musical forms and guides for improvisation could emerge.

Combinatorics and Musical Objects

Naturally, this kind of thinking blended well with the post-Schoenberg serial composition techniques of the mid-twentieth century. The scope was broadened considerably, however, when principles of combinatorial mathematics were brought to bear on musical objects. A particularly influential textbook from which I drew ideas for compositional techniques at the time, especially with respect to recurrence relations among permutations and combinations of elements in pseudorandom series, was C. L. Liu's *Introduction to Combinatorial Mathematics* (Liu 1968). There were other important sources of ideas for pseudorandom number generation surfacing at that time (e.g., Carnahan, Luther, and Wilkes 1969; Hemmerle 1969; Kruskal 1969; Payne, Rabung, and Bogyo 1969). Some of these ideas, which could be applied to both formal elements of a composition and the generation of sounds, were shared with Martirano.

What were the musical objects? That question would be answered by returning to the first primary principle described: choosing what would be defined as musical objects and which ones would be included in the primary set for compositional attention. Over the years, I developed a practice called "propositional music," which contains elements that can be traced back to ideas in 1960s discussions I had with Martirano (Rosenboom 2000).

Gann (1997) has referred to this as a "conceptualist paradigm," particularly prominent in (but certainly not limited to) the American Midwest, an expansion of European serialism to include making rows not just of pitches but of any musical objects one could define. It was clearly a feature of new-music life around UIUC during its extraordinarily fertile time as a garden of experimental music emergence during the mid-twentieth century (Rosenboom 2017).

Though combinatorial thinking was clearly applied to all conceivable parameters of sound generation and musical structures that could be reasonably controlled, pitch remained dominant in actual practice. Evidence of this emerges in many aspects of Martirano's music, also reflecting his great ear and sensibility. It is poignant that he used an example from his deep involvement with serial techniques in previous works, which was imbued with a keen sense of interval qualities and their uses, in describing early visions for the SalMar Construction's design. So, in his *Progress Report #1*, we first encounter a description of pitch controls via hierarchical clocks in digital signal generation, followed by a description of a particular 12-tone pitch matrix he devised, from which rich intervallic structures and beautiful musical results emerged (Martirano 1971). Martirano considered this analogous to an underlying combinatorial approach, found throughout the SalMar Construction's musical architecture. To my ear, Martirano's serialism always sounded particularly musical, never dry in its abstractions. Though these may be vague terms, it is hard not to hear them in the music.

Early Compositional Schemes Presaging System Designs

A few selected examples from Martirano's early work will be pointed to here because, to my ear, hints of his musical sensibilities that we can hear in them persist unmistakably in his later work and are embedded in the SalMar Construction's musical qualities. Many others could have been selected as well.

First, in the work *Contrasto* for orchestra (Martirano 1960), one can find closely positioned, chromatically meandering line forms that feel as though they are infused with jazz ears, with interval skips that outline extended chord forms, even though they may also have been influenced by dodecaphony.

In figure 6.3, the violin line demonstrates the chromatic lines typical of Martirano's style. They show up in many compositions and could be heard in improvisations. Note the contrapuntal imitation appearing in the first eight notes of the second phrase,

Contrasto

violin line starting at bar 10

Salvatore Martirano (1960)

Figure 6.3

A violin line from *Contrasto* for orchestra, characteristic of the meandering chromatic lines that were typical of Martirano's style, copied from Martirano (1960).

which are a downward, perfect-fifth transposition of the first eight notes of the first phrase, and other features, such as alternating whole and half-step constructions (hinting at octotonicism) appearing in later bars (Martirano 1960).

Next, *Cocktail Music* for solo piano (1962) and the *Octet* for instrumental ensemble (1963) are two beautiful examples of dodecaphonic music (Martirano 1963; Martirano 1989; Martirano 1998; Burge 1966). They can be treated as one, however, because they are in large measure the same piece. *Cocktail Music* was twisted and morphed into *Octet*, as one can easily hear. Many passages are directly translated into one another. The ways in which they are reorchestrated in *Octet* (figure 6.4), however, can be quite intriguing. Some sound particularly SalMar-like to my ear.

Underworld (1964–1965), for actors, percussionists, two string basses, tenor saxophone, and two-channel tape, was a breakthrough piece (Martirano 1967; Martirano 1995). Complex notation, extended techniques for percussion and saxophone, improvised interpolations, and innovative electronic sounds were all involved. Influences from jazz and Latin rhythms are prominent. Two heroic instrumentalists, saxophonist Ron Dewar and percussionist William Parsons, contributed a great deal in the process of developing this piece.

In retrospect, *Underworld's* electronic part presaged the development of hybrid synthesis techniques, digital data being used to articulate macrostructural components of a composition, with analog circuitry generating some or all the sonic materials. This hybrid approach later became a cornerstone objective in the design of the SalMar Construction. For *Underworld*, Martirano devised a unique method. In brief, he programmed a digital mainframe, an IBM 7094 computer in UIUC's Coordinated Science

Figure 6.4
A sudden burst of reorchestrated triplets with jagged leaps and close interval clusters from *Octet* (Martirano 1963).

Laboratory, with punched data cards specifying the time entrances in seconds of musical events he distinguished in the piece according to a "carefully devised, complex rhythmic scheme" (Martirano 1966). The IBM 7094 produced a digital magnetic tape that could be read by another computer, called CSX-1, which could use data from the digital tape to produce an audio tape. The result was a "rhythm gate" tape containing bursts of 6 kHz tones that could then be used in the UIUC Experimental Music Studio to gate a variety of prerecorded concrete and/or synthesized sounds. The process resulted in gated sounds that were broken up into nine separate channels and then combined in a tape montage. Reverse engineering this process to recover the original rhythmic scheme, with only the final tape to work with, would be very difficult. However, the electronic collage that resulted, combined with the orchestrations and dramatic events of the final mixture, offers a very rich listening experience indeed.

One of the most important analog synthesis components used in this process was the innovative Harmonic Tone Generator developed by James Beauchamp, an early example of a voltage-controlled, additive synthesis machine that is now archived in the Sousa Archives and Center for American Music at UIUC. Other sound sources and processing equipment in the Experimental Music Studio were, no doubt, also employed. This was not yet real-time electronic music, but this hybrid, digital-analog approach would later influence the design of real-time components of the SalMar Construction. The musical results were very interesting and engaging. Again, in retrospect, listening to the sounds of the electronics in *Underworld* now makes it easy to imagine how both the integrative capabilities of the human ear and the brain's audio cognitive capacities for parsing complex sounds would inevitably lead to *sensibilities* that reappear in the output of the SalMar Construction.

The compositional procedures employed in *Underworld* naturally influenced design thinking in the SalMar, particularly those emphasizing its combinatorics. Dodecaphonic techniques were employed in creating the pitch materials. Combinatorial thinking was also applied to other materials in the manner of the conceptual paradigms pointed out by Gann (1997). For example, *Underworld* deploys collections and permutations of four wailing sounds and five laughing sounds, arranged and rearranged in sets of two, four, six, and eight repetitions. The makeup of the four live percussion setups and choices of playing techniques were also guided by combinatorial processes.

Another component of the *Underworld* composition process relevant to the SalMar's design was a focus on hierarchical structuring. In his description of *Underworld*, Martirano emphasizes a hierarchy of sections, subsections, subsubsections, and subsubsubsections. The music moves through a progression of three main sections plus "buffer sections": Introduction, Wailing, Laughing, Improvisation, YEAS and NAYS, and Coda.

Each has its own musical quality and texture: very dense and dynamic, somewhat pointillistic, Latin rhythm references, improvisational interpretations, and calmer, quieter textures. Electronic sounds on tape weave in and out of the ensemble textures. These sections and the roles of ensemble members have metaphorical relationships to the "organization of the family" (Martirano 1966). Percussionists and other instrumentalists take on the personality characteristics of specific family members, and actors or actor-musicians deliver various kinds of laughing and wailing, with particular qualities assigned to each. The piece has a narrative form that moves from tragedy to comedy and, finally, to a mixture of comedy and tragedy.

Martirano lists 96 subsubsubsections in *Underworld*. These are characterized especially by theatrical elements that appear in combinations and permutations articulating sections, subsections, subsubsections, and subsubsubsections: yes, no, laugh (HE, HEE, HO, HU, HA), wail, father, mother, son, daughter, sets of rhythmic repetitions, and five specified physical gestures. This scoring of physical gestures presages Martirano's (1968; 1995) later multimedia work, *L's G.A.*, for which the score specifies physical actions to be performed by an actor. We will return to the notion of structural hierarchies later, when discussing compositional choices made in designing the SalMar Construction.

Influence of Pitch and Harmonic Combinatorics

Of all the documents available describing the design of the SalMar Construction, the one that is the most revealing about Martirano's compositional thinking guiding its design, in my opinion, is his *Progress Report #1* (1971), written as he progressed from creating early versions to the final version. *Progress Report #1* served as a stepping-stone toward an eventually more refined SalMar product, and several particularly striking parts of it are quite revealing about approaches to design and electronic materials that were always thought of as musical. We can associate this directly with *Underworld*, since Martirano chose to include a detailed description of its dodecaphonic combinatorics in a section of the paper titled "General description of the instrument." The fact that he chose to include this description in a report about the design of a new hybrid electronic music instrument is telling. It is worth at least a cursory examination.

Before describing what Martirano refers to as a multidimensional matrix for pitch control, he brings up the potential of using pseudorandom number sequences for musical applications—which will become fundamental in the SalMar Construction— and draws an analogy with traditional tonal systems by pointing out that a C major triad functions as a I chord in the key of C, a V chord in F, a IV chord in G, and so on, and then refers to contemporary composers of the time working with sets and subsets. Later, in personal conversations while visiting my home and using my piano to work

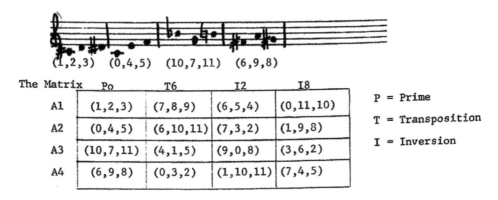

The Matrix

	P0	T6	I2	I8
A1	(1,2,3)	(7,8,9)	(6,5,4)	(0,11,10)
A2	(0,4,5)	(6,10,11)	(7,3,2)	(1,9,8)
A3	(10,7,11)	(4,1,5)	(9,0,8)	(3,6,2)
A4	(6,9,8)	(0,3,2)	(1,10,11)	(7,4,5)

P = Prime

T = Transposition

I = Inversion

Figure 6.5
Martirano's drawing from his *Progress Report #1* showing the row divided into trichords and the matrix from which the combinations of trichords are drawn.

on his solo piano piece *Stuck on Stella*, Martirano joked about all the permutations he could make with seventh chords (Rosenboom 2017). In *Progress Report #1*, he then goes into considerable detail describing the combinatorial possibilities of a set of trichords (three-note groups) contained in a particular 12-tone row arranged in a kind of magical square (figure 6.5). Four trichords from the original row, or prime (P0), are arranged in a column, along with one transposition (T6) and two inversions (I2 and I8).

It is of prime importance here to note the intervallic qualities and thus the sound and feeling of each trichord. There are four basic trichord identities defined by the intervals they contain. The trick is to observe all the combinatorial possibilities for combining trichords to create new 12-tone rows with particular qualities. Four rows made up of only one kind of trichord result from following the horizontal rows in the matrix. There are eight rows containing all four types of trichords that are obtained by following the columns and four possible diagonal or diagonal segment pathways. Then, there are 12 rows that can be obtained from various rectangular arrangements among cells. Martirano provides more details and concludes the section with the following:

> The important consideration here in regard to music is that if the gamut of change from identity to novelty can be defined, a composer can control the gradations between. In music, Newton's first law of dynamics is only partially true. What goes up only occasionally comes down. Set combinations can be biased to stress certain pitches by repeating them. And as well by withholding certain other pitches for a time, provide intrinsic contrast which can be used at will.
>
> At any rate the analogy to tonal music of the past holds true if one considers that the character of A1(P0) changes depending on the context that is created by the particular segment with which it is associated.

Such a method for the control of pitches is economical and efficient in as much as it could be programmed with eighteen 4×4 random-access register files, or with two-hundred and eighty-eight bits of READ ONLY MEMORY. (Martirano 1971)

Martirano used this technique in *Underworld* and subsequently in *Ballad* (1966), written for the incredible jazz singer Donald Smith with instrumental ensemble (Martirano 1998).

SalMar Construction—Concepts and Principles Emerging in Its Development

With all this in mind, we now delve into the SalMar Construction itself, albeit still remaining within the perspective of compositional schema and how compositional decisions influenced the hardware design. For reference, figure 6.6 shows Sergio Franco's condensed overview of the final SalMar Construction design. He notes that "orchestras" also interact with each other. Those possibilities are not shown in the figure, however, because detailing all the possible interconnections among the "orchestras" would make the diagram too complex and confusing.

We will preface the discussion of the SalMar Construction with some background commentary on attitudes emerging from a kind of cybernetic optimism of the time about the potential offered by technology in music.

One of the objectives in the SalMar design was to combine composing processes with performance in real time. In the extraordinarily fertile interdisciplinary environment of the time at UIUC, especially from approximately the mid-1950s to the mid-1970s, it was

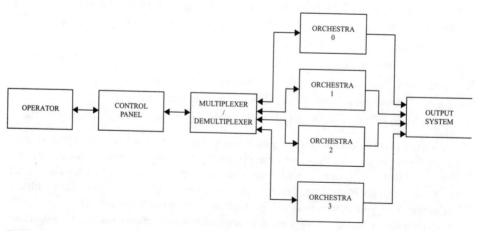

Figure 6.6
Sergio Franco's system block diagram for the final SalMar Construction design (Franco 1974).

natural to speculate about the future of interactive technology. At the time I was working with Martirano in the mid-1960s, we knew that even with the then-limited computing power and speed, we could imagine how, as technology advanced, what we thought of as composing, or precompositional, processes could eventually be embedded inside the workings of "intelligent" or "quasi-intelligent" instruments. This started a continuous quest (Rosenboom 1992). By now, considerable successes have been achieved!

Of course, some essential questions inevitably arise: What are composing processes? What is real time? How can composing processes be embedded in real-time systems? Martirano asks the question

> Does anyone know or ask why a shoemaker makes shoes? Music is as necessary as a pair of shoes: the process for the crafting of each is similar though not necessarily identical.
>
> Part of the difference between music composed for electronic and automated circuitry and music composed for instrumentalists and vocalists is this: the emphasis, in the first case, is placed only on a study of the limits of human perception whereas in the second case, a study of the performer's capability is the subject which de facto sets the limits of perception. (Martirano 1971)

He goes on to soften this by acknowledging that composers always work within limits, and he emphasizes the collaborative nature of the SalMar project. This was not a process of a solitary composer working alone.

The years 1969 and 1970 were critical. In 1969, intrigued by the possible relationships of digital logic systems to combinatorial compositional thinking, Martirano audited a summer course in digital electronics for scientists taught by Howard V. Malmstadt. Also in summer 1969, Martirano invited me to be a resident composer in UIUC's Summer Workshops in Contemporary Music. Previously, I had developed a unique electronic instrument capable of voltage-controlled, nonlinear frequency division (Rosenboom 1996). In Martirano's garage, we soldered together a duplicate of this instrument so that we could play duets together. We further expanded these circuits by connecting patchable digital logic modules to them. Malmstadt had loaned Martirano a couple of his Heathkit Analog-Digital Designers, a very useful device with patchable digital logic modules that was primarily used for teaching. A close friend, schoolmate, and collaborator of mine, William Rouner, had also taken Malmstadt's course and had one of these units, which he loaned to me. Martirano and I connected them to my nonlinear frequency dividers to generate cyclical control patterns—probably with shift registers and simple logic patches in feedback arrangements—and rolled out the whole setup publicly during a concert that a group of us arranged to occur simultaneously with the first landing on the moon by *Apollo 11* on July 20, 1969. A few years ago, John Martirano recovered a recording of this duet, which I digitized and released (Rosenboom 2012a). It is called *B.C.–A.D. (The Moon Landing)*. One of the Heathkit Analog-Digital Designers and a panel with my voltage-controlled, nonlinear frequency dividers are shown in figure 6.7, in a photo that was taken during a concert of my music at The Electric Circus in New York in early 1970. William Rouner and I later incorporated my circuit into a modular system we attempted to commercialize in a business effort we called Neurona Company. Unfortunately, neither of us was skilled at business, and the effort was short lived, though the overall design concepts were documented (Rosenboom 1972).

The piece of equipment in the lower right corner of figure 6.7 is the Heathkit Analog-Digital Designer. On its left is a Heathkit Analog Computer made with vacuum tubes. To its left is an equipment rack in which the second panel down from the top contains the voltage-controlled, chaotic frequency divider circuits, a copy of which was made for Martirano in 1969.

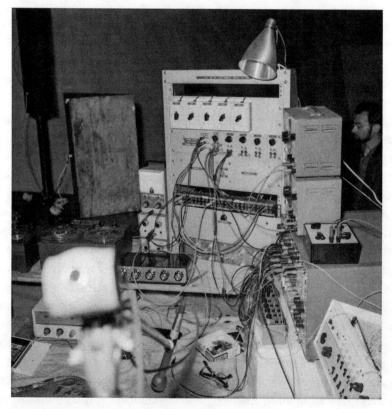

Figure 6.7
David Rosenboom's live electronic performance setup in 1969–1970, shown here ready for a concert at New York's Electric Circus on a multimedia series called The Electric Ear. Photograph by the author.

In November 1969, Dominic Skaperdas of UIUC's Coordinated Science Laboratory designed digital circuitry for sound distribution for Martirano, and in September 1970, he met James Divilbiss. Together, they designed and built the Mar-Vil Construction, which was first presented in a concert at Automation House in New York City on March 5, 1971, part of a legendary series of multimedia events produced by the Intermedia Institute in New York in 1970–1971.

After that, an extraordinary team of engineers assembled at UIUC and contributed to the final, visionary design and realization of the SalMar Construction. As far as I have been able to determine, these included, in no particular order, Dominic Skaperdas, James Divilbiss, Sergio Franco, Richard Borovec, Jay Barr, and, later, Josef Sekon and Terry Mohn. Much later, in 2004, an interdisciplinary and intercultural conference was organized by the Division of Musicology in the UIUC School of Music, spearheaded by ethnomusicologist Bruno Nettle with Gabriel Solis and William Kinderman, called New Directions in the Study of Musical Improvisation. I was invited to give a lecture-demonstration-performance with the SalMar Construction for this conference, exploring the meanings of improvisation on various hierarchical levels of musical structure. The SalMar had fallen into disrepair before this and was not functional. Through the heroic efforts of engineer Greg Danner, the machine was brought back to life enough to make this presentation possible. Though the performance level of Martirano himself with his machine could only be approached, and then only with lots of practice, it was gratifying to be able to play or, better put, interact with the SalMar Construction for this conference on April 1 (see figure 6.8). Greg Danner remained instrumental in completing the renovation. The machine is now functional and on display at the Sousa Archives and Center for American Music.

Programmable Pseudorandom Number Generators in the SalMar Construction

It is important at this point to pay particular attention to Martirano's fascination with pseudorandom numbers and sequences. It is not possible for finite-state machines, such as a digital circuit or computer, to produce true randomness. They are limited to producing pseudorandom sequences. These sequences may appear unpredictable, and indeed very long nonrepeating sequences can be produced, but, in the end, they will eventually cycle. This repetition has musical value. Depending on the length of a sequence, it can generate intriguing, partially predictable rhythms or, when read out at high speeds, harmonic tones with complex spectra and interesting timbres.

Pseudorandom sequences are completely determined by their starting values, called seeds. Identical generators that start from the same seed will produce identical sequences. When pseudorandom sequences are used to produce musical control

Figure 6.8
David Rosenboom playing the SalMar Construction at UIUC in 2004. Photographer unknown.

information, varying the choice of seeds can affect the perceived predictability of the results. When the sequences are generated at high speeds and converted to audio samples, the integrative properties of auditory perception mechanisms cause them to be perceived as colored noises.

The usual method of producing them with relatively simple circuitry is to employ feedback shift registers, in which the output bits of the register are combined in some network of logic gates and the result is fed back to the register's input. If the shift register holds n bits, the maximum length of its output sequence before repetition is 2^n-1. For practical reasons, at the time of the SalMar, Martirano was limited to relatively short pseudorandom sequence generators. These were adequate and interesting for controlling musical structures, though somewhat limiting for creating waveforms.

This observation led to the idea that a continuum of perceptibly predictable qualities among musical elements could be created, ranging from completely deterministic and fully predictable sets, through partially predictable permutations, to maximally unpredictable pseudorandom sets. Furthermore, it might be possible to implement something like a scale of transitional steps along this continuum that could be traversed with quantifiable interval jumps, just as in a traditional musical scale of pitches. The quantification of these intervals would enable comparisons to be made along with similarity and dissimilarity judgments. This was exciting. In the SalMar Construction, it would lead to networks and hierarchies of pseudorandom generators feeding each other as primary mechanisms for generating both musical control data and digital audio waveforms.

The digital circuitry of the SalMar also included digital window detectors. These were circuits that would compare the outputs of pseudorandom sequence generators and detect whether they fell between a minimum and maximum that could be set by the operator. For example, window detectors could be used to create information-filtering schemes that admitted only values that lay within set limits. In the end, judgments were made through listening, and pseudorandom sequence generation produced lots of musically interesting results.

Interest in pseudorandom techniques spread rapidly through the electronic music community. In my archive, I have found handwritten notes I made during the 1970s about a range of techniques to explore. Some might have been shared with Martirano, though the feedback shift register, the hardware implementation employed in the SalMar Construction, was fixed relatively early on.

Key Questions

Here is a list of some key questions that arise when designing a system on the scale of the SalMar Construction:

1. What does it mean to "play" an instrument? (For more discussion about what "play" means in this context, see Rosenboom 1992).

2. How are hierarchies of control best arranged?

3. How are improvisation, composition, and performance related, and can we collapse distinctions among them?

4. What is a compositional algorithm? This is not a trivial question.

5. What does real time mean?

6. How do we delineate and make choices among what can be predetermined and remain predictable and what is fundamentally indeterminate and unpredictable?

7. What presumptions about musical possibilities are implied in an instrument's design?

SalMar Construction First Principles and Compositional Schemata

Let's consider what might be described as first principles in the SalMar Construction when viewed as a composition in the broadest sense. The instrument would be the materialization of compositional schemata, collectively thought of as a compositional world materialized in circuitry. No general-purpose computer would be used, partly because at the time they were too slow and partly because the need to have one's hands on the circuitry remained palpable. In this case, however, the hands-on aspect would be directed not to physical gestures shaping individual musical events but rather to letting fingers touch the data of larger-scale musical forms. The system would have to be a real-time machine. The need for real time emerged in reaction to presumptions about the composer versus performer paradigm of Western classical music, in which improvisation was relegated to a composer's trying out of sounds and developing aural images in the process of perfecting a composition. A composition was a fixed object icon to be interpreted by performers via notation with instruments of relatively fixed, built-in features: timbre, attack, decay, pitch, and so on. Therefore, notation of the iconic musical object was sufficient representation of the composition. In electronic music, however, this fundamentally changed. The control systems that could be embedded within instruments could operate on any hierarchical level of compositional structure. As a result, quoting Franco, "the distinction between composer and performer ceases to exist" (Franco 1974).

The SalMar design required musical decisions to be made about the best allocation of system components to the timescales of improvisation. Ironically, a conductor-to-orchestra model rather than a player-to-instrument model was thought to be the best way to achieve that. Of course, large ensemble improvisation is difficult to coordinate unless a control structure is employed. A single controller with some kind of Conduction® system like that of the late Lawrence D. "Butch" Morris is one solution. A means of coordinating decisions made by ensemble members, such as with the "Prompter" in John Zorn's elaborate Cobra system, is another. In any case, the SalMar was conceived as a collection of orchestras that needed to be controlled in the time of improvisation and to make sound in the time of sound waves.

Referring back to experimental orchestration, even before describing the SalMar's electronic systems plan, Martirano described it as being made of four orchestras, each with a soloist, as he illustrated in figure 6.2. Martirano was steeped in orchestral thinking and often talked about ways to arrange instruments in groups. We can recall that the idea of multiple orchestras was in the air in mid-twentieth-century music. The most famous example is probably Karlheinz Stockhausen's *Gruppen* (1955–1957) for three orchestras. Later, postdating the SalMar, Anthony Braxton (1978a; 1978b) would produce an extraordinary work for four orchestras, four conductors, and instructions for spatialized sound, *No. 82*. In his description of the work, Braxton refers to influences on what he calls "multiple-orchestralism," citing Charles Ives; Stockhausen's *Gruppen* and *Carré* (1959–1960), the latter for four orchestras and four choirs; Iannis Xenakis's techniques for spatialized sound and music, known as polytopes; and Sun Ra's work from the late 1950s and 1960s "involving spatial implications of multi-orchestralism" (Braxton 1988). The concept of segmenting large groups of players into interacting subgroups was in the atmosphere of ideas at the time, and many were breathing it. To this, Martirano brought combinatorial thinking, and thus he ensured that the SalMar Construction's four orchestras could run independently or be linked in a variety of ways with a system of hierarchical clocks (described in more detail later).

Careful choices were made about allocating tasks in this hybrid digital-analog context. In general, digital controls were allocated to structure generation, and analog circuits were used for sound generation. This relegation did not, however, extend to creating waveforms. The SalMar did not use oscillators in the typical synthesizer sense. Rather, sets of waveform memories were filled with data derived from the digital controls. Performers' actions were focused largely on steering or guiding the evolution of the system over the time frames of musical structures. Alternatively, the system was capable of playing by itself. This was an example of what I would classify as *emergent form*.

Thus, dynamic control of compositional elements was relegated to automatic control inside the system with a collection of feedback shift registers and memories. Again, the SalMar Construction was perfused with pseudorandom sequence generators, some of which could be interconnected with others.

To relieve the operator of the burden of too much control on the microstructural level, in the time frame of 1 to 100 events per second, operator control was implemented primarily on the macrostructural level—events of 1 to 100 seconds in duration, the level of unfolding musical forms. The system was conceived hierarchically, allowing sequences to be controlled by other sequences. Franco (1974) refers to "automatic co-operation," allowing the balance between human and machine to vary continuously under the control of the operator. This was decided by information steering. Figure 6.9 illustrates how this was implemented in the SalMar. Subsystems could share

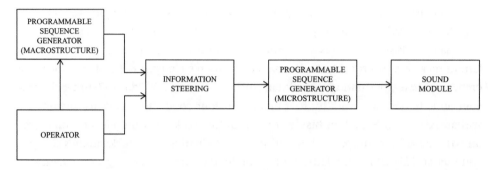

Figure 6.9
Sergio Franco's block diagram of a sound module showing the concept of information steering (from Franco 1974).

information and be put into hierarchical relationships. Thus, to maintain maximum fluidity, the operator was in control of the balance between manual and automatic operation.

The SalMar Construction's control panel consisted of 291 touch switches—Martirano called them TOUCH FLOPS—and corresponding lights with metal rings around them, enabling individual digital system bits to be turned on or off. It was used to control one of the four orchestras at a time. Too much information would otherwise have been required—along with potential operator overload—for the panel to control all four orchestras at once. The panel was therefore multiplexed bidirectionally among the orchestra group. The buttons and rings served as control inputs, and the lights served as system state displays for the operator.

In the final design, each of the four orchestras had two "voices," as commonly thought of in electronic instrument terms—the resulting eight voices could be coupled in various ways for cross modulation of control parameters—, and two of the orchestras had 16 percussion instruments added. In my view, adding dedicated percussion instruments with circuits that produced damped oscillations when "struck" with impulse signals was not just for convenience and efficiency in circuit design. Martirano had exhibited a fascination with new percussion techniques in various prior compositions. He liked percussion instruments and talked about them often. After all, UIUC was a hotbed of contemporary percussion activity at the time, a very inspiring atmosphere indeed (Rosenboom 2017). From my point of view, adding these percussion circuits to two of the orchestras was a musical decision, through and through.

Another first principle of the SalMar's design was to broaden the spectral pallet of electronic sounds beyond those offered by typical subtractive synthesis schemes with the standard oscillator waveforms employed in synthesizers. This approach required waveform memories that could be filled with arbitrarily designed or generated waveform sample data. In order to achieve smooth, dynamic transitions among timbres, a pair of memories was required for each voice. The outputs of a particular pair could be crossfaded to enable one memory to be loaded with new data while the other one was sounding, or data could be loaded while both were sounding in some mixture if that was desired. Martirano called this crossfading system the SEE-SAW.

Data for the waveform memories again came largely from pseudorandom sequence generators. This was achieved at what we would regard today as very low resolution, only 16 amplitude levels per sample and 32 samples per waveform period. Yet, with clever filtering designed to follow the fundamental frequencies being output, a huge range of musically interesting sounds emerged. In his *Progress Report #1*, Martirano (1971) projected being able to generate 4,095 or $(2^{12}-1)$ waveshapes to replace the standard ones commonly used in typical analog synthesis at the time. The original design plan included provision of read-only memories (ROMs) to hold fixed data that could be preloaded for things like percussive or speech-like sounds, though it isn't clear how much of this was implemented and used.

This design scheme with dual waveform memories had spinoffs. In 1979, I joined forces with Donald Buchla to design what became a powerful hybrid digital keyboard instrument, called the Touché. Sound synthesis in this instrument was based on nonlinear waveshaping techniques. Dual memories were employed to hold samples for waveform transformation functions, and a scheme of crossfading was also implemented. The interface software for the Touché facilitated creating "instrument definitions" that included dual waveshaping functions and initial mix states for the outputs of these functions, which could be dynamically varied in performance. Though the synthesis scheme for the Touché was different, the dual memory concept was analogous.

It should be acknowledged that the analog circuit designs made for the SalMar Construction were very sophisticated, elegant, and innovative for their time. Franco emphasized the use of current control, rather than voltage control, because it was more manageable over wider ranges. He felt that current control was not emphasized enough in electronic music circuitry of the time (Franco 1974). In the SalMar, operational transconductance amplifiers (OTAs) were used in critical places, like programmable filters.

Continuous analog function controls in the SalMar (i.e., envelopes) were generated in the form of sequences of piecewise linear line segments. The data for these again originated in pseudorandom feedback shift registers. Segments were programmed with four bits to specify amplitude ordinates, or breakpoint targets, and four bits to specify slopes. When applied to sound amplitudes, this provided 3 dB resolution over a 50 dB range. If finer control was desired, small line segments could be connected together. A voltage follower circuit with programmable slew rate and polarity reversibility—so that segments could go up or down—was used to generate continuously varying control signals. Up slopes (attacks) had a range of 1 volt/millisecond to 1 volt/second, and down slopes (decays) were 2 volts/millisecond to 2 volts/second. Here again, a musical choice was made to have up slopes move faster than down slopes. Based on musical snap judgments, the operator could capture in digital registers emerging envelope control data that were considered desirable. Martirano (1971) also described using pseudorandom sets to modulate the least significant bits (LSBs) of the envelope data to produce "dimples and pimples to one's heart's content," another qualitative design decision resulting from musical sensibility.

Some ideas for envelope generating schemes appear in Martirano's *Progress Report #1* (1971) that don't appear in Franco's (1974) system design. They are mentioned here only because they illustrate more of Martirano's compositional decision-making. In his document, a HOLD control is described that would freeze an envelope at a particular amplitude. Perhaps even more musically interesting is his description of a REST control. When activated, the amplitude of an envelope would decay, with its state determining decay time, and then stay at zero. Martirano imagined "a striking musical effect" when the REST control was activated and deactivated. I assume that he was also thinking of these activations as coming from programmable pseudorandom sequence generators. Then, Martirano states, "Simple counterpoint results from [a] group of music signals whose rest controls are independently programmed."

The SalMar Construction was famous for its spatial distribution features. For normal daily studio use, the outputs of the four orchestras were distributed across four channels. For a significant period of time, Martirano had a four-channel, quarter-inch tape recorder in his home studio, with which he captured some good examples. For public performances, each of the four orchestras could be routed to any combination of 24 loudspeakers, each fed by a quadruple audio gate and a switching power amplifier.

Another key compositional scheme came into play here. It was called SOUND TRAF-FIC. For each public performance, Martirano would carefully scrutinize the architecture of the venue and come up with a design for placing the 24 loudspeakers throughout the space. The original speakers were inexpensive, flat, "polyplanar" speakers that cost $6.55 each in 1969 dollars—these were probably designed to be hung on walls, occupying no greater depth than a typical framed artwork. They were set in bubble-like plastic housings that could easily be suspended. The result was remarkably effective. Typically, the bubbles would be suspended in different regions and at different heights in a performance space. Martirano's father was a builder of public spaces, and perhaps his influence can be inferred. In any case, a SalMar performance was also, and very importantly, a sound installation. From the control panel, combinatorial thinking was applied again to realizing sets of sound traffic patterns around and through the performance space. Martirano's architectural and sound-space sensibilities were keys to generating suitably immersive experiences. Usually, four larger speakers would be added to boost bass frequencies. These were often pointed upward in performance spaces to reduce any perception of directionality. In later years, the "polyplanar" speakers were abandoned and replaced by speakers designed for car stereo systems. Though more expensive, these were also more physically robust, reliable, and less prone to being damaged during transport.

Sounds from each particular orchestra—which originated as mono signals—could be routed to any combination of the 24 speakers, specified by 24 bits of data. Audio gates opening and closing signal pathways required only one bit each, or 96 bits in all.

For clarity, and recalling that the control panel addressed one orchestra at a time, it is easiest to understand the distribution control system by thinking of just one orchestra. The contents of a circular, 24-bit shift register determined the distribution of sounds from an orchestra. Individual bits could be set or reset with the panel TOUCH FLOPS. As bit patterns moved around the register, sounds moved through the speaker array along particular sound traffic pathways. To make things more interesting and offer more choices, the 24-bit register was broken down into a series of six shorter registers: two three-bit, two four-bit, and two five-bit registers. Next, a means of connecting the output of any of these registers to the input of any other register via a six-by-six interconnection matrix was provided. In this way, the operator could break up the 24-bit register into subregisters and connect them to each other to make a wide variety of sound traffic patterns. A short register could be connected to itself to make local traffic loops. Registers could be interconnected to implement spatial jumps in a variety of ways. The combinatorial possibilities for sound traffic patterns were extensive enough to satisfy musical needs, ranging from simple predictable patterns to very complex movements around the sound space. Furthermore, each of the four orchestras had its own distribution controls, so varieties of sound traffic patterns could be set up individually for each orchestra and run simultaneously.

Why were the 24-bit registers broken down into subregisters of three, four, and five bits? Again, this must have been a musical choice. The number 12 was under a strong spotlight at the time, of course. Breaking it down into divisions of two prime numbers, three and five, and the minimally composite remainder, four, provides interesting possibilities for interlocking counterpoint: all the combinatorial possibilities of three, four, and five taken individually or together and the possibilities multiplied with the four

Figure 6.10
The control panel for the SalMar Construction after the buttons and lights were labeled during the restoration. Photo by the author.

independent orchestras. Why not apply this to movements of sound in space to create sound traffic counterpoint? I am convinced that Martirano was keenly aware of the possibilities enabled by his choices.

Figure 6.10 depicts the restored SalMar Construction. In the lower center area, one can see the six-by-six matrix for interconnecting the subregisters for sound distribution. The subregisters themselves appear just above and just below the six-by-six matrix. The ones above are in left to right order: three-bit, four-bit, and five-bit. The ones below are in the order five-bit, four-bit, and three-bit. The metal bar along the bottom of the panel was placed so that the operator could keep a hand on it, making a necessary circuit connection with their body. This was needed for the TOUCH FLOPS to work properly.

Control Hierarchy

The control hierarchy of the SalMar Construction may be summarized as follows. Performing with the SalMar involves making decisions about how data will be steered toward microstructural components (1–100 Hz range) of the music and how they will influence data driving the evolving macrostructure (0.01–1 Hz range). In addition, the performer may adjust balances among elements that will become the responsibility of the machine and those that will remain the responsibility of the operator. The operator will directly interact with programmable sequence generators (pseudorandom) that affect the musical macrostructure. The nature of this interaction may range from direct control to subtly influencing processes already running. The operator will also directly interact with an information steering mechanism, which can determine how data from macrostructure sequence generators will be directed to affect microstructure sequence generators. The microstructural data are then transferred to primarily analog sound-generating circuits. With the information steering mechanisms, the operator also determines whether particular data-generating components will run in automatic mode or be relegated to manual control.

Another very important aspect of hierarchical control is found in the SalMar's system of clocks. Each orchestra had its own primary duration clock. These could run independently or be slaved to each other in a top-down arrangement. The highest-level clock could drive the three other clocks. The second highest could drive the remaining two below it, and the third-level clock could drive the fourth-level clock, which could not be connected to drive any of the higher-level clocks. The operator could either determine the possible hierarchical clock slaving options or leave that to the behavior of circuits. Timing signals for other parts of the system could be derived from the master clocks in complex ways. For example, programmable (pseudorandom) binary sequence generators controlled circuits for synthesizing subaudio frequencies for duration controls and for generating waveshape data. The outputs of the subaudio frequency synthesis circuits could also be fed back into the clocking inputs of pseudorandom sequence generators. The results could become very complex very quickly. One of the points of this hierarchy of clocks was to enable generating relationships among simultaneities and nonsimultaneities to create a kind of counterpoint. Here again, we have a fundamentally compositional idea determining the system design architecture.

A massive patch bay provided complete reconfigurability among components in the system's hierarchy. It was used for interconnecting them and was critical for routing digital data to the analog components. Routing voltage-control signals among analog components was also done this way. A typical SalMar patch was so complex that it was necessary to preserve it while transporting the machine from place to place. It has now become common to consider the development of a patch over time as analogous to traditional composition. This was partly the case with the SalMar, though much of this was made necessary by the sheer number of independent circuit components, how they had to be patched together, and how the control panel of 291 TOUCH FLOPS had to be connected to the digital logic arrays.

Figure 6.11
The SalMar Construction patch bay as it appeared in 2014 at the Sousa Archives and Center for American Music at UIUC. Photo by the author.

Performing and Performances with the SalMar Construction

Martirano would usually drive the SalMar Construction, housed inside a trailer hitched to his car, from location to location for performances. Somehow, the machine made it to France and back for a stint in Paris. That was, no doubt, quite a logistical feat to pull off. Sometimes, after heroic installation efforts, Martirano would be a bit parsimonious in his subsequent musical offering. Reynolds describes a challenging circumstance at Avery Fisher Hall in New York's Lincoln Center when, after a particularly stressful setup and in a difficult event-programming environment, Martirano finally came out to deliver the final item in a long program. He bowed, sat down, and played for a little over seven minutes (Reynolds 1996). I recall one concert at Mills College when, after very complicated and extended efforts were devoted to installing the instrument, including suspending the 24 loudspeakers in a beautiful arrangement inside the Mills Concert Hall, Martirano's performance that followed seemed to most of us around to be surprisingly short. In just about every performance or installation with the SalMar Construction that I witnessed directly, the instrument would require considerable servicing before performance time. Martirano always traveled with test equipment and, when possible, an engineering assistant.

Playing the SalMar effectively required learning to think in terms of binary data words, just as one might need to think in terms of scales, intervals, chords, and rhythms in traditional improvisation. It is telling to see how Martirano went to significant lengths in his *Progress Report #1* (1971) to tabulate the cycling collections he could produce with four-bit, feedback shift registers. In addition, one must always pay attention to making decisions about perceived periodicity versus unpredictability. Determining how data are transferred to various memories around the system is a key arena of SalMar performance practice. It is critical for one to become adept at sensing musical qualities in pseudorandom data sequences and biasing them in particular directions, what Reynolds (1996) referred to as "chains of contingency." Reynolds's comment is important because it raises notions about models of evolution and self-organizing emergent forms, which I have also explored extensively in musical models (Rosenboom 2018). For example, I have developed nondeterministic musical notations and composing systems that explore what evolution theorist Stephen J. Gould (2002) calls the *contingent possible* and alternatively what Stuart Kaufman (2000) refers to as the *adjacent possible*. These are fundamentally different paradigms that can have important musical meanings.

As Michael Robinson puts it in his overview, this instrument was optimized for "improvisation of highly complex musical structures by a single musician/composer" (Robinson 1978). Disciplined improvising—and disciplined practice is emphasized here— could be thought of as composing in real time. It is appropriate in our time now to collapse the traditional distinction separating improvising from composing.

Very little one-to-one performing activity is ever involved in a SalMar performance. Rather, the focus is on thinking about performing-composing musical structures that emerge and evolve over time. The primary performing actions are macrostructural. I remember an amusing day in which Martirano was challenged to see if he could make the SalMar with its TOUCH FLOPS play "Happy Birthday." If memory serves me, he was able to make an approximation of the pitches in the song emerge, albeit very, very slowly.

The vast spectrum of possible input structures for performing with electronic instruments is still fertile territory to explore. After all we've accomplished, the surface has still only been scratched (Rosenboom 1987). For example, new developments in gesture recognition, multi-agent BCMI (Brain-Computer Music Interface) (Rosenboom and Mullen 2019), and new analysis techniques for biometric data are emerging at a fast pace. Perhaps the malleability of electronic media will cause a lean toward individuality in system design as standard practice. We can look back at the SalMar Construction as a landmark in embedding an individual artist's compositional world inside circuitry.

The designers of the SalMar Construction broke fertile ground by significantly pushing forward the hybrid digital-analog electronic musical instrument paradigm. Franco closed his 1974 thesis on the SalMar with the prophetic statement, "In light of these remarks, it seems appropriate to speculate that the electronic music systems of the next generation will be based on a central, general-purpose computer controlling a collection of peripheral, special-purpose computers whose task is the synthesis and processing of sounds." As new technologies emerged later, levels of integration would be reached in which such hybridity could be embedded in musical instruments so thoroughly that the digital-analog distinction has now become nearly invisible.

Collective Composition, Recordings, and Duets

In the 1970s, Martirano gave several tapes to me on which samples of the SalMar were captured in his home studio in either four-channel or stereo mix-down format. He labeled them sequentially, *SalMar #4*, *#5*, and *#8*. To me, this indicated that he was taking audio snapshots of the SalMar's output over time. He repeatedly said things to me that emphasized that he did not consider any particular recording to be an individual composition. Any particular recorded audio snapshot of the SalMar was just that, like an individual frame from a long movie that was unfolding over time. Martirano was concerned that if sample recordings were publicly released, they would become fixed in the minds of audiences as the quintessential representations of the SalMar concept. Thus, he resisted releasing recordings of the SalMar for some time. The complete "composition" known as the SalMar Construction included all its emanations from the time its power was first turned on to sometime in the future when it could no longer emit sound. Thus, an analysis of any one SalMar recording remains an analysis of only a sample, like looking inside only one boxcar on a long train moving across the prairie and trying to infer a complete description of the train.

Many advances in musical circuitry came from work on the SalMar Construction, some of which are highlighted in this chapter. However, one of Martirano's most powerful achievements lies in showing how a physical medium—in this case, interactive technology—can be used to materialize a creative individual's artistic practice in the form of a *life composition*, existing not as a series of differentiated works of art but rather as a dynamical, generative system, the very functioning of which manifests that practice continuously. The SalMar has inspired many and continues to exhibit Martirano's musical practice to this day.

Nevertheless, at this point in history, analytical observations can be a useful resource. Readers should be aware of Peter Roubal's important and comprehensive annotated catalog of Martirano's works, which includes a comparative analysis of large-scale forms presented in selected performances with the SalMar Construction (Roubal 2000). In the end, qualitative listening easily reveals unmistakable commonalities and threads of consistency in Martirano's musical sensibilities and tendencies in shaping musical gestures: manipulation of combinations and permutations of sounds while maintaining a sense of lyricism, playing fluidly with expectancy and surprise in both subtle and dramatic ways, a kind of sonic theatricality, moving in and out of momentary harmonicities, and other ineffable musical propensities that are best discovered through listening.

Martirano did selectively experiment with playing the SalMar in improvisations with others. I was fortunate to engage in several such improvising sessions, in which my setups were wide-ranging. Recorded ones included Fender Rhodes electric piano with signal processing and a unique opportunity to use the Sayles Hall pipe organ at Brown University during the 1975 19-Mile Festival organized by Gerald "Shep" Shapiro. I have already referred to *B.C.–A.D. (The Moon Landing)*, with my voltage-controlled, chaotic frequency dividers. On another occasion, in 1977, Martirano and I captured a duet improvisation session in his home studio, in which he played the SalMar and I played a collection of electronic music modules, including a Buchla Music Easel and 200 Series Electric Music Box, that were being driven by homemade digital controls. Both instruments became hardware-software embodiments of compositional thinking made available for spontaneous activation. This event was a particularly rewarding example of what might be very aptly termed *spontaneous collective composition*. A stereo mix-down excerpt from a four-channel tape recovered by John Martirano from this special event is available (Rosenboom 2012b). I called it *B.C.–A.D. II*.

This way of improvising, informed by long experience with disciplined, spontaneous composition employing electronic instruments designed as compositions, is truly distinctive. *B.C.–A.D. II*, like many other musical collaborations among experienced musicians who know each other well (Martirano engaged in many of these), did not begin with any specification of common musical materials, such as themes, pitch structures, scales, rhythmic forms, and timbre specifications, but neither was it what I consider to be commonly misconstrued as "free" improvisation. It was improvising with knowledge of each other's musical worlds, understanding the nature of the interactive instruments involved, and trusting in each one's ability to bring their entire musical self to bear on every moment of the music that would emerge. I assert this to be one of the most demanding practices in which one can engage in music. It all begins with listening. Judging the quality of the outcome is up to the musical sensibilities of each individual. A famous saying attributed to Duke Ellington and Robert George "Joe"

Meek may bear on this: "If it sounds good, it *is* good." Active imaginative listening is the best means to gain deeper comprehension of this kind of music.

Post SalMar

Martirano was a rising force in the time of the SalMar Construction's emergence. Subsequently, his practice evolved on to new software-based composing tools with which to generate data for instrumental scores and driving synthesizers. Clear lines of development from ideas motivating compositional choice in the SalMar Construction to the designs of these new tools can be seen. The scope of this chapter does not permit examining the technical intricacies of these post-SalMar developments in the depth they deserve. It would be remiss of me, though, not to at least mention some that also contributed important new ideas to the music technology arena of their time.

From around the end of the 1970s into the early 1990s, Martirano developed innovative software toolkits for composition and performance. Significant among them was his Sound and Logic (SAL), written in the Le_Lisp language. Sound and Logic 80, a variation translated into Smalltalk-80, was used to drive an early version of the Kyma computer music system from Symbolic Sound Corporation. Martirano often improvised with this setup by initiating events with a Yamaha DX-7 MIDI keyboard. In the late 1980s, he developed a system called yahaSALmaMAC in which Sound and Logic (SAL) programs linked live MIDI signal sources with an elaborate bank of Yamaha MIDI synthesis hardware. Martirano used these new tools to create an array of powerful electronic and instrumental compositions and improvisations imbued with his typically diverse approaches to musical style.

Note on Archiving Electronic Music Artifacts

We live in a time during which the nature of the artifacts in which music history resides is hard to define. Scores, paper notes, and even recordings and videos cannot tell the whole story. Retrospective analyses can help, but they never tell the full story and are always created from the perspective of the analyst. This is especially true with respect to electronic music, computer music, electroacoustic music, sound art, and related forms. Some of the key artifacts documenting artistic creations in these arenas include installation objects, hardware circuitry, one-of-a-kind instruments, and software. Notating electronic music is a fascinating and mercurial subject, though often nearly impossible and possibly not relevant. In 1997, I tried to interest the Getty Research Institute for the History of Art and Humanities in acquiring, restoring, and displaying the SalMar

Construction. Though certain key individuals were interested, the idea was deemed impractical and turned down. It is therefore very important to acknowledge the efforts of the Sousa Archives and Center for American Music (SACAM) at the University of Illinois at Urbana-Champaign in preserving and displaying the SalMar Construction. I would like to draw attention to an important case study documenting this effort (Cuervo 2011). I hope that it might inspire other institutions to seriously consider new ways to address the mounting need to preserve for future study some of the most important artifacts documenting the creative breakthroughs of our time.

Concluding Commentary

What is real time? When considered deeply, this can be a vexing question. Much of the life of the SalMar Construction revolves around that question. In the end, each composer-performer will provide their individual answer. Martirano ends his *Progress Report #1* with this comment:

> Does real time only exist when you think of it? Have you, who have skimmed through, thought of a better way to say it? Are you aware that the process that allows a real musical time to happen is a real musical? Where's the trance? Can you sing and dance? Where's the reflex? Is Wagner's idea to put all the melodies together at the end of the overture less of an inspiration than the melodies themselves?
>   The best is A HEAD. (Martirano 1971)

Martirano relished the vast range of structures he could coax the SalMar to produce. One day in his studio, sometime in the early or mid-1970s, he set up recirculating patterns activating the "percussion instruments" attached to two of the SalMar's four "orchestras." They sounded like invocations of certain strands emerging in 1970s American minimalism, which was becoming increasingly popular at the time. While we listened, Martirano quipped, "See, I can be hip, too!" But it was the structure that intrigued us in listening, a kind of vigor applied to hearing forms, not the visceral physicality associated with pounding out shifting rhythms. One day, while listening to particularly complex sound arrays coming from the SalMar, Martirano said, "I hear everything." He was referring to a very particular kind of deep listening, the parsing out in perception of the parts in extremely complex structures.

Martirano frequently used sensual terms to describe musical experiences. One day at CalArts, while Martirano was in residence, we listened to a noon-hour concert of highly serialized music by Mel Powell. Martirano said, "What delicious relationships." He was referring to the structural details in pitch relationships he could hear that Mel had worked out. A story illustrates how strictly calculated these relationships were.

One day, Mel showed me a score he was working on, and I jokingly said, "But Mel, how will you determine whether that B-flat will be pizzicato or arco?" Mel replied, "That's a day," meaning it would take a full day's work to determine the answer. That was the level of detailed structural determinism that was applied to every item chosen for compositional control. What Martirano was referring to was his feeling that he could "hear everything" in such superdetermined forms.

Finally, to illuminate Salvatore Martirano's humorous, infectious spirit, here is his "MEMOGRAM" from *Progress Report #1* (1971). Throughout what is purported to be a technical document, Martirano's penchant for spicy words is amply evidenced by his verbal peppering, popping up again and again.

MEMOGRAM

To: Page of expletive

From: Monolithic Speakers

one-shot RAM's ROM STOP EX OR's

pair, NANDS ODD STOP SHIFT SCHOTTKY'S pot STOP

(TUBE)

(GO input AND multiply)

ADD ADDADDAD DAD DAD DAD DA D-DA D-DA D-DA D-DA D-DA D-DA

(RE, MI, FA, SOL, LA, TI)

(DOUGH)

cc: L.S.I.
       M.S.I.
       S.S.I.

Notes

1. The author's copy is a manuscript with hand written corrections given to him by Martirano. A copy dated circa 1972 is listed in the Salvatore Martirano: Personal Papers and SalMar Construction 1927–1999 collection of the Sousa Archives and Center for American Music at the University of Illinois. The online finding aid can be found at https://archives.library.illinois.edu/archon/index.php?p=collections/findingaid&id=5829&q=Martirano&rootcontentid=73882#id73882.

2. Though inspired by computer-electronic instruments, Michael Robinson's work broadened greatly, including immersion in South Asian music. See Meruvina: Composition and Performance Coalesce, 2017, at http://www.azuremilesrecords.com/meruvina.html?feature=watch. It is not known whether his manuscript on the SalMar Construction was ever published.

References

Braxton, Anthony. 1978a. *No. 82*. Copy of manuscript in the author's personal archives. (Note: Braxton's actual title for this work is a graphic diagram, not reproduced here.)

Braxton, Anthony. 1978b. *Anthony Braxton/3 Record Set*. New York: Arista Records.

Braxton, Anthony. 1988. *Composition Notes, Book D*. Oakland, CA: Synthesis Music (original) and Dartmouth, NH: Frog Peak Music.

Burge, David. 1966. *David Burge Plays New Piano Music*. Vinyl LP, FGR-3. Advance Recordings.

Carnahan, B., H. A. Luther, and J. O. Wilkes. 1969. "Poisson Distribution Random Number Generator." In *Applied Numerical Methods*, edited by B. Carnahan, H. A. Luther, and J. O. Wilkes, 545–546. New York: Wiley.

Cuervo, Adriana P. 2011. "Preserving the Electroacoustic Music Legacy: A Case Study of the SalMar Construction at the University of Illinois." *Quarterly Journal of the Music Library Association* 68 (1): 33–47.

Franco, Sergio. 1974. *Hardware Design of a Real-Time Musical System*. PhD thesis in Computer Science, UIUCDCS-R-74-677. Urbana: University of Illinois, Department of Computer Science.

Gann, Kyle. 1997. *American Music in the Twentieth Century*. New York: Schirmer Books.

Gould, Stephen J. 2002. *The Structure of Evolutionary Theory*. Cambridge, MA: Harvard University Press.

Hemmerle, W. J. 1969. "Generating Pseudorandom Numbers on a Two's Compliment Machine Such as the IBM 360." *Communications of the ACM* 12 (7): 382–383.

Kaufman, Stuart. 2000. *Investigations*. Oxford: Oxford University Press.

Kruskal, J. B. 1969. "Extremely Portable Random Number Generator." *Communications of the ACM* 12 (2): 93–94.

Liu, C. L. 1968. *Introduction to Combinatorial Mathematics*. New York: McGraw-Hill.

Martirano, Salvatore. 1960. *Contrasto for Orchestra*. London: Shott.

Martirano, Salvatore. 1963. *Octet*. Manuscript in the collection of CalArts Library, California Institute of the Arts, Valencia, CA.

Martirano, Salvatore. 1966. Manuscript of program notes for *Underworld* contained in the author's personal archives. These notes were later reproduced in a program booklet accompanying the CD (Martirano 1995).

Martirano, Salvatore. 1967. *Underworld*. In *Electronic Music from the University of Illinois*. Vinyl LP, H/HS-25047. New York: Heliodor, MGM Records.

Martirano, Salvatore. 1968. *L's G.A.—Ballad—Octet*. Vinyl LP, 24–5001. New York: Polydor.

Martirano, Salvatore. 1971. *Progress Report #1, an Electronic Music Instrument which Combines the Composing Process with Performance in Real Time*. Manuscript with handwritten corrections in the author's archive.

Martirano, Salvatore. 1989. *Cocktail Music*. Sharon, VT: Smith Publications.

Martirano, Salvatore. 1995. *CDCM Computer Music Series Volume 22, the Composer in the Computer Age—V: A Salvatore Martirano Retrospective: 1962–92*. CD, CRC 2266. Baton Rouge, LA: Centaur Records.

Martirano, Salvatore. 1998. *Salvatore Martirano, O, O, O, O, That Shakespeherian Rag*. CD, 80535–2. New York: New World Records.

Melby, John. 1996. "Sal's G.A." *Perspectives of New Music* 34 (1): 190–198.

Payne, W. H., J. R. Rabung, and T. P. Bogyo. 1969. "Coding the Lehmer Pseudorandom Number Generator." *Communications of the ACM* 12 (2): 85–86.

Pellegrino, Ronald. 1982. *The Electronic Arts of Sound and Light*. New York: Van Nostrand Reinhold.

Reynolds, Roger. 1996. "… Taste, Boundaries, Relevance, Purpose, Risk … (About Salvatore Martirano)." *Perspectives of New Music* 34 (1): 200–206.

Robinson, Michael. 1978. *The SAL-MAR CONSTRUCTION: A Hybrid Digital/Analog System for Real-Time Musical Performance*. Manuscript in the author's archive.

Rosenboom, David. 1972. "In Support of a Systems Theoretical Approach to Art Media." In *Proceedings of the Fifth Annual Conference, April, 1970*, edited by Barney Childes and Paul Lansky, 56–68. New York: American Society of University Composers.

Rosenboom, David. 1987. "A Program for the Development of Performance-Oriented Electronic Music Instrumentation in the Coming Decades: 'What You Conceive Is What You Get.'" *Perspectives of New Music* 25 (1–2): 569–583.

Rosenboom, David. 1992. "Interactive Music with Intelligent Instruments—a New, Propositional Music?" In *New Music across America*, edited by Iris Brooks, 66–70. Valencia, CA and Santa Monica, CA: California Institute of the Arts and High Performance Books.

Rosenboom, David. 1996. "B.C.–A.D. and Two Lines: Two Ways of Making Music While Exploring Instability in Tribute to Salvatore Martirano." *Perspectives of New Music* 34 (1): 208–226.

Rosenboom, David. 2000. "Propositional Music: On Emergent Properties in Morphogenesis and the Evolution of Music." In *Arcana: Musicians on Music*, edited by John Zorn, 203–232. New York: Hips Road and Granary Books.

Rosenboom, David. 2012a. *Roundup Two: Selected Music with Electro-acoustic Landscapes (1968–1984)*. Two CDs, 001. Mashiko, Japan: Art into Life.

Rosenboom, David. 2012b. *Life Field*. CD, TZ 8091. New York: Tzadik.

Rosenboom, David. 2017. "'2 + 2 = Green' Innovation in Experimental Music at the University of Illinois." In *Engine of Innovation, the University of Illinois*, edited by Frederick E. Hoxie, 121–134. Urbana: University of Illinois Press.

Rosenboom, David. 2018. "Propositional Music of Many Nows." In *Tradition and Synthesis, Multiple Modernities for Composer-Performers*, edited by Dusan Bogdanovic and Xavier Bouvier, 121–142. Lévis, Québec: Les Éditions Doberman-Yppan.

Rosenboom, David and Tim Mullen. 2019. "More Than One—Artistic Explorations with Multi-agent BCIs." In Brain Art, Brain-Computer Interfaces for Artistic Expression, edited by Anton Nijholt, 117–143. Cham, Switzerland: Springer Nature Switzerland.

Roubal, Peter J. 2000. *A Complete and Annotated Catalog of the Works of Salvatore Martirano*. DMA thesis, Theses-UIUC-2001-Music-Composition, University of Illinois.

Appendix: Note on Mentions of the SalMar Construction in Other References

The SalMar Construction, the yahaSALmaMAC system, and the Sound and Logic (SAL) software are referred to, mostly in brief terms, in a wide range of sources. Readers are cautioned that some of these descriptions are inconsistent regarding technical details. Nevertheless, it may be useful to have the following list of selected references available for future research. These are in addition to the sources listed under References that served as more informative sources for this chapter.

Collins, Nick, and Julio d'Escriván, eds. 2007. *The Cambridge Companion to Electronic Music*. Cambridge: Cambridge University Press.

Dean, Roger T., ed. 2009. *The Oxford Handbook of Computer Music*. Oxford: Oxford University Press.

Dodge, Charles, and Thomas A. Jerse. 1985. *Computer Music, Synthesis, Composition, and Performance*. New York: Schirmer Books.

Manning, Peter. 2004. *Electronic and Computer Music*. New York: Oxford University Press.

Roads, Curtis, ed. 1989. *The Music Machine: Selected Readings from Computer Music Journal*. Cambridge, MA: MIT Press.

Roads, Curtis. 1996. *The Computer Music Tutorial*. Cambridge, MA: MIT Press.

Roads, Curtis, and John Strawn, eds. 1985. *Foundations of Computer Music*. Cambridge, MA: MIT Press.

7   Invisible Influence: An Analysis of Bülent Arel's *Fantasy and Dance for Five Viols and Tape*

Margaret Anne Schedel with Taylor Ackley

I heard Bülent Arel's work long before I ever knew his name—one of the pieces that made me want to become an electroacoustic composer was Edgard Varèse's *Déserts*. In honor of Varèse, every laptop I have ever owned, including the one I am using to type this chapter, has been called Edgard. I think *Déserts* was the first piece of truly timbral music I ever heard, and I was utterly fascinated by the juxtaposition of chamber music and tape. I especially love the three tape interludes and have always been confused about how their stark elegance contrasts so deeply with Varèse's more famous work for tape, *Poème Électronique*. I discovered that Varèse's final studio engineer for *Déserts* was Bülent Arel and that Arel edited most of the seven minutes of electronic sounds heard on the tape, while Varèse's contributions were mainly to shout, "*Sec, Sec!*" (Davidovsky 2016). Varèse started the piece in New York, working with Ann McMillan, who "help[ed] him prepare the beginning of the first tape version of *Déserts*, to make suggestions as to what [she] thought would be possible and what would not be possible within the confines of tape machines: cutting and rearranging the already recorded sounds, going uptown to record an organ fragment, and so on. The first tape interpolation and part of the second one were done when Pierre Schaeffer invited [Varèse] to complete the tape parts at the Musique Concrète studio of the French Radio (RDF) in Paris" (McMillan 2004, 3).

The tape part was finally completed under the direction of Arel, with the help of Mario Davidovsky and Max Mathews, at the Columbia-Princeton Electronic Music Center. Eric Chasalow provided an interview with Max Mathews in personal correspondence with the author on August 8, 2015, where Mathews said, "Varèse trusted 'scientists' to make the tape parts of his compositions." Later in the interview, Mathews said that "Arel would direct us [Mathews and Davidovsky] how to make the sounds drier, using the analog studio, filtering the tape, changing beats but not loops." Davidovsky recalled that Varèse had lost some of his hearing and kept asking for the recording to be louder and louder, so he and Arel had to pop aspirin during their sessions. Davidovsky described the engineer/composer relationship as "Varèse would make a noise and then the technician would have to make it." Edgard Varèse, Max Mathews, and Mario Davidovsky are legends in our field, yet the man who taught them how to use the resources of the Columbia-Princeton Electronic Music Center (CPEMC) has been largely forgotten by our community.

The legend of the CPEMC looms large in the history of electronic music in the United States, if not the world. Composers who worked there have become revered as founding members of a tribe who "compose music directly in sound" as Vladimir Ussachevsky so eloquently wrote (Ussachevsky n.d.). After nearly a decade of informal experiments in electroacoustic music composition, the center was officially founded in 1958 with a grant from the Rockefeller Foundation. The composers who worked at the CPEMC in the early years are now recognized as pioneers, and a huge number of publications have been devoted to its founders, Ussachevsky and Otto Luening, as well as the musicians who worked there, including Jon Appleton, Luciano Berio, Wendy Carlos, Mario Davidovsky, Charles Dodge, Halim El-Dabh, Kenjiro Ezaki, Max Mathews, Daria Semegen, Alice Shields, Edgard Varèse, and Charles Wuorinen. Many of these composers were featured on the seminal recordings put out by the CPEMC, the eponymous *Columbia-Princeton Electronic Music Center* LP from 1964, and the 1976 compilation *Columbia-Princeton Electronic Music Center 1961–1973*. Only one composer appears on both recordings, the Turkish-born Arel. He also has three tracks on the 1963 recording *Son-Nova 1988: Electronic Music by Bülent Arel, Mario Davidovsky, and Vladimir Ussachevsky Electronically Realized at the Columbia-Princeton Electronic Music Center*. Yet, until I started working at Stony Brook University, I had never heard anything about this fascinating composer who was one of the founding members of CPEMC.

Because there isn't very much written about Arel in English, most of the information for this chapter comes from interviews with my colleague Daria Semegen, who was first Arel's student, then his collaborator, and then his colleague at Stony Brook University. Although Arel spent most of his life in the United States, he is much better known in his home country of Turkey. There is an entire book in Turkish, *Elektronik Muzigin Oncusu Bülent Arel*, by Filiz Ali, published in 2002. His *Postlude from Music for a Sacred Service* was recently included on *An Anthology of Turkish Experimental Music 1961–2014* (Various Artists 2019), and he is name-checked by Turkish composer Erdem Helvacioglu in *The Cambridge Companion to Electronic Music* (Collins and d'Escrivan 2017).

Arel is included in Neil Butterworth's *Dictionary of American Classical Composers* (2013) and Hugh Davies's foundational *International Catalog of Electronic Music* (1968). Robert Moog (1981) interviewed him for an article about the CPEMC for *Keyboard Magazine*, and Robert Gluck (2007) wrote extensively about him. He is also included on a long list of composers who "Have Contributed Materially in Many Ways to Make

Our Music What It Is. Please Do Not Hold It Against Them" in liner notes for the debut album by Frank Zappa and the Mothers of Invention, *Freak Out* (1966). An often-repeated story in electronic music is that Zappa wrote an entire article about Edgard Varèse for *Stereo Review*. Zappa almost certainly sampled Arel's *Stereo Electronic Music No. 1* in "Nasal Retentive Calliope Music" on *We're Only in It for the Money* (Lewis 2008), and *Stereo Electronic Music No. 1* is the final track on the 2010 CD *Frank Zappa's Classical Selection—The Dissonant Classics That Informed and Inspired Zappa* (Various Artists 2010). Arel has largely been forgotten, but he directly impacted numerous highly visible actors in computer music, and he had an undeniable impact on both my compositional voice and my academic career at Stony Brook University.

Arel was born in 1919 in Ankara, Turkey, to a well-off artistic family, and died in 1990 in Stony Brook, New York. His life spanned nearly a century of incredible change in music technology. He was not only a founding member of CPEMC; he also founded electronic music studios at Yale, where he taught from 1965 to 1970, and Stony Brook University. Between his time at Columbia and Yale, Arel returned to Turkey and directed the "Ankara State Radio middle-wave music programs, and found[ed] and direct[ed] a Madrigal Chorus for the State Radio" (Composers Recordings Inc. 1970). Arel was also a notable painter and sculptor, whose works are collected in the Turkish National Gallery (Shields 1998); his mother was a painter, whose work is also in Turkish museum collections. Mario Davidovsky specifically remembered Arel's mobiles as ingenious combinations of engineering and sculpture, and Semegen recalls him as an avid painter. He was known to link his visual and music senses, for example, using the structure of a fourteenth-century Chinese painting for his 12-tone composition *For Violin and Piano*. Of the relationship between his painting and his music, Arel wrote: "A thin branch, curving slightly, begins the painting from the left. The branch is the solo violin part; tiny leaves, attached later, represent the percussive introduction of the piano. Then several branches intertwine in various directions and combinations, and there are two climactic episodes. A restricted improvisation in both violin and piano parts, followed by a rhapsodic episode, leads into the soft ending, that disappears like the branch in the drawing" (Composers Recordings Inc. 1970). The scores for his tape pieces are works of art in themselves, and Ussachevsky commissioned him to create a detailed score for *Stereo Electronic Music No. 1* for the cover of the first CPEMC recording (figure 7.1). The brilliant graphic design details many musical parameters at work over the five-track stereo work. This score was created after the composition was completed in order for Arel to claim a copyright. Ironically, he is not credited with creating the image on the record jacket, although he had the idea of cover art in mind while he was designing the graphics for his score.

Figure 7.1
Album cover of Columbia-Princeton Electronic Music Center recording featuring Arel's score for *Stereo Electronic Music No. 1*.

Arel's formal musical education was in composition, conducting, and piano at the Ankara Conservatory, founded under the direction of Paul Hindemith. Arel later taught at the conservatory and, according to his biography, cofounded the Helikon Society of Contemporary Arts. The phrase Helikon Society of Contemporary Arts is used in multiple versions of his biography, but I haven't been able to find information about this anywhere else. Perhaps this difference in name is a result of the Turkish to French to English translation of Helikon Derneği Galerisi. Arel was fluent in French from a young age because of his schooling at the famed Galatasaray Lisesi, and he was known to teach composition lessons in French to students who were more familiar with that language. Davidovsky said Arel's English was structured more as a word-by-word translation from French; the accepted English translation of Helikon Derneği Galeris is the Helikon Association Gallery, which is known as the second art gallery in Turkey. Its mission was to expose unschooled audiences to avant-garde art forms in order to advance the cultural sophistication of Turkey (Smith 2016). Arel might have also tried to widen the scope of the name in his translation; in addition to art exhibitions, Helikon held concerts, meetings, and conferences.

Radio Ankara sent Arel to Paris to learn about sound engineering so he could become their music engineer, and there he learned about theoretical sound engineering with Joze Bernard and Wilfred Garret (Composers Recordings Inc. 1970). He then worked at Radio Ankara from 1951 to 1959, and in 1957 he wrote one of his first pieces incorporating electronic sound, *Music for String Quartet and Oscillator*. Semegen believes this piece brought Arel to the attention of the Rockefeller Foundation. Arel claimed that he sat under a table manipulating the oscillator in real time as the string quartet played, but Semegen admits he could have also prerecorded the sounds onto tape. Not long after a performance of *Music for String Quartet and Oscillator*, the Rockefeller Foundation invited Arel to become the first research assistant at the CPEMC. He revised this seminal work in 1962 at the CPEMC and retitled it *Music for String Quartet and Tape*.

Davidovsky spent a year studying electronic music under Arel; he said they found common ground in the studio but were very different musically, with Davidovsky preferring the German school (synthesis) while Arel leaned more toward the French (sampling). Davidovsky also said that Arel was not an "intellectual teacher"; he preferred the immediacy of the studio and would spend hours showing techniques, walking around and talking, while Semegen said that Arel wasn't pedantic or pseudoscientific and was perceived as less intellectual because he believed in embodiment and intuitive expression in addition to rigorous technique. Many of the musicians I asked about Arel mentioned his physical dexterity, the elegance of his movement, and the clarity of his conducting. Davidovsky said Arel could do things that required a lot of physical coordination, making up for the fact that we didn't yet have technology advanced enough to easily create the sound he wanted—and if he couldn't do it physically, he would engineer a mechanical solution. Stony Brook University still has Arel's custom splice blocks created to make tape loops and splices easier to create and control.

Unlike many pieces created in analog studios for tape, Arel's electronic music doesn't sound dated to my ears. James McCartney, the original programmer of the audio programming language SuperCollider, is a big fan of Arel's music, writing, "Those were my favorite tracks on the Columbia Princeton LPs—they just sounded good, rather than sounding like an exercise of formal possibilities" (McCartney, personal correspondence with the author, July 31, 2015).

Richard Teitelbaum believed "Mr. Arel possesse[d] both that intangible gift for 'sound vision' in the electronic medium and an unusual technical ability to realize his vision which mark him as one of the most successful composers of this kind in electronic music" (Teitelbaum 1964, 129). Mel Powell (1997) said that Arel had the most natural gift for the medium at that time and that "he managed to make electronics sound like music, not fakery, not noise, something else. He had that knack."

Eric Chasalow has been conducting oral history interviews with the pioneers of electronic music and regrets that he wasn't able to interview Arel before his untimely death. Chasalow wrote that "Bülent was really the one who brought attention to fine details in the studio to the US. It is hard to say how much he invented and how much he adapted, but he did invent a lot. When I did those interviews in the 90's, virtually everyone mentioned him fondly and gave him credit for being the true pioneer. I remember him as very kind and demanding at the same time" (Chasalow, personal correspondence, August 8, 2015). Semegen thinks his *Stereo Electronic Music No. 2* is one of the finest works for tape ever composed. When researching his compositional oeuvre for this chapter, I fell in love with his 1974 *Fantasy and Dance for Five Viols and Tape*, commissioned by the New York Consort of Viols. The piece is on the promotional CD of the Arel biography *Elektronik Müziğin Öncüsü Bülent Arel*, with the copyright held by Semegen, and is also available on YouTube. All timings referenced in this chapter come from the YouTube recording. Arel composed the work at Stony Brook University using the studio facilities he had modeled on the CPEMC. Unlike much of his earlier work, the electronic sounds in this piece are synthesized. Arel developed much of the sonic material using the newly purchased Buchla 200 (figure 7.2). The studio, with its custom standing desks, quadraphonic speakers, and analog gear, is still operational and looks much the way it did when Arel was working there. I was able to use the Buchla 200 to help with the following analysis of *Fantasy and Dance for Five Viols and Tape*.

The Buchla 200 is a direct descendant of the Modular Electronic Music System, better known as the Buchla Box, that engineer/inventor Don Buchla developed for the San Francisco Tape Music Center (SFTMC) between 1963 and 1965. While many historians refer to his invention as a synthesizer, that was not a word he used to describe his collection of circuits. "Rather, Buchla was building exactly what he said he was building: a modular electronic music system, making possibilities for both radically new sounds and radically new ways to control those sounds in real time" (Gordon 2018, 19). The Rockefeller Foundation may have given the SFTMC money toward the new machine; a line item for their 1964–1965 season includes US$5000 for "Research & Development, for new visual-optical apparatuses as well as audio equipment engineering" (Gordon 2018, 45). In this first instrument, as in later instruments, users "patch" various modules together in order to create a complex sound. Buchla's first modules were modeled on existing equipment such as oscillators and ring modulators; his advancement was to create a single large box with a standardized power supply in the back and

Figure 7.2
The Buchla 200 at Stony Brook University on its custom stand. Taylor Ackley found the upper modules in storage and added them to the system at a later time. Photo by Margaret Schedel and Kevin Yager.

consistent control and line-level audio voltages for input and output. The Buchla Box shipped with two kinds of cables: 0.141 inch "tiny-jax" connectors for audio signals and stackable banana plugs for control signals. The stacking plugs meant that control voltages could easily be routed from one source to multiple inputs. Musicians simply used uniform connectors soldered onto colored wires to connect one module to another, "configuring the flow of signal through the Buchla, upending familiar, unidirectional models of music-compositional authority, in favor of complex, non-linear, and unstable circuits between human and instrument" (Gordon 2018, 48). Semegen agrees that the flexibility and ergonomics inherent in Buchla's design make his synthesizers a remarkable creative resource.

The Buchla synthesizer was unique for its time; not only was it one of the first commercially available voltage-controlled synthesizers, but it also featured a monochromatic touch plate keyboard, not a three-dimensional black and white imitation piano as found on Moog and Serge equipment. Unlike simple switches, these keys generate both pulsed and steady-state variable voltage-control signals. Later models also included a ribbon that changes voltage based on position, with another separate output for pressure, enabling complex performer mappings. Buchla worked closely with the musicians—notably Morton Subotnick, who used it to compose *Silver Apples of the Moon*—at the SFTMC to create an entirely new musically expressive machine. As Suzanne Ciani, Buchla's employee and famous Buchla artist, recalled, "He did it all—he designed the instruments, he did all the graphics, he designed all the cases, he worked out how they could be transportable" (Friedlander 2017). These voltage-controlled synthesizers went out of fashion because they were large and prohibitively expensive, and their pitch would drift dramatically based on the weather. Although Buchla intended that his instruments be used for live performance, they became known more as studio instruments, and very few people played them live in concert. With the advent of digital synthesizers, starting with the Yamaha DX7, many studios abandoned their analog roots altogether. For a period of 30 years, modular synthesizers were seen essentially as historic remnants and occasionally useful teaching tools. With the advent of the Eurorack format, "invented by German company Doepfer in the late 90's, … many users [returned to] the flexibility and heuristic nature of the modular format, forgoing preset sounds for a mutable patch architecture and increased control over sound" (Rohs 2018, 2). When I first started at Stony Brook, no one knew what the Buchla was; now students, with their own Eurorack setups in tow, come here specifically to work on our synthesizer. *Fantasy and Dance* appeals to me on the surface level of the music itself, its combination of ancient instruments and tape, as material history because we still have the original machine it was composed on at my school and because of my friendship with the iconoclastic inventor Buchla himself when I was living in the Bay Area before I started my position at Stony Brook.

Arel designed Stony Brook's Buchla 200 system himself. When Semegen arrived at Stony Brook in 1974, she found the Buchla 200 sitting on a tabletop in the studio. They decided to build the large wooden frame with rolling casters that it sits on today. One of the stories told about our system is that it was the largest one made at the time. Since then, collectors have assembled larger kits, but this instrument was assembled by Buchla and was the centerpiece of Stony Brook's studio. Seen in person, the instrument is imposing but human scaled. It is easy to reach all the modules, and the curved case is now a standard design. Arel had worked with smaller Buchla systems at CPEMC. "Around 1965–66, the first Buchla analog synthesizer appeared at the Center, causing quite a bit of excitement, as its voltage-controlled sequencer permitted for the first time the creation of a sequence of notes without splicing" (Shields 1998). Buchla named the sequencers "sequential voltage sources." Arel specifically chose the modules for the system to express his musical vision, including two of these 16-step sequencers and one five-step sequencer. Each module has programmable voltages at each of four outputs and the ability to turn the sequence on or off. "Buchla is generally credited with having invented the analog sequencer, which was conceived of first as a device for eliminating numerous tiny tape splices by allowing a single oscillator to be programmed to sound a desired sequence of pitches" (Aikin 1982). Arel made full use of the Buchla in his signature piece for the instrument, *Fantasy and Dance for Five Viols and Tape.*

Fantasy and Dance is a polystylistic romp with a somber introduction in the viols, quoting the *Dies Irae* with the open fourths and fifths of the early Renaissance played *senza vibrato* (Intro A, 0:00–1:45; see figure 7.3. This section ends at mark "M1" in the figure). The texture slowly thickens, and then the treble line trills over a final cadence while the other viol lines fade out. A single high, synthesized tone that almost seems like a detuned overtone takes over from the upper voice. There is a very typical sounding 1970s abstract electronic music solo (Intro B, 1:45–3:35), which still retains a strong sense of phrase and cadence. Toward the end of this second introduction (M2), a very strong beat emerges from the electronic texture, and then the beat becomes faster, clearer, and more active (M3). The rest of the piece (M4 onward) is in this tempo, a duet between the viols and the tape. This tightly synchronized dance is made possible by the

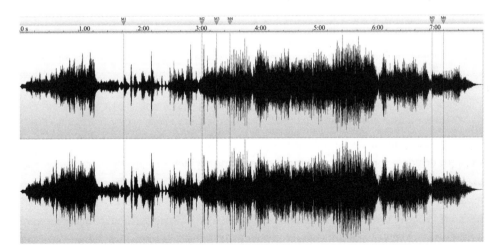

Figure 7.3
Waveform image of Arel's complete *Fantasy and Dance* showing sectional divisions.

steady beat, with the electronics playing complex Anatolian rhythms (section C, 3:35–7:50) grounded in larger motives. Arel told Semegen that he didn't actually transcribe the rhythms of his homeland but had participated in several festivals and wanted to capture that rhythmic spirit where the product of stacking several simple rhythms is a resultant complex rhythm. After several of these rhythmic exchanges, the viols finally land on a large cadence at 7:00 (M5) and hold while the electronics have one last flourish (M6) before fading out. Despite the contrasting character of the three sections, the piece is unified by Arel's musicality, phrasing, and virtuosic use of reverberated and dry textures. The piece did not come out of the Buchla "raw" but had detailed adjustments and editing in the studio after the Buchla output was recorded onto tape.

If I heard this piece today for a composition competition or festival, I would absolutely program it, and I am working on getting a new performance of the piece. I must acknowledge musicologist Matt Brounley for scanning Arel's handwritten manuscript of the parts, entering them into the Sibelius notation program, and assembling a score and typeset parts for a new performance and my analysis. Our former audio engineer, Andy Nitolli, was able to digitize the tape part from a second-generation reel-to-reel tape for the performance. Unfortunately, the original version was too weak at the splices to run through the machine, so there is a higher noise floor on the digitized recording than there would be if we had been able to use the original.

In the hands of experts, the Buchla is a true instrument, and Arel clearly learned how to make the Buchla create the sounds he wanted and then used his knowledge of studio techniques to edit the pieces together through multitracking and splicing and careful use of reverberation. Ciani stated,

> The beauty of the Buchla is that it has an open architecture—all these modular systems do. There is nothing defining about the way you use it—you create your own instrument within the instrument. You could choose your modules, you could connect them the way you wanted, you could design the way you used them. If I made music on the Buchla, it was absolutely nothing like the music that somebody else made on the Buchla. The way Buchla used it was not anything like the way I used it. It was a tool that you could customize to a great degree. (Friedlander 2017)

I asked my student Taylor Ackley, who uses the Buchla 200 in his own compositional work, to do some forensic musicology to determine which of our Buchla modules Arel likely used to create the source material for the electronic sounds. The rest of the chapter is drawn from his listening and decoding which modules were used, with additional research into the units Ackley believes Arel used. The following three paragraphs were written by Ackley; I have lightly edited them. Ackley also showed me how to use the sequencer and lowpass gate, which feature prominently in the third section of the piece. This was an invaluable experience of physically interacting with the system and hearing sounds similar to those found in the tape part of *Fantasy and Dance*.

The first phrase of the electronic section begins at 1:45 with the entrance of the single synthesized pitch over the top of the solo viol. The first phrase grows into a triggered rhythmic sequence of seemingly randomized pitches, which flow with an almost recitative-like rubato. This serves to introduce the character of the Buchla in a way that grows very naturally out of the ritardando cadence, which closes the viol section of the piece. [In all probability, Arel set up the patch and recorded several versions of the generative result and chose his favorite, a kind of "soft generative" (Schedel and Rootberg 2009) composition not possible in live performance.—MS] At 2:06, a series of driplike filtered noise sequences build in intensity, culminating in the first clear cadence of the solo electronic section from 2:14 to 2:24.

The second phrase begins at 2:25 with a slightly more urgent feel. Here, Arel made excellent use of the Buchla's highly expressive voltage-controlled bandpass filters. He most likely added frequency modulation built into the dual oscillator modules. When these processes are combined with a wide variety of rather extreme envelope filters and the characteristically acoustic sound of the Buchla's voltage-controlled lowpass gate, a complex electronic polyphony emerges. The sounds in this section were probably triggered by using the 217 touch keyboard module, as opposed to the generative sequences of the first section. That said, there is almost certainly a sequencer connected to the sample-and-hold module, which introduces random voltage in parts of Arel's patches. It is this interaction of analog sequencing, random voltage from the Buchla's Source of Uncertainty, and human touch that creates the bridge between acoustic performance and electronic sound production on which this piece is constructed. The phrase cadences at 3:00 with a long, perhaps sampled, bell-like sound, which fades into the final portion of the purely electronic section of the piece.

At 3:03, a steady, dancelike rhythmic sequence begins to emerge from the previous arrhythmic material. It is extremely quiet and devoid of all but low frequencies, and at first it comes across as a bubbling cacophony barely audible under the more active material. Long tones lie over the top of this texture, accented by percussive stabs. This creates a tension from which a dance feel emerges at 3:20. This is brilliantly accomplished through a shift in filtering that allows a drumlike sound to arise from the sequence. Arel then uses a convenient series of switches on the Buchla's sequential voltage source to shorten the length of the pattern into the beat of a Turkish dance, which sets up the reentry of the viols.

The dance section is a brilliantly conceived partnership between the unrelenting rhythmic sequences of the Buchla and the sectionalized melodic material in the viols. The breaks in the acoustic part enable the instrumental players to realign their internal clocks to the beat of the tape part, which could be difficult to hear while playing. On the surface, the fast, rhythmic sequence in the electronics is fairly consistent, containing foregrounded pitched-percussion passages with short attacks and quick decays, embellished by occasional swooping pitches in the same timescale but with longer attacks and sustains on a separate channel. The rhythmic material enters at 3:21, and there is a gorgeous 15-second minimalist process as the phrase gradually shortens from four repetitions of an eight-note sequence with a short pause to two repetitions of a six-note phrase, created by removing the rest and the first two notes of the eight-note sequence. An equal-length phrase follows from three repetitions of a four-note sequence similarly created by removing the first two notes from the six-note sequence. Finally, eight repetitions of a two-note sequence, which focus attention on the subtle variations in the backing swooping pitches, lead directly into the viol entrance. This section begins and ends with a larger percussive hit, bounding the larger period.

On the Buchla, this process of subtraction is easily achieved by turning off switches under each column of the step sequencer (see figure 7.4, bottom right). Arel most likely performed the maneuver of turning off the switches in real time while the tape was recording; he had both the dexterity and the musicality. By "performing the studio" instead of recording the sequences individually and then splicing tape, he kept the rhythm totally synchronized as the pattern became shorter. This is a clear moment

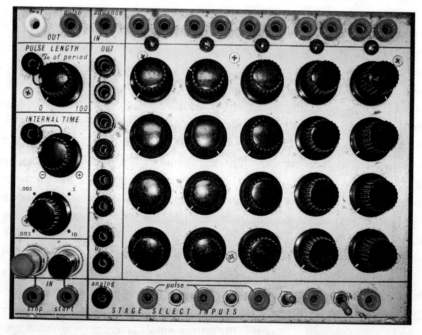

Figure 7.4
Close-up of the five-step sequencer, with the block between the fourth and fifth steps turned off. Photo by Margaret Schedel and Kevin Yager.

where the machine influenced Arel's composition, the tool of the switches on the sequencer shaping the hand and cognition of the user. Simon Penny writes, "Tool use, generally speaking, involves an artifact tuned over time to [a] specific task domain, combined with equally attuned skill. Skills and tool are complementary and isomorphic. In order to effectively use a specialized artifact, specific skills must be deployed. The skill with no tool is dormant, while the tool with no skilled user is worthless. No cognitive extension performs its task without a tradition of complementary bodily practice" (Penny 2017, 253). Using the sequencer in this manner is a natural and easy process to create on a Buchla; however, the rhythmic material and attention to sonic detail mark this passage clearly as Arel's work.

The dance has very clear sections demarcated by cadences in the strings. The first phrase is the electronic intro detailed in the previous paragraph. From 3:35 to 3:46, falling angular viol lines alternate with the electronics in a tight feat of synchronization from the performers. Just as the viols change their line, a longer swoop emerges from the electronic texture signaling the end of this section. The next phrase builds intensity, with a rising sequence in the viols accented by a gradually more prevalent percussive electronic accompaniment. At 3:57, the viols sustain a chord, and the electronic accompaniment once again bubbles to the surface, reminding the listener of how the beat emerged from the electronic texture in section B. The electronics become a steady force as the viols abandon their long notes and begin to punctuate the electronic soundscape with trills leading to accents.

Throughout the dance section, Arel makes full use of the capabilities of the sequencer units. On the YouTube recording, it is possible to hear that the beat is ping-ponging between the left and right speakers. Listening to the tape part alone, it is clear that there are distinct patterns in each speaker that are coupled in order to create a more complex resultant rhythm. Stony Brook's Buchla is a quadraphonic system, and it is trivial to route audio from its oscillators to separate outputs. There are even joysticks that allow you to pan signals between multiple outputs in real time, although Arel did not exploit that capability. In the previous solo electronic section, the left and right channels play similar material at any given moment as expected, but in the dance section, the right and left channels are offset in a tight and joyful hocket. This distinct panning aids in the definition of the release portion of the envelope on the drum hits, which otherwise could have become muddy, with the start of one sound masking the decay of the other. In figure 7.5, it is very easy to see that the left and right channels are distinct, with the left channel containing a steady rhythm and the right channel alternating between longer swoops and offset rhythms resulting in a double-time feeling at the end of this excerpt. Arel was well aware of the power of spatialization in his music—*Stereo Electronic*

Figure 7.5
Detail of tape part of *Fantasy and Dance for Five Viols and Tape* clearly showing stereo separation.

Music No. 1 and *Stereo Electronic Music No. 2* use spatialization to aid in the clarity of the mix throughout their composition, as well as for expressive purposes in specific passages.

At 4:15, the first viol begins a recognizable melody that is swiftly imitated in the other string voices. In this recording, the thick texture of the viols nearly obscures the tape part, but still the occasional swoop can be heard at the ends of notes, keeping an off-kilter energy going. There is a huge string cadence at 4:35, and the electronics once again have a short solo with a repeated four-note pattern. Two seconds later, we hear a sudden change in the electronics for the first time, as a steady eighth-note beat is introduced with swoops on the downbeats and some almost incidental shifting crackles. Two phrases of jagged viol material follow, while the electronics continue in the same pattern.

All the rhythms in this section were most likely created by manipulating the knobs on the sequencer unit of the Buchla. The sequencers function almost like analog memory, capable of storing intricate patterns with four variables in each stage of the matrix. Arel probably used the five-stage sequencer to control both 16-stage sequencers at the same time. He likely recorded several loops of each sequence, adjusted the knobs, recorded another variation, and then spliced the result together. He would have sent the control output of each step of the sequencer to one of ten oscillators, stacking the banana plugs to create the same timbre at different steps in the sequence. He also clearly used a variant of what we now call side-chaining, tying one element in a mix to another. Side-chaining's original use can be dated to the 1930s, when Doug Shearer "first developed the idea while working at MGM Studios at the birth of film sound. Originally it was developed to 'de-ess' sibilant voices which were problematic to record as they could easily overload the electronics of the day" (Southall 2011). The concept has expanded since "Shearer conceived of a compressor with a 'side' signal chain (separate to the main trigger signal) with an EQ slapped on it—rather than evenly compressing the incoming signal, this 'de-esser' would only be triggered when the specific sibilant sounds appeared" (Ableton Tutorials 2019). Side-chaining most often refers to side-chain compression popularized by EDM, where a kick drum cuts through the mix, but in its most general definition a side-chain signal acts as a reference to a modulator and links two signals.

Put another way, the output of one track is used to control the modulating action on another track. It is clear that Arel linked many parameters in *Fantasy and Dance*; most obviously, there is a self-similarity in the pitch and the decay around the 2:00 mark, which are likely side-chained using an envelope generator.

There are two hardware envelope generators on our Buchla 200. The 245 has only attack and decay, which are dramatically variable between 1 millisecond and 10 seconds. The 246 has delay, attack, duration, and decay. It also has a sustain switch, which when activated continues the envelope's duration as long as a pulse is received (for instance, by holding a key on the 217 touch keyboard module). Both circuits follow through the whole decay and release cycle, even if they only get a short pulse. With the ease of duplicating signals using the stacking banana plugs, it made sense to use the same envelope to control multiple units, but there are several possible ways Arel could have used these envelope generators:

1. One envelope to multiple voltage controls (for example, gate and pitch). An example is audible around 2:35, in which both the lowpass gate and the pitch of an oscillator seem to be controlled by the same envelope.

2. Two or more independent envelopes controlling different aspects of the same signal (for example, independent or uncorrelated control of gate and timbre). It is hard to tell with certainty exactly when this is happening, but a likely moment is the first entrance of the electronic part at 1:45–2:05, where the array of long evolving sounds briefly transition into smaller notes. This could have been accomplished by triggering sequencers (and connected envelope generators) via the keyboard.

3. Two or more independent but correlated envelopes controlling different voltages in the same signal path (for example, one short envelope chopping up individual notes with a longer envelope controlling pitch). This is likely how the percussive sounds of the dance are being produced. While this could be accomplished by a single sequencer, this percussive sound is also often accompanied by a continuous softer sound following the same melodic contour. This sound (which is clearly audible at 3:20–3:35, among other places) cannot be produced using only the stages of the sequencer, as Stony Brook's Buchla does not have a gliss/slew-control module. Instead, it is likely that Arel created the rhythm (as well as the pulses for the short envelope) of the percussion sound with the sequencer but used a single stage to send a pulse triggering an envelope, which controlled the pitch of both the percussive sounds and the pitch of the softer accompanying sound.

At 4:59, there is another break, and the electronics turn decidedly darker, while the viols play violent five-note phrases in various registers. This time there is a longer electronic interlude with more querulous swoops that are overtaken by an explosion in the viols. The section culminates in a held chord; then the viols get increasingly frantic until 5:49, when there is another short Buchla solo followed by even more urgent tremoloing strings. The tremolos turn into a short downward gliss reinforced by the tape part, one of the first times the electronic and acoustic parts truly merge. The electronic pattern then starts to fade away with an odd and satisfying stutter at 6:01. At 6:07, the viols come in with pizzicati, reinforcing the rhythmic tape part. Another long melody spins out in the upper viol, with more ornaments added to vary each phrase. A tutti interruption in the strings at 6:34 gradually breaks down into scalar passages while the electronics continue their playful, occasionally stuttering line. At 6:58, there is another cadence, with a fade-out of the Buchla rhythm continuing after the strings stop.

This section really exploits the sonic characteristics of the Buchla with the classic pitched percussive sound of a lowpass gate. A lowpass gate combines aspects of audio amplifiers and lowpass filters. NerdAudio asserts that the original Buchla Music Box had three lowpass gates, each with "its own capacitor [sic; probably vactrol] type, giving a unique sound to each module" (NerdAudio 2017). One distinctive sound of the Buchla comes from the behavior of these *vactrols*, which are photoresistive, electrically coupled, optically isolated devices, essentially a tube with a light-emitting diode at one end and a light sensor at the other. "Vactrol" is a generonym for this particular electro-optical circuit from the trademarked product produced by Vactec in the 1960s. Vactrols are now popular among Eurorack designers, with some companies referring to them as vactrol drums because of how easy it is to create a pitched percussion sound with this electronic schematic. According to one electronic music site, the "sole supplier of new vactrols is Perkin-Elmer, which markets about ten different types with different response characteristics" (ElectronicMusicFandom n.d.). In the 1970s, both Buchla and Serge used these somewhat slow, nonlinear circuits, which enable voltage-controlled cutoff frequencies of filters to rise and fall smoothly, making them useful as gates. According to Rohs, "One ... characteristic of the Vactrol response is the fact that the 'attack' and 'decay' times of the Vactrol's 'envelope' are determined by the level of the vactrol current. ... For example, a higher control voltage (and therefore, current) will result in a quicker rise time and a slower decay time" (Rohs 2018, 9). This behavior, combined with the other physical characteristic of the vactrol, that resistance decreases rapidly in response to increasing light but builds up slowly when the LED is turned off or down, enables a user to create tuned percussion sounds by sending a short impulse, which results in a quick on/off of the LED. The light received by the detector opens a voltage-controlled amplifier and also controls the filter cutoff at the same time. Another result of this filter design is that sounds at low amplitude are not just quieter but are also duller. This is most likely how Arel controlled the darkening timbre at the start of this section.

It should be noted that a number of other components make up this percussive sound, including some sort of modulation (likely applying FM to an oscillator), filtering, and voltage control of the waveform of at least one oscillator. The complexity of this patch is hard to imagine on any contemporaneous equipment other than the massive Buchla system Arel designed. This synthesizer boasts a remarkable ten oscillators (in the form of five 258 dual oscillator modules), eight envelope generators, and incredible analog memory and sequencing potential from the two 246 sequential voltage source modules and single 245 sequential voltage source module. This is why our analysis of this piece required such careful study of the specific instrument Arel used to create it. The type of patch he created for each sound would hardly be possible on anything but a Buchla system of this size. To our knowledge, Stony Brook's 200 series was a superior system at the time this piece was composed.

In the final large phrase, the Buchla plays softly as the viols hold long notes, which almost completely mask the electronics. In this recording at least, the tape part seems to add a grainy texture to the held viol notes. At 7:14, the tape part comes to the front with clearly pitched material that is built from the previous swooping pitches. The percussive rhythm at the start of the dance has been transformed into a pitched sequence at the same tempo, whose frequency content is gradually constrained as it fades out under the held strings.

When the tape part comes to the fore in all its pitched glory, it is clear that Arel is using multiple envelope generators for pitch, length, shape, and modulation of the oscillators. He cleverly routed the signal from the sequencer to unique oscillators and then from each oscillator to distinct outputs so each note can ring fully, utilizing the signature "round" sound of the Buchla. Even though the entire dance is essentially at a single tempo with a uniform density of percussion notes, the tape part is a virtuosic display of the timbral possibilities of the Buchla. Arel was well aware of the limitations of the Buchla; he and Semegen did not like the way trills sounded on the Buchla because the attack is too round. They created a "trill study" using very short tape splices to achieve the kind of sustained presence an acoustic instrument has while trilling. This round attack may have led Arel to use two channels for the fast passages. Throughout the dance, Arel very slowly transitions from a very limited set of pitched percussion sounds, through somewhat less constrained and brighter pitched percussion, to a fully realized synthesized melody created from the same building blocks, before moving back into constrained pitch material in a higher register at the end.

To quote Stefan from *Saturday Night Live*, this piece has EVERYTHING. Arel showcased his facility with acoustic and electronic techniques, incorporated rhythms from his homeland of Turkey, and used his mastery of studio techniques gained working at Radio Ankara and RDF to create an engaging tape part. The electronics have his characteristically careful attention to the mix of dry and reverberated sounds, which can also be heard in the tape part for *Déserts*. Arel's time conducting madrigal choirs is reflected in the open harmonies of the viols in the introduction and the brief moments of canonic imitation in the dance. His experience at the CPEMC studios is fully realized in the electronic introduction of section B, and there is even a reference to the minimalist process music of the 1960s in the transition between sections B and C. Arel's polystylistic swirling dance of strings and machines is a masterful fusion of electronic and acoustic worlds that has stood the test of time.

References

Ableton Tutorials. 2019. "Sidechain Compression: Part 1—Concepts and History." https://www .ableton.com/en/blog/sidechain-compression-part-1/.

Aikin, Jim. 1982. "The Horizons of Instrument Design: A Conversation with Don Buchla." *Keyboard Magazine*, December. https://www.keyboardmag.com/artists/the-horizons-of-instrument-desi gn-a-conversation-with-don-buchla.

Ali, Filiz. 2002. *Elektronik Müziğin Öncüsü Bülent Arel*. İstanbul: Türkiye İş.

Butterworth, Neil. 2005. *Dictionary of American Classical Composers*. New York: Routledge.

Collins, Nick, and Julio d'Escriván, eds. 2017. *The Cambridge Companion to Electronic Music*. Cambridge: Cambridge University Press.

Composers Recordings, Inc. 1970. Liner notes for CD recording *Bülent Arel / Olly Wilson / Robert Stern*, CRI SD 264. New York: Composers Recordings.

Davidovsky, Mario. 2016. Telephone interview with Margaret Schedel, March 19.

Davies, Hugh. 1968. *International Catalog of Electronic Music*. Paris: Groupe de Recherches Musicales de l'ORTF.

ElectronicMusicFandom. 2019. "Vactrol" (wiki). https://electronicmusic.fandom.com/wiki/Vactrol.

Friedlander, Emilie. 2017. "Don Buchla's Modular Revolution, Remembered by Suzanne Ciani." Vice (website). https://www.vice.com/en_us/article/59pm45/don-buchlas-modular-revolution-remem bered-by-suzanne-ciani.

Gluck, Robert J. 2007. "The Columbia-Princeton Electronic Music Center: Educating International Composers." *Computer Music Journal* 31 (2): 20–38.

Gordon, Theodore Barker. 2018. *Bay Area Experimentalism: Music and Technology in the Long 1960s*. PhD thesis, University of Chicago.

Lewis, Saul. 2008. Music and Film blog. http://lewissaul.blogspot.com/2008/02/140-frank-zappa -nasal-retentive.html.

McMillan, Ann. 2004. "Celebrated Villager: Edgard Varèse 1883–1965." *Contemporary Music Review* 23 (1): 3–9.

Moog, Robert. 1981. "The Columbia-Princeton Electronic Music Center: Thirty Years of Explorations in Sound." *Contemporary Keyboard Magazine:* 22–32. https://www.keyboardmag.com/miscellaneous /the-columbia-princeton-electronic-music-center-thirty-years-of-explorations-in-sound.

NerdAudio. 2017. "Patching with a Low Pass Gate." https://nerdaudio.com/blogs/news/wired -wednesday-patching-with-a-low-pass-gate.

Penny, Simon. 2017. *Making Sense: Cognition, Computing, Art, and Embodiment.* Cambridge, MA: MIT Press.

Powell, Mel. 1997. Interviewed by Eric Chasalow. https://ensemble.brandeis.edu/hapi/v1/cont ents/permalinks/Ri9x8G4F/view?fbclid=IwAR1ox7RV5YyrNtK9LPQ6Fm0rB23T5e6m-SbuB4cy oi9jZZXtpz9mW84KNzc.

Rohs, Josh. 2018. "A Matlab Implementation of the Buchla Lowpass Gate." McGill University student paper. http://www.music.mcgill.ca/~gary/courses/projects/618_2018/rohs/MUMT618 _Buchla_LPG_Report.pdf.

Schedel, Margaret, and Alison Rootberg. 2009. "Generative Techniques in Hypermedia Performance." *Contemporary Music Review* 28 (1): 57–73.

Shields, Alice. 1998. Liner notes to *Columbia-Princeton Electronic Music Center 1961–1973.* CD. New York: New World Records.

Smith, Sarah-Neel. 2016. "Introduction to 'Artistic Awakening in Ankara,' 'The Artist and Politics,' and 'The Burden of the Intellectual' by Bülent Ecevit." *ARTMargins* 5 (1): 108–120.

Southall, Nick. 2011. "A Brief History of Side-Chaining." Sick Mouthy (blog): https://sickmouthy .wordpress.com/2011/03/14/a-brief-history-of-side-chaining/.

Teitelbaum, Richard. 1964. "SON-NOVA 1988: Electronic Music." *Perspectives of New Music* 3 (1) (Autumn–Winter): 127–130.

Ussachevsky, Vladimir. n.d. Typescript notes on the arrival of the Ampex 400 tape recorder. https://exhibitions.library.columbia.edu/exhibits/show/music-centennial/electronic-and -computer-music. Accessed August 2019.

Various Artists. 2010. *Frank Zappa's Classical Selection—The Dissonant Classics That Informed and Inspired Zappa.* CD. New Malden, UK: Chrome Dreams.

Various Artists. 2019. *An Anthology of Turkish Experimental Music 1961–2014.* Brussels: Sub Rosa.

Zappa, Frank. 1966. Liner notes to *Freak Out.* LP. New York: Verve Records.

8   *Nuo Ri Lang* by Zhang Xiaofu

Marc Battier

Electroacoustic music spread quickly from its modest beginnings on French Radio in 1948. As it grew and diversified around the globe, some countries kept their doors closed to the winds of modern art and music. This has been the case with China, where young composers were not able to gain access to contemporary music scores and recordings until the early 1980s. At the same time, they became aware of the use of technology in music. Some of these young composers decided to travel abroad to receive instruction in new composition and in electroacoustic music. This is what Zhang Xiaofu did after some early experiments dating back to 1984.

Nuo Ri Lang is probably Zhang's best-known piece, having received many performances around the world, although several other pieces by the composer have also been quite successful. It must be noted that all those pieces belong essentially to the category of mixed music, while Zhang considers that the latest performances of *Nuo Ri Lang*—the piece having been through several incarnations—allow it to be categorized as a *multimedia symphony*.

The Nuo Ri Lang God

According to the composer, the title invokes the name of a god of masculinity.[1] In Tibetan Buddhism, there are several gods of masculinity, called *pho-lha*. Coleman and Thuuten (2005) describe the various families of gods as mostly spirits "who are said to accompany an individual throughout his or her life, like a shadow, protecting the vitality (*bla*) of the individual. Five types of lifelong companion gods (*'go-ba'i lha lnga*) are specifically identified: the gods of the life essence (*srog-gi-lha*), the gods of masculinity (*pho-lha*), the gods of femininity (*mo-lha*), the gods of the countryside (*yul-lha*), and the gods of inimical force (*dgra-lha*)."

The name of Nuo Ri Lang is also associated with an impressive waterfall located in the northwest of Sichuan province, not far from Tibet. According to Zhao Bai (2017,

146), Zhang visited this region for a couple of weeks as early as 1983. In any case, he was so impressed by what he saw there that he collected many photos and recorded various examples of singing, including chanting monks, which were used in the tape of the piece.

In Buddhism, masculine gods have several functions. Some of them belong to the fierce deities category, in which the gods are wrathful and frightening. Their role is to protect, by force if necessary, against the forces contrary to the dharma, the teaching of Buddha. While there are also some wrathful female deities, masculine figures are numerous and are commonly represented in Buddhist temples. Nuo Ri Lang is classified as a strong and powerful yet majestic god.

The Life of *Nuo Ri Lang*

The first performance of *Nuo Ri Lang* took place in 1996 in the Radio France auditorium in Paris, with live percussion played by Jean Pierlot. This was the shortest version of the piece, lasting 14 minutes 20 seconds, matching the length of the electroacoustic part. This is the version that can be heard on the CD *Nuo Ri Lang: Selected Electroacoustic Music Works of Zhang Xiao Fu*. In the years since, Zhang has continually updated and expanded the work.

A second version was presented in the Forbidden City concert hall in Beijing in September 1999. There was still only one percussionist, but a dancer was added (Wan Su). That year, it was performed at the Beijing Central Conservatory, with a video made by Wang Xi. In that form, the piece was also presented in the United States and in Greece. In 2004, *Nuo Ri Lang* was played as an acousmatic piece, first in France during the Bourges festival of experimental music and then in China, Cuba, and Belgium, following the itinerary of the International Confederation of Electroacoustic Music (ICEM), founded in France in 1981, of which Zhang is an active member. In the same year, another multimedia version with a new video, made by Ma Ge, was performed in China and Italy. French percussionist Thierry Miroglio began to tour with this version in China and Europe. In 2010, the Beijing Modern Dance Troupe, with choreography by Liu Yifeng, performed it at the Beijing Mei Lanfang Grand Theatre. In 2014, the piece acquired full multimedia status for a performance at the Poly Theatre in Beijing, in an extravagant concert with lights, dance, and projection in front of a packed audience. This time, the choreography was made by Wan Su for the dancers of the Beijing Dance Academy Dance Troupe. The percussionist was Thierry Miroglio. Then, two years later, the score was rewritten for three percussionists. This version was performed on various occasions with the three musicians and a video by Ma Ge. We will discuss this score later. It must be noted that it is from that moment that the piece received its subtitle of *Multimedia Symphony for 3 Multi-Percussionists, Digital Image and Electroacoustic Music*. Its duration reached 20 minutes. Finally, a new version, for one percussionist and video, was scored in 2018. In this incarnation, *Nuo Ri Lang* has been performed on various occasions in China as well as in Bordeaux, France. With almost 30 performances on three continents, *Nuo Ri Lang* is the most successful electroacoustic music piece by a mainland Chinese composer.

Electroacoustic Music as Seen by Zhang Xiaofu

Zhang sees four well-defined trends in the practice of electroacoustic music, which he names acousmatic, mixed, multimedia, and interaction (Zhao Xiaoyu 2016). The first three may use a fixed medium to hold the sound elements. This is certainly true for the first. The term *acousmatic music* has now been used for over 40 years, and its meaning— a piece for fixed media, such a magnetic tape or a digital audio file, without any live instrument or visual counterpart—is generally accepted and does not lead to any misunderstanding. The use of the word *mixed* by Zhang is more ambiguous. Today, it is common for it to designate a piece combining live instruments or voice with electroacoustic or electronic components, either fixed or generated in real time. In fact, the technology today is such that the distinction between fixed and live electroacoustic material has lost any clear meaning. However, Zhang seems to define mixed music as a combination of fixed media and live instruments. This is how *Nuo Ri Lang* has remained across several external transformations, such as adding choreography, visual elements, or live instruments. In fact, other pieces by Zhang have similar characteristics. More generally, such a specific definition of mixed music can be applied to a majority of Chinese electroacoustic music. Leigh Landy (2018) discusses this aspect and proposes several hypotheses. In any case, it is true that the presence of skilled and willing performers in China has created a strong incentive for composers to augment their electroacoustic works with live instruments.

The third category, multimedia, seems well tailored for *Nuo Ri Lang*. Indeed, the piece became a multimedia work—or intermedia, in certain aspects—when choreography, video, projected images, and lights were added to the performances. It should be stressed that despite Zhang's calling *Nuo Ri Lang* a multimedia symphony, it is essentially a mixed piece. The presence of live performers playing with fixed electroacoustic elements remains the foundation of the piece; its essence, so to speak. By placing pieces with multimedia elements in a separate category, Zhang implies that electroacoustic music reaches a new stage when combined with external layers such as images, videos, lights, and dancers. For him, the superimposition of planes of perception creates a new form of performance that transcends the conventional categories of acousmatic and mixed.

Finally, the fourth category, interaction, has strong appeal for Zhang. Using real-time digital systems that respond to gestural and visual controls is a significant evolution of electroacoustic music. However, until now, *Nuo Ri Lang* has remained a mixed piece with multimedia elements, even though the composer has sometimes allowed a performance of the unaccompanied tape.

The reader will find a comprehensive discussion of Zhang's aesthetic views in the long article the composer wrote for an issue of *Contemporary Music Review* (Zhang 2018), republished by Routledge (Battier and Fields 2019).

The Road to *Nuo Ri Lang*

Born in 1954, Zhang Xiaofu was part of the first generation of young composers to be admitted to the composition class at the Beijing Central Conservatory of Music. This group of students is now known as the "Class of 1978." Although the number of young applicants varies according to several testimonies, it is estimated that between eleven thousand and eighteen thousand students tried to enter the reopened conservatory, which had been closed for almost 10 years during the Cultural Revolution. According to Wu Zu-qiang, the vice president of the conservatory at the time, only one hundred had been accepted, and then another hundred were added. Wu himself began teaching a composition class, and Zhang became his student, along with others who also later became quite famous, such as Chen Yi.

Wu is a composer who, during the 1950s, belonged to a group of young, innovative musicians (Liu 2010, 366). An example of Wu's music can be found in Liu's *A Critical History of New Music in China* (Liu 2010, 319). Wu Zu-qiang had been a celebrated composer prior to the Cultural Revolution, and his music was again published after the end of this episode of Chinese history.

When I visited the Beijing Central Conservatory in November 1982, I was surprised, while walking alongside classrooms toward my meeting with some of the leaders of the school, to hear traditional Chinese instruments. Indeed, not only were some students learning them, but the composition students were asked to study Chinese music alongside their classes on several aspects of Western music. Furthermore, among the students accepted to study composition in 1977, many had only had the opportunity to practice Chinese instruments. This was true of Zhang, who had been playing the two-string erhu from an early age before taking up the bassoon.

Electroacoustic music was not part of the curriculum. I can attest to this as, during my 1982 visit to the Central Conservatory, where I met some people who were curious to meet that French musician who had been recommended by the Chinese embassy in France, I was asked by them to send documentation and music examples of the sort of musical projects undertaken at Institute for Research and Coordination in Acoustics/ Music (IRCAM), where I worked at the time (Battier 2018, 86). Upon my return to Paris, I immediately sent them a packet of documentation and several magnetic tapes of computer music realizations from the IRCAM repertoire of the time, but apparently none of this material was made accessible to the students, who remained in the dark regarding the field of electroacoustic music for several years, at least until the arrival of MIDI synthesizers after 1984. The only experience they might have witnessed were the concerts made by popular electronic musician Jean-Michel Jarre during his 1981 public events in Beijing and Shanghai. The concealment of this material can be explained by the careful attitude of the conservatory authorities after the Cultural Revolution, which is discussed by Barbara Mittler. At the time, there were many fierce discussions among the faculty as to which trends and styles were suitable for the curriculum (Mittler 1997, 141).

At the same time, violent criticisms of the political choices in the arts at the time of the Cultural Revolution were openly made by Deng Xiaoping. In October 1979, he addressed the Fourth Congress of Writers and Artists with these words after having firmly condemned Lin Biao and the Gang of Four: "Leadership doesn't mean handing out administrative orders and demanding that literature and art serve immediate, short-range political goals. It means understanding the special characteristics of literature and art and the laws of their development and creating conditions for them to flourish" (Deng 1979a, 218).

Shortly thereafter, Deng developed the concept of socialism with Chinese characteristics, writing that "China's socialism had its own characteristics ever since the founding of the People's Republic" (Deng 1979b, 238). The insistence on Chinese characteristics, still very much in force today, has come home to practicing artists. In a theoretical article, Zhang has amply commented on the issue (Zhang 2018). This attitude, combining aesthetic freedom and Chinese roots, reflects an interesting change in communist ideology toward the arts. Mao Zedong had dictated rules for artists in a talk he gave at Yenan in 1942 (Mao 1967). Even during the movement launched in 1956 under the banner "Let a hundred flowers blossom. A hundred schools of thought contend," it was made clear by Lu Dengyi (Lu 1974), then director of the Department of Propaganda of the Chinese Communist Party (CCP), that this call for artistic and thought freedom was to be guided by the CCP. Mao (1977, 409) had earlier insisted that only an ideological struggle could determine the course to be taken.

This led to compositions inspired by studies many composers had made in the USSR. In Russian conservatories, they were taught excellent orchestration, but they carefully stayed away from innovation. Not until after World War II did composers, some of whom later became professors at the Beijing Central Conservatory, such as Wu Zu-qiang, Zhang's professor in Beijing, undertake more daring works. That drew violent reactions from conservatives and led to their condemnation during the first years of the Cultural Revolution, where they lost any possibility of making any music, at least for several years.

In any case, one element remained despite the various sources of inspiration and musical styles, and that is the omnipresence of Chinese elements, as can be observed in the influence of Chinese traditional popular music. For many years after the 1949 establishment of the People's Republic of China, it was mandatory to write works that pleased the public, be they for orchestral performance or for ballet, while at the same time nationalistic elements, such as the frequent use of pentatonic scales, gave the works an indisputable Chinese flavor.

Throughout the 1950s, composers often included Chinese traits in their new works. These elements not only gave their music an air of "Chineseness" but also maintained a link between new music and popular culture, particularly that of the peasant population, an important principle of government ideology. Even though many composers studied Western technique in the USSR during that time, they wrote music filled with vernacular elements. No one has better explained the dilemma facing composers during the development of the socialist regime in mainland China than sinologist Barbara Mittler (Mittler 1997).

It must be observed that the integration of Chinese cultural elements was very much part of the teaching of Chou Wen Chung (Zhou Wenzhong) in his composition classes at Columbia University. Chou had left China in 1946 to live in the United States, where he became a student of Edgard Varèse before becoming a professor at Columbia.

Following visits to China between 1972 and 1977, in October 1978 Chou established the Center for US-China Arts Exchanges in New York. Thanks to this institution, he was able to bring several young Chinese composers to further their studies with him at Columbia University. There, he strongly and repeatedly encouraged his Chinese students, such as Zhou Long and Chen Yi, both products of the Class of 1978 of the Beijing Central Conservatory, who had graduated, respectively, in 1983 and 1986. Both had obtained scholarships to go to New York thanks to the efforts of Chou and his center. Other musicians from those post–Cultural Revolution classes followed the same program, such as Tan Dun and Qu Xiaosong, also thanks to the efforts of Chou.

Longtime Hong Kong resident and musician Samson Young warns of the danger of forcing vernacular elements into a work of art. As he put it, "Authenticity as a demand places an enormous symbolic weight upon Chinese composers, as well as reviewers of their work to 'perform Chineseness' in music and in analysis, reducing Chinese composers into local informant, shaman, and conjurer" (Young 2014, 269). It may seem artificial, at times, to constantly blend Western music language with Chinese material or cultural allusions. However, several factors ought to be taken into account. The Class of 1978, for instance, went through the almost 10 years of the Cultural Revolution (1966–1976) without proper musical training and, in particular, were kept ignorant of Western music techniques, but they could experience songs and instruments from local traditions in the countryside. They had exposure to traditional music, thanks to their being exiled to remote parts of the country to work with peasants, and some played with musical groups on Chinese instruments. In fact, that was the only music they could hear or play, apart from the model works put forward by Jiang Qing, the wife of Mao Zedong and promoter of the revolutionary musical symbolism of that time (Mittler 2010, 378). After having spent their early formative years with music from the countryside, it may not have been artificial for composers to express their desire to create music with deep roots in the local cultures of China. Indeed, Zhang has taken the opportunity to declare on several occasions that contemporary Chinese composers should create music without copying the West. In his case, because his main medium of expression is electroacoustic music, which relies heavily on technology conceived in Western countries, this quest has led him to include explicitly elements from his native land.

Interestingly enough, Zhang undertook studies in electroacoustic music at the Music Conservatory of Genevilliers, on the outskirts of Paris, with Jean Schwartz. It so happened that Schwartz was a member of the Groupe de Recherches Musicales (GRM), which he had joined in 1969, but he also worked at the Centre National de Recherche Scientifique (CNRS), where he was an engineer in the ethnomusicology department of the Musée de l'Homme, also in Paris. Thus, Zhang studied the theory and practice of the GRM approach to electroacoustic music, but with someone who was close to traditional music of other cultures and who incorporated some of these influences into his own music.

In New York, Zhang's classmates Chen Yi and Zhou Long were advised by their teacher Chou Wen Chung to investigate Chinese culture and art practices, such as calligraphy and poetry (Chen, Zhou, and Radice 2018). Zhang also studied with someone open to the living culture of other civilizations. He took advantage of being in Paris to follow classes at École Normale de Musique de Paris, a private school founded in 1918 by Alfred Cortot and attended by many foreign students. Zhang arrived in France in 1989 and, while taking classes at École Normale, enrolled at the Conservatory of Genevilliers. In 1993, he obtained his doctorate in composition from the École Normale and then decided to return to China, where he soon began to work at the Beijing Central Conservatory.

As a professor at the Central Conservatory of Music, Zhang Xiaofu soon assumed important roles for the development of electronic music in his country. Not only did he train and tutor several generations of young composers, which he continues to do today, but he became the director of the Centre for Electroacoustic Music of China (CEMC) as well as the president of the Electroacoustic Music Association of China (EMAC).

In Zhang's music, often for live instruments and electroacoustic material, Chinese references, such as instruments or recorded sounds, are interwoven with abstract timbres and textures. In his studio, these are further blended and transformed, but without ever totally obliterating their nature. The listener feels the Chineseness of his music, despite the modern surface resulting from the use of technology. This is certainly the case with *Nuo Ri Lang* (figure 8.1).

Figure 8.1
Nuo Ri Lang, with one percussionist (Thierry Miroglio), dancers, projections, and lights, 2016 (Photo: Zhang Xiaofu).

Sounds Identified in the Score

What follows is a taxonomy of the sounds included in *Nuo Ri Lang* in the electroacoustic part, as identified in the score. Having spent several years in France, Zhang often wrote his indications in French. I have kept the original markings in italics, along with an English translation. Note that, in the score, the term *electro* is often used by the composer to denote an electroacoustic processing of recordings. I have kept this term, which sometimes appears with a precise mention of the source sound. All the original sounds fall into two broad categories: voices, in the form of chanting for males and singing for females; and percussion, either skins (timpani and bass drums), metal (cymbals and ritual metal bowls), or wood. Several of those sounds were recorded by the composer himself during a two-week trip to Tibet before the realization of the piece.

Bell [*cloche*]

Tibet (deep percussion)

Chime

Buddhist voice (low chanting)

Voice (glissando)

Electro bells, Low—ECB [*Electro-cloches Basse*]

Electro bells, High—ECA [*Electro-cloches, Aigue*]

Wind electro [*Vent electro*]

Melody

Woman's voice [*Voix femme*]

Man's voice [*Voix homme*]

Electro high [*Electro aigu*]

Large drum [*Grand Tambour*]

Small drum [*Petit Tambour*]

Low voice [*Bass voix*]

Analysis

Nuo Ri Lang was conceived from the start as a mixed music work, with a percussionist playing along with a stereo tape. There have been a few instances where only the tape was performed, but it is the mixed version that underwent several transformations and, as such, has obtained a favorable reception, as over 30 performances have been produced, which, for an electroacoustic piece, is quite remarkable.

The tape part was realized in the studios of the Groupe de Recherches Musicales, located in Maison de la Radio on the right bank of the Seine in Paris, as well as in China. The studios offered specific equipment, with sound-processing software developed at GRM since the mid-1970s, implemented on the SYTER real-time digital processor before being rewritten as pure software and available under the name of GRM Tools (Teruggi 1998). At the time of the realization of *Nuo Ri Lang*, Zhang had obtained a copy of GRM Tools. A few sounds had already been processed in the Conservatory of Genevilliers, in particular the loops, because the studio there had many tape recorders, which made this operation quite efficient. However, most of the sounds came out of a computer running the GRM Tools software.

I will discuss the score for the version that has been released on CD, along with other pieces by Zhang Xiaofu. This is the original version, the same as was presented in the first performance in Paris in 1996. However, the latest scores show some verbal indications at important transitions, such as at the beginning of a new section. I will mention these, as they shed some light on the composer's intention regarding how the performance ought to be conducted.

I will start by describing the acousmatic material. This is because no matter the version, the tape remains constant. Recent versions of the piece have their own score, because of the diversity of the instrumental parts and the increasing duration of later performances. However, on those recent scores, the acousmatic part is only thoroughly notated on the first page, at least on the documents provided by the composer. However, the original score (figure 8.2) proposes graphical notation and some verbal indications of the nature of the sounds on the tape. Unlike the 1996 score, which is notated by hand and uses graphical symbols to denote the gestures and the types of sounds, later versions are entirely written using music notation software.

Figure 8.3 shows the first system of the latest version, performed in 2018. It is written for only one percussionist, even though the instrumental part is distributed on two groups of staves.

The 1996 score has nine rehearsal marks, marked A to I. As they are intended for the percussionist, they do not necessarily correspond to particular events on the tape. For instance, mark B occurs at 1:08, measure 18, during a very soft and continuous background of a low drone in the acousmatic part.

Subsequent scores have a different distribution of rehearsal marks. This is partly because the percussion parts have been rewritten, and this also reflects the augmented duration of the piece. In the recent version, the tape starts eight seconds after the beginning of the performance. There are 15 rehearsal marks in those versions.

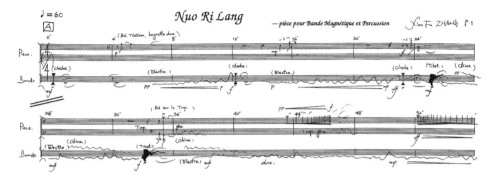

Figure 8.2
Nuo Ri Lang. First two systems, 1996.

Figure 8.3
Nuo Ri Lang. First system, 2018 version for one percussionist.

"Solemn"

The tape part starts with five strong percussive sounds. Let's call them P1 to P5 (figure 8.4).

P1, the first sound on the tape, is played pianissimo. It is repeated as P2, a bit louder, at 0:12. At 0:23, the third percussion sound brings a clearer, metallic sound. It is soon followed, at 0:25.5, by P4. In the decay of this event, a resonance appears, swelling briefly. We will call it RES1. This is a mixture of several sustained sounds, including what seems to be a male voice. The last of this series of percussive sounds is P5, which is heard at 0:34. It, too, is followed by a resonance—RES2—which has the same vocal component mixed with layers a semitone higher.

This introduction is labeled "Solemn" by the composer, as noted in the 2018 score.

This serves as an introduction. Its duration is 40 seconds, which is 10 measures. The vocal element that is part of the two RES events will be heard again in the long crescendo, which starts at 0:42.

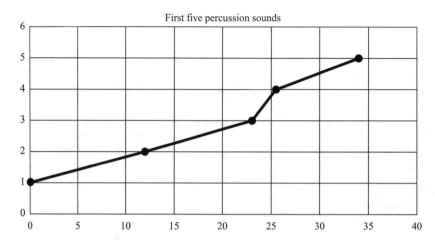

Figure 8.4
The first five percussive events on the tape of *Nuo Ri Lang*, measured in seconds (*y*) and their respective number (*x*).

"Deep and Mysterious"

A new section, labeled "Deep and mysterious," starts right at the end of the decay of P5 and RES2. The beginning of the long event emerges from the resonance of RES2, triple piano. It is based on a short loop of males chanting on a low G2. These are blended with a sustained metallic sound, which does not relate to the percussive material but is a looped resonance from what seems to be a Tibetan bowl transposed in a lower register. This constitutes a drone, while the percussionist plays short gestures, accelerando and decelerando, on a timpani. The score identifies the electronic layer as "chime" as well as "electro."

At 1:16, at measure 20, a recording of a group of males chanting in a low voice can be heard. This element is in fact a loop with a duration of one and half seconds. While starting in the pianissimo nuance, it slowly increases. Its occurrence is preceded at measure 18 by the percussionist, who plays with hard sticks on a wooden drum, starting triple piano and increasing to mezzopiano at measure 20, coinciding with the subtle entrance of the voices, now chanting on G-sharp2.

"Wide, Increasing"

At 2:25, just before measure 40, another male chant appears, stronger, clearer, centered on B2, a minor third above the original drone. It quickly reaches the forte dynamic at measure 41. The 2018 score identifies this section as rehearsal mark B2 and gives as verbal indication "Wide, increasing."

The long crescendo, which lasts 3:56, ends on a short decay of sounds processed with a harmonizer, whose pitch is E-flat3. While increasing in loudness, its texture becomes more noisy and jagged. The four-second event vanishes into silence, opening a new section of the piece.

"Passion Surging"
This new section starts around 4:45, in the middle of measure 72. It is marked B3, "Passion surging," in the 2018 score, and C in the 1996 score. It also is based on loops, but this time they are of singing bowls, all in the medium and high registers. They start on E-flat and E-natural and then diversify into multiple pitches. This represents a very quiet moment of the piece, where time seems suspended. While short, this is a very quiet moment, with only a few subtle accents.

"Solemn Silence"
A low pulsation, at the metronome tempo of 96 BPM (beats per minute), starts and links to the next section, which occurs around measure 76, at around 5:00. Marked C1 (2018), the section is a continuation of the previous one, so soft it's almost inaudible. The percussionist is asked to play a few strokes of ritual bell sounds and, around measure 80, at 5:16, to play with two stones. Progressively, the tape includes some percussive sounds of temple bells on top of the background layer of looped bowls. A motive of two resonances emerges, one on E4 and the other, louder, on E-flat4. Both have a strong tremolo resulting from the effect of a beating, and this motive is in the foreground. This layer disappears at the beginning of the next section, but the same motive will reappear later in the piece.

"Chanting and Meditation"
At 6:00, the electroacoustic layers made of looped resonances swell slightly and become more complex. The low pulsation is gone and the bell sounds cross the stereo space.

The 2018 score identifies this moment as "Chanting and meditation," although no voices are heard on the tape.

From this point onward, the scores do not add any new verbal indications, so I will simply use the types of electroacoustic material to divide the paragraphs that follow.

Female Voices and Tibetan Cymbals
For the first time in the piece, recordings of female voices appear at 7:28, at measure 113. Almost inaudible at first, their amplitude increases progressively, while some very low components of the resonating bells become prominent. This is still a very slow movement, but the resonances become louder. In particular, a beating of cymbal

sounds on a loud E4 is played 12 times, appearing and vanishing every six seconds, until it resolves on a similar pattern on D-sharp4. At 8:52, around measure 134, whenever a temple bell decays, one can perceive, very far away and quite pianissimo, what sounds like female voices. Indeed, at 9:00, at measure 136, the voices enter clearly.

Terry Jay Ellingson (1979, 395–397) classifies the Tibetan voices according to their "place of origin." Compared with the low, deep, and full voices, categorized as "body-cavity voices," the "throat voices," produced by controlling the throat muscles, give a thin sound, contrasting with the former. The other type of voice on the tape is the "nose voice," used to produce nasal resonances. Also, according to Ellingson, female voices in Tibet are often devoted to thin, fluctuating sounds. In fact, what is heard from measure 136 are jagged, piercing female voices, not unlike female singing from other parts of China.

Unlike the previous section, this texture, composed of temple bells, Tibetan cymbals, and female voices, decreases progressively over 30 seconds, to give birth at around 10:00 to long, sustained loops of bell resonances in the middle register, centered around C4.

Meditation

The 1996 score marks this moment with the letter F, at 10:04, at measure 152. The percussionist rubs a tam-tam while playing small Tibetan cymbals. This goes on as a long, meditative passage lasting 1:30 and ends on a sustained, continuous, low D3 over a deep F-sharp1.

Climax

At around 11:25, at measure 172, a new section starts with a series of percussive sounds. There are seven distinct percussive events (P6–P12), which become more and more complex. They are distributed on each channel with a hard pan right or left, while the D3/F-sharp1 drone plays in the background.

P6, the first percussion of this section, sounds like a bass drum with some reverberation. It appears hard right. It is followed by P7, a repetition of the same sound. P8, played hard left, is a series of four identical skin percussive sounds. P9, hard right, is a fast repetition of the same skin sample as P6 and P7. The spatial distribution of events continues with P10, an isolated stroke of the same sound as P8. It is followed by a dry roll, apparently on a wooden instrument. From that point on, the density of events becomes high, with the same samples being played, always hard right or left, mixed with the roll, which itself swells and moves between the two channels while increasingly occupying the stereo space.

At 12:08, at measure 183, sounds of Chinese cymbals appear and contribute to the tense and dense texture of the passage. The intensity increases and so does the loudness, because of the richer materials that compose the various layers.

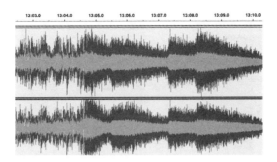

Figure 8.5
Nuo Ri Lang. Transition to section "Vanishing Bells" at around 13:04.5.

As often occurs in this piece, a new layer of sound starts appearing very discreetly in the background. This happens at 12:32. Its tempo is fast, around 160 BPM. It is composed of a loop made of filtered noisy percussion over a layer of very rapid wooden percussion. The amplitude of those rhythmic layers increases into a climax of a dense, pressed texture, suddenly cut off at 13:05, at measure 197, by a new layer (figure 8.5).

"Vanishing Bells"
This starts a new section. It is made of highly processed Chinese cymbal sounds, their attack blurred or compressed, their resonances mixed with those of other cymbals. The nuance is fortissimo, but the whole cymbal sequence is diminuendo. The previous rhythmic material has disappeared, and this cymbal section quickly decreases in amplitude. Figure 8.6 shows how the 1996 score represents this transition.

There are 15 discernible strokes. Each one is followed by a secondary one, sometimes more, resembling tolling Western church bells. The strokes appear at quasiperiodic intervals of two to three seconds, but some are further apart. Their amplitude progressively fades out, so the last stroke, number 15, is almost covered by a pulsating drone of male voices (figure 8.7).

A recording of males chanting in a low voice on B-flat appears at 13:25. As it swells upward, it becomes noticeable that it is processed by a periodic amplitude modulation, like a tremolo. Its amplitude increases until 14:20 and then decreases rapidly.

Ending
As already seen in this piece, a new layer appears very softly and gradually swells. This happens at 14:54. Female voices emerge, while the low male chanting slowly fades out. As it disappears, the female layer becomes more audible. Its effect is gripping: the voices are shrilling and constantly in motion. Even though their amplitude on the tape is soft,

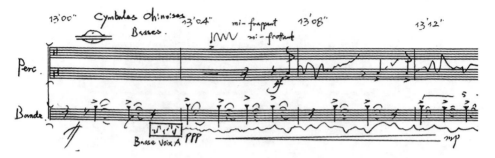

Figure 8.6
Nuo Ri Lang. Transition to the "Vanishing Bells" section of the 1996 score.

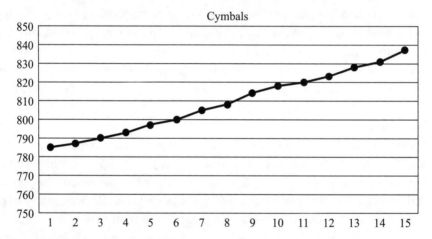

Figure 8.7
Nuo Ri Lang. Rhythmic progression of the cymbal strokes. Time is measured in seconds.

they originally were emitted in a loud, powerful manner, adding to the captivating impact on the listener.

The drone centered on C-sharp4 reappears at 15:28. It will be sustained until the end of the piece (figure 8.8) and, as earlier, is accompanied by a low F-sharp1 layer. The female voices fade out and disappear at 15:48, leaving space for the C-sharp4/F-sharp1 drone, which in turn fades out slowly. The score indicates that, during the last seconds of the fadeout, the performer leaves the stage (*"quitter la scène"*).

Subsequent versions have their own scores. Figure 8.9 shows the beginning of the 2016 version for three percussionists, image projections, and lights. The tape part starts eight seconds after the beginning, which actually is a complete silence. It is the first

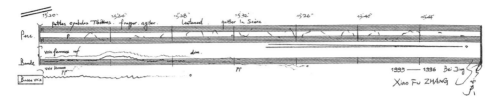

Figure 8.8

Ending of the 1996 version of *Nuo Ri Lang*.

Figure 8.9

Nuo Ri Lang. First system, 2016 version for three percussionists.

tape percussion that triggers the entry of a tam-tam and then a vibraphone and Chinese gongs together, as can be seen in figure 8.9.

The percussion instruments are a blend of Chinese and Western ones. In addition to a vibraphone and a marimba, there are two timpani and several other skin instruments. As for the Chinese instruments, there are numerous cymbals, Chinese and Tibetan, bowls, gongs, and tam-tams of various sizes. Each player has a pair of stones, and one has suspended glass tubes. Thus, the percussion is composed of objects of metal, wood, skin, and earth.

The 2018 version, for one performer, has a set of instruments similar to the original score but adds a vibraphone and a marimba, and additional skin percussion instruments and metal bowls. The duration of these recent versions is also much longer, almost 20 minutes for the 2016 and 2018 scores.

Conclusion

If we follow the taxonomy established by Yayoi Uno Everett, *Nuo Ri Lang* would offer a perfect example of "distinctive synthesis of Western and Asian musical idioms" (Everett 2004, 16). Zhang had already mastered the electroacoustic music idiom, as this was a piece completed after long studies and several realizations in studios, in France as well as in China. While in France, Zhang composed several acousmatic as well as mixed pieces, such as his first electroacoustic piece, *Chant Intérieur (Yin)*, composed in 1988 for a Chinese bamboo flute and tape (Zhao Rui 2016, 126; Li 2018, 144–145). Other pieces from this period include *Terre et ciel* and *Homme et nature*, both parts of the suite *Dialogues entre des mondes différents* (1992), and *Ciel cent réponses*, for male voice, percussion, and tape (1992). The last piece received first prize in composition at the Conservatory of Genevilliers. At the same time, Zhang composed several pieces for instruments at the École Normale, such as *Fontaine de la montagne* for two sopranos and piano and *Mort* for five percussionists and orchestra (Zhao Rui 2016, 126; Zhao Bai 2017, 144). *Fontaine* received a first prize in composition at École Normale. Some of these electroacoustic compositions were realized at the Genevilliers conservatory, where he studied, and La Muse en Circuit, a center established by Luc Ferrari near Paris.

When he composed *Nuo Ri Lang*, Zhang had already founded, in 1994, a festival at the Beijing Central Conservatory. After several years of being held biannually, the event would become the Beijing-Musicacoustica festival, which since 2004 has been held each year at the conservatory (Wang 2018). *Nuo Ri Lang* reflects the preoccupation of the author with making room for elements of Chineseness alongside a Western idiomatic language.

That the vernacular material, the inspiration, and the overall mood of the piece pertain to Tibet, as opposed to the dominant Han culture, should not be misinterpreted by the reader. On the contrary, China is nowadays composed of multiple ethnic groups, which are officially counted as 56 nationalities, and all contribute to Chinese cultural diversity. Zhang did find in Tibet strong sources of inspiration. His composition is modeled after the emotions and the spiritual feelings gathered during his travels to that region. For instance, the use of tape loops in *Nuo Ri Lang* can be linked to what Zhang saw in Tibetan temples he visited in 1983, where the worshipers rotate sets of prayer wheels while others are placed so that the wind activates their movement. Each one is inscribed with a mantra, and their cylinders contain other prayers. Every rotation corresponds to a reading of the prayers. By using loops of fragments of recordings, Zhang transposed this practice into an electroacoustic material while retaining the concept. Because the prayer wheels should be rotated gently, the pace of the composition is calm, meditative at times, and it only reaches a climax for a short moment.

Another factor contributing to the effect of the piece on listeners is its use of harmonic fields. The composer chose metal bowls that gave certain pitches. Many of them have resonances around E4 and include C4, C-sharp4, E-flat4, and E4; other strong and recurring pitches are D3 and the low pitches: a deep F-sharp1, made of resonances, and the G-sharp2 of the male voices chanting sutras.

These pitches define harmonic fields in the low and middle registers. Their reiteration throughout the piece contributes to a certain homogeneity that enhances the meditative moments. The source material is also quite consistent: male voices on a single low pitch and contrasting females singing in a strong and high manner, resonances of singing bowls, and Chinese cymbals. Not only do these textures relate to Tibetan cultures, they also ensure that the piece unfolds in a consistent and dreamlike manner. At least the success of *Nuo Ri Lang* shows that the audience has been receptive to the mood instilled by this composition.

Notes

1. Most of the information on the composer comes from an interview with Zhang Xiaofu conducted by the author on June 17, 2019, at the Beijing Central Conservatory.

References

Battier, Marc. 2018. "Building Bridges; Nourishing the Soul—Ten Years of Musical Activities in China." In *Musicking the Soul*, edited by Kimasi Browne and Zhang Boyu, 86–97. Beijing: Central Conservatory of Music Press.

Battier, Marc, and Kenneth Fields, eds. 2019. *Electroacoustic Music in East Asia*. London: Routledge.

Chen, Yi, Zhou Long, and Mark A. Radice. 2018. "Radice in Conversation about Chou Wen-chung." In *Polycultural Synthesis in the Music of Chou Wen-chung*, edited by Mary I. Arlin and Mark A. Radice, 255–267. London: Routledge.

Coleman, Graham, and Jinpa Thuuten, eds. 2005. *The Tibetan Book of the Dead: First Complete Translation*, translated by Gyurme Dorje. New York: Penguin Books. https://archive.org/stream /TheTibetanBookOfTheDeadPenguinClassicsEditionTranslatedByGrahamColeman/The%20 Tibetan%20Book%20Of%20The%20Dead%20-%20Penguin%20Classics%20Edition%20-%20 Translated%20by%20Graham%20Coleman_djvu.txt.

Deng, Xiao Ping. 1979a. "Speech Greeting the Fourth Congress of Chinese Writers and Artists." October 30. In *Selected Works of Deng Xiaoping*, vol. 2 (1975–1982), 213–219. Beijing: Foreign Language Press.

Deng, Xiao Ping. 1979b. "We Can Develop a Market Economy under Socialism." In *Selected Works of Deng Xiaoping*, vol. 2 (1975–1982), 235–239. Beijing: Foreign Language Press.

Ellingson, Terry Jay. 1979. *The Mandala of Sound: Concepts and Sound Structures in Tibetan Ritual Music*. PhD thesis, University of Wisconsin-Madison.

Everett, Yayoi Uno. 2004. "Intercultural Synthesis in Postwar Western Art Music: Historical Contexts, Perspectives, and Taxonomy." In *Locating East Asia in Western Art Music*, edited by Yayoi Uno Everett and Frederick Lau, 1–21. Middletown, CT: Wesleyan University Press.

Landy, Leigh. 2018. "The Three Paths: Cultural Retention in Contemporary Chinese Electroacoustic Music." In *The Routledge Research Companion to Electronic Music: Reaching Out with Technology*, edited by Simon Emmerson, 77–95. London: Routledge.

Li, Qiuxiao. 2018. "Characteristics of Early Electronic Music Composition in China's Mainland." *Contemporary Music Review* 37 (1–2) (February–April) : 135–146.

Liu, Ching-Chih. 2010. *A Critical History of New Music in China*. Translated by Caroline Mason. Hong Kong: The Chinese University of Hong Kong.

Lu, Ting-Yi. 1964. *Let a Hundred Flowers Blossom. A Hundred Schools of Thought Contend!* (1956). Beijing: Foreign Languages Press.

Mao, Tse-Tung. 1967. *Talks at the Yenan Forum on Literature and Arts* (1942). Beijing: Foreign Languages Press. Also in *Selected Works of Mao Tse-Tung*, volume 3. Beijing: Foreign Languages Press, 1965, 69–98.

Mao, Tse-Tung. 1977. "On 'Let a Hundred Flowers Blossom. A Hundred Schools of Thought Contend' and 'Long-Term Coexistence and Mutual Supervision'" (1957). In *Selected Works of Mao Tse-Tung*, vol. 5, 408–414. Beijing: Foreign Languages Press.

Mittler, Barbara. 1997. *Dangerous Tunes: The Politics of Chinese Music in Hong Kong, Taiwan, and the People's Republic of China since 1949*. Wiesbaden: Harrassowitz Verlag.

Mittler, Barbara. 2010. "Eight Stage Works for 800 Million People: The Great Proletarian Cultural Revolution in Music—a View from Revolutionary Opera." *Opera Quarterly* 26 (2–3): 377–401.

Teruggi, Daniel. 1998. *Le système SYTER: Son histoire, ses développements, sa production musicale, ses implications dans le langage électroacoustique d'aujourd'hui*. PhD diss., Université de Paris 8.

Wang, Hefei. 2018. "Exploration and Innovation, the Chinese Model of the Musicacoustica-Beijing Festival." *Contemporary Music Review* 37 (1–2) (February–April): 147–160.

Young, Samson. 2014. "The Possibility of Authenticity: Sounding Socialist in the Buddha Machine." In *Contemporary Music in East Asia*, edited by Hee Sook Oh, 267–283. Seoul: Seoul National University Press.

Zhang, Xiaofu. 2018. "The Power of Arterial Language in Constructing a Musical Vocabulary of One's Own: Inheriting the Inspiration and Gene of Innovation in Electroacoustic Music from Chinese Culture." *Contemporary Music Review* 37 (1–2) (February–April,): 126–134.

Zhang, Xiaofu. *Nuo Ri Lang. Selected Electroacoustic Music Works of Zhang Xiao Fu.* CD. ISRC CN-M35-06-0002-O/A.J6.

Zhao, Bai. 2017. *Influences étrangères dans la musique contemporaine des compositeurs chinois exerçant ou ayant exercé en France et en Amérique du Nord.* PhD diss., Université Paris-Sorbonne.

Zhao, Xiaoyu. 2016. "Zhangxiaofu duomeiti jiaoxiangyue 'nuo ri lang' chuangzuo duihua" (A Dialogue on the Creativity Process of Zhang Xiaofu's Multimedia Symphony *Nuo Ri Lang*). *Music and Technology* 2: 49–55.

Zhao, Rui. 2016. *Les renaissances et les innovations de la culture traditionnelle chinoise dans la musique contemporaine chinoise depuis les années 1980.* PhD diss., Université Paris-Sorbonne.

9   Seeds and Mutations: Connections and Divergences in the Materials of Unsuk Chin's *Xi*

Kerry L. Hagan

Introduction

Unsuk Chin (b. 1961) is a composer based in Berlin, Germany, who was born in South Korea. Her early education was mostly informal, but her later education included studying with György Ligeti. Her Western education led to a number of important premieres (promoted by Kent Nagano and Sir Simon Rattle, and performed by major orchestras around the entire world), commissions (e.g., the Ensemble InterContemporain, EIC), and awards in Europe (e.g., Gaudeamus Foundation, 1985; Concours Internationaux de Musique et d'Art Sonore Electroacoustiques de Bourges, 1999; Wihuri Sibelius Prize, 2017).

Her critical supporters often speak positively of her commitment to avoiding "stylistic or geographical classification" [1] (Bernd Stratmann in Ehrler 2001; my translation). Ehrler states that this is a conscious choice on Chin's part: "I find it very annoying that, because I am of Korean origin, my work is automatically subjected to the stereotype of Asian music"[2] (Unsuk Chin in Ehrler 2017; my translation). Paul Griffiths even stated that "any local color, in the work of one born in Seoul in 1961, is much harder to find—nor, one might add, does Chin's music proclaim a specifically female sensibility" (Griffiths 2014). Griffiths also wrote text for Boosey and Hawkes's official page for Unsuk Chin, again asserting that "Her music makes no parade of national flavour: her preferences for the sounds of plucked or struck strings, for slowly drifting glissandos and for arrays of bells and gongs all carry no specific cultural overtones, and that indeed is one of her strengths" (Griffiths 2012).

In light of this, it is hard to determine precisely why Chin meets with so much critical success yet barely any broader notice. Her most supportive commentators still want to situate her as a Korean composer or as a woman. She is lauded, but often as a token. She features in the *Washington Post*'s "Top 35 female composers in classical music" (Midgette 2017) and in special concerts for Korean composers in Paris (Auditorium Marcel Landowski du CRR de Paris, November 28, 2015). Regardless of her Western music "credentials" or her applauded escape from a feminine or Asian identity, she is almost always contextualized by the journalistic media as a female, Korean composer.

Though Chin works with both acoustic and electroacoustic media, she did not "seek an integration of the two strands" as late as 1995 (Babcock 1995). However, in 1998, Chin composed *Xi*, commissioned by the EIC, for ensemble and tape. Chin remarked that she already felt that working with electronic music in Technische Universität Berlin in the 1980s changed the way she worked with acoustic instruments because she was able to work microscopically with sound (Varga 2017). It seems natural that she would turn to granular synthesis when computers allowed for the technique.

Xi (씨, spelled Ssi in Revised Romanization) is defined by Chin as "core, source, origin or the smallest unit of things"[3] (Chin 1998; my translation), though several dictionaries translate it more commonly as "seed" first. The tape part is constructed primarily through granular synthesis from the sound of striking a piano on its soundboard (Unsuk Chin in Ehrler 2001), and the instrumental parts grow from the seeds of the tape and cells within the instrumental writing (Harders-Wuthenow 2011).

This chapter analyzes *Xi* to examine the aspects of sound Chin works with microscopically. *Xi* exemplifies, in an iconic way, how Chin uses electronic techniques in her acoustic writing (Hanno Ehrler, Ruth Jarre, and Bernd Stratmann in Ehrler 2001) with side-by-side acoustic and electronic materials.

The official program note for *Xi*, available in English from Boosey and Hawkes (translated by Howard Weiner) and in French from the EIC (translated by Beatrix Raanan) comes from a short description of the piece by Frank Harders-Wuthenow in *Im Spiegel Der Zeit: Die Komponistin Unsuk Chin* (2011). It provides a basic overview of what is immanently perceivable in the experience of the piece. The first section begins with noise, from which Chin extrapolates pitches. The second section is a series of harmonies triggered by initial articulations in one form or another. The third section consists of pulsing layers of varying durations. The fourth section is a dense, frenetic section of diverse pitch clouds. Chin indicates a fifth section in the score that acts as a climax, which Harders-Wuthenow considers part of the fourth section; the experience of the piece justifies this elision. Finally, the last section is a recapitulation of the opening section, transformed by the developments preceding it. Harders-Wuthenow explains that the title of the work is a reference not just to the musical technique of granular synthesis but also to the technique of using sonic materials from specific instruments as cells from which the rest of the work grows, as evidenced by the progression of the four sections (Harders-Wuthenow 2011).

Although Chin says the electronics come primarily from granular synthesis on a struck-piano sound (in Ehrler 2001), and Harders-Wuthenow identifies the sonic cells of the piano, cello, and contrabass (Harders-Wuthenow 2011), it is interesting to listen to the piece as if it grows from *two* acoustic sources: the struck piano and a bowed tam-tam. What Harders-Wuthenow (2011) and Chin describe as a "breathing sound" is the resonance of the struck piano with its attack cut away (Ehrler 2001).

The piece begins with this sound, a quiet noise that fades in and out, appearing twice before the actual tam-tam is bowed in the ensemble. The recorded and acoustic sounds are so similar that the tam-tam is almost imperceptible. Given its similarity to the bowed tam-tam in the ensemble and the role that recorded instrumental samples play in the electronics throughout the work, it serves an analytical purpose to consider this sound a bowed tam-tam.

Missing Information on the Electronics

If an analysis is intended to provide the exact circumstances for a work's recomposition, then the available materials for *Xi* do not allow it. With information from Boosey and Hawkes and from the EIC, who commissioned and premiered the work, I made some assumptions about the electronics. This chapter relies on the score by Boosey and Hawkes (Chin 1998), information provided by the EIC, and the recording by the EIC (Chin 2011). A great deal of the discussion of Chin's electronics, especially spatialization, is based on educated guesses, speculation, and piecing together the most likely conditions of the original performance. Unfortunately, Chin was not available to answer questions definitively.

The score for *Xi* indicates two electronic parts, a fixed-medium part (*tonband*) and a sampler. From the EIC's documentation, it is clear that the sampler is performed live, and Chin performed this part on both the recording and premiere. Boosey and Hawkes has two versions of the electronics available. The 12-channel version is the fixed-medium part alone, while the six-channel version consists of a mix-down of the fixed-medium part and a recording of the sampler part, also distributed around the six channels. There appears to be no existing documentation for the placement of the six or 12 channels, though one naturally assumes that they surround the audience. Not only that, but there is no indication as to which channel is assigned to each speaker. The EIC provided a stage diagram revealing that Chin used a Kurzweil K2500 sampler with eight output channels sent to a front-of-house mixer, which then went to 12 speakers. The diagram, however, ends at the stage. Additionally, the ensemble instruments were amplified and sent to the house mixer, but there is no indication of spatial placement. The EIC recording does not have any special electronic spatialization of the acoustic instruments.

None of this information is available in the score. There is no mention of instrumental amplification. The score calls for two percussionists, but the EIC elected to split

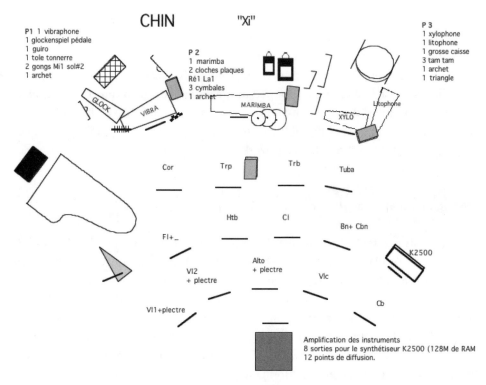

Figure 9.1
The stage diagram from the premiere of *Xi* (courtesy of EIC).

the two parts into three. The score does not indicate any particular pick or plectrum for the string instruments, but the EIC's document shows that the high strings used them.

Based on the K2500 manual (Kurzweil n.d.), a close listening of the electronics, and comparing the scored sampler part versus the elements of the fixed medium that are notated in the score, it seems that Chin used the sampler in order to ensure that certain electronic elements were precisely performed with the ensemble, either synchronously or in complex cross-instrumental rhythms. She also appears to use some of the digital signal processing available in the K2500, perhaps some pitch shifting, time stretching, reverse playback, and real-time pitch bending. It is also possible that using all eight outputs of the K2500 enabled individuated spatial diffusion for each sample, suggested by the separate placements of samples in the tracks provided. However, other technologies used in the premiere and recording could also produce these elements.

The use of space is perhaps one of the most relevant aspects of multichannel electronics. The available sources provided no information to indicate the track arrangement.

This chapter refers to the six-channel version, since it includes the sampler part. Predicated on presumptions of spatial behavior and an analysis of each track's content, the best arrangement of the channels appears to be as shown in figure 9.2.

The first assumption leading to this arrangement was that Chin was not attempting anything particularly innovative with regard to spatial audio. Given that assumption, fairly normative and practical uses of space are:

1. a predominantly frontal perspective, where the majority of sounds and complex behaviors occur around the front and sides of the space (at the stage);

2. a combination of point-source and trajectory-based spatialization;

3. in the case of point-source spatialization, a relatively balanced distribution of sounds around the space;

4. in the case of trajectory-based spatialization, coherent types of movement conducted primarily through panning;

5. any cross-center panning occurs in opposite pairs of speakers (e.g., track 1 to 4, 3 to 6, and so on);

6. and with cross-center (diametrically opposite) panning, possibly more front to back pairings than back to front, but movement from right to left and left to right would be relatively equal in occurrence.

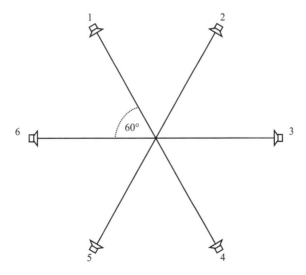

Figure 9.2
Six-channel track assignments.

In the arrangement in figure 9.2, all assumptions but the sixth were satisfied. There appeared to be more movements from right to left than left to right. However, any rotation of the circle made the static, complex spatial assignments occur mostly on the left side. Given that this arrangement is a best guess, we cannot draw any real conclusions regarding any aesthetic or intentional use of right-to-left movement.

For a secondary check, the 12-channel version was similarly spatialized,[4] and the spatial attributes of the fixed medium were considerably similar. As much as can be determined by this arrangement of tracks, Chin resorts to four spatial behaviors that she consistently uses with certain materials:

1. point-source spatialization, where similar materials are distributed evenly around the audience but do not move;

2. slow circular movements, especially for long drones or sustained timbres;

3. faster movements that appear to fly out of the space;

4. and cross-center rebounds, where an echo or repercussion of a sharp attack occurs in an opposing speaker.

Finally, a critical circumstance of this analysis is that it arises from a close listening of the recording published by the EIC (Chin 2011). Like other works that intentionally link timbres between acoustic instruments and recorded instruments on tape parts, such as Davidovsky's *Synchronisms* or Risset's *Songes*, a kind of forensic listening is needed to conclusively determine what is being provided by the sampler and what is being performed by the ensemble. The published recording blends the two parts far better than any live performance would be capable of, even if the instruments were amplified and distributed into the performance speakers, as suggested by the EIC's stage diagram. One can only assume the spatial relationships between the sampler and the instruments, and without definitive track assignments, those assumptions would be flimsy at best.

An Overview of Sections A through F

Harders-Wuthenow's description of the sections is sufficient for an introduction, but a more detailed description of the sections and their relationships is needed before proceeding further. Chin divides the 23-minute work into six sections by using rehearsal marks (A through F). More relevantly, these rehearsal marks indicate significant material changes that one can hear immediately. After section A, section B begins around 5:45. Section C starts approximately at 8:43, and D begins almost precisely at 14:00, though the nature of the electronics makes it difficult to be sure. Section E has the

Figure 9.3
Proportions of *Xi*.

shortest duration, starting at approximately 17:12, with F following closely at 19:08. The metronome markings, including metric modulations, have the quarter note nearly always at 60 BPM (beats per minute). Section E stands out, again, as having a continuous accelerando of a quarter note at 107–115 BPM.

As indicated by the visualization of *Xi*'s proportions shown in figure 9.3, each section has a linear continuity, despite their unique characteristics. The figure also shows that there is symmetry to the work, both in sectional length and in material.

Section A consists of slowly swelling sounds reminiscent of a bowed tam-tam, which is also the first acoustic sound to be heard. There is a quality of spectral writing to the materials of section A, where pitches that emerge in the electronics have relationships to sustained and indeterminately detuned pitches in the ensemble.

In the transition to section B, some more iterative gestures appear. In this analysis, I distinguish between a rhythmic gesture, one where individual articulations are singular events in a larger pattern, and an iterative gesture, one where a series of short, fast articulations combine in a single event, much as a bowed tremolo is still considered a "sustained" note. In section B, the iterative gestures accrete, and eventually some short melodic figurations appear.

By the time section C enters, these figures have grouped and changed their temporal nature to layer superimposed, independent tempos. Rather than iterations, repeated gestures in C take on the role of pulses in each temporal plane.

Section D scatters the pulses, creating a denser but pointillistic section. In section D, the points spread among the ensemble in a fairly equally distributed manner overall. In the brief section E, an accelerando race to the climax of the work, the material retains the pointillism of section D, the layered qualities of section C, and the melodic figurations of section B, yet maintains an independent musical identity for itself.

The final section, F, recapitulates section A. The nearly identical reiteration of the tam-tam swell signals a return to the opening materials, with a curious dyad drone emerging and overtaking other materials near the end of the piece, with ghostly, plucked sounds and piano figures suggesting timbres from older algorithms of granular synthesis.

Although a visualization of a work's form may be informative, it is also important to remember that the temporal experience changes one's perception of form. Repeated material, when repeated literally, feels longer in duration the second time. An event that occurs two-thirds through a piece may seem to be the midpoint of the form in one's recollection and review in the mind's ear. In the experience of *Xi*, section A feels quite monumental, a slow and considered development of a sound source. Sections B, C, and D feel more equivalent to each other in their weight, while the two-minute section E, which gathers speed as it reaches the climax of the work, barely registers temporally. With F almost literally repeating section A, its slightly shorter duration feels equivalent, and the introduction of new material prevents it from sounding longer. This function almost ascends above the musical resolution that section F must accomplish. These factors together further impart the sense of classical symmetry that the recapitulation of section F incurs.

The Sound Archetypes

Both a struck piano and a bowed tam-tam will have an identifiable sound and behavior. The nature of activating these instruments with extended techniques, however, ensures that they will not have precisely the same significant perceptual components from instance to instance. Repeatedly playing a C4 on the piano keyboard will, despite the minute physical differences, sound like the same C4 played on a piano. Striking the inside of a piano, even in the same location, will create an unpredictable variety of resonances. Though it retains the perceptual identity of a piano strike, different pitches may emerge from strike to strike. Each strike's evolving sounds have as much to do with the vagaries of human inconsistency as with how the instrumentalist strikes the piano. After all, instrument builders strive to make the piano sound as reliably consistent as possible when played traditionally (by mechanical means). There is little ability to control the sound if one chooses to slap the lower strings with an open palm.

The sound of a bowed tam-tam varies with several factors that are difficult to control, quite like the struck piano. Depending on the bow and its properties, the size of the tam-tam, the speed and pressure of the bow, how the tam-tam is mounted, and the completely unpredictable and uncontrollable variety in construction of different tam-tams (which are, after all, not machined but crafted), a bowed tam-tam can give a swelling, noisy sound or a screeching series of inharmonic or quasiharmonic partials.

Both sounds have distinctive characteristic spectromorphologies.[5] The piano attack has a loud, almost percussive noise spectrum that quickly resolves to a lingering series of resonances consisting of the pitches of the strongest components of the noisy hit. The bowed tam-tam always starts from little to no sound, swells loudly, and possibly increases to include screeching pitches from higher modes of vibration. Once bowing stops, the tam-tam will ring for quite a while, with higher frequencies typically decaying faster than lower ones. If these two sounds are the grains from which the rest of the piece emerges, we can abstract these two opposites as

- hit then resonance (harmonic partials) and
- swell to noise, then possibly screech (random partials), and then ring for a protracted decay.

Their timescales are significantly different, their frequency contents are vastly dissimilar, and their behaviors over time are perceptually and affectively divergent. These abstracted spectromorphologies are the two kernels propagating development and direction in the work.

These models lend themselves to a particular use of multichannel space, and Chin consistently diffuses them in complementary spatialization. Even as she develops variations on each archetype, the spatial development rhymes with the new articulations.

This chapter looks at the musical materials in *Xi* as belonging to one of the two archetypes' timbral characteristics (their spectra) and amplitude characteristics (the gesture implied by their morphologies).

Gesture Categories: Morphologies

Since music is an embodied experience, the use of "gesture" as a descriptor is almost no longer metaphorical but instead denotative. One can define a musical gesture without having to liken it to a human gesture. It is, however, useful to qualify musical gestures with associated characteristics of physical ones.

Variations on Attack and Response

Acoustically, every sounding body has an attack-and-response morphology. How we imagine the proprioceptive action to create the attack and the instrument's response changes the way we experience the sound.

In its quintessential form, the struck-piano morphology of attack and response may qualify as hit then resonance. A hit is percussive and requires a physical action that may be quite violent. Even a marcato attack on a clarinet implies a different kind of energy. The response qualified as "resonance" implies an unmediated physical behavior, lacking human interaction and providing unconscious information about the struck body and the space it inhabits. The response of a piano strike is significantly different from the response of a clarinet, for example, which requires human effort to sustain it.

Gestural and timbral variations on the piano strike occur throughout *Xi*. These variations become metaphorical "hits" in different instrumental and electronic materials.

Early in the piece, a struck sound, possibly a processed piano strike, appears in less or more pitched versions coinciding with plucked string sounds; for example, in measure 49. The piano strike sounds pitch shifted well below the piano register in measure 60 and is then played in reverse a few seconds later. Fast crescendo "hits" (*sfp*, or accented, sustained tones) in the brass imitate the gesture, connecting an abstraction of the struck piano to the live ensemble. The analogy reappears much later, around measures 422 to 426, where the acoustic piano and xylophone parts imitate plucked or short metal string sounds. Some pulsed layers in section C, though described as bells or metal strikes elsewhere in this chapter, connect through variations to plucked or struck strings in other layers.

Some of the struck, staccato, or plucked sounds in section C and elsewhere appear to be highly processed piano sounds, while others appear to be unchanged samples of string *pizzicati*. In the extended, sweeping timbral modulations in section D, some of the highly processed piano sounds approach the sounds of the "hits" on other acoustic instruments, obviously the plucked string or piano sounds but also a modified flute staccato.

Split into its parts, *Xi* presents variations on hit and resonance. A discussion of resonance continues in the next section, Sound Categories: Spectra. This section focuses on hits and what occurs in iterations or repetitions of hits.

When multiple articulations can be grouped as an iterative gesture, the speed and regularity determine the categorical perception of the iterations. Slow, regular iterations form pulses. Faster iterations lasting a shorter duration create flutters. Even faster, longer iterations border on a timbral effect or a tremolo. The relatively consistent perception of these categories is even reflected in Western notation, which Chin employs. This notation is particularly revelatory in the tape part because she is not required to conform to a standard for performers' execution but instead only needs to allow the conductor to quickly recognize a timbre or sound for cueing with the tape, as in the excerpt shown in figure 9.4.

The transition from a single attack and response to iterative hits begins with Chin's use of a rebound or echo of the attacks and responses at the start of *Xi*, which Chin typically spatializes in facing speakers. Perceptually, we hear these as two articulations, but their causal relationship binds them as an experience of a single incident.

In the early parts of section A, Chin might spatialize a hit in one speaker but place the resonance cross-center to the attack. Similarly, when an echo or ricochet follows the hit, the echo might appear cross-centered. This behavior happens early in the work, in measures 49 and 53, introducing the iterative nature of hits rather quickly. Even in section B, where the staggered partials after each hit draw one's attention, there can be echoes to the hits that appear to trigger each broader gesture.

Figure 9.4
Chin notates a flutter with a slashed grace note, a tremolo as traditionally notated in strings, and a pulse as regular rhythms in the fixed-medium part (Chin 1998, 16).

These hit-and-echo ricochets introduce a recurrent formal device that groups multiple events into a unified sound object. Chin develops this ricochet device further, creating gestures that live between echoes (i.e., identifiable events belonging to a single sound object, and multiple similar events that, while occurring as part of the same gesture, still may be activated by multiple impulses). On several occasions, a flutter or a scratching sound appears in the work, the circumstances of this appearance linking it to the echo/ricochet.

Flutters tend to be spatialized by something like orbital slingshots, using the circle to shoot off into the distance. This spatial treatment helps to group these iterative articulations into a single flutter identity, even as the articulations themselves vary.

Chin rhymes this flutter in electronics with instrumental writing, for example, in measures 107–108, where the strings perform a *col legno battuto* ricochet accompanied by the flutters in the electronics.

Together, the flutters and the echoes prepare the listener for notated "errors" in attacks appearing later. Combined with aleatoric pitch variations, notated by an arrow pointing up or down on an accidental, Chin writes grace-note entrances or unrelated tuplets that blur both pitches and onset times. This device works especially well when repetitions of attacks gather to form pulses. Intentionally staggered attacks, in some cases sounding like errors, prevent the layers of pulses from appearing mechanical or machined.

When the regularity of a flutter slows to individuated, recurring events, the material escapes the percept of a single gesture to exist as separate temporal markers. Evenly spaced markers engender a sense of pulse. In section C, Chin creates layers of pulses inhabiting different temporal planes that sporadically intersect when pulses align.

Starting measure 148 (section C)

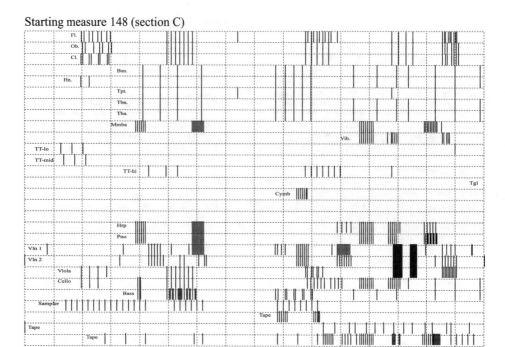

Continuing measure 164

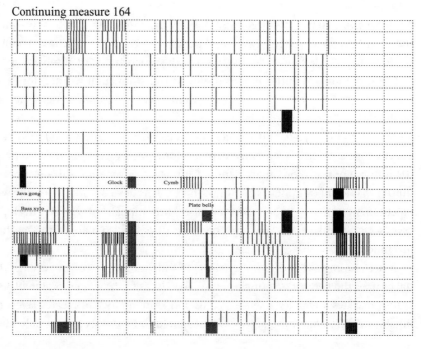

Figure 9.5
The notated pulses of section C, transcribed to scale. Dotted vertical lines indicate measures.

Rather than notating the pulses as layers of meters or tempi, Chin sets the meter of section C to a simple 4/4 measure at 60 quarter notes per minute. Section C is the only place in the score where the notation can be read clearly as a measure of time against the tape part. Chin does not use the sampler in this section. She only notates some of the pulse layers in the tape part, though many more layers exist.

In a foreshadowing of the use of space in section D, each layer of pulses in the electronics appears in a different spatial location surrounding the listener, but the sounds do not move dynamically. Instead, Chin spatializes each layer as a fixed point source.

Section B prepares for section C to some degree. The hits and responses of section B are somewhat regular but occur too far apart for a listener to hear as a pulse or to determine the degree of regularity. Instead, one experiences the hits in section B as repetitions of a formal event, connecting the large-scale experiences of hits or hits and echoes in section A to the pulses of section C.

Pulse and Pointillism

The experience of a pulse arises from regularly spaced sonic points. However, articulated sounds with similar but irregular temporal spacing might be usefully compared to pointillism in the visual domain.

Chin employs this type of pointillism in *Xi*, especially in sections D and E. Whereas section D has no perceptible pulse, the sonic points of section E congeal into more repetitive and regular gestures, verging on pulses again. The irregular rhythms of section D are foreshadowed by the slower, irregular sustained sounds of section B. The short attacks and faster tempo, however, qualify section D as pointillistic.

There is a unique quality to the pointillism of section D that coheres with the hit and response of the piano strike. Each phrase starts with an articulated low A anchor, or "hit," that sets off a constellation of short, articulated sounds in the tape and ensemble. These points of sound are a staccato variation on section B's harmonic clouds. Throughout section D, they increasingly take registral form, arching up and then falling to the next low A nadir. The speed of ascension, hesitation, and then acceleration downward begins to suggest the rise and fall of a pendulum. With some variation, the upward gestures tend to be orchestrated in the electronics, while the acoustic instruments tend to articulate the fall back to the low As. One can almost begin to hear these arches as a kind of arpeggio.

As the gestures cement into these arching shapes, they naturally lead to the faster, measured, articulated, pointillistic runs of section E. Section D ends with rising and falling, indistinct arpeggios, but section E is a more solidly formed allusion to descending arpeggios. Beneath these articulated runs, pulses reminiscent of section C swell in and out. The climactic intensity of section E is achieved by a combination of the faster, irregular pointillism of section D with the emerging pulses of section C. The electronics connect this pointillism to granular synthesis and prepare the ear for the descending granular sounds, suggesting falling ping pong balls in a reverberant space, that signal the end of the climax before the recapitulation in section F.

Although there is no clear indication of elevated speakers in any instructions or stage diagrams, the compelling physical metaphor of the pointillistic arches and runs in sections D and E progressively imposes an imagined elevation. Quite convincingly, one begins to hear the ascending and descending pitches as moving physically up and down in space. However, Chin spatializes the pointillistic materials themselves as point sources. The space in section D especially is created not by sound movement but instead by envelopment within multiple voices playing in counterpoint in timbre, rhythm, and space.

A pulse and a flutter are related through regular iterations but differ in speed, and a flutter and tremolo possess a similar relationship. While iterative in behavior, like a flutter, a tremolo exists as a sustained, single action, unlike the flutter. In several cases, the tremolo acts as a bridge between the morphologies arising from the struck piano and the bowed tam-tam.

When a sustained tone has the amplitude fluctuation speed of a flutter, then the effect is better classified as a rattle. The rattle's iterative character is quite compelling. In close listening, the rattles in *Xi* are slightly slower, with sharper attacks, than tremolos. Likewise, a rattle is generally more suggestive of noisier, less-pitched tones. Functionally, however, the rattles in *Xi* behave like tremolos in the creation of sustained tones with amplitude variations. Unlike the tremolos, the amplitude fluctuations in the rattles may be less regular. However, the spatialization of the rattles in prolonged circular movements is identical to the spatialization of the sustained timbres with tremolo ornamentation. The spatialization of these sustained rattles and tremolos is somewhat straightforward, and it helps articulate the imaginary space of the electronics while leaving room for the more active layers above them, almost acting like the ground beneath the other materials.

There is a trajectory of hit-and-response developments from section A through section E. Starting with section A, where Chin introduces the piano strike and then quickly plays with the echo or ricochet, the responses of the hits in section B are staggered partials or harmonic clouds. In section D, the clouds begin to take registral shape but become more articulated and pointed. In section E, the arching points of section D lead to more regularly articulated descending runs, and the hits are no longer acoustically present. Pulses replace the hits. Therefore, it is the variation of iterations that connects the materials, quite linearly, from start to climax.

Variations on Swells

The characteristic morphology of the bowed tam-tam in *Xi* is "swell" and "decay." In the same way that the variations of hit and response arise from speed and scale, the variations of swell and decay depend on the timescale in which they occur. In a single event, swell and decay describe the amplitude envelope. When dynamics indicate a swell and decay over a lengthier musical unit, they become a phrase envelope. When phrases join or overlap, so that density accretes or erodes, a structural envelope can be experienced as a swell and decay. In *Xi*, where the sections are connected by a quiet, sustained, stable tape part, the overall swelling and decaying of each section provides a kind of formal envelope.

The variation on the swell-and-decay amplitude envelope occurs in the electronics of section A, made more salient by the actual tam-tam's accompaniment. Compared to the tam-tam, its electronic counterpoint has a more symmetrical swell and decay. It can also occur in a much shorter duration without losing its timbral identity.

Section A begins with measured swell-and-decay amplitude envelopes in the electronics and tam-tam. This sets the stage for the ensuing envelopes. As the swells increase, the instrumentation thickens and resonates. The sustained pitches in the instruments are all notated with hairpin crescendos and decrescendos. These begin to conflate with hit gestures, with *fp* markings into crescendos, or with crescendos that sound like reversed hits. However, longer sustained tones all have crescendo and decrescendo dynamics. These amplitude envelopes are most exposed in section A, where larger musical structures do not exist. In section B, these amplitude envelopes continue in the instrumental parts under the hit and response of the attacks with staggered partials.

Musical phrases often have dynamic envelopes. Given the variety of ways in which one can mark a single musical phrase, Chin's frequent use of crescendo and decrescendo in phrases that contain multiple gestures is a variation on swell and decay. In some regards, earlier, long sustained notes prepare the experience of the phrase envelope.

The phrase envelopes introduced in section C are a natural extension in time of the single notes in sections A and B. Although the most immanent feature of section C is the layered pulses, these pulses fade in and out, rarely appearing suddenly.

On a larger timescale, swells of passages operate as structural envelopes. These structures extend beyond single phrases or gestures. Structural envelopes are not only made as a swell of material in loudness or density but also rely in part on a kind of resolution of the swell.

In section D, dynamics are used to create structural envelopes that are too long to be considered phrases. As the pointillistic gestures gather into ascending and descending arches, the swell occurs on the descent, landing at the low A attack, and the decay occurs as the points ascend through the registers. The arches double as hit and response and as swell and decay, bridging the struck piano's morphology to the bowed tam-tam's morphology at the level of the structural envelopes.

Finally, at the formal level, where sections transition, Chin uses the electronics as connective tissue to link different musical materials. The absence of instrumental parts contributes to the work's overall swelling and breathing quality. These exposed periods of electronics-only sounds delineate each formal section, acting as the quiet moments between each swell.

Sound Categories: Spectra

The sound world of *Xi* is exceptionally diverse considering how tightly the sounds hold together. No sound is extraneous or out of place, but the types of sounds range from nearly sinusoidal to complex timbres and noise. The timbres in *Xi* originate in the archetypes' spectra similarly to the way gestural categories derive from the archetypes' morphologies.

The most fundamental component of any pitched sound is the sinusoid. Considering the title of this work, no license need be taken to connect sinusoidal timbres to the theme of *Xi*. However, as Chin transitions from sinusoids to more complex timbres consisting of multiple sinusoids, the relationships between the partials begin to connect the timbres to one of the two archetypes.

In fact, the construction of the piano, intended to ring at frequencies tuned to equal temperaments, guarantees that the ringing partials in a struck piano will tend to have harmonic relationships. On the other hand, metallic instruments constructed for noise and loudness, such as the tam-tam, will resonate at much less harmonically related frequencies when bowed.

Returning to the initial discussion on the variations on "resonance," the difference between the resonance of the struck piano and the bowed tam-tam engenders a different use of language. Though, acoustically speaking, any sounding body can resonate, in common parlance we reserve the term *resonance* to describe a ringing sound, in many cases implying harmonicity. This usage is more evident when we use *resonance* opposite words such as *clang* or *screech*. Therefore, discussing the sounds on a scale from sinusoidal timbres to anharmonic noise situates the sounds between the two archetypes.

Sinusoids or Simple Harmonic Spectra

Although most timbres in *Xi* are complex, there are a few occasions where Chin uses sinusoidal or relatively simple timbres as part of the spectral composition. The most striking example is in section B, where fused timbres from section A are staggered in time. Individual partials emerge as pitches within a tonal or harmonic cloud. The timbres in the electronics are very spare, nearly sinusoidal. There is more complexity in lower-pitched sounds, perhaps a consequence of having more bandwidth for overtones. However, the connection to section A spectra, the spectral characteristics of the clouds themselves, and the contrast with the instrumental timbres evoke a kind of purity in the electronic tones of section B. The references to the noise of the bowed tam-tam and the short, pitchless articulations of the flutters in section B further accentuate the sinusoidal nature of the staggered partials.

Complex Harmonic to Quasiharmonic Spectra

In *Xi*, when the sinusoids layer and fuse, they are sometimes resonant and at other times edgy and metallic, and the distinction alludes to different archetypes. When the component frequencies in a sound are nearly integer related but not precisely so, one still perceives a pitch, but the timbre becomes internally dissonant. Through varying degrees of quasiharmonic spectra, timbres belong to one of the two archetypes but, paradoxically, also link the archetypes. The degree of harmonicity and the fusion of the partials of complex tones result in three categories of timbres, which, for descriptive purposes, I refer to as didgeridoo, train whistle, and motorboat.

A few instances of timbres occur that are unlikely to be perceived in a single listening of *Xi*, since they occur briefly and behind layers of other sounds. For lack of a better descriptor, these sounds have the rough but harmonic spectra of a straight, tubular wind instrument activated through lip vibrations such as the didgeridoo. The didgeridoo timbre in *Xi* metaphorically connects the embodied drones of the swells to the harmonicity of a struck piano.

One particular example is in measures 236–237, and in comparing the 12-track and six-track versions, the sound appears to come from the sampler. Although Chin notates this sound as an A2 and E3, it is more like a single timbre than a dyad. One can only assume that this is a kind of processing that the K2500 can perform, but the source and the processing are hard to determine. There is, however, a quality to the timbre's spectral characteristics that connects it to the motorboat timbre found in the drones. This quality probably does not come from audio processing, as Chin most likely achieves the motorboat sounds through granular synthesis and not the functions available in the K2500.

In the six-channel electronics, the sound moves slowly from right to left. In the EIC stereo recording, the movement is less clear. In either instance, however, this sound is rare, easy to miss on a first hearing, and yet possibly makes a connection between behaviors and timbres preceding section F that prepare for the long, droning glissando.

On the other hand, a wind instrument relying on the pressure of air through a narrowed gap, such as a whistle, can be perceived as extrahuman when it implies a mechanical device such as a train whistle. In *Xi*, one may readily notice a few instances of this type of whistle.

A significant aspect of a train whistle that differentiates its timbre from, say, that of a pipe organ is that the spectrum of the train whistle is often mistuned, with spectral energy distributed broadly between relatively few peaks. The train whistle could be heard more as an unresolved harmony than as a single whistle. One can choose to listen to a train whistle for its components or listen to it as a timbre by merely changing one's attention. Quite similarly, the timbres of the winds playing multiphonics behave similarly in the ear. Though one can single out the individual pitches within the spectrum of the multiphonic, it still borders on a complex timbre rather than an ostensible harmony.

Chin ties the train whistle sounds to the metallic sounds through the use of more or less screechy partials. Multiphonics in the winds accompany the metallic spectra of the bowed tam-tam between measures 45 and 55. The multiphonics prepare the ear for when the more distinctive multiphonic quality of the train whistles emerges later. Later still, the multiphonics in the winds connect the sirens and bells in section C.

These examples of sounds are more or less inharmonic but related to equal temperament for their frequency content. At a particularly isolated moment, in measure 225, Chin uses the metallic swell notation of section A, but the sound is the siren or train whistle. This measure also contains an A-minor chord that connects section C to section D. This moment exemplifies particularly well the conflation of roles that partials, tones, harmonies, and timbres take in *Xi*, where one could hear a sound as having any of the functions, depending on the way the material leads the ear in that hearing.

The final drone in the last section borders on amplitude modulation synthesis, but the slow speed of the modulation imitates the dissonant, beating relationships of frequencies in engines for boats or airplanes. Though it may be more conceptual than perceptual, this characteristic of amplitude modulation synthesis bridges the resonance of harmonic piano spectra to the quasiharmonic or inharmonic spectra of the tam-tam.

Quasiharmonic to Inharmonic to Anharmonic Spectra

When activated with more traditional techniques, the tam-tam is a noise-producing instrument, where the spectral energy is random and constantly changing from moment to moment. However, a performer can emphasize specific modes of vibration when bowing a tam-tam by changing the bow speed, pressure, and location. When this happens, the high and unrelated partials of the tam-tam can be likened to a screech or described as metallic.

In the swell gesture, Chin highlights the partials that give a sound its edgy, metallic property, as seen in the opening section. In fact, in the EIC recording, screeching partials emerge from the bowed tam-tam as the performer increases dynamics. However, the performer cannot reliably control the resulting pitches, which means that the spectral writing of the screeching sounds can only be, at best, allusive to this behavior.

In the first few entrances of pitched ensemble writing, the strings and the metallic sound are coincident, and the pitches of the strings are related to spectral peaks in the electronics. Chin does not, however, compose these parts entirely faithfully to those partials. Though they are related, the instrumental parts often flesh out the complex spectrum, and the electronics and instruments together fuse to create an overall crystallized timbre. Especially at the start of section A, the electronics nearly mask the instrumental parts in the recording entirely. In a live performance, the amplification and live sound may overcome this effect. In any case, this is just a further indication that Chin achieves a combined timbre from all parts rather than a polyphonic accumulation of individual parts.

By creating these metallic and screech sounds by using added quasiharmonic partials, Chin provides herself with the opportunity to detach these partials as individual sounds as well. By decorrelating the partials in measure 40 and spatializing them more independently, Chin prepares the scene for the staggered partials forming the pitch clouds of section B.

Chin combines these spectral characteristics with the morphological characteristics of the struck piano in measures 170–180, where somewhat metallic, clanging pulses range from anvil or factory sounds to bell sounds. They rhyme rather closely with piano and harp clusters appearing in other layers, strengthening the connections between the metallic spectrum and the struck morphology.

Despite similarities in the bowed tam-tam and the struck piano, the tam-tam's potential for noisiness sets the archetype apart from the more harmonic spectrum of the piano. Therefore, the last sound category is that of varying noise-based sounds, all fairly imitative of the tam-tams in the ensemble.

Noise

One can think of the sound of a bowed tam-tam as a kind of spectrally shaped noise. In this regard, other similarly constructed noises in the electronics and instruments refer to the bowed tam-tam sound.

The first electronic sound appears with little variation throughout *Xi*. It is the source of the materials in section A and reappears at moments in section B in measure 106 and, especially, in measure 115 and later, where the sound refers to its appearance in section A through nearly literal repetition. There are occasional pulse layers in section C that consist of noises in different bandwidths contributing to the overall texture of the section while alluding to the bowed tam-tam sound. Chin also creates variations on the bowed tam-tam in the percussion section with brushed or bowed cymbals. The use of colored noise in sustained materials allows less-pitched gestures such as the rattling or fluttering sounds to fit within the overall sound world of the work. It also serves to bridge between sustained gestures and attack gestures through spectral similarities.

Perhaps the most striking difference between the sustained spectral categories of sounds and the faster gestural categories is the way Chin spatializes them. Sustained tones move slowly, if at all. Faster, articulated gestures bounce across the audience or fly off into the distance. Even the static point-source spatialization of the pointillistic elements occurs so quickly that the alternations between speakers create a fast, spatial movement. In comparison, one can easily follow the sustained materials in space. This facet of spatialization reflects the organization of sounds into categories of spectromorphologies.

The Tonal Center(s) of *Xi*

Despite Harders-Wuthenow's (2011) assertion that the pitch content in *Xi* develops from instrumental musical cells, only two pitches function, somewhat equally, as tonal centers. In section A, the instrumental parts more closely align with upper partials in the tape part, but more extended fundamental frequencies at or around E underlie the more active sustained tones. Most of section A appears to respond to the E as a fundamental frequency. Although the noise may blur the fundamental to some extent, Chin signals its importance in measure 63, where the sampler and the contrabass play a clearly articulated E1. Although a section based on a fundamental A follows the E1, Chin resolves this A in measure 74 with an E2. In measure 64, the tuba and sampler introduce the A as a powerful tonal center that tends to dominate the rest of the piece. The E does reemerge at points as a tonal center in section B—for example, in measure 88—but it lessens in importance compared to the A.

The A plays crucial roles in marking points between sections or phrases at other points as well. For example, in the last measure before section B, the horn plays an A4 solo against the noise and an A4 in the electronics leading to the new material introduced in section B.

Throughout section D, the pointillistic material can be heard as a hit and response, as the fall to the low A1 (most often in the tape and piano) and a pointillistic flourish in response. The repeated As, though sufficiently spaced in time to be reminiscent of the regular pulses of section C, still create an uneven meter by anchoring the material with each articulation. Chin may blur the anchor through grace notes and detunings, but the A is ever-present throughout the section.

After sections A through D so carefully prime the ear for A and E as tonal centers, the repetitive, measured pointillism of section E may seem less centered, but the As and Es keep emerging as familiar pitches. The electronics support this by being more recognizable as granular synthesis than in any other section and therefore the least likely to distract from or undermine pitch recognition.

Occasionally, Chin undermines this dual center by including a substantial C, creating a distinct A-minor harmony. More forcefully, Chin lays out the importance of A, E, and the A-minor chord in the last section. The end of section C resolves with an A4 accumulating with a C5 and E5. With timbres evocative of section A, E6 and D6 emerge briefly to resolve with an E6 and C6 over A4, C5, and E5 a clear, if slightly detuned, A-minor chord, signaling the entrance of section D.

While all the other materials in section F form a recapitulation, almost a literal repetition of the materials, of section A, the two drones starting at A1 and E6 (both slightly flat) are a remarkable new addition. The A1 slowly glisses up several octaves, while subtly the E5 becomes an E6. The movement reestablishes the A/E tonal center. However, the final recognizable pitch material in the instrumental part is a slow ascending whole-tone scale in the piano, starting at an E6 and ending at C8. The whole-tone scale is a fascinating device, considering that the one pitch of the A-minor triad that is missing is the A.

Resolution in *Xi*

The tension points and subsequent releases establish the overall form of *Xi*. In this sense, each release is a kind of musical resolution. A particularly striking feature of the work is that the resolutions are not always tonal or harmonic. In effect, the roles of the spectromorphologies and their variations create levels of tension and release, or resolutions. In that regard, some musical resolutions in *Xi* are "gestural" or "spectral."

Gestural Resolutions

A gesture has a start, an end, and some action between those points, but what does it mean to have a gestural resolution? Some gestures imply a kind of movement that is effortful or unstable. The gesture resolves when that movement stops; the impetus that kept the gesture effortful or unstable disappears.

The term Chin (Ehrler 2001) and Harders-Wuthenow (2011) use for the swell gesture is more embodied: "breathing." Unlike a swell, which perhaps implies a force of nature providing energy, human effort drives breath. Release often accompanies exhalation, since the primary muscular effort in breathing is for inhalation. In this regard, the swell gesture is one way in which phrases, structures, and formal sections resolve in energy.

In section D, Chin inverts this figure. As section D prepares for section E, the pendulum swings upward, to the maximum of potential energy, and through anticipation, the moment of highest tension. However, it is in this upswing that the dynamics diminish. The release of potential energy into the downswing to the low A attack is where the swell occurs. If one extends Harders-Wuthenow's analogy, then the tension and silence occur at the top of one's breath, held uncomfortably until a release of air and immediate reinhalation.

Another way in which one may perceive a resolution in a gesture is when layers or pulses synchronize. The simplicity of coincident events compared to the complexity of layered temporal planes may be perceived as a reduction in instability. Despite the lesser degree of embodiment, the moment of a stable coincidence is a release or relaxation of metaphorical tension, another gestural resolution.

Tonal Resolutions

In many sections, the blurred tonal centers or dense spectral and harmonic clouds resolve to the tonal centers of A and/or E. Chin occasionally achieved periods of stability within materials through octaves or fifths with those fundamental pitches.

One notable example is measure 74 in section A, where the building of spectral content gives way to tonal content. At the fading away of the complex tone, the E1 emerges as a brief resolution or pause between materials, orchestrated in the tuba, contrabass, and sampler. This momentary pause becomes the backdrop for the first flutters, which then lead to section B and the staggered articulation of spectral content. More importantly, this E functions almost like the tonal dominant to the A that appears in measure 78 and persists until the start of section B.

Formal Resolutions

When each section's materials and densities erode to transition to the next section, gestural resolutions converge with spectral and tonal resolutions to create a formal resolution between each section. The more complex instrumental materials disappear, exposing stable, sustained electronic material, which presents a tonal center. The tape's spectral content simplifies in conjunction with the tonal center. These triple-weighted releases establish the formal markers that one hears clearly in the work.

Intentional Error

The highly formalized approach to spectral content and gestural content, especially layers of pulses, might imply a level of precision that would result in mechanical music. Although the influences of Ligeti are apparent, the machine-like materials of his crystallized structures or counterpoint do not appear in Chin's writing. In the case of *Xi*, it is because Chin notates indeterminate alterations in attack and pitch that introduce what we may perceive as a human component: human error.

Chin often uses arrows to specify indeterminate detuning of pitches, despite relationships between the pitches of the ensemble and the spectral content of the electronics in, for example, section A. The performance instructions in the score only indicate a "little" adjustment up or down from the indicated pitch.[6] One can only suppose that Chin is looking for an almost coloristic change in pitch. When these pitch changes accumulate across parts, either on similar pitches or in otherwise consonant intervals such as perfect fifths, the result is a kind of detuning that seems like inaccuracy.

In section C, where the regularity of rhythms engenders layers of pulses, Chin still introduces errors that break the patterns in small ways. These adjustments are not immediately perceptible, but they do prevent this section from sounding derivative of Ligeti. For example, the flute, oboe, and clarinet often contribute to the same layer, articulating pulses in unison, but in some phrases, one or more instruments are slightly misaligned. In figure 9.5, it is clear that the first grouping at measure 150 consists of misaligned patterns similar in rhythmic contour. However, at measure 153, the group plays in unison. The same kinds of misalignments or unsystematic articulations occur across other groups, such as the brass section (the bassoon is part of this section) or the piano and harp duo.

In section D, where the low A acts as the anchor point from which the pointillistic arches emerge, Chin initially aligns the attacks. As the section develops, Chin employs grace notes for some instruments articulating the A. Like the arrows for pitch, grace notes have indeterminate durations, and the variability of human performance prevents the attacks from being precise or predictable. These "flubbed" attacks become more pronounced and less aligned as section D progresses.

Drones: The Spaces Between

In *Xi*, Chin uses drones that live in spaces between states. The drones in *Xi* exist between the two archetypal spectromorphologies and balance between tension and release, depending on their timbre, placement, and function.

Between the Archetypes

Occasionally throughout the work, Chin employs drones or dronelike tones with various functions. The drone occupies a shared space between the struck piano and bowed tam-tam. It is quite easy to imagine a drone as a swell that has an extended peak, even if the connection is tenuous. After all, a swell occurs when a sustained tone expands and contracts, not when it remains unchanged. The connections to the other swelling, sustained tones can associate the drone with the swell.

However, the connection to a hit and resonance may be harder to make. The tremolo transforms sequential iterative hits into a single sustained tone, but not all sustained tones become drones. Chin makes this connection by increasing the rate of tremolo, creating a tone most obviously present in the final section, which begins to take on timbral characteristics of amplitude modulation. The drone is also an intriguing union of a gesture category defined by the archetypes' morphologies and a spectral category defined by the archetypes' spectra.

In this way, a drone in *Xi* has roots in the two archetypes, so that when the prominent drones at the end of the work appear, they still manage to fit within the sound world that Chin creates.

Between Tension and Release

The final drones in section F are remarkably distinctive as the only instance of that timbre and extended gesture. The sound itself lives between tremolo and an amplitude-modulated timbre. It appears to be created by synchronous granular synthesis, in which the duration and speed of the grains create regular amplitude envelopes at the perceptual boundary between tremolo ornamentation and separately audible sidebands.

The bass drone in section F glisses up two octaves over long minutes, a behavior unprecedented in the work. Its existence in the recapitulation underscores the development and variations of the archetypes in the preceding sections.

The movement from a slightly flat A1 to a fifth with the slightly flat E6 also creates a slow drift in and out of tension or possibly a protracted modulation of tension and release that slides between resolutions until the final pitch. The moving tone is a paradox, perhaps a Shepherd tone, which, though glissing over the entirety of section F, commences and terminates at the interval of a detuned A1 against a detuned E6. The conflict between the tonal resolution and the instability of the glissando ensures that this drone lies in the space between tension and resolution. As noted earlier, the instrumental lines ascend a whole-tone scale leading to the final fifth, thus avoiding A. After all other As in the instruments disappear, the drone remains as the fundamental A underneath everything else as the piece ends.

Speculative Conclusions

In this analysis, one hears this work as a formal, linear development involving two archetypal sounds. Although Chin specifies that the struck piano and granular synthesis generate the sounds in the piece, many of the materials align with the opening bowed tam-tam sound. The spectral content of the sounds used in *Xi* and the accompanying instrumental writing can relate to one or the other. It may be reasonably obvious that sounds will fall on a spectrum from harmonic, to inharmonic, to noise, but it is the relationship of the categories in this spectrum to the two sound archetypes that makes the distinction salient here.

Chin coordinates these relationships with gestures that appear to arise from the morphologies, or characteristic amplitude envelopes, from these two archetypes. The dynamics, phrases, structures, and formal units all build and erode with a swell and decay like that of a bowed tam-tam. Many gestures are congruent with a model of hit (or attack) and response. In section D, where the swell/decay formal gestures are combined with the attack of the anchoring A followed by an upward rebound of electronics and falling decay of the instruments, one hears the combined gestures as an extended intermingling of the two archetypes.

As a result of the broader gestures, one can experience a series of tension-building and tension-releasing moments that lead from one to the other. Harders-Wuthenow (2011) refers to the original bowed tam-tam as breathing, and indeed the variations on the sound, as they intensify and relax, can give an impression of inhalation and exhalation. But the original archetypal sound does not necessarily suggest that metaphor. In and of itself, the original sound is abstracted rather than embodied.

Nonetheless, tension and release is a driving force throughout the work. In many instances, Chin relies on veiled tonal centers to reinforce the resolutions between each peak of tension. The fundamental pitch of A figures predominantly, but E functions autonomously as well as in relation to A. The dominant/tonic function of these two pitches frequently appears, though stretched in time and hidden within complex timbres. As the piece develops, the introduction of the C nearly engenders a key of A minor. This impression emerges after multiple auditions, even if it is not immediately perceptible in the first one.

These characteristics of *Xi* give rise to questions I cannot answer but to which I can only imagine a response. On the surface, a work that relies on spectromorphological behaviors and granular synthesis suggests a vocabulary of sounds that today are quite ossified and recognizable. Many more recent works using these techniques are clichéd. Yet, this work from 1998 sounds neither dated nor hackneyed. I believe this is because of the technology available to Chin versus technology today.

Chin started working with electronics in the tape medium, which gave her microcontrol over her sounds. This experience can lead a composer to approach sound manipulation differently than younger composers who learn with off-the-shelf software that provides only macrocontrols to the user. What little off-the-shelf software was available in 1998 was far from ubiquitous. Chin relied on bespoke granular synthesis programming, attributed to Thomas Seelig on the recording. Current software that provides built-in granular synthesizers, such as SuperCollider, produces sounds like those made familiar in works by Truax and Roads. Historically, granular synthesis timbres were more varied, especially when composers used them to transform sounds in ways more commonly accomplished with digital frequency-domain algorithms today.

In *Xi*, Chin relies heavily on the processing techniques available in the Kurzweil K2500. Without access to the internal algorithms of the K2500 or even the programs that Chin used on the sampler, it is difficult to draw conclusive comparisons, but the use of dedicated hardware, specifically hardware that is not that common, would naturally lead to a unique sound. The time stretching and pitch shifting in the K2500 are not as recognizable as the phase vocoder algorithms in, say, Cycling '74's Max.

A second question that naturally arises from this work and Griffiths's critique of Chin's music is, what in this music is so unfeminine or un-Asian? I believe this arises from a Western classical approach to the material. On the surface, one can easily imagine the symmetry of the work and its teleological development of exposition, development, climax, and denouement emerging from a Western sensibility. The formalized development of two small units, almost like a subject and countersubject in a fugue, also speaks clearly to a Western ear. A distinctive A-minor tonal center, however veiled, cements a Western tonality. Perhaps this is why this piece does not sound so "Asian." Given, too, that music associated with classical symmetry, clear teleological development, and formalized structures is associated with Western male composers, it makes sense that this piece does not sound feminine either. To be somewhat less generous to the critics, if feminine music implies "pretty" timbres and consonant sounds, then Chin's use of granular synthesis, noisy and anharmonic spectra, and extended instrumental techniques would certainly not sound feminine, even though a pretty A-minor chord hides beneath it all.

However, analyses by musicians who enjoy Western and Asian heritage or education call into question this assertion. On a more general level, the thesis work of Hae Young Yoo describes the complex social context of Korean traditional music in Korean musical education and the ambivalent role it plays in Westernized classical music in Korea (Yoo 2005). Yoo also discusses the role women musicians play in contemporary Korean music. Yoo asserts that the impact of Japanese music and the feminized study of music in Korea contributed to the circumstances of Chin's music and career. In her subsequent analysis of Chin's *Six Piano Etudes*, Yoo identifies timbral and rhythmic influences of Korean, Indian, and Javanese music, as well as influences of Bartók, Messiaen, and Ligeti. Some etudes exhibit the use of "numerical puzzles and symmetry" (Yoo 2005, 106), which Yoo attributes to a twentieth-century Germanic tradition.

Similarly, Eunhee Kim (2016) attributes Chin's use of rhythm to Gamelan influences and German counterpoint, especially in her piano music. Kim also identifies the influence of spectral composers, such as Gérard Grisey, in Chin's sonic textures. Although Soo Kyung Kim's analysis of Chin's *Piano Etudes* (Kim 2012) makes observations similar to those made by Yoo and Eunhee Kim, Soo Kyung Kim's analysis more heavily discusses the Western influences of Ligeti and others.

Jong Eun Lee analyzed Chin's *Double Concerto* and paid similar degrees of attention to Chin's Western music education in Korea and with Ligeti. However, Lee asserts that the use of "seeds" and the "organic emergence of large and complex forms" found in *Xi* are present in Chin's *Double Concerto* and in the etude named *Grains* (Lee 2014, 17). Lee presents this technique as a device Chin uses alongside, but not together with, the Gamelan influences in her music.

The analyses by these Korean musicians educated in both the West and Korea suggest that it is as much the Western ear that associates Chin's work with familiar twentieth- century Western music than anything inherently un-Asian in Chin's music that affords her the questionable compliment of not being Asian sounding in Western writing. Chin's assertion that she does not wish to portray any particular Korean identity promotes this perspective further. This fact does not, however, preclude Chin from achieving an integrated, multifarious identity whose individual components are recognized by the ear that beholds it. Therefore, this is yet another conclusion I cannot make, as my ear is entirely Western in its training and experience.

Notes

1. In the original German, Die Musik Unsuk Chins entzieht sich jedem Versuch einer stilistischen oder geographischen Klassifizierung.

2. In the original Portuguese, Pelo contrário: "Acho muito irritante o fato de que, por eu ser de origem coreana, minha obra automaticamente seja submetida ao estereótipo da música asiática," diz ela.

3. In the original German, "Xi" ist, ausgesprochen wie "C" im Englischen, ein koreanisches Wort, und bedeutet Kern, Quelle, Ursprung oder die kleinste Einheit der Dinge.

4. The 12-channel media appear to have speakers arranged at approximately 30° angles, with channels 3 and 4 as the front stereo pair and all tracks arranged sequentially in a clockwise direction. However, less can be ascertained regarding the 12-channel version because the track names suggest that tracks 9–12 are arranged in some other fashion, despite the spatial coherence of a simple clockwise configuration.

5. *Spectromorphology* here means the time-varying frequency spectrum defined by Smalley (1997) to be the most salient descriptor of timbre.

6. Original: "etwas höher/tiefen greifen" or "ton un peu plus haut/bas."

References

Babcock, David. 1995. "Korean Composers in Profile." *Tempo* 192:15–21.

Chin, Unsuk. 1998. *Xi pour ensemble et électronique*. Boosey and Hawkes.

Chin, Unsuk. 2011. *Xi*. CD. Kairos, 0013062KAI. Paris: Ensemble InterContemporain.

Ehrler, Hanno. 2001. "Ordnung, Chaos und Computer." Transcription of comments from radio broadcast, DLR Berlin, August 26, 2001. http://www.hanno-ehrler.de/downloads/s-chin_dlr.pdf.

Ehrler, Hanno. 2017. "Unsuk Chin: Ordem, Caos e Computadores." *Essay for Orquestra Sinfónica Do Estado São Paolo*, March 1, 2017. http://www.osesp.art.br/ensaios.aspx?Ensaio=61.

Griffiths, Paul. 2012. "An Introduction to the Music of Unsuk Chin." http://www.boosey.com /pages/cr/composer/composer_main?composerid=2754&ttype=INTRODUCTION.

Griffiths, Paul. 2014. Program notes in "Composer Portraits: Unsuk Chin." Miller Theatre, Columbia University, March 13, 2014. http://www.millertheatre.com/uploads/images/Unsuk_Chin_Composer_Portrait.pdf.

Harders-Wuthenow, Frank. 2011. "Xi für Ensemble und Elektronik (1998)." *Im Spiegel der Zeit: Die Komponisten Unsuk Chin*, edited by Stefan Drees. Mainz, Germany: Schott Music, 74–76.

Kim, Eunhee. 2016. "A Study of Unsuk Chin's *Piano Concerto*: The Influence of György Ligeti's *Piano Concerto*." DMA diss., Ohio State University.

Kim, Soo Kyung. 2012. "A Study of Unsuk Chin's *Piano Etudes*." DMA diss., University of Georgia.

Kurzweil. n.d. K2500 Performance Guide. Kurzweil Music Systems. http://kurzweil.com/product /k2500/downloads/. Accessed September 8, 2019.

Lee, Jong Eun. 2014. "Inside the Hyper-instrument: Unsuk Chin's *Double Concerto*." DMA diss., University of Washington.

Midgette, Anne. 2017. "The Top 35 Female Composers in Classical Music." *Washington Post*, August 4, 2017.

Varga, Bálint András. 2017. *The Courage of Composers and the Tyranny of Taste: Reflections on New Music*. Rochester, NY: University of Rochester Press.

Smalley, Denis. 1997. "Spectromorphology: Explaining Sound-shapes." *Organised Sound* 2 (2): 107–126.

Yoo, Hae Young. 2005. "Western Music in Modern Korea: A Study of Two Women Composers." DMA diss., Rice University.

10 The Collaborative Process of Re-creation: Anne La Berge's *Brokenheart* (2007) for Performers, Live Electronics, and Video

Pamela Madsen

Brokenheart (2007) is a work by Anne La Berge for computer-controlled electronics, acoustic instruments using small loudspeakers, and live video. The resultant work exists in multiple realizations of guided improvisations created through a process of collaboration. It was first commissioned and performed in 2007 by the LOOS ensemble, re-created in 2009 in collaboration with Jane Rigler (flutist/electronics), Pamela Madsen (pianist/electronics), and Anne La Berge (typist/electronics), and recorded in 2011 by Cor Fuhler (piano/electronics) and Anne La Berge (flute/electronics) for La Berge's CD *Speak*. The generations of the work resulted in multiple evolving perspectives of interpretation of the concept of "broken heart" syndrome through the use of guided improvisation, text, and electronics. What is unique about La Berge's work is her generosity in sharing her creative process and the openness to diverse perspectives during her engagement in the moment. I will discuss La Berge's collaborative process of re-creation, her aesthetic of guided improvisation and electronics, and the subsequent multiple generations of the work and their divergent results.

About Anne La Berge

Anne La Berge's passion for the extremes in both composed and improvised music has led her to the fringes of storytelling and sound art for sources of musical inspiration. Bob Gilmore asserts, in the booklet of La Berge's CD *Speak*: "Her performances bring together the elements on which her international reputation is based: a ferocious and far-reaching virtuosity, a penchant for improvising delicately spun microtonal textures and melodies, and her wholly unique array of powerfully percussive flute effects, all combined with electronic processing" (Gilmore 2011).

La Berge was born in the United States and moved to Amsterdam in 1989. Her early compositions (collected on her first solo CD, *blow*) pioneered new approaches to the flute—percussive, noise-filled, microtonal, sometimes aggressively physical performances. She worked with new lip techniques, breathing, and use of the micro-phone, developing the amplified flute as an instrument in its own right. She has worked with interactive computer systems and digital processing techniques in live performance, using programs such as Max, LiSa, Imagine, and the Clavia MicroModu-lar synthesizer (on the CD *United Noise Toys* with Gert-Jan Prins). Currently, La Berge primarily uses the Kyma Sound Design System. In 1999, together with drummer Steve Heather and synthesizer player Cor Fuhler, she founded Kraakgeluiden, an improvi-sation series based in Amsterdam, exploring combinations of acoustic instruments, electronic instruments, and computers, and using real-time interactive performance systems. La Berge's own music has evolved in parallel, and the flute has become only one element in a sound world that includes computer samples and the use of spoken text (La Berge n.d.).

La Berge's Aesthetic of Guided Improvisation, Electronics, and Text

To understand how to approach La Berge's work *Brokenheart*, we first must understand her aesthetic of guided improvisation, use of electronics, and how text is involved in the creation and generation of the performance. La Berge creates compositions that work with a flexible combination of imposed musical situations and electronics, where per-former/improvisers are an integrated part of the music-making process, dividing her time between "conjuring up concepts, structures and scores and showing up on stage to play" and thriving on a precarious balance between creating and performing (La Berge 2010).

In her article "On Improvising," La Berge discusses her perspectives as a composer/performer and gives further insight into her own unique aesthetic of hearing and play-ing. Her approach is investigative, often scientific, and curious, exploring sound as an acoustic phenomenon to be discovered and expanded. She explains, "We live in a field of ears. It is known that the little hairs in our ears, the cilia, respond to sound by vibrat-ing in patterns that undergo various psychoacoustic interpretations in our brains" (La Berge 2006).

La Berge's studied perspective of interpretation, respect for the composer's inten-tions, and mastery of skills give us clues as to how she also composes and intends her guided improvisation to be heard within the context of their codes and intended performance practice. As she put it, "Full use of performance practice resembles impro-visation. Creative use of performance practice makes room for imagination, invention, and taste" (La Berge 2006).

La Berge's aesthetic of improvisation has often been one of rebellion, as an out-sider or outlier, and to create improvisations that don't quite fit. As she describes it, "I love to improvise material in places where it might not fit. That means playing very softly, very loudly, very brutally, very simply, very virtuosically, very naively, so that the sounds have their own clear musical identity. It is then up to the sounds to find out if they will be artistically useful or even magical in the moment. In some cases, they find themselves as a driving force in a larger structure. In other cases, they live and die in a breath" (La Berge 2006).

The basis of her compositional and improvisational language is intimately linked to her playing and the performance history of the flute as a classical instrument:

> I play the flute. My flute is a tube with a series of holes sized and placed in a highly sophisticated and innovative way (give or take some instinctual departures). When I play my flute, I blow and occasionally suck through my body's tubes—that is, my lungs, my windpipe, my nose, my mouth, my lips. While playing my flute I love to imagine those little cilia vibrating away in that enormous field of ears, responding to whatever I can get my flesh and metal tubes to do. When I start to sense that those ears are not getting enough information, enough articulation, enough clarity, enough ideas, I make up new sonorities, new envelopes, new timings, new juxtapositions to keep my sonic language fresh and keep those ears alert. (La Berge 2006)

Her perspective as a performer/composer developed from her mastery of her instrument and her performance of composed music. In her words, "When I play composed music, I try to support the ideas, the fantasies and the structures of the composer. Playing composed music takes a lot of trust. It is a three-way trust between composer, performer(s) and the field of ears" (La Berge 2006).

In her mastery of composers' intentions, she reflects on the need for an understanding of performance practice—and the tacit codes surrounding it: "I do my best to trust composers' intentions and I like to learn music so that I can attempt to replicate it from performance to performance. There is no perfect performance although the ambition to create one often comes with composed music. I suppose perfection is something that accompanies notated music. I once thought that ink was holy. As performer, I feel responsible for not only understanding composed music but for making use of the tacit codes surrounding it. That is, performance practice" (La Berge 2006).

For her insights on improvisation, La Berge explains her understanding of past music and how she hears new music: "When I improvise, I mess with orchestration, with style, with timbre. I prefer to experiment with sounds, rhythms, shapes that may or may not work. I like to stumble on new places by establishing familiar territory and getting lost. If I go to a place I've been before, I pretend that the field of ears has not yet tasted these sounds, this music, at least not quite like this before. I work to renovate and transform my fantasies about my flute, my body, my wind, the field of ears, the millions of cilia per millimeter each ear hosts" (La Berge 2006).

La Berge developed her improvisational approach in various ensembles, exploring extended techniques as a researcher for other composers. She also collaborated in improvisational performances with composer/flutist John Fonville and composer/guitarist/singer David Dramm. Through her work as a performer/improviser, she evolved to become a composer/improviser. She explains, "As a result of those collaborations with other musicians (and dancers), documenting my work became a necessity. It was at that point that someone called me a composer. I saw it as freezing improvisations on paper" (La Berge 2010).

These "frozen improvisations" became a system of notation to document the work that La Berge was creating in performance. As she asserts, "We had no desktop computers in those days. Notation was ink on the page. Looking back at those early documents I remember a couple of obstacles that took years to solve. One was finding a notation for the extended techniques, some of which were unique to my playing, and the other was how to construct a work where anarchy and control had equal footing. In other words, how could I compose music that sounded like me? Or even more accurately, how could I enable a performance environment where everyone involved sounded like an organism composed of separate musical personalities?" (La Berge 2010).

These concerns for composing a music that sounded like an improvisation, that captured the essence of a real-time realization, are not new, but La Berge was, and is, at the forefront of attempting the realizations of these processes, still striving for a way to solve issues of communication and collaboration. In her words, "Give me until 2050 and I think I may get close enough to be satisfied. Improvisation, experiment, experience, technology, colleagues and failures have all been my saving graces. Regardless of the obstacles, I continue to compose and perform because I need to and I simply can't and/or won't give up one or the other. Why not have it all? Or in this case, why not have a portion of both to get on with making art?" (La Berge 2010).

Rebekah Wilson summarizes the unique, powerful nature of La Berge as performer and improviser/composer, and her use of technology, in her review of La Berge's work for Institute for Media Archaeology:

> The powerful nature of Anne La Berge isn't just that she is a virtuoso performer, or that she embraces technology: it's that she visibly has fun with it. She mocks and circles around the question, her scientist-daughter mind so sharp that you know she is fully aware of the audience and its perceptions and yet she is not so self-absorbed that she misses being in the moment. Her music and performances do not suffer from cynicism or that kind of post-modern criticism that chides itself from being joyful. Her music is engaging and infectious. As a listener you marvel at her technique and want to know if her stories are true and how she is inspired. As a composer/performer you want to be on stage with her. (Wilson 2015)

Anne La Berge on Intermedia Composition: Image, Music, Text, and Technology

La Berge also engages in intermedia: using image, music, and text to approach a social or political topic in her work. Her real-time use of intermedia allows her to embed social and political dimensions within the metanarrative of the composition/improvisation. Her primary interest in creating intermedia digital scores is to take her audience "through personal narratives where they are given the opportunity to learn about science, history, social theories, and psychology" and to experience an opportunity for "learning on an emotional level." She also has a playful side in her scores, saying, "In my pieces I like to inject some confusion, so people have to redirect their attention and reassemble either their own story, or come to terms with elements of the story that I haven't led them through" (Vear 2019).

She aims to have the audience "fit things together" for themselves, and, in doing so, she invites people's imagination into the rich mediated stories she presents through abstract, visceral sound and the complex semiotics of language (Vear 2019). Within the flow of musicking, creating new music in the moment, La Berge considered the behavior of the digital electronic elements (sound, image, algorithms, and the network of interconnections) as if they were the "other living being making aesthetic and structural decisions throughout the performance" (Vear 2019). She said that throughout a performance she stays "hyper-alert to their activities and actions," as they help determine her decisions to "function as either support or as steering member of the ensemble." This changed the nature of her role and her perception of the role of the digital elements. At times, she felt that she functioned as a "side-person" and at others the "front-person in an improvising band" in which the electronic digital elements were the other "members" of the band. Overall, she perceived her role as "co-architect, co-composer, co-designer, co-poet," in which her "brain and body were active as were the digital others." To facilitate this, La Berge imagined that "we are all in it together, the digits and me" (Vear 2019).

The interplay generated through the digital score in the flow of musicking creates a work that feels like you are "performing with an improvisation ensemble" but also that it clearly defines "strict aesthetic boundaries." The presence of the generative functions made her feel like she was "playing a score with rules" and that the evocation of its moment-to-moment decisions called on her to "interact, steer and follow all the media." Within the flow, she feels that each medium had the opportunity to be playful, dominant, and fluid, depending on the here-and-now combinations of "pre-sets, juxtapositions of sound and image and what the data flow was doing." Although she chose a minimal approach in her realization of the work, it did entail jumping between somewhat athletic changes and pauses to give the audience a mazelike path to follow while still enjoying her own performance (Vear 2019).

Discussion and Analysis of *Brokenheart* (2007)

For the discussion and analysis of *Brokenheart*, I will consider the specific elements that influence La Berge's process of realizing the work:

1. Creation of work: inspiration based on scientific exploration and text
2. Technology: specific systems used
3. Guided improvisation: strategies for realization
4. Discussion of multiple generations of *Brokenheart*

Creation of Work: Inspiration

For La Berge, her works involve careful research, which she uses as material to generate the work:

> I construct most of my works after a lengthy period of research on social, psychological, political, and/or scientific issues that the piece will be based on and then I sort out what the audience needs to see and hear in order to grasp the artistic messages I am focused on. The mixed medias I work with in this stage are text, sound, and image. The usual way for me to create a piece using text is to research the subject(s) that have inspired the piece and collect facts, quotes, and my own responses to what I have read and then create a reduced poetry. My process is gathering and harvesting information followed by a ruthless killing of my darlings. (Madsen 2019a)

As inspirational material for *Brokenheart*, La Berge used information on broken heart syndrome. Broken heart syndrome is a condition in which intense emotional or physical stress can cause rapid and severe heart muscle weakness. This condition can occur following a variety of emotional stressors such as grief, fear, extreme anger, and surprise. It can also occur following physical stress such as stroke, seizure, difficulty breathing, or significant bleeding. It primarily affects women and occurs most frequently in middle-aged or elderly women, with the average age about 60. While it can also occur in young women and even in men, the vast majority of the patients are postmenopausal women. The exact reason for this is unknown.

The heart muscle is overwhelmed by a massive amount of adrenaline that is suddenly produced in response to stress. The precise way in which adrenaline affects the heart is unknown. One of the main features of this syndrome is that the heart is only weakened for a brief period, and there tends to be no permanent or long-term damage.

Broken heart syndrome can easily be mistaken for a heart attack. Most of the people with broken heart syndrome appear to have fairly normal coronary arteries with no severe blockages or clots. The heart cells of people with broken heart syndrome are "stunned" but not killed, as they are in a heart attack. This stunning heals very quickly, often within just a few days. Even though a person with broken heart syndrome can have severe heart muscle weakness, the heart completely recovers within a couple of weeks in most cases, and there is no permanent damage.

First described medically in 1991 by Japanese doctors, broken heart syndrome was originally called takotsubo cardiomyopathy. When doctors take images of a person experiencing broken heart syndrome, part of his or her heart resembles the shape of a Takotsubo pot, used by Japanese fishermen to capture octopuses. La Berge used these medical descriptions and history of this condition as inspiration for the text she wrote to be recited for the work and as the elements that guided the creation of the score, technology, and choices to be made by performers in their approaches to improvisation (La Berge 2007).

La Berge's text about broken heart syndrome is used for the chat material to be inserted in the live video. This text needs to be typed in real time during the performance of *Brokenheart*. The choice of timing, screen position, font, and words is left up to the "typing" performer. For La Berge, the use of text is integral to her process of guided improvisation:

> Text brings us into a special cognitive, psychological space that is different than when we listen to nontext sounds or music. We create meanings that are deeply personal, and our emotions are touched differently when text and music are combined. … In my work, I use a semi-narrative use of text that can range from abstract poetry to lists of facts. The text is meant to inspire improvisers to pay attention to their music making in a different way than when they only relate via sound. It is also meant to inspire the audience to listen and receive the meanings and sounds I have created in their own ways. I find using text is a way to shuffle improvisers' musical habits and listeners' expectations. … I use text to startle people, to *jump-start* them out of their habits and truly experiment. (Madsen 2019a)

The text for *Brokenheart* is a set of poetic and narrative texts that La Berge made up as she delved into the science and personal accounts of broken heart syndrome. The texts relate specifically to each individual section, where video, sound, and live improvisations create a total experience. This is the text created by La Berge from which the "typing" performer chooses:

attack
The pain was somehow completely different than the sorrow.
But it still felt like some kind of attack.

although I couldn't describe what or where the pain actually was. But I remember it as an over-whelming attack from the inside out. I just wanted to find a way to ease away from all of it.

blood
There was an old and deep trust that my heart would get through it.
Or at least that my blood would find its way back to where it wanted to be. it moved with quiet power.—constant blood stopped its twisted route There inside me where belief was sup-posed to be safe.

breath
Something in my heart went very very wrong
but nothing in my breath has changed.
another way to solve it was not to have loved at all.

chest
found its way into the darkest corners of my chest—there in the back of my chest Too scary. Can't even put it into words.
black noises throbs strange loud gushes—dagger tingles and strange twinges

extreme
flash moments and long spans of extreme—surge of extreme sharp internal tears

muscle
such a faithful muscle waiting to be heard
flailing muscle that claimed to be more than just a bodypart never asked why they hid there in the corner

mystery
the mystery kept trying to sneak into my heart hated the mystery because it was so dark screaming mystery would find silence

nostalgia
had an old wish that floated up—hope squirting in all directions Sometimes after it hap-pened my heart seemed better. Time could not find its way back into power. There was a period when only simple pangs bounced against it.

stress
never quite sad enough to fully break—pushing the sadness from room to room

stun—(no typing)

ventricle
A silly shaped heart with too many beats.
Named after a super old Japanese pot.
It generally hits the left side when it finds a heart. only the favorite ventricle gets so weird
Takotsubo is the name of the old pot
(La Berge 2007)

Technology of *Brokenheart*

Brokenheart uses computer-controlled electronics, acoustic instruments using small loudspeakers on and in their instruments, and live video. The audio samples played by the computer are recordings of instruments built by Wessel Westerveld, recordings of Anne La Berge reading text, and sine tones generated by the Clavia Nord synthesizer.

La Berge's technology is intentionally direct and simple so that it can be easily duplicated by others:

> To perform the work one needs the audio samples and technology to synthesize sine tones. The audio needs to be played through small and robust speakers that are wired where the performers can put them in or on their instruments and relocate them. The video needs to have the heart video clips with options to process them similar to the way the Max patch does. And finally, the live typing of the text would have to be projected preferably on the same screen as the heart videos. At this time, in 2019, this could be done in Ableton Live using Processing for the video. Or in SuperCollider with another new video program. Currently, in 2019, there are many options, and I anticipate many more will appear as technology becomes more and more advanced. (Madsen 2019a)

La Berge uses technology as a way to free the performer from previous conceptions about work and provide another way of interacting. She explains, "I have also found that using technology to guide performers is less confronting and has less historical baggage than when using a conductor and/or a human cueing system. Using technology and algorithms to guide an improvisation gives the performers equal responsibility because they are all responding to the computer's random generation of instructions and sounds rather than waiting for and responding to another human" (Madsen 2019a).

The technology for the original version of *Brokenheart* consists of a Max patch, playing sections of sampled material. Each section contains samples that are played randomly with random envelopes, which gives the computer a somewhat structured improvisational role. Even though the volume of the samples is set for each section, the Max patch allows MIDI control to tweak the volumes of each sample during the performance. La Berge states, "Many of my pieces are in the form of a Max patch or Max app that informs the performers when and when not to play and suggests musical parameters to focus on. The cues that the Max patch gives can be either visual, aural, or both. ... The advantage of using touch-sensitive devices is that the communication is two-way between the device and the main computer" (Madsen 2019a).

For each section, the acoustic performers are given specific instructions as to the material they should play, while the introduction and coda are roughly notated. Specifically, commenting on her use of technology in *Brokenheart*, La Berge notes that, "I am interested in using the computer as a third party, as another personality in the performance. The computer/typist in Brokenheart chooses which text to type and when to move on to another section in the piece. In each section, the Max patch plays samples and/or sine tones using a scaled random control of envelopes and volumes and also chooses which samples to turn on and off. One could even say that the computer is improvising the sound material within a strict set of rules" (Madsen 2019a).

For La Berge, engaging this particular form of improvisation and electronics provides a way to level the playing field and engage both performers who are professional acoustic improvisers and performers who are at home with technology. As she puts it,

Many professional acoustic improvisers are still shy about engaging with technology whether that is using hardware or software or just cueing sound files on a device. Performers who are at home with technology have often given up playing an acoustic instrument. What a pity that these parallel worlds are taking so much time to share the stage together! Much of my career has been invested in creating works where virtuosic electroacoustic performers can play with creative pleasure and abandon and where music technology nerds can do the same. And they can perform with one another, sharing the same musical space. (Madsen 2019a)

La Berge believes that prerecorded fixed media scores (such as playing along to a backing sound track) are confining, as in-the-moment decisions can't be requested, whereas responsive and cooperative digital scores bring a "personality into the music similar to that of another performer." As noted by La Berge, "The practice of responding to real-time changes in situations promotes an alertness and responsibility to make decisions that I find valuable to people" (Vear 2019). Her focus on digital scores that respond to the here and now of musicking is grounded in the ethos that wishes to create cooperative social partnerships between the machines, the media, and the musician.

La Berge's narrative flows are equally open. She does not fix the trajectory of a digital score to go from "A through to Z." Instead, she believes that the media and the score should evolve with each fresh interpretation of the score. According to La Berge, "I want to start a piece at A, and for it to finish on Z, but what it does in-between can go along many routes, or any number of different pathways. ... [I]t can be a surprise, even to the programme itself" (Vear 2019).

Improvisation: Performer/Composer Choice

For *Brokenheart*, the order of the sections can be controlled by a computer player or can be chosen by the computer. In the latter case, the sections have been programmed to occur in random order, with each section lasting randomly between 30 seconds and three minutes. Performers can cancel the proposed sections or request new sections. Each performer is given one or two small Monacor loudspeakers. The audio played by the computer is played exclusively through these speakers, with each player having a unique speaker part. They are required to interact with the audio coming from their individual speakers, using the audio and the physical vibrations of the speakers to help generate and filter sounds using their own instruments. For example, low frequencies set the speakers in quite a dramatic motion. These "vibrating" speakers can be used inside the piano to generate sound from the piano strings and on the snare drum to make the drum "rumble." The audio coming from the speaker placed inside the tenor saxophone can be filtered by using different combinations of fingerings and playing different notes.

As part of the live performance, there is also video material of hearts, with one performer typing text as chat material that is inserted into the live video. The choice of timing, screen position, font, and words is left up to the "typing" performer. The random sample playing gives the computer a somewhat structured improvisational role in each section. Even though the volume of the samples is set for each section, the Max patch allows MIDI control to tweak the volumes of each sample during the performance (La Berge 2007).

For each section, the acoustic performers are given specific instructions as to the material they should play, with the introduction and coda materials notated. However, *Brokenheart* can also evolve to be played as a free improvisation once the performers become familiar with the sections, the samples, and the text. *Brokenheart* can last any length of time. After some experimenting, La Berge indicates that performers will find a length that is appropriate for them and the material and find different lengths that are fitting for different performance situations (La Berge 2007).

La Berge discussed her process of constructing her guided improvisation—what parameters are fixed and what are free, and how this differs in each performance, specifically of *Brokenheart*:

> The fixed parameters in the score or in the materials are different for each piece. Audio files, samples, and images are usually played using Max, where I can set up weighted random orders of start and stop and then use scaled random envelopes, volumes, filters, EQs, and other forms of audio processing. The compositions have predetermined sections that are ordered to support a narrative or a seminarrative function. I also like to structure pieces where beginnings and endings are set and the order of the other structures is random. That way, the narrative can take different paths from performance to performance while still supporting the meaning and the musical content of the piece. (Madsen 2019a)

Specifically, stopping and listening is a requirement of La Berge's works in guided improvisation, as she explains:

> My guided improvisation pieces require performers to periodically stop playing and listen to the evolution of the piece they are part of. I also encourage them to play their instruments more freely than from when they would be reading a notated score. That way surprises and

unexpected juxtapositions of material are built into the piece. Some pieces allow the performers to control the structure, such as controlling when to move on to another section; give yes or no responses to parameter and timing issues; vote on a question; or control the volume of a sound. Stop and listen! What I've found when I work with groups is that improvisers are waiting for their next chance to play rather than listening for how they could contribute to the real-time composition that is unfolding. To strategize how they could steer it further or drive an unexpected change is key in my music. (Madsen 2019a)

Multiple Generations of *Brokenheart*

Currently, there exist three different versions of *Brokenheart* that work with various instrumental settings. Version 1 was originally for Peter van Bergen (saxophone), Gerard Bouwhuis (piano), and Johan Faber (drums). Version 2 was originally for Peter van Bergen (tenor saxophone) solo. Version 3 is for one to three players. All versions are for a computer running a Max patch and the performer(s) playing a guided improvisation. This work can be played by any small improvising ensemble. For the purpose of this chapter, I will discuss the three versions performed and recorded by specific ensembles: version 1, the original version for the LOOS Ensemble (2007); version 2, the recorded solo version for pianist Cor Fuhler (piano/electronics) and Anne La Berge (electronics), which is available on Anne La Berge's CD *Speak*; and version 3, for three players, as realized by Jane Rigler, Pamela Madsen, and Anne La Berge (2009). I will briefly introduce the two versions by the LOOS Ensemble and by Cor Fuhler and Anne La Berge. I will discuss in detail the third version of *Brokenheart*, the one I am most familiar with since I performed this work with Anne La Berge and Jane Rigler. According to La Berge, each of these different versions strives to "create musical situations that change, either dramatically or at unpredictable moments in time. I am interested in giving music extreme lengths, short or long, and extreme sonic expression, sometimes horribly rough and other times sublime." She says she is "less interested in creating logical and formal transitions when creating a piece." Rather, she enjoys "slamming and juxtaposing contrasting materials and seeing what the improvisers and the audience do to make transitions." This results in music that is created out of "not knowing what will happen" and can be very exciting for both the musicians and the audience (Madsen 2019a).

Version 1: LOOS Ensemble Performance of *Brokenheart* (2007), a Guided Improvisation by Anne La Berge   The timeline and score created by the LOOS Ensemble provide an example of how a guided improvisation of this work would proceed with a fixed order, where the work is given section names and specific guidelines for performers. The specific performers in the LOOS Ensemble for this performance are Peter van Bergen (composer, clarinet, and saxophone), Johan Faber (percussion), and Gerard Bouwhuis (piano), with Anne La Berge cueing computer sounds and guiding the improvisation.

Performers in the LOOS Ensemble worked together to create a specific plan and strategy for working together in real time based directly on the unfolding sections of the text. This realization is the most structured in that the timings and relative sound material were predetermined to create a specific guided trajectory of form in time.

LOOS Ensemble timeline/score

1 **attack** (computer plays machine sounds; Anne La Berge, computer)—00:00–01:30. intro—play notated material—develop material *ff*—make transition to blood

2 **blood** (computer plays sine tones)—01:30–03:00 Gerard (piano)—ebow inside piano. Johan (percussion)—bowed cymbals evolving into solo material. Peter (saxophone/ clarinet)—*ppp* airy long tones—3 sec play—3 sec rest

3 **breath** (computer plays very soft sine tones) 03:00–04:00 Johan's (percussion) solo evolves into low rhythms—*p* to *f*

4 **chest** (computer plays grinding sounds) 04:00–06:00 Gerard (piano)—sparse rhythmically driven clusters—*mf*, Johan (percussion)—continue low rhythms—*mf–f*, Peter (saxophone/clarinet)—abstract pitch material on long tones w/sines—*mf–f*

5 **extreme** (computer plays clicks) 06:00–08:00—Gerard (piano)—dampen strings—*prestissimo ppp* with accents, Johan (percussion) —knitting needles—*prestissimo ppp* with accents, Peter (saxophone/clarinet)-*prestissimo ppp* with accents

6 **muscle** (computer plays low sines which vibrate the speakers) 08:00–10:00 Gerard (piano)—use the speaker on your instrument, Johan (percussion)—use the speaker on your instruments, Peter (saxophone, clarinet)—solo will continue into next section

7 **mystery** (computer plays text and only sine tones in saxophone) —10:00–12:00 Peter (saxophone, clarinet) solo—taking advantage of the filtering possibilities of the saxophone

8 **nostalgia** (computer plays text and sine tones)—12:00–13:30 Gerard (piano)—solo—*mp*, Johan (percussion) —soft articulations—only brushes—5 sec play—5 sec rest—*p* Peter (saxophone/clarinet)—soft squeaks that develop later into multiphonics—*p*

9 **stress** (computer plays text and sounds)—13:30–14:00 Gerard (piano)—still playing solo, Johan (percussion)—noisy paper or other soft objects—interrupt Gerard (piano)—*mf*, Peter (saxophone, clarinet)—multiphonics—interrupt Gerard (piano)—*mf*

10 **stun** (computer plays no samples) 14:00–15:00 LOOS ensemble solo that evolves into sustained clusters

11 **ventricle** (computer plays combinations of various machine sounds) 15:00–15:30 sustained clusters using the rhythms of the coda notation—Peter (saxophone, clarinet) cues end. (La Berge 2009a)

Version 2: Recording of *Brokenheart* for Anne La Berge CD *Speak* (2011)   The second version of this work is for solo piano/electronics with electronics and flute. The recording of this work by Cor Fuhler (piano/electronics) and Anne La Berge (flute/electronics) is available on Anne La Berge's CD *Speak*. For this work, the spoken voice of La Berge reading text of a poem about *Brokenheart* provides structure and clarity to the guided improvisation performed by Cor Fuhler. According to the liner notes, a performance of this work will normally involve computer-controlled electronics, any small ensemble of improvising acoustic instrumentalists using small loudspeakers on and in their instruments, and live video. As with all the works recorded on this CD, any two realizations might vary considerably—although not totally—from each other, and what we hear here is only one, albeit highly polished, studio version. For this work, much of the instrumental material in this recording was improvised by La Berge's longtime collaborator Cor Fuhler on the inside of a piano. The starting point for his version of the piece was based on a response to the text for the phenomenon that doctors call "broken heart syndrome," a condition in which intense emotional or physical stress can cause rapid and severe heart muscle weakness similar to that experienced in a heart attack but not life-threatening. In this version of *Brokenheart*, the computer patch played a random selection from a bank of samples (with random "envelopes" that cut and shape the sounds in unpredictable ways). The samples include prerecordings of instruments built by Wessel Westerveld, recordings of La Berge reading a text describing broken heart syndrome, and sine tones generated by a Clavia Nord synthesizer. The small speakers were used almost as performers in their own right, and the musicians interacted with them (Gilmore 2011).

Version 3: Performance of *Brokenheart* (2009b) by Jane Rigler, Pamela Madsen, and Anne La Berge   *Brokenheart* was performed as a version for instruments, electronics (loudspeakers), and video, for a trio consisting of Jane Rigler as flutist, myself as pianist, and Anne La Berge as typist/video performer during the Annual New Music Festival at California State University, Fullerton, in February 2009.

As a performer, I asked La Berge to suggest a work that I might be able to play with others as improviser and pianist. As a composer, pianist, and improviser, I had recently developed peripheral neuropathy in my hands and was looking for pieces that could reactivate my sense of touch. She suggested her work *Brokenheart* because as a player I would be able to hold the vibrating loudspeakers in my hands and feel the sensation of sounds being generated as I applied them to the internal mechanism of the strings on the piano. I also was very attracted to the meaning of the work and the physicality of its subject matter, broken heart syndrome, which I was to embody and interpret through my choices of materials in the act of improvisation.

The work was created through a series of meetings, collaborations, improvisations, and discussions, where a version evolved over time. Rigler and I worked collaboratively with the text and the directions of the score, consciously discussing the text, creating responses to the guided improvisation, and devising a plan for triggered cues. We developed a map of a sound world within which we worked well, but we left the direction of where and when we would move along the way to the realization of the work in the present moment. La Berge fed us triggers of typed text randomly on the video screen, which we reacted to. She also fed samples of machines and sine tones that had weighted random processing to the loudspeakers we held in our hands. The result was an 11 min interactive guided improvisation that became a coherent piece we executed in performance.

For our 2009 performance of *Brokenheart*, our trio discussed the meaning of the texts, the possible triggers for cues of sounds, and how these might interact. We shared our process of creation freely, collaboratively making decisions about the most effective cues for specific texts and sound samples that were being sent. While we came to a consensus about what the work might be about and how we might approach this, we were also open to the spontaneity of the moment. The process of creating *Brokenheart* came from a concerted effort at precomposition, preperformance discussion on the part of all players. The end result was tied to conversation, dialogue, energy, and mutual respect for the performers/composers' process. During the performance of *Brokenheart* as a guided improvisation, the decision-making came from a careful balance between listening to yourself and the other players. Internal and external decision-making was in constant flux. For Rigler, this includes "being in the flow, recalling/storing phrases heard/played; spontaneous decision-making (the critical, yet playful game of fighting personal 'judgments'); and a constant awareness of your presence with others (i.e., audience, players); and letting go" (Madsen 2019b).

The electronics were decided by La Berge: sounds fed into loudspeakers that we could use to distort or amplify our instruments. These were not controlled by us as players but were sent to us randomly by La Berge as typist and cuer of electronics. For Rigler, as a flutist/improviser/composer, electronics are part of who she is as a musician, so there was no boundary between her instrument and the electronics. In her words, "We have become hybrid beings—we've become cyborgs. When I'm playing, the electronics are me, my voice and my body" (Madsen 2019b).

Rigler and I discussed our process of preparing for the performance of guided improvisation in *Brokenheart*. This work required skillfully thought-out, predetermined decisions in order for the spontaneity to manifest freely. Rigler explains:

> I work on specific techniques in order to bring out the best aspects of the phrase or gesture. I don't predetermine the time—but give myself options for the transitions between sound

worlds, movements, or gestures. I love performing and creating in this way because I am fascinated with the process. We have a theme and a topic, but no conclusions, and maybe some grandiose ideas emerge along the way. ... Guided improvisation compels creative artists to focus on the moment to allow for new connections. It allows us all as a community to give permission to explore new ideas. The guided improvisation is merely a map, or blueprint, to create opportunities for something unexpected to emerge. (Madsen 2019b)

We discussed the resultant work of our guided improvisation. In Rigler's view, "*Brokenheart* can have many outcomes—it could heal or create more brokenness. For this reason, I respect the process of the piece. It comes into being throughout time. It reiterates itself into many new meanings. The piece tells me how to begin, and the outcome is a channel for creative outlet, for us, the performers as well as the audience. The piece is like a living being, always on its way toward becoming. Maybe this work is still in its infancy, waiting to be constantly reborn" (Madsen 2019b). Rigler sees *Brokenheart* an object that is seeking a new life from life itself, and we as performers offer to give this piece a life form. A potential for the piece to become its own life form—a life after that will always exist. *Brokenheart* will always be there and exist as an impetus, a challenge for us to listen and create. Sound will always be there, whether we are there to do it or not. (Madsen 2019b)

This version of *Brokenheart* (2009) with La Berge, Rigler, and me was recorded during the performance and served as recorded material and cues for subsequent layers of new improvisational works. The resultant recording became the impetus for another series of works created in collaboration with my longtime collaborator video artist/poet Quintan Ana Wikswo. This work became a video installation for her cycle of work *Prophecy of Place: "On the Sofa a Vilnius"* (2011, Yeshiva Museum, New York City) using the backing track of the recorded improvisation. Subsequently, I composed another guided improvisation with a new layer of spoken text for voice, piano, and saxophone on top of the video installation, text to perform with the recorded audio, and Quintan Ana Wikswo's *Prophecy of Place* video in live performance. The result is an ever-evolving concept of guided improvisation, generously shared by La Berge as a sequence of layered improvisations stemming from the original concept of *Brokenheart*.

Ten years later, in 2019, I conducted phone interviews with La Berge and Rigler on our process of performance/realization of *Brokenheart* and the strategies for realization of this work involving extended techniques, technology, and improvisation. This discussion was essentially an extension of our process of creation—since it is in this discussion process and openness to collaboration that the work *Brokenheart* resides—in that moment of questioning and creation. The very process of unfolding questions and directions, the selection of words spoken and exchanged by both creator and performer, and the discussion about the content and choices made after the realization of a work became yet another part of the evolving work.

Conclusions

La Berge's creative process, aesthetic of guided improvisation, and electronics informed the subsequent multiple generations, divergent results, and evolving perspectives of interpretation of the concept of broken heart syndrome. What is unique about La Berge's *Brokenheart* is the generous sharing of this work and the blurring of the boundaries of creator, composer, performer, and electronics. The work, in its various forms, exists each time, in its own time and unique perspective. La Berge and the collaborating performers of *Brokenheart* generously shared their creative processes without reservations or claims of ownership but rather forged new ground to create a porous process of generation in each new performance, with the use of technology as an integral member of the improvising ensemble. *Brokenheart* asks the performers to tell the story aesthetically, conceptually, emotionally, and musically in the ways that work for each specific performance situation. Technology became a kindred spirit that supported and inspired performers to play different material than they would without the *Brokenheart* computer cues of texts and sounds.

Brokenheart also created the sense of engaging in a new experience each time it was performed. La Berge's interest is in the act of musicking—and the extremes in the process that guided the improvisation. For La Berge, technology is an extension of her technique of performance and acts as a facilitator, becoming another body to improvise with. Technology, for La Berge, meant access to power and the empowering of others through technology.

Her strategies of guided improvisation seek to engage performers in the process, dissolving boundaries and inviting others to play, to engage with technology and the act of musicking. She strives to have performers be alive in the moment of her work. This engagement with technology, guided improvisation, and the collaborative process of re-creation creates works that seek to exist in time beyond the present moment. As La Berge puts it, "I make art that explores the thoughts and feelings we have that continue to resonate after we have thrown something away, after we have moved on from one thing to the next thing" (Madsen 2019a).

La Berge's work, through its intensity, extended techniques, and extremes of expression, text, technology, and guided improvisation, presses us as performers. She encourages us "to let go and then remember what we hold, use and dispose of as resonances from one experience to the next, and how we do that in unpredictable and fascinating ways" (Madsen 2019a). And, in doing so, we experience the intention and emotion behind the meaning of "broken heart syndrome" and reengage in real time in the expression of what it must feel like to become brokenhearted.

La Berge has been deeply engaged in the world of guided improvisation and electronics for over 40 years. She has stayed the course, with her work, aesthetic, devotion to musicking, and the process of experimentation. She has made her work available through continued performance and recording and established her work in a community of performers and improvisers worldwide. Her work is now being analyzed and discussed as a historical object, with active curatorship of her past and present works. She continues to work in the interarts collaboratively and is true to her mission: engagement in process as a composer/performer striving to be alive in the moment of her work and forging new ground in music technology. La Berge says that, "Technology is the human body including the organ we call our brain. Technology is the machines we play with that help us further understand ourselves. Technology is forever changing" (Madsen 2019a).

References

Gilmore, Bob. 2005. "Anne La Berge, Interview with Bob Gilmore, Amsterdam, Summer 2005." *Paris Transatlantic Magazine-Global Coverage of New Music*. Summer 2005. http://www.paristransatlantic .com/magazine/interviews/laberge.html.

Gilmore, Bob. 2011. Liner notes to Anne La Berge's CD *Speak*, 80717–2. May 3, 2011. New York: New World Records.

La Berge, Anne. 2006. "On Improvising." *Contemporary Music Review* 25 (5/6) (October/December 2006): 557–558.

La Berge, Anne. 2007. *Brokenheart* score.

La Berge, Anne. 2009a. *Brokenheart* performance notes for LOOS Ensemble.

La Berge, Anne. 2009b. *Brokenheart* recording of Anne La Berge, Jane Rigler, and Pamela Madsen performance, CSUF New Music Festival, Meng Concert Hall, February 2009.

La Berge, Anne. 2010. "Composer/Performers in the Netherlands: The Nuts and Bolts." *The Ear Reader*, December 2010. http://earreader.nl.

La Berge, Anne. 2011. *Brokenheart* recording for CD *Speak*, 80717–2. May 3, 2011. New York: New World Records.

La Berge, Anne. n.d. "Biography." https://annelaberge.com/bio/. Accessed May 1, 2019.

Madsen, Pamela. 2019a. Recorded interview with Anne La Berge, Santa Fe, New Mexico, June 2019.

Madsen, Pamela. 2019b. Recorded phone interview with Jane Rigler, Santa Fe, New Mexico, June 2019.

Vear, Craig. 2019. *The Digital Score, Musicianship, Creativity and Innovation*. London: Routledge.

Wilson, Rebekah. 2015. "Interview Portrait." Institute for Media Archaeology. https://ima.or.at /en/imafiction/video-portrait-07-anne-la-berge/.

11   *Taras su tre dimensioni* by Teresa Rampazzi: Documenting the Creative Process

Laura Zattra

Introduction

Taras su tre dimensioni [Taras on three dimensions] is a work composed in 1971, during a transitional phase in Teresa Rampazzi's career. In particular, this period corresponds to her evolution from analog to digital music technology. It also marks the last activities of the collective laboratory NPS (Nuove Proposte Sonore, New Sound Proposals, 1965–1972) group, which she founded, and her strategic moves to open an electronic music course at the Conservatory of Music in Padua (one of the first electronic music courses in Italy).

The approximately 11-minute work is unique in Rampazzi's repertoire because of its compositional material. It is made from the juxtaposition of three typologies of sounds: analog, concrete, and computer-made.[1] It is also the only piece in her catalog that incorporates concrete sounds.

A former avant-garde pianist, Teresa Rampazzi (October 31, 1914–December 16, 2001) had originally fallen in love with electronic music at the age of 40, after listening to a frequency generator at the 1952 edition of the Darmstadt International Summer Courses for New Music (Zattra 2002; Zattra 2003).[2] On that occasion, she had the chance to hear Herbert Eimert's speech in which he presented the equipment from the Studio for Electronic Music of West German Radio in Cologne.[3] She understood that sound synthesis would have been the only way to go beyond the rigidity of tonal music and to bend the rules of instrumental avant-garde music. A few years passed, and she continued to play piano, perform avant-garde concerts (one with John Cage and Sylvano Bussotti in Padua in 1959) and be in contact with Bruno Maderna, Heinz-Klaus Metzger, Luigi Nono, Franco Donatoni, Niccolò Castiglioni, and Karlheinz Stockhausen, among others. In 1963, she met a young artist, Ennio Chiggio, and their encounter was disruptive. He was a member of the visual-kinetic Gruppo Enne, a collective founded in 1959 by Chiggio with Alberto Biasi, Toni Costa, Manfredo Massironi, and Edoardo Landi, plus other architecture students. Rampazzi was almost 50 and tired of being a pianist. She needed a "mixer" to edit some electronic music pieces to be presented during a concert for the conservative public of the city of Padua. She finally realized her plans in 1964. Rampazzi and Chiggio's first experimental work was a sound collage that served as musical background for the vernissage of an exhibition by the Gruppo Enne at the Venice Biennale. On May 22, 1965, with the arrival of Serenella Marega, Gianni Meiners, and Memo Alfonsi, the NPS group was established.[4] The studio was located at Rampazzi's home, as in the case of other Italian studios of the second generation: the S2FM (Studio di Fonologia Musicale) created by Pietro Grossi in his Florence home in 1963 and the SMET (Studio di Musica Elettronica Torino) in Turin by composer Enore Zaffiri in 1964.

Not until later did Grossi, Zaffiri, and Rampazzi donate their instruments to the conservatories of music in Florence, Turin, and Padua, respectively, and start electronic music courses within those institutions (Rampazzi from October 1972). Rampazzi approached computer music in the early 1970s, thanks to her close friend and colleague Pietro Grossi; at the time, she was 60 years old. While she taught analog techniques, she began to learn digital music. Her first piece was *Computer 1800* (1972), realized at Grossi's CNUCE (Centro Nazionale Universitario di Calcolo Elettronico) in Pisa during the same period as *Taras su tre dimensioni*. She later composed with the computer at CSC (Centro di Sonologia Computazionale at the University of Padua) funded by Giovanni Battista Debiasi, Giovanni De Poli, Alvise Vidolin, Graziano Tisato, and James Dashow. In 1976, Rampazzi realized one of the first two works made at the center: *With the Light Pen*. In 1980, she realized *Atmen Noch*, which won the second prize at the Eighth Concours International de Musique Électroacoustique in Bourges. After the death of her husband in 1984, she moved to Assisi and later to Bassano del Grappa (Vicenza), where she continued to compose.

In 1999, Rampazzi's adult children Leonardo and Francesca donated their mother's archive to the University of Padua. Rampazzi, then 85 years old, was in a precarious state of health and had withdrawn from musical activity. The collection consisted of approximately 50 tapes with her music (including final versions and makeup tapes; a digitization was made later by Laboratorio Mirage in Gorizia, Italy).[5] The physical items include a couple of letters, a binder holding working notes, some texts she wrote describing her pieces, and a printed digital "score" made with a computer program named ICMS (Interactive Computer Music System).

The Teresa Rampazzi Collection (TRC) is not large and allows only a partial look at the production and life of this composer, pedagogue, and pioneer of electronic music in Italy. Rampazzi was forward looking and modern (for instance, she loved contemporary architecture and interior design). She was interested in new developments and was ingenious in seeing how music was supposed to evolve. She duly discharged everything that could remind her of past times or nostalgia, including letters and photographs (she disliked being photographed), because her thoughts and interests were projected into the future. This life vision, unfortunately, has caused a certain silence over her production during the last period of her life, a fate Rampazzi has in common with other women composers "either ignored or thought to be marginal," as Frances Morgan put it (Morgan 2017, 238), such as Delia Derbyshire or Constança Capdeville, among others.

As is the case with many electroacoustic music pieces, there is no score for *Taras su tre dimensioni*.[6] However, my analysis will use methods borrowed from source criticism in order to study the creative and (hypothetical) revision process that Rampazzi carried out in the realization of this piece, a method I already used (Zattra 2007; Zattra 2015) in the study of the assembly of *Stria* by John Chowning. This is made possible by textual scrutiny and interpretation based on different recordings, short writings by the author, and oral communications from her collaborators and friends I collected over the years.

Background: Historical Circumstances and Methodology

Taras su tre dimensioni was composed in 1971 and probably finished in December of the same year, as she wrote in an unpublished source (TRC). The premiere performance was held in Paris on January 26, 1972, at the American Center during the Festival International de Musique Electroacoustique (January 24–29, 1972). The title of the concert was "Studio di Fonologia Musicale Padua, Gruppo NPS; Direction: T. Rampazzi." The concert included several NPS works, as we see in the unpublished book compiled by NPS members titled *NPS 65–72: Sette anni di attività del gruppo nuove proposte sonore nello studio di fonologia musicale di Padova* (NPS 1977, 104–106).[7]

According to my research, *Taras* was aired two times. The first time was probably at the end of 1971, but this is purely speculative. The book *NPS 65–72* (NPS 1977, 115) mentions a broadcast over the national radio program Terzo Programma (on Radio RAI) in 1971 for the series of programs titled "Incontro con la Computer Music," although I have not been able to verify this information in any other sources, and the month and day it aired is unknown. However, this participation is echoed in another handwritten source by Rampazzi, but this time with the wrong year. In December 1982, she wrote, "Surely enough the RAI, by broadcasting it (1968? [*sic*]) gave proof of courage, that it has now completely lost. In fact, this is a piece of primitive and savage brutality" (figure 11.1). The broadcast could have taken place in 1971 but probably not before December, because in the quadraphonic magnetic recording of *Taras* Rampazzi wrote that she completed her work in December 1971. Again, her inscription could be a

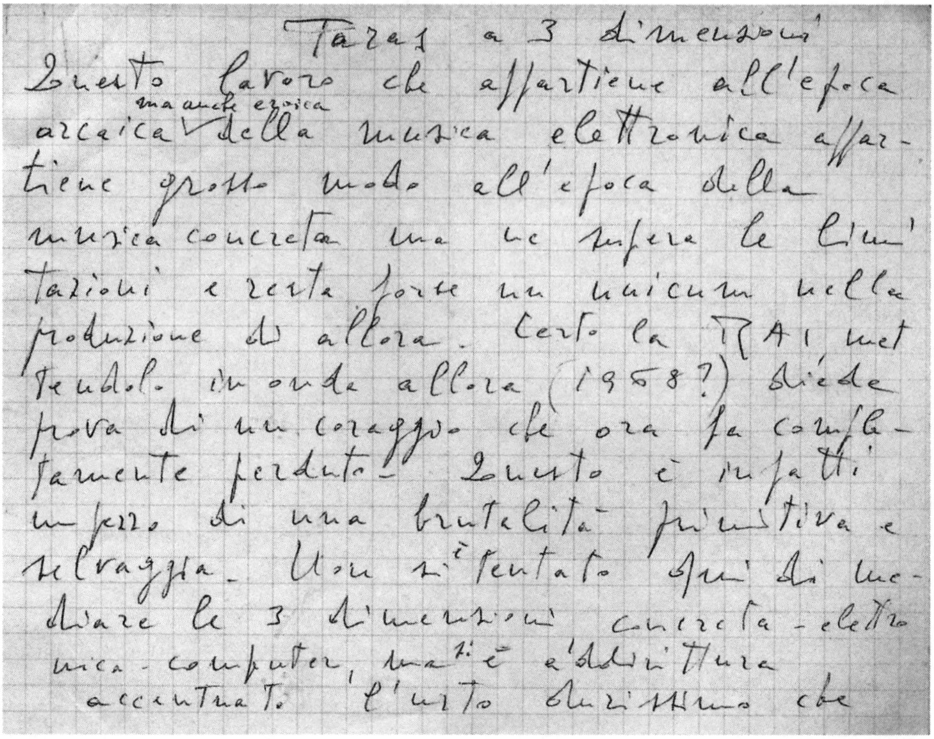
Taras a 3 dimensioni
Questo lavoro che appartiene all'epoca arcaica ma anche eroica della musica elettronica appartiene grosso modo all'epoca della musica concreta ma ne supera le limitazioni e resta forse un unicum nella produzione di allora. Certo la RAI mettendolo in onda allora (1958?) diede prova di un coraggio che ora fa completamente perduto! Questo è infatti un pezzo di una brutalità primitiva e selvaggia. Non si è tentato qui di mediare le 3 dimensioni concreta-elettronica-computer, ma si è addirittura accentuato l'urto durissimo che

Figure 11.1
Taras a [*sic*] *3 dimensioni*, handwritten manuscript, three small pages, dated December 1982, enclosed inside source 1, quadraphonic tape (Teresa Rampazzi Collection, University of Padua).

mistake. Only the RAI archives may solve this uncertainty, by revealing the exact date the piece aired.

The second airing of *Taras* was in spring 1985 (the exact date is not known). A partial audio excerpt (the beginning) was broadcast, preceded by Rampazzi's introduction, during the program *Le nuove frontiere della musica* (*New frontiers of music*; directed by Tonino Delfino). The program consisted of 10 episodes of about half an hour each, from December 1984 to spring 1985, with Rampazzi and Delfino discussing the evolution of electroacoustic music and audio excerpts from the most famous works.[8]

Authorship

A small text introduces the piece *Taras* in *NPS 65–72* (NPS 1977, 111): "*TARAS SU TRE DIMENSIONI*, 10'50" (De Poli, Menini, Rampazzi, Vidolin)—it was the first and probably the last attempt to bring together the three dimensions concrete, electronic, and computer. The strident contrast between the brutal element (concrete) and the "romantic" element (electronic) is resolved by the advent of the computer, which, with its precision, seems to prevail over the former dimensions" (NPS 1977, 111; my translation from Italian).

This source clearly marks the presence of four authors: Giovanni De Poli, Luciano Menini, Teresa Rampazzi, and Alvise Vidolin. As strange as it may seem, the piece was instead made entirely by Rampazzi. It was indeed signed by everyone, in the collaborative spirit of the NPS, but she was the one who realized it. This is not the first case of "collaborative work" that was actually created by one specific person. Other works of the NPS have the same discrepancies.

I asked De Poli and Vidolin for clarification. Vidolin confirmed that "as for *Taras*, I think the name of 4 people followed the approach of the NPS Group, but did not correspond to a[n] 8-hands work. Maybe there was a technical-operational support from us, but it was surely a work by Teresa on the compositional level" (Vidolin, personal communication via e-mail, June 20, 2015). In a separate communication, Vidolin repeats that "as for *Taras*, I cannot find anything beyond the few lines written in the unpublished book [NPS 1977, 111]. It might be something in one spiral notebook with checkered paper that we used at the time, with a pale green (or was it azure) cover. But the presence of all our names was part of the ideological choice of our group NPS, which was still valid in 1971" (Vidolin, personal communication via e-mail, June 25, 2015). Finally, Alvise wrote me that he "asked Gianni [Giovanni De Poli] regarding what you asked, and he too thinks that *Taras* was realized by Teresa, in full autonomy. The notebook was kind of a diary on which we used to annotate our work in progress, in order to coordinate our collective activity when we operated separately. I am not sure I have seen it recently, maybe it was just a dream. I even searched in my home, but it was not there unfortunately. I don't think even Ennio [Chiggio] has it" (Vidolin, personal communication via e-mail, June 26, 2015).

Title

The title *Taras su tre dimensioni* is a tribute to the city of Taranto, a coastal city in Apulia. In ancient times, the Greeks of Sparta called the city Taras, after the mythological son of Poseidon. Ennio Chiggio recalls that Rampazzi used to spend summers in Taranto, in Martina Franca to be precise. She stayed in a hotel or sometimes at the house of Vittorio Prosdocimi. Prosdocimi was a craftsman from Padua who had a small workshop near Taranto and made jewelry by hand (Prosdocimi, personal communication, February 21, 2008). During summer 1971, she was hosted by Prosdocimi. Also staying there were Ennio Chiggio, with his young daughter Claudia, and Manfredo Massironi (from the

Gruppo Enne), with his young son Michele. Although Claudia and Michele have no clear memories about that summer because they were toddlers (both were interviewed on May 31, 2019), Chiggio recalls that Rampazzi was completely absorbed by her new musical project: "She even ate alone, or even did not eat at all. She was interested in Prosdocimi's laboratory and the sounds that she could hear there. She was also very close to Prosdocimi because he loved music and they both shared an interest in the Potere Operaio (Worker Power) group" (Chiggio, personal communication, February 21, 2008).

Prosdocimi, who currently lives in Tunisia and creates design furniture, remembers that summer vividly. He had a small laboratory, very well equipped, with several employees. Regarding Rampazzi, he recalled: "I knew her more as a result of our mutual political interest than for artistic or musical reasons (I personally prefer and love jazz and classical music). We used to distribute political leaflets in and around Padova. I remember she came to record some sounds, that she wanted to use for a musical piece. There was a young employee who helped her in the recording sessions. He was interested in music and recording techniques. I don't remember his name. I remember that summer intensely. We had great barbecues" (Prosdocimi, personal communication, May 31, 2019).

Taras is a tribute to a city, to that summer, and—as concerns the concrete sound materials—to the sounds Rampazzi could hear in that jewelry laboratory.

Sources

My study of Rampazzi's collection, held by the University of Padua, has given me insights into the story of this piece. There exist two audio sources of *Taras*. I will call them source 1 and source 2 (annotations are translated from Italian). Source 1 is quadraphonic, and source 2 is stereophonic (of course, I discovered this only after the digitization of the tape). Source 1 contains only the piece *Taras*. Source 2 contains three pieces: *Insiemi*, *Taras*, and *Computer 1800*. None of the sources have ever been published.[9] A third audio source (source 3) is an excerpt (the beginning of the piece) aired during the program *Le nuove frontiere della musica*, given to me by Tonino Delfino.[10] Table 11.1 provides information on these sources.

The following are the transcribed texts of the documents included within the boxes of source 1 (see Figure 11.1 for the first page of three) and source 2. One thing worth noting right away is the discrepancy among the dates. This is a clear and common problem in all material sources pertaining to Rampazzi's life and work, as can be seen in many passages of this chapter. Rampazzi was more interested in her present and future experiences than in the past, of which she maintained conscious of the general facts but not the precise chronology.

Table 11.1

Audio sources for Rampazzi's *Taras su tre dimensioni*

Source 1 (TRC): quadraphonic	Location: case no. 1/4
	Tape no.: 2 (my numbering created in 2001)
	Medium: magnetic tape
	Annotations on the box/packet [handwritten; Rampazzi's calligraphy]
	[Front of the box]
	Title: *Taras su 3 dimensioni*
	Author: *NPS*
	Duration: *11'05"*
	Date: *December 1971*
	Tracks: *Stereo* [sic]
	Reel-to-reel tape speed: *19 cm/s*
	[Spine of the box]
	Original / Original version not "stereo-phonized" / Copy on 4 tracks, 1984
	[Back of the box]
	Taranto 1971—Padua
	Annotation on the magnetic tape [Rampazzi's handwriting]
	Taras / 1971 / Stereo [sic] / 19 cm/s / original version
	Additional notes
	The box contains three small photocopies of a handwritten document, with Rampazzi's handwriting, dated December 1982 (See figure 11.1). The original manuscript is held in the archive.
	The digitization is named R02 by Laboratorio Mirage.
Source 2 (TRC): stereophonic	Location: case no. 1/4
	Tape no.: 19 (my numbering created in 2001)
	Medium: magnetic tape
	Annotations on the box/packet [handwritten; Rampazzi's calligraphy]
	[Front of the box]
	Title: *Insiemi / Taras / Vade Mecum*
	Author: *TR / NPS*
	Duration:—— [not mentioned]
	Date:—— [not mentioned]
	Tracks: *Stereo*
	Reel-to-reel tape speed: *19 cm/s*
	[Spine of the box]
	Insiemi / Taras / Vade Mecum
	Additional notes:
	The box contains one handwritten document, in Rampazzi's handwriting.
	The digitization is named R19 by Laboratorio Mirage.
Source 3 (radio program)	Location: my personal archive (and Tonino Delfino's archive)
	Medium: digital file
	Typology: Excerpt (first minutes of the piece) aired during the program *Le nuove frontiere della musica* [New Frontiers of Music], spring 1985
	Digitization made by Tonino Delfino.

Annex to Source 1 [my translation from Italian]

[first sheet]

Taranto—Padua 1973 (9?) [blue ball-point pen]

Taras a 3 dimensioni [*sic*]
This work that belongs to the archaic epoch [she inserted here "but also heroic"] of electronic music belongs more or less to the era of concrete music, but it also exceeds its limits and stands perhaps as *unique* in the production of that time. Sure enough, the RAI, by broadcasting it (1968? [*sic*]), gave proof of courage, [a courage] that it has now completely lost. In fact, this is a piece of primitive and savage brutality. There was no attempt to mediate the three dimensions, concrete—electronic—computer, indeed it even accentuated the very hard impact that

[second sheet]

is happening in the opposition between one dimension and the other. Concrete signals bring us back to the animal, still not human, of the stone age, in which the struggle with the adverse forces of nature took place on the basis of the ~~strength~~ [*sic*, strikethrough] necessity, brute and muscular—without adapted tools, without conscious purposes. Electronic music makes us jump over the eras—men own and construct sophisticated instruments and not for principles of self-preservation but for pure phonic delight. Their singing has no practical goals—it is an end in itself—signals always belong to the callback, ~~but~~ [*sic*, strikethrough]

[third sheet]

and are repetitive, but their timbre must be attractive for itself and undergo subtle variations.—At this point we are doing again another big jump, and from the terrestrial human dimension, we are passing without mediation to signals that already are way beyond our known speed and space.—They are suspended from the ether—they dance vertically and explore the whole present acoustic space with the suggestion or hypothesis of the existence of other worlds where communications have meaning that we still do not decipher, where the evolution of men into robot has already occurred.

Dec. 1982

Compositional Process

According to oral sources and my hypotheses, Rampazzi recorded the concrete material used in *Taras* during summer 1971. Unfortunately, I was not able to establish whether she returned to Padua to compose the electronic parts (with oscillators, filters, etc.) in her home studio, where the NPS worked, or whether instead she had previously prepared these two materials and did not put them together until the fall.

Annex to Source 2 (Rampazzi's handwriting; the original is in English)

For Madrid [in Italian: per Madrid; the reason of this inscription is not clear]

I think it is better to say something else about "Insiemi" "Taras" "Computer 1800."

The form of Insiemi is: A B AB C ABC. At the beginning the A and B are opposed: the [first is] more heavy and aggressive, the other lighter and lyrical.

The third almost tonal is a kind of catholic element, finally the three are "together," a single Insieme.

Taras on three dimensions is the first and surely the last attempt to work on three dimensions with nothing in common: concrete, electronic and computer music. The aim was to enhance the difference and nevertheless to compose something organized.

In Computer 1800 only the duration of the signals is focused; the form is traditional: a mirror form.

We cannot account for many of the decisions, ideas, and thought processes that went into the creation of *Taras*. However, Rampazzi's short writings (mentioned earlier) are illuminating. At least it is possible to know what she wants us to hear—the "battle" between the concrete, the analog, and the computer sounds—more specifically, the animal and prehistoric level (that corresponds to concrete sounds) with brute and muscular stratagems; a more sophisticated level, where pleasure and delight are self-referential and one can take pure gratification in listening to the analog electronic sound; and finally, the computer era represented by cyborg entities, where sounds are still not completely clear to our comprehension but will win over the two others.

What follows is Rampazzi's presentation of *Taras* given during the radio program *Le nuove frontiere della musica* in 1985.

Taras is the name of Taranto. This is a rather autobiographical story, because I was in Taranto without my instruments and I was quite unhappy. I had a friend who had this mania for recording natural sounds. He used to go into the fields during the night, he recorded crickets. But he was a jeweller and he had a laboratory with many motors and machines. It was them I was interested in, not so much in crickets. So I went to the factory, and I started recording sounds that I thought to be useful in one composition, and had concrete character. I had been somewhat against the concrete element until that time, as scarcely controllable, but in this piece I had already planned to use three dimensions: the concrete one, and I could of course not neglect it; the electronic one as an almost romantic element; and the computer one which was the final stage, the one which would prevail over the other two. (Rampazzi 1985)

It is worth noting that Rampazzi is not interested in soundscape recording, but on the contrary in the sounds of machines. She also romanticizes her story somewhat by making us believe that the person who helped her make the field recording was the same person who owned the factory. According to Vittorio Prosdocimi (the craftsman jeweler), one of his employees helped her.

Because written sources do not refer to it, the typology of concrete sounds is not completely evident. It could have been an aesthetic choice not to reveal them; nonetheless, Rampazzi claims that she specifically decided not to transform them in any way, leaving us the pleasure of source bonding any concrete sound: "Here you will listen to an alternation of noises from motors from the factory, that naturally I recorded isolated and I decided not to manipulate at all, in order to emphasize even more the impact force of the three dimensions. The concrete level stays just concrete" (Rampazzi 1985).

I have asked Prosdocimi to recollect what machines and tools he used at the time (Prosdocimi, personal communication, May 31, 2019). He told me that he used

> a centrifuge for blending gold or silver; this machine used to make a lot of noise, particularly in the starting phase;
> a jeweler working counter: here lay a blow torch with continuous fire used for welding gold and silver; the blow torch produced a very fascinating hiss;
> hammers and files, to smooth and polish jewels; these tools inevitably produce beating, rhythms, or flutters and scrapings;
> mechanical presses, lathes, and sandblasting machines.

My analysis tried to detect concrete sounds and their provenance.[11] Analog sounds have the same characteristics we found in previous analog pieces. The likelihood is that Rampazzi reused materials produced earlier. Chiggio recalls that, "We used to experiment and produce several tapes when working on a piece, or sound objects. If we liked something, we kept it and used it. The discarded sounds would end up as functional music, for example soundtracks. Teresa would also stretch previous discarded material" (Chiggio, personal communication, February 21, 2008).

Analog sounds used in *Taras* were therefore produced with the NPS instruments. At the time, Rampazzi used oscillators, impulse generators, and filters. She owned two two-track tape recording machines, a Sony 777 and a Sony 521, and two Revoxes, two low-frequency EICO generators, and one long-wave radio receiver for colored noise (Chiggio, personal communication, February 21, 2008). Alvise Vidolin (her collaborator during the second phase of the collective group, from 1968) specifies that in 1970 they had "six oscillators with manual control, six oscillators for frequency modulation, a white noise generator, an octave filter, a filter with changeable band, an amplitude modulator, a time-controlled sound gate, a reverberator, a 10-channel mixer, an audio signal switchboard, four tape recorders, a stereo amplifier and a frequency meter" (Vidolin 1989). Renato Tassinari, another collaborator from 1968 to 1972, says he had set up some oscillators for Rampazzi to produce glissandi (Tassinari, personal communication, July 2, 2008). Tassinari also recalls they had a problem with a constant hiss produced by cables. He equipped the studio with a filter to cut this hiss over 10,000 Hz, adding, "However, this would not have seriously compromised music creation, because of the threshold of normal human hearing, which loses precision in high frequencies" (Tassinari, personal communication, July 2, 2008). This technical (and historical) fact is confirmed in figures 11.2 and 11.3, where the highest frequencies of the spectra reach only 8,000 Hz.

Lastly, computer sounds were almost certainly the same ones Rampazzi was experimenting with in Pisa at the Centro Nazionale Universitario per il Calcolo Elettronico (CNUCE-CNR, Consiglio Nazionale delle Ricerche), an Italian national research laboratory. In fact, in 1972, right after *Taras*, she would complete *Computer 1800*—her first computer music piece, even before the opening of the CSC—during her visit to her friend Pietro Grossi. *Computer 1800* is important in this context because it allows me to establish the compositional process of the digital sounds used in *Taras*. The same sounds are recognizable in both pieces. *Computer 1800* was "realized at the CNR with the program PLAY 1800 on an IBM system 1800,"[12] with an alternation or fluctuation of fragments of extremely short sounds and longer fragments (from 1/200 of a second to a few seconds), hence from "noise" to "notes." Grossi was experimenting and programming in deferred time using an IBM 360/67 (with a program called DCMP, Digital Computer Music Program, which produced square-wave monophonic sequences), an IBM 1800 (with a program called PLAY 1800, which allowed control over timbre and loudness), and an S/7 with a D/A converter (he had also already started to use real-time computer synthesis) (Bertini 2007, 102–104; Leonello Tarabella, personal communication, August 7, 2019). Sounds similar to the ones used by Rampazzi in *Computer 1800* and *Taras*—made with the PLAY 1800—are part of a series of sound examples by Pietro Grossi published in 1972 by Fonos Musical Editions in a double LP called *Computer Music* (a demonstration of works made by Grossi).

The Analysis

Taras, like most other pieces of electromagnetic tape or fixed media, does not have a score. The two unpublished recordings (sources 1 and 2) and source 3 (broadcast on the radio) are the only texts that can be analyzed. Hence, it is unavoidable to take into consideration only the recording (or better, the digitization of the tapes) and thus the sonogram, a two-dimensional representation of frequency and amplitude as a function of time that helps match the aural analysis with the actual depiction of the signal.[13]

My methodological approach is based on philology, historical facts, and documentation. In fact, while Robert Cogan and Pozzi Escot pioneered the use of the sonogram for analysis (and let us not of course forget the work by Emile Leipp and the spectral composers who used the sonogram for compositional purposes), the analyst is still important for understanding the sonogram's meaning. As Cogan and Escot detail: "Spectrum photos display sonic formations vividly, but they do not quite speak for themselves (a tempting illusion). The commentaries, therefore, direct the reader's attention to those elements that are essential for an understanding of the photos" (Cogan and Escot 1984, 5). This is why a combination of several different approaches is best, in my opinion.

My analysis has tried to correlate spectrograms with my perception in order to discriminate where concrete, analog, and computer sounds occur. I also have tried to understand the identifiable source-bound elements in the concrete parts.

Audio Source of Reference

Documentation, archiving, and preservation are not priorities for many composers. Rampazzi was not alone in this respect. She was not precise in writing titles or dates or in cataloging her work, because she was simply not interested (she sometimes even altered dates and facts, as we read in the box of source 1). However, when studying her music, this becomes a serious complication. *Taras* is conserved in three different sources. Alas, they are all audibly different. The first step in doing an analysis of *Taras* has to be to choose the most appropriate audio source of reference.

In source 1, the quadraphonic version, *Taras* is 11 minutes 23 seconds as measured from the beginning of its digitization by Mirage laboratory to the end of the final decay of the last sound. The audio file has a six-second silence at the beginning. This means that the piece is 11 minutes 17 seconds. Figure 11.2 presents the spectrogram of

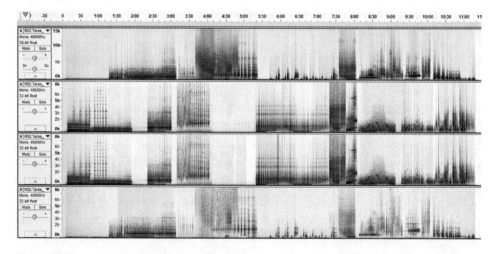

Figure 11.2
Taras su 3 dimensioni, quadraphonic version (source 1); channel from top to bottom: LF (left front), RF (right front), RR (right rear), LR (left rear) (Teresa Rampazzi Collection, University of Padua; digitization by Laboratorio Mirage, Udine).

the entire piece. The four channels were realized separately for reproduction through amplifier and speaker systems; each track was named differently by the author: LF (left front), LR (left rear), RF (right front), RR (right rear). The order of the four tracks in figure 11.2 is arranged as follows from the top down: LF, RF, RR, LR.

In source 2, the stereophonic version, *Taras* is 11 minutes 8 seconds as measured from the beginning of its digitization by Mirage laboratory to the end of the final decay of the last sound. The audio file is the one I selected from the entire tape, which contains three pieces: *Insiemi*, *Taras*, and *Vade Mecum*. *Taras* starts with two seconds of silence, which means the piece is 11 minutes 6 seconds.

It goes without saying that the durations are different: 11 minutes 17 seconds (source 1) versus 11 minutes 8 seconds (source 2). Even if we merge the left front and rear channels of source 1 down to a single left channel and the right front and rear channels down to a single right channel for a stereophonic file (with software such as Audacity), it is clear that the audio content is altered. This difference is less in the timbre domain—which we can recognize and is preserved in the micro and macro forms—than in spatialization. This implies two things. First, source 2 is not a direct mix-down to a stereo "copy" of the piece, and its spatialization is meant as a creative act. Second, from a compositional viewpoint, source 1 was the first to be created, with a precise idea of timbral content and of its distribution around the four channels, which in fact makes a very separate positioning of the three typologies of sounds (concrete, electronic, and digital). Only later did Rampazzi produce the stereophonic version, with new spatial movements, and a less radical distribution than the one in source 1. These observations and others (discussed later) have led me to base my analysis on source 2, the stereophonic version.

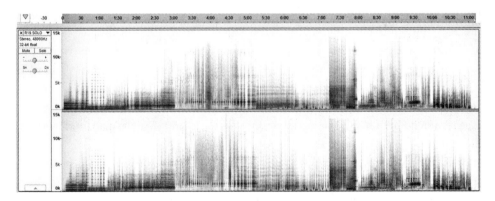

Figure 11.3
Taras su 3 dimensioni, stereophonic version (source 2) (Teresa Rampazzi Collection, University of Padua; digitization by Laboratorio Mirage, Udine).

Source 3 is the excerpt from the program *Le nuove frontiere della musica* that I selected from one of the 10 episodes aired in spring 1985. This source, the beginning of the piece, runs 2 minutes 33 seconds. The tuning is imperceptibly flat compared to source 2, but the audio content is definitely the same. This slight flatness could be a problem of digitization or could be embedded in the original version aired during the program.

Rampazzi's approach to spatialization of sound is worth mentioning to fully understand the discrepancy in audio sources, particularly between sources 1 and 2. Vidolin (via e-mail, March 25, 2009) recalls that Rampazzi owned two or even three TEAC tape machines. She made the spatialization autonomously, but she preferred an acousmatic listening experience during concerts. Her musical works would thus be diffused without any further changes, because she disliked the human gesture in live electronic music (as she disliked improvising electronic groups; she was part of one, the Arke Sinth, with Vidolin and De Poli, but only participated for a very short period).

If we believe what is written on the spine of the box of source 1 ("Original / Original version not 'stereo-phonized' [*sic*] / Copy on 4 tracks, 1984"), this is the original version. This is an important fact that implies that *Taras* was originally realized for quadraphonic listening. Not until later did Rampazzi realize a stereophonic version for more traditional listening venues (a radio broadcast and a conventional concert hall). We might thus conjecture, with some certainty, that source 1 is the original version, the *Ur-Text*, which reflects the composer's intention (although the tape is a copy from the original, as we read in the box with Rampazzi's handwriting). In fact, it was in the early 1970s that she started producing four-track works. Hence, source 2 is a variant, a new realization from the primary original version.

What interests me here also is the fact that the stereophonic version is not simply a mix-down of tracks but a meticulous work of reinterpretation from the original mono tracks. Mauro Graziani—one of Rampazzi's students from 1975, who later worked as a composer/researcher at the CSC in the production of *Prometeo* by Luigi Nono and became a composer and electronic music teacher on his own—was not working with Rampazzi on *Taras*. However, he recalls that "even later in the 1970s, spatialization was made directly on tape. When we were students, we had two TEAC 4-channel reel to reel tape recorders. With her, we set up the sounds on tracks and then we made rudimentary movements. It could happen that we started from monophonic tracks and left them as they were. Sometimes we realized the movements from the single tracks initially in a stereo dimension, and afterwards again from two already spatialized tracks" (Graziani, personal communication, March 25, 2009). Taking into account Graziani's words, it is likely that *Taras*'s spatialization may also be the result of the same process performed by Rampazzi in 1971. A few years later, in the late 1970s, Graziani continues, "we did not have personal computer[s] with sound cards. So everything was made onto the magnetic tape, and manually. She was very good with mixing and cutting the magnetic tapes. I also remember that we jotted down some schemes with the sound movements, but unfortunately we discarded everything after we were done" (Graziani, personal communication, March 25, 2009). Vidolin likewise recalls that sometimes they made sketches with movements (always thrown away) and at other times they improvised the spatialization.

The spatialization in source 2 is very fast, at the beginning even mind-blowing (the sound travels around with sudden and alternating movements, jumping from the left to the right channel so much it almost pulls me off balance). This leads me to believe that Rampazzi's spatialization in *Taras* was improvised. On the other hand, her complex spatialization can be considered in the light of her aesthetic thought. As Chiggio recalls, Rampazzi had always been interested in Medieval and Renaissance music. Chiggio recalls that they used to listen to the Notre Dame school of polyphony, the madrigals, and the complex polyphony of Gesualdo da Venosa. A demonstration of this cultural and musical interest is found in a passage from one of Rampazzi's essays: "In a mass by Josquin Des Prez in which the behavior of each individual voice is highly differentiated, complex, though coordinated, what matters for the ear is not so much the individual behavior but the overall effect" (Rampazzi 1977, 458).

For the purpose of my analysis, I consider source 2, the stereophonic version, the same that was aired during the program *Le nuove frontiere della musica*, since the fact that it was broadcast implies that it can be considered an official release. Yet, I also refer to source 1 when appropriate.

Form, Typology of Sounds, and Spatialization
Taras continues without interruption from the beginning to the end, in an unbroken flux of sound. In spite of this, six parts can be identified in relation to the use of different sound materials. The battle between analog, concrete, and computer sounds actually begins very early in the piece.

Part I extends from 0:02 (the piece starts after two seconds of silence) to 1:12 (figure 11.4). *Taras* opens with analog sounds. A drone enriched with inharmonic contours centered on A3 (215 Hz) begins in the left channel, followed after three seconds in the right channel and continuously passing from left to right until a slow glissando of three seconds at 0:35–0:38; the same drone starts again at 0:41, an octave lower (A2 at around 110 Hz). After 8 seconds from the beginning, a recurrent and reverberated D-flat4 at around 280 Hz, progressively shorter, begins to emerge in iteration. After the glissando, the D-flat jumps an octave higher. All this part stays on the left channel (front and rear) in source 1.

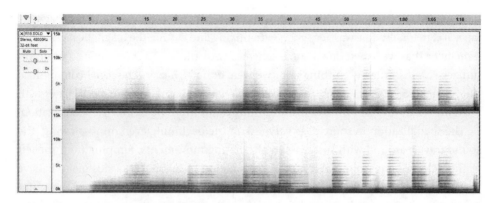

Figure 11.4
Part I of *Taras su tre dimensioni*, from 0:02 to 1:12.

At 1:12, the concrete material makes its appearance (figure 11.5). Part II begins at 1:12 and ends at 3:03. It is characterized by an accumulation of isolated and short objects, like the falling of stones, or perhaps the use of hammers, among the tools Prosdocimi indicated he used in his factory. At 2:40, there appear a series of sounds of file tools, used for filing and polishing external or internal surfaces of jewels; it is a fascinating series of flutters and scrapings. Hammer (or stone falling) sound objects continue in an accumulation of polyphonies. During the entire section, the drone from part I continues with an A2 pitch (around 110 Hz). This drone is slowly filtered and moved from the center to the left and right. It disappears toward 1:48 and reemerges, this time centered on A4 (around 432 Hz). My listening has identified this drone as an analog sound, but this could also be the sound of a machine that produces continuous sound. The subsection between 2:40 and 2:54 is the richest part in terms of polyphony and saturation of spectra. In source 1, there is silence in the left channels (front and rear) from 2:00 to 2:23.

Part III (figure 11.6) starts at 3:03 and ends at 5:16. This is the central part of the piece. Here, the analog but above all concrete and computer dimensions are struggling together and against each other. This is also a very dense part. In fact, whereas parts I and II are silent above 10,000 Hz (we should recall the filter introduced by Tassinari in order to avoid the hiss), in part III the spectral window, especially when computer sounds emerge, expands over 10,000 Hz and reaches 15,000 Hz. Of course, the creation of digital sound in a digital environment permitted production of more "clean" sounds (and the analog tapes after the D/A conversion contain sounds up to 15,000 Hz).

Part III is divided into sections A, B, and C; from my listening, I think I can state that it is composed only from concrete and computer sounds. Section A starts with

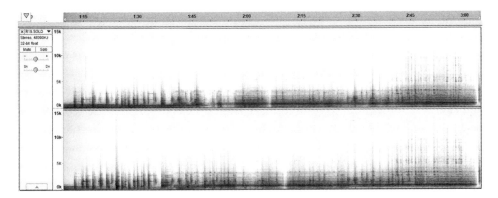

Figure 11.5
Part II of *Taras su tre dimensioni*, from 1:12 to 3:03.

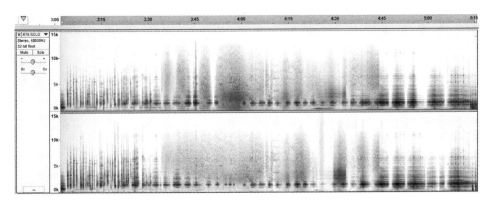

Figure 11.6
Part III of *Taras su tre dimensioni*, from 3:03 to 5:16.

resounding objects (metal cups, chains, stones, small objects) falling and slamming against each other, from 3:03 to 3:34. From 3:24 to 3:34, we can hear drone sounds certainly produced by machines in the background (possibly the blowtorch). In section B, from 3:34 to 4:24, computer sounds emerge, while concrete sounds continue as a counterpoint, and a low sound of a machine (centrifuge?) plays slow, repetitive "notes." The computer sounds are identical to those we hear in Rampazzi's work *Computer 1800* from the same period; that is, an alternation of fragments of extremely short sounds (almost granulated; at 3:34 it is reminiscent of the sound of a buzzer) and longer fragments (from 1/200 of a second to a few seconds). Section B is reminiscent of a counterpoint between slow, long events and very fast, high-pitched computer sounds. Section C starts at 4:24.

Here, small, isolated, very high-pitched computer sounds disappear gradually. What appears here are clouds of sounds produced by machines (presses or lathes?), each event separated by silence. In source 1 (quadraphonic original version), there is complete silence in the left channels (front and rear) from 4:00 to 5:20.

Part IV (figure 11.7) has a completely new character: it is a dialog between concrete and analog sounds, and it has a rhythmic charm. It extends from 5:13 to 8:01. At the beginning of the section, beating hammers (I think) alternate between the left and right channels, slowly decreasingly in tempo. At 5:45, the analog microtonal pitches return. They oscillate between a sinusoidal bichord and a sinusoidal pitch (almost a modal suggestion, on a defective scale). The bichord is formed with a B-flat4 (around 470 Hz) and an E-flat4 (around 320 Hz); the second pitch is formed (again, as in part I) by the D-flat4 at around 280 Hz. This is realized in continuous interplay with the beating hammers, which gradually continue their *rallentando*. At 7:13, a new section starts with fast groups of seven notes (beatings, like a hammer) in a loop, sometimes formed by six beats, at other times by eight; they are filtered over time and accompanied by the two bichords.

Part V is a quieter part (8:01–10:03) (figure 11.8). It alternates computer sounds (this time longer, similar to what Rampazzi described in *Computer 1800* as "from noise to note") and concrete objects (saw blades, scrapers, etc.). This part is not reverberated.

The sixth and final part is the dreamiest and most reverberated section. It is also the shortest. To me, it stands alone and anticipates further pieces by Rampazzi, those that she realized using frequency modulation. In fact, this part is realized with slow and low masses of sound. The closure of the piece seems to stand isolated from the rest of

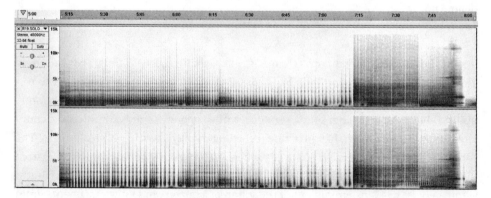

Figure 11.7
Part IV of *Taras su tre dimensioni*, from 5:13 to 8:01.

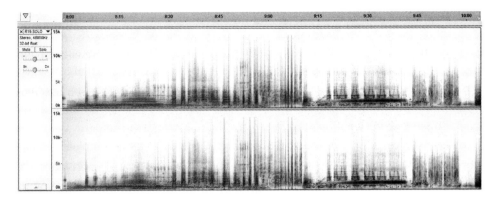

Figure 11.8
Part V of *Taras su tre dimensioni*, from 8:01 to 10:03.

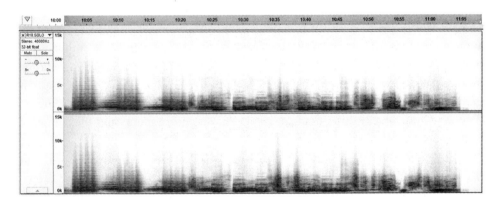

Figure 11.9
Part VI of *Taras su tre dimensioni*, from 10:03 to 11:06.

the work, almost as an open question, a doubt Rampazzi has over the predominance of concrete, analog, and computer materials. I am not sure that computer sounds win the battle, as she says in her writing; at least this is not clear from the aesthetic result of this finale.

Taras su tre dimensioni has specific parts centered around the idea of repetition of rhythms, often gradually decelerating. Unfortunately, spectrogram visualization bears the typical spectrogram problem: accuracy in the frequency domain, which does not correspond to the time domain, and vice versa. This analysis follows the overall sound material treatment and macro form. Further analysis would be appropriate in order to better investigate spectra, sound objects, and spatialization.

Conclusions

Taras is the only piece in Rampazzi's catalog that includes concrete sounds, as she strenuously stresses in many statements, as though it were almost a misstep or a failed experiment. It is so unique that in 1980 she did not include it in a list of "selected works" from 1968 to 1980 ("Lista delle opere principali composte da Teresa Rampazzi 1968-1978-1980," unpublished document, TRC).

In fact, only later, during the late 1980s and 1990s, does she use a completely different concrete material—the voice. In works such as *Almost a Haiku* (1987) and *Polifonie di Novembre* (1988), the voice recites excerpts of texts or poems, with a small experiment early in 1975 called *Canti per Checca* or *Canti di Checca* (again, Rampazzi's precision is poor when we read the titles written on magnetic tapes). *Canti per Checca* used the voice of her daughter Francesca, who sang long notes in the high register to make a mixture with sinusoidal sounds.

Taras also seems to translate the ideological engagement of Rampazzi in the creation of sounds. To her, the electronic medium was an instrument to unhinge the traditional, stagnant (and Catholic, in the particular case of Padua, the city where she lived) Italian musical system (Di Capua 1993; Rampazzi 2007). The NPS manifesto, for example, proclaimed the suppression of old-fashioned musical instruments. Of course, they were not alone in this crusade. Analog electronic instruments and the computer were revolutionary.

There is another component in this ideological battle, however. It must be placed in the political context of the period, the late 1960s to early 1970s. Rampazzi was deeply involved in students' and workers' demonstrations. (Previously, from 1956 to 1960, she also had become a member of another group, Circolo Pozzetto, a cultural and political circle founded by Ettore Luccini, an intellectual engaged in the Communist Federation of Padua). Prosdocimi recalls their mutual active engagement with enthusiasm (Prosdocimi, personal communication, May 31, 2019). Therefore, I propose here that the concrete sounds recorded in a jewelry workshop can by themselves form the idea of an active, operational, and physical commitment in the composition of electronic music.

Notes

1. Analog sounds are made with electronically produced sound. Concrete sounds are realized from recorded sounds as raw material. Computer-made sounds are synthesized by computer algorithms.

2. For more information and writings on and by Teresa Rampazzi, see http://www.teresarampazzi.it/bioteresarampazzi/ , the blog/website I've been curating for almost 12 years.

3. Teresa Rampazzi mentions this anecdote in her interview with Michela Mollia (Mollia 1979, 122). Herbert Eimert's speech ("Probleme der elektronischen Musik," July 21, 1952) is briefly summed up in Trudu (1992, 81) and mentioned in Iddon (2013, xvi).

4. The choice of the name shows a firm decision to eliminate any artistic aspiration. This was pure research, and each result, named "oggetto sonoro" (sound object), would have been anonymous, at least during the first years of activity (1965–1968). These "oggetti sonori" were reminiscent of the Schaefferian sound research (Rampazzi had a copy of the first edition of Schaeffer's *Traité des objets musicaux*, autographed by the author) but were intended to be an evolution, a scientific investigation of sound electronic techniques: timbre, impulses, density of events, and glissandi. Since 1968, when Chiggio left the studio, sound objects began to be signed and started to be real pieces reflecting each single personality (Zattra 2003). Ennio Chiggio says in this regard that "on one hand, collective control was claimed, on the other hand, this was felt to be demeaning for personal freedom and individual creativity, and everybody was reacting more or less 'romantically' to the harsh discipline of the rational postulates of the group" (Chiggio 2002, 1).

5. The collection also contains about 150 tapes with music she received from colleagues and friends, and music she recorded from the Radio Third program of the RAI, the national public broadcasting company of Italy.

6. The lack of scores is typical of her overall production. However, during the period 1965–1972, the NPS members discussed the importance of notation, and they succeeded in creating scores they called Audiogrammi (Audiograms). These scores were schematics with amplitudes, frequencies, and blocks of sounds, similar to Stockhausen's scores made in the Cologne Studio. The Audiogrammi were used as operational schemes but also as graphic and listening scores. They were so precise that Ennio Chiggio has recently been able to resynthesize them with modern software.

7. This unpublished typewritten book *NPS 65–72: Sette anni di attività del gruppo nuove proposte sonore nello studio di fonologia musicale di Padua*, was compiled in January 1977, a few years after the NPS had stopped its activities. It is signed by members Ennio Chiggio, Serenella Marega, Teresa Rampazzi, Giorgio Lovischek, Luciano Menini, Alvise Vidolin, and Giovanni De Poli. It is available at the Library of the Conservatory of Music in Padua.

8. Rampazzi explaining her piece and the audio excerpt that was aired are available at https://soundcloud.com/laura-zattra/teresa-rampazzi-taras-su-tre-dimensioni-presentation-and-audio-excerpt. Delfino says that Rampazzi had just arrived in Bassano del Grappa in October 1984 and asked him to install a small studio in the retirement home where she had recently moved in order to continue her musical activity. He became her assistant. Delfino was working at the Radio Verci in Bassano as technician and curator (Delfino had founded the first free radio in Bassano, called Radio Sturm, in 1975; in 1980, it was incorporated by Verci Publishing Company and became Radio Verci. Radio Verci was closed down in 1985) (Baggio 2019). Delfino recalls that, "We did not want to miss the opportunity to have such a great and important figure in our radio

shows; so the person responsible for the entire radio programming immediately agreed to do this programme and supported us. The episodes started airing in December 1984" (Tonino Delfino, interview with the author in 2007).

9. Only two pieces by Teresa Rampazzi were published during her lifetime: *Fluxus* (1979) and *Atmen noch* (1980), both synthesized with the computer. Other works were broadcast over the radio, along with interviews. One important radio program was the 1993 show *Teresa Rampazzi: Fino all'ultimo suono*, curated by Gianni Di Capua and completely dedicated to Teresa Rampazzi, with interviews with the composer and her collaborators (Di Capua 1993). Starting in 2008, I have curated three issues (CDs and vinyl records) for the Milan-based label Die Schachtel in a project aimed at preserving her music.

10. *Taras* recordings that I used for this analysis (sources 1 and 2) were digitized as part of a project of active preservation of Rampazzi's magnetic tapes, enabled by the musicological and technical consulting of the Mirage Laboratory (University of Udine). Sergio Canazza and Antonio Rodà have been responsible for this project. As Rodà writes, "Special care has been reserved during all the phases necessary for the creation of a digitally preserved copy of the tapes: from the carrier restoration to the documentation of each intervention made, from the playback of the audio signal to the storing of the data on a digital carrier" (Rodà 2008). The digitization of source 3 was realized by Tonino Delfino.

11. The internet shows interesting videos with sound recordings within a jewelry workshop. Examples include "Goldsmith saw," 2015 (https://www.youtube.com/watch?v=7WbWmn5mPZ8) and "Goldsmiths' Fair 2018 (with sound)," 2018 (https://www.youtube.com/watch?v=FebVe5H8ANQ).

12. This presentation text is held at the TRC and in NPS (1977, 111).

13. Historical precedents for the use of sonograms in electroacoustic music are well documented and do not need to be listed. Among the most famous examples, suffice it to cite the founding work in this field by Cogan and Escot (1984), some of the essays contained in Licata (2002), and Simoni (2006) and the software EAnalysis by Pierre Couprie.

References

Baggio, Gianfranco. 2019. "Tonino Delfino, la prima voce bassanese in radio," *Bassano Week*, May 11, p. 9.

Bertini, Gaziano. 2007. "Il terminale musicale polifonico TAU2: Il progetto, la realizzazione e il suo ruolo nella computer music." *Musica/Tecnologia* 1 (1): 97–131.

Chiggio, Ennio. 2002. *Oggetto sonoro*. Lectures. Musica elettronica—Fonologia no. 7. Padua: Edizioni multimediali del Barbagianni.

Cogan, Robert, and Pozzi Escot. 1984. *New Images of Musical Sound*. Cambridge, MA: Harvard University Press.

Di Capua, Gianni. 1993. "Teresa Rampazzi: Fino all'ultimo suono." Radio program, RAI-Radio3, March 10.

Iddon, Martin. 2013. *New Music at Darmstadt: Nono, Stockhausen, Cage and Boulez.* Cambridge: Cambridge University Press.

Licata, Thomas. 2002. *Electroacoustic Music: Analytical Perspectives.* Westport, CT: Praeger.

Mollia, Michela. 1979. "Piccolo discorso con Michela: Teresa Rampazzi." In *Autobiografia della musica contemporanea,* edited by Michela Mollia, 122–126. Cosenza: Lerici.

Morgan, Francis. 2017. "Pioneer Spirits: New Media Representations of Women in Electronic Music History." *Organised Sound* 22 (2): 238–249.

NPS (Nuove Proposte Sonore). 1977. *NPS 65–72: Sette anni di attività del gruppo nuove proposte sonore nello studio di fonologia musicale di Padua.* Unpublished typescript (available at the Library of the Conservatory "C. Pollini" in Padua).

Rampazzi, Teresa. 1977. "One Parameter Adrift, Another on the Horizon." In *Music/Technology I,* edited by Paolo Zavagna, 458–465. Firenze: Firenze University Press. Originally published in Italian as "Un parametro alla deriva: Un altro in avanzata." In *Quaderni del Conservatorio "G. Rossigni" di Pesaro,* Tecnomusica/1, Creazione musicale e tecnologia, Pesaro, May 1977, 1–17. Original typewritten source dated April 1973 (TRC collection, University of Padua).

Rampazzi, Teresa. 1985. Presentation of *Taras* given during the radio program *Le nuove frontiere della musica.* Bassano, Italy: Radio Verci.

Rampazzi, Teresa. 2007. "Raccolta di articoli." In *Music/Technology I,* edited by Paolo Zavagna, 183–244. Firenze: Firenze University Press.

Rodà, Antonio. 2008. "Sound Tracks to Be Rediscovered." Article in the booklet of the CD *Teresa Rampazzi: Musica endoscopica,* DS9. Milan: Die Schachtel.

Simoni, Mary Hope. 2006. *Analytical Methods of Electroacoustic Music.* Abingdon, UK: Routledge.

Trudu, Antonio. 1992. *La "scuola" di Darmstadt: I Ferienkurse dal 1948 a oggi.* Milan: Ricordi Unicopli.

Vidolin, Alvise. 1989. "Contatti elettronici: La linea veneta nella musica della nuova avanguardia." In *Venezia Arti 1989/3,* Bollettino del Dipartimento di Storia e Critica delle Arti dell'Università di Venezia, 97–107.

Zattra, Laura. 2002. "Storia documenti e testimonianze." In Vent'anni di musica elettronica all'università di Padova. Il centro di sonologia computazionale, edited by Sergio Durante and Laura Zattra, 13–102. Padua: CLEUP / Palermo: CIMS, Archivio Musiche del XX secolo.

Zattra, Laura. 2003. "Teresa Rampazzi: Pioneer of Italian Electronic Music." In *Proceedings of the 14th Colloquium on Musical Informatics,* edited by Nicola Bernardini, Francesco Giomi, Nicola Giosmin, 11–16. Florence: AIMI (Associazione Informatica Musicale Italiana). .

Zattra, Laura. 2007. "The Assembling of *Stria* by John Chowning: A Philological Investigation." *Computer Music Journal* 31 (3): 38–64.

Zattra, Laura. 2015. "Génétiques de la computer music." In *Genèses Musicales,* edited by Nicolas Donin, Almuth Grésillon, and Jean-Louis Lebrave, 213–238. Paris: Presses universitaires de Paris Sorbonne.

12 Luciano Berio and Cathy Berberian's *Visage*: Revisiting Late Modernist Composition and the New Vocality

Juliana Snapper

Introduction

In 1961, Luciano Berio and Cathy Berberian created *Visage*, a work for magnetic tape using electronically generated sounds and studio recordings of Berberian's voice. It was the last piece Berio made at the Studio di Fonologia in Milan and the final collaboration between the two as a married couple. The work of both artists, together and separately, is well known and solidly fixed in the canon of post–World War II music, but to some degree, that fixity has also resulted in a kind of stuckness regarding the analysis of their work and has left some key aspects of their work together unexplored. This chapter explores the creation of *Visage* as an extension of Berio's compositional ideas. I examine the collaboration between Berio and Berberian and its upset of traditional compositional processes. I detail the charged reception of their work together and those aspects that render *Visage* distinct from other electronic and experimental vocal works. Within this, I look at Berberian's ideas about experimental vocalisms and the essential relation to the bel canto instrument as a component of meaning. Through this analysis, I hope to lay the groundwork for new ways forward in our understanding of creative collaboration between Berio and Berberian, its implications for contemporary vocality, and its relevance to a broader culture of radical performance in the second half of the twentieth century.

Visage has not received the kind of attention that Berio's other works have. The work is infrequently addressed in any depth in critical literature or featured in fixed-media concerts. It was released on vinyl a few times in the 1960s (mostly as B-sides to his other works) and reemerged on CD, mostly in reissues and electronic music compilations early in the new millennium. Most of the reissues are out of print, and the piece has only a trace presence on common web-based streaming sources such as YouTube and Spotify. It takes a little digging to find *Visage*, whereas other works by both artists are copiously available. *Visage* is a challenging listen, but that quality in itself does not particularly distinguish it from other contemporary works. So what makes *Visage* the exception?

Berio intended *Visage* as a work for radio. However, immediately after its premiere on Italian National Radio (RAI), public reaction led to its immediate ban from the airwaves for its "obscenity." The censure of experimental work from the radio was not so exceptional at the time: that same year, a work by Antonin Artaud on the topic of a final judgment of God was also banned. What makes the censorship of *Visage* so strange is that there is essentially no text, no narrative, no quotations or overt references, and no visible body. What is there to censor? What is it that is obscene? *Visage* evidently upset listeners in a way that either personally offended them or seemed to breach the boundaries of social decency. David Osmond-Smith writes that the reactions of audiences during subsequent live presentations of the fixed-media work validated RAI's call to some extent (Osmond-Smith 2004). Somehow, *Visage* was abject in a way that other similar pieces were not.

A Brief Tour of *Visage*

Visage crystallizes the tension between the contextless sound source and the excessively connotative source. Like many early adopters of electronic music, Berio was fascinated by the intersection of voice and electronic music. New sound technologies offer(ed) the capacity for generating as yet unheard sounds, devoid of reference or context. As Berio describes it, "In electronic music … we use sound as an acoustical phenomenon regardless of its origin. Superficially, it might appear as though this would deprive it of an important characteristic—its meaning. In reality, however, exactly the opposite is the case: when analysed, new strata of meaning come to the surface" (Muller 1997, 16–20).

Berio's fascination with the voice, on the other hand, lay in its resistance to abstraction. He described the traces of the everyday as "dirt": sonic residues tracked onto the musical surface by the body burdened by day-to-day human existence. As he explains, "I have always been very sensitive, perhaps overly so, to the excess of connotations that the voice carries, whatever it is doing. From the grossest of noises to the most delicate of singing, the voice always means something, always refers beyond itself and creates a huge range of associations: cultural, musical, emotive, physiological, or drawn from everyday life, etc." (Berio 1985, 141–143).

The compositional components of *Visage* are identifiable through the sonic gestures of voice and electronics, the affective flow of the voice, and the dramaturgical axes of the voice and electronics, both individually and in relation to one another. I suggest a partial list of these intersecting elements in table 12.1.

Table 12.1

Intersecting elements of the compositional components of *Visage*

Sonic axes	Vocal palette	Affective palette
Pitched/Unpitched	Breath: panting, gasping, sighing	Tentative
Aspirate/Focused timbre	Phonemes, Vocables	Driven
Sustained/Percussive	Laughter (varied)	Straining
Atmospheric/Eventful	Crying (varied)	Raging
Sudden or gradual onset/offset	Moans/Whines	Wounded
Organic/Inorganic	Vocal	Aroused
Texture: single or multiple layers	Speech and speechlike sounds	Amused
Independent/Integrated	(varied)	Anguished
Processed/Unprocessed	Humming	Taunting
Panning	Singing (bel canto)	Imploring
Perceived spatial proximity to listener	Silence	Playful
		Chatty
		Curious
		Secretive
		Conjuring

Interactive axes	Dramaturgical axes
Instigative/Reactive	In control/Out of control
Independent	Performative/Unobserved
Parallel activity	Acting/Reacting
Fusion	
Alternating	
Atmospheric	

Visage began with a series of studio improvisations by Berberian that Berio recorded and then edited, adding electronic sounds generated in the Studio Fonologia. Berio reorders and resituates the performed content but leaves the raw immediacy of the voice intact. His manipulation of the recorded voice is limited to placement of the sonic body in space (degrees of reverberation, panning), some layering, and speeding up or slowing down of the magnetic tape. Berberian's voice maintains the central role in the work as subject, which, in Berio's words, is "constantly amplified and commented upon by a very close relationship, almost an organic exchange, with the electronic sounds" (Berio 1961).

Visage resists linguistic analysis because within its vast array of vocal phenomena there is only one actual word, *Parole*, Italian for "words." Nor is there a consistent musical (melodic, rhythmic, harmonic, or timbral) organization on which to establish a conventional musical analysis. For the most part, the sonic content of the vocal layer is familiar. We know these sounds from our own lived histories. The difficulty arises when we attempt to organize them or even to orient ourselves to their source or context. The nonlanguage that Berberian utters compels the ear to make sense from it, and the rapid shifts of emotional content make that desire more urgent. Beyond wanting to know what she is saying, we want to know why. We want to know what the hell is going on! In this way, the listener is continuously seduced to construct a narrative, to establish character(s), to put a motive behind the varied sonic behaviors, organic and inorganic, only to be frustrated over and over again.

To some extent, the piece is episodic. Distinct sonic dynamics begin to jell, only to pivot into a different expressive texture with varying degrees of abruptness:

(a) At about 6:00, a woman chatters playfully, a little tipsy maybe, to an unheard suitor. "Hmm," she purrs, then giggles, and speaks a challenging "Ohhh?"

(b) A sudden blast of metallic violence lashes in and shots follow. A(nother?) woman's grunts and shrieks follow in agitated retreat.

(c) Her voice is suddenly very close, as if we share a small, dampened room. She whimpers and mutters to herself in soft, hiccupped Italianate syllables.

(d) We are now at around 7:30, or a third of the way, into the piece. We hear another entity but the same voice: laughter, low and mocking, descending into a gravelly fry, echoing from deep in her gullet. Her own overlapping voice sucks in an ingressive growly incantation, uncanny, too fast, not entirely human. A manic whisper of radio static surges into the space around her.

These episodes begin to suggest narrativity of a situational nature, but each emerges after the other from a highly fractured flow, unanchored by any explicit expository structure or coherency of character.

Berio consciously courts the listener's inclination to fill in the gaps left by the author, our ingrained compulsion to generate a story or even to format a genre by which to listen, in essence to "make sense" of the work as a whole. Berio's attention to the way a listener participates in the assignation of meaning to a work derives in part from his well-documented interest in the ideas articulated by his friend and collaborator Umberto Eco; in particular, the concept of the "Opera aperta," or Open Work (Eco 1962), which explores the dynamic relationship between author and reader. The "openness" of the work acknowledges the cues by which an author leads his imagined reader through a text, but more importantly, it makes room for the active subjectivity of the person reading, or in this case listening (the listener's experience, mood, and personal associations), in the formation of meaning in a text as it unfolds. This is not to be confused with indeterminacy in the Cagean sense, or a lazy definition of postmodernism as unlimited possibility. The Open Work is a composed work that recognizes the subjectivity of the reader in the formation of any single "reading" (that is, the reader's reception) of a text or performance.

By organizing the expressive content in such a way that a coherent narrative never quite jells, Berio requires the listener to consciously and continuously reevaluate what is happening. This invokes a kind of crisis of interpretation that the listener must ultimately resolve. In this way, we are not only spectators but also participants, but Berio does not provoke this crisis for its own sake. In a way, he lets us in on the game. At four points in the 21-minute piece, the vocalist utters the word *Parole* to signal, to share with, and to remind the listener of what is in play, why the work happens as it does, and how to listen (or how to avoid getting caught up in any single episode). *Parole*. And all around the word *Parole*, nonwords brim with expressive import.

The notion of the "extraconnotative" voice as a force independent of and constantly in friction with language is reinforced by two distinct episodes that bookend the piece. You can trace the bare physical morphology of the first three minutes with your own mouth. Tap the tip of your tongue against the roof of your mouth, near your gum line. Say [t], "tuh." Now, [d], "duh." Now, [z], "zzzzzz," with your tongue vibrating on your hard palate. Now let your breath out and say [tʃ], "ch," as in "chop," and [ʃ], "shhhh-hhh." Press the back of your tongue up against your tonsils: [k], "kuh," now deeper in, [g], "guh." Berberian draws the building blocks of language into her mouth, first between her tongue and teeth, then trapped against her tonsils, then finally reaching from deep in her throat, engaging her lungs, then her diaphragm, the deep muscles of her core.

The final five minutes of the 21-minute work recall its opening, but now it is the listener who is being consumed. A metallic swarm sneaks in behind an ambivalent aria. Insects? Machines? Voices? Increasing reverberation opens a hollow void in the center of the swarm. Somewhere from the outskirts comes a memory, a trace of the soprano. A bassy vocal droning layer rises up and overtakes the texture, then a slightly higher choir surges in, and then another. An empty, ambivalent "Ahhhhhhhh," a swelling, disembodied, multithroated human/inhuman gullet closes around us and fades. The opening episode enacts the intrusion of language on a single subject's body. The ending shatters subjectivity and swallows us whole.

Beyond a Compositional Assembly Line

Rather than training the listener to hear differently, as other modernist composers sought to do via new tonalities and other explicitly musical (mechanical or syntactic) systems, Berio's work leverages the way we already listen to activate an expanded field of meaning. But more than this, Berio extends the active exchange of creation and receptivity into his creative work with Berberian. We tend to refer to the process of musical composition as a kind of procreative assembly line: the composer has an idea, he notates that idea, he gives the score to a performer, the performer works the musical text into her body, and then she delivers the musical product to an audience. With electronic music, of course, the composer may act as both creative author and manufacturer of the final product, but within that process we generally assume the resulting work is the product of passive machines and sonic objects that the composer manipulates. Berio's work with Berberian, however, complicates any simple understanding of the compositional process. A closer look at the making of *Visage* suggests the extension of Eco's theory of codetermined meaning as it manifests before the audience even gets a shot at it. A play of creativity, receptivity, interpretation, and reinterpretation in the construction of *Visage* allows the full importance of Berio's project to come to light. Osmond-Smith writes, "In Visage, Berio ... dispensed with texts altogether, and allowed Berberian's fertile imagination its head. In the recording studio, she improvised a series of monologues, each based on a repertoire of vocal gesture and phonetic material. ... (One exhausting session was devoted entirely to different types of laughter, an obsession to which Berio was to return in Sequenza III)" (Osmond-Smith 1991, 63). Carol Plantamura adds, "Cathy told me of the making of the monumental tape piece 'Visage' (1961) and how Luciano asked her to go to the Studio di Fonologia in Milano where he asked her to just go into the recording booth and record ... anything ... being born, whatever. And this is what Cathy was really great at: Conjuring! (Plantamura in Snapper 2014, 205–212).

Berbarian's creative agency, until quite recently, was generally ignored or underestimated. Berio names Berberian as the voice of *Visage* and details other works as having been written for her. He also referred to her more than once as his "Second Studio di Fonologia." Yet while it is notable that he recognizes her role as a specific voice and a singular interpreter, we can now see that these are inadequate terms. A muse, a space of experimentation, or an instrument to be played can only inspire or be acted on, not create. But what is authorship if not giving one's "fertile imagination its head" or "conjuring?" To accurately and adequately address Berberian's creative role, we need a better understanding of the spectrum of compositional processes. We need a more nuanced generative taxonomy.

Carol Plantamura, a contemporary and close friend of Berberian, describes the way Berberian would vocalize at home, playing around and improvising while cooking, for example. John Cage's inspiration for *Aria* (1958) came after having dinner at Berio and Berberian's home and hearing her improvise in the kitchen as she worked, jumping genres seamlessly (Plantamura, unpublished, partially reproduced in Snapper 2014). Such accounts suggest that Berberian in fact initiated many works. Plantamura continues:

Stockhausen described hearing a tape of me singing "Sequenza III" that Vinko Globokar had played for him, and told me that he'd felt these were sounds that had come from his (Stockhausen's) pen. And I said: "Well, from what I understand, it was Cathy Berberian who had these sounds in her." I mean was the source of Luciano's vocal writing. And this is something I am adamant about … her laugh [she imitates it]. Berio notates it as it progressively went up in pitch. That's one of the first things I noticed as I got to know Cathy. I thought about "Sequenza III" and realized he actually notated her laugh! … [H]e notated everything else that she did too. I mean, her sigh [Carol demonstrates]. (Snapper 2014, 205–212)

Recognizing Berberian's authorship within the compositional process is significant in its own right, but the implications for her collaborators are fascinating. Those composers who drew directly from her improvisations, such as John Cage and Sylvano Busotti, as well as Berio, must now be understood as interpreters of *her* work as well. Their interpretations are performed not on stage but in the act of composing itself. (Composing for Berberian!) Recognizing the true complexity of the compositional process in (and beyond) *Visage* reroutes the compositional conveyor belt; it disrupts the predominant procreative model by making husband and wife coactive as seed planter and incubator for the musical work.

A Small Digression

This creative dynamic extends beyond *Visage* into Berio's later related work for unaccompanied solo voice, *Sequenza III*. *Sequenza III* shares essential sonic and dramaturgical aspects with *Visage*. The roughly seven-minute work is structured through 40 affective cues that shift rapidly, taking the singer from states of high agitation to sensual dissociation. In addition to sung tones, the vocalist mutters nontext under her breath, gasps, sighs, and releases cadenzas of laughter. Berberian's body and her ideas are diagrammed in *Sequenza III*. The sonic palette is established by Berberian. Berio interprets, builds on, and scores these sounds and then gives them back to Berberian to interpret in performance. In a way, *Sequenza III* visually maps out the creative exchange between Berio and Berberian. Whereas *Visage* records Berberian in the studio, *Sequenza III* "records" Berberian's unique vocal behaviors in the notated score. This has interesting implications for the evolution of contemporary vocalism. If *Sequenza III* is central to the contemporary vocal canon, so is a transaction between Berberian and classical vocalists who follow in her footsteps. A voice is more unique to its person than a fingerprint is. We can hear the internal architecture of a person through their voice, along with traces of their history and enculturation. Learning *Sequenza III* entails taking Berberian's voice into our throats, a very intimate transfer. At the heart of classical entrainment, then, is a kind of voluntary "possession" by Berberian.

Alongside this process of embodying the voice of Berberian, the singer who takes on *Sequenza III* must also delve into the core of her own specific voice and psychic makeup. Carol Plantamura, an early and influential interpreter of *Sequenza III*, describes the piece as both physically and psychically demanding, requiring the vocalist to "probe her plumbing" (Plantamura, personal communication, ca. 2014). One must investigate her personal relationship to the 44 affective cues and then draw them to the surface in rapid and regimented sequence. Berberian compares the work to virtuosic coloratura work. Like a bel canto "mad scene," the singer must demonstrate complete control over her instrument while acting out a loss of control. With Berberian's laugh in her throat, she must contact her own emotional past while maintaining a connected presence; that is, an openness to and awareness of her audience.

Accounts from both singers and audience members indicate a shared vulnerability that results. Even her collaborator, composer Louis Andriessen, describes an uncanny intimacy in Berberian's performances: "She made you feel very close when she sang. The openness and intimacy was almost embarrassing" (de Swaan 1994). Berberian conveys the transference she considers part and parcel of the performing act. "When you sigh, the audience sighs," she tells a student, "They are just as tense" (de Swaan 1994). This visceral connection between singer and listener may linger even in the transcription of Berberian's sighs. Plantamura recounts extreme compulsive responses from audiences in early performances of *Sequenza III*:

> When I was on tour in New Zealand, I was singing Sequenza and I began to hear strange sounds coming from the audience (Carol moans abjectly to demonstrate, "ehhhnnnnn-uhhhnnnnnnnnn …"). I just kept performing. I couldn't think about it. But according to John and Marijke who were on stage watching the audience while I was performing it, a woman seemed to have lost it. She was moaning, and then she started giggling! And the person with her took her gently out. I heard it when it was happening but you know, when you're performing you don't stop! … The other incident occurred during an Arts Council tour in Great Britain. We were in a town north of England, in Scotland. … I was performing Sequenza in a church. And a gentleman, the only way I can describe him, tall, elegant-looking. Somewhat elderly. Got up and walked up the tiled aisle of the church. I could hear the clink clink clink [of his shoes] and I thought, "Oh that's interesting." He wasn't trying to be quiet. And when he got to the door he turned around—I was still performing Sequenza—and looked at me and said: "SHAME!" And then walked out. [Carol laughs] Yes it was a procession. (Snapper 2014, 205–212)

The Voice Unleashed from Language

In his analysis of Berio's *Sequenza III*, Jean-François Lyotard (1993, 15–36) identifies a singular quality of musical vocalism that rings from cracks between the deliberate and accidental vocal utterance. He describes it as a "sonority of the affect." Full of feeling, yet ambiguous in meaning, this sonority erodes the "meaningful units" of language and opens "a figural space of anxiety at the heart of discourse." Eco's interest in the meanings in and around a composed text was shared by (and influential to) many other philosophers and critical theorists. It may be useful at this point to have some concrete terms for what can be a very messy topic. Sometimes described as "liminal semiotics," it can be tricky to put into words the meanings that emerge from the slippage of voice and language. Stutters, faltering, and hesitations mark measures for humans to cope with failures in the process of verbal communication and the recurrent inadequacy of words alone to encapsulate meaning. Where the voice makes sounds between words, or beyond the bounds of language, we register them nonetheless as units of meaning. Julia Kristeva (1975) considers these interstitial sounds a secondary text that she calls "geno-text," the expressive noise that emerges from the breakage in coherent sentences (pheno-text). Roland Barthes has extended Kristeva's categories of structured vocality and the vocality of the "everything else" to singing. Pheno-song is the composed musical text and the culturally entrained instrument that interprets it. Geno-song encompasses the particularity of the individual voice—the "grain" of the voice. Geno-song encompasses those acoustic qualities that distinguish one tenor from another, the ineffable affective content that marks one singer's interpretation of a Schubert lied from another's. In those performances where it emerges, the vocal "grain" connects with the listener outside genre and syntax. The "grain," wrote Barthes, is "the body in the voice as it sings" (Barthes 1977). It opens an erotic channel between listener and singer by which extradiscursive information can transfer. Those aspects of voice that exceed symbolic systems (language, music) seem to have an immediacy that words can only aspire to. Since most human listeners share the basic physiological dynamics of vocality, we recognize and register degrees of tension in another's body: the constriction of an angry throat or the abdominal pulse that powers a shout. Our bones also vibrate with the frequencies transmitted by another's voice in the places our own voices rattle: chest, neck, head. This visceral exchange is especially noticeable when witnessing a body in extremis; that is, a body temporarily overcome by sensation or loss of sense. The sounds humans make under various states of physical and emotional duress carry across linguistic barriers. Like clearing our own throat when someone speaks to us with a "frog" in their throat, or crying out when we see another person stumble, our bodies may mirror, to some degree, our perceived state of the affected body. The sounds we experience outside language have the potential to bypass the critical brain of the hearer, upsetting the relative orientation of our bodies, however briefly.

Back to Visage

There are key differences between *Visage* and *Sequenza III*. In the live solo vocal piece, the sonic palette and affective scope are more constrained. The voice is grounded in a poetic text and mediated by the presence of the body vocalizing. In conventional concert or theater settings, several factors may mitigate the immediacy of our response. The material and ritual elements of the classical performance, proscenium/setting/ritual, narrative, other actors, and so on, orient the audience in relation to the performing body. But when these factors are not present in the usual way, the listener's orientation vis-à-vis the sounding body may lose its moorings. We become literally disoriented. Linda Dusman explains that within the fixed media of the tape piece, the absence of the expressive body exacerbates the impact of the text on the listener: "No interpreter or mediator stands between the sound of the music itself and the body of the listener," leading to what she describes as an "extreme" and even threatening transfer of awareness onto the body of the listener in the public space (Dusman 2000). Richard Causton describes a transfer of the metaphorical spotlight, in the absence of a visible performing body, onto the listener's body, generating "an endless feedback loop of psychic disturbance between the person (becoming intermittently the subject) who apprehends it, and the sound source itself" (Causton 1995, 19).

The Body at Stake

So what makes these works enduringly upsetting, embarrassing, or even obscene, whereas other works playing at the edges of language and song are not? Kurt Schwitters's *Ursonate* (1932) is a rhythmic solo voice work composed entirely of nonlanguage. Arnold Schoenberg's *Pierrot Lunaire* (1912) smears song into speech and back again on expressionist texts. These works were shocking in their time but have since been absorbed into the classical canon. And what of other pioneers of New Vocality, both contemporary with and following on the heels of Berberian, such as Joan La Barbara and Meredith Monk? Their experimentations and new virtuosities of voice are just as radical, but their critical reception is not charged with descriptions of loss of self or accusations of obscenity. La Barbara quotes Berberian: "I'll tell you something that my experience with people with extended vocal technique is just that it's a fabulous source of research. But it—for the moment—it has hit an impasse. … I doubt that most of the people involved can really sing in the true sense of the word, you see. And they're kind of—I don't want to be offensive because I don't intend this—but they're, in a way, they're freaks, they're phenomena—what they used to call me. But it wasn't true in my case because I can also sing, you see" (Berberian in La Barbara 1976).

La Barbara's use of this quotation in her piece "Cathing" sets up a kind of challenge to Berberian's seeming dismissal of extended vocalists, but if we carefully unpack Berberian's statement, we begin to see a constructive differentiation between Berberian's ideas and a largely undifferentiated repertory of experimental vocality within Western classical music. What does she mean by extended techniques in isolation versus extended vocality from a performer who "also sing[s]"? La Barbara and other extended vocalists are singing, too! But digging a little deeper into Berberian's ideas reveals that she is speaking about a specific relationship to entrainment and experimentation with substantive implications for the performative act (and, I confess, ideas that have been key in my own creative work).

Berberian refers to the need for the contemporary vocalist to maintain a relationship to the classical instrument and repertoire in order for her departures from those conventions to be meaningful within classical music: "In order to understand the New Vocality it is essential to establish that art must reflect and express its own era; and yet it must refer to the past, accepting the weight of history … it must, while apparently creating a break, provide a continuity which belongs to the present and at the same time leaves the door open to the future" (Berberian 2016, 48).

In addition to her work with contemporary composers, Berberian performed repertory opera and recital repertoire from the seventeenth to nineteenth centuries. She cultivated and maintained her traditional bel canto instrument alongside her experimental performances, and thus the intact operatic body was also at stake when she vocalized outside the boundaries of bel canto practice. Meredith Monk and Joan La Barbara share with Berberian some degree of classical vocal training, but their aims and application of the trained instrument diverge. Monk and La Barbara use classical vocality as a springboard for developing new sonic palettes. They articulate their creative practices in terms of musical and vocal research and the cultivation of a singular compositional vocabulary.

Contemporary singer and composer Kristen Nordeval discusses both artists in the context of interviews with them:

> [La Barbara] created a vocabulary of breath sounds, multiphonics, circular singing, ullulation, and glottal clicks that became her signature sounds … but rather than simply presenting the sounds fully formed, La Barbara preferred instead to fragment them, pull them apart, and even create what she calls "impossible sounds" such as a series of inhales [without?] exhales.
>
> Though Berberian and Monk are often grouped together as experimental new music vocalists, the contrast between them is stark. As much as Cathy Berberian enjoyed imitating different folk traditions, she was very much a product of the opera world. She prized the traditions of coloratura and Bel Canto singing technique, and she measured other singers according to their mastery of those traditions. Meredith Monk, on the other hand, considers Western classical

traditions in both ballet and opera to have imposed a codified system of standardizations that leaves little room for appreciation of unique and fascinating variations in each individual performer. ... Monk again: "I've made my own style, my own vocabulary." (Nordeval 2014, 185–204)

The body of a singer must be understood as both an explicit and implicit instrument. The classical relationship to formal entrainment prepares a musical-dramatic context, a set of expectations that shapes meaning. By separating themselves from the operatic voice, La Barbara and Monk free themselves from these associations. The virtuoso of extended techniques sets up no expectations, refers to no stable traditional use of the instrument. As such, no matter how far from the classical instrument they "extend," there is no implicit conflict. A sonic gesture on the tongue of the vocal sound artist, a vocal fry for example, comes to meaning differently than that same vocal fry from an operatic body. The latter violates the boundaries of operatic entrainment and convention and potentially puts the vocal instrument at risk. Here lies the difference between extended vocality as its own practice and extended vocality from the performer who "can also sing." Her implicit body, the fact that she is an opera singer, changes the stakes. The opera singer who digresses from the seamlessly rich and vibrant bel canto aesthetic signals, on some level, physical failure or a psychic break; in either case, a ruinous loss of control or a violation. In the words of Amelia Jones and Marin Blazevic, the expressive crux is exactly here, where the disciplined body performs in friction with the drive to rebel: "the hinge between explicit and implicit embodiment—between a body constrained by habit, disciplines, techniques or regulatory practices and one driven to expose, violate, trouble, parody or shatter these constraints" (Jones and Blazevic 2014, 140–143).

Body Art with No Body There

In order to fully apprehend *Visage*, we must take into consideration the exceptional nature of its generativity, its reception, and the relative stakes of the performing body as components of the total work. This opens up some interesting analytical territory and unexpected bedfellows. Neither their cohort nor aesthetic concerns overtly connect them to emergent modes of performance art. On the surface, they are not obvious allies, but if we take into consideration Amelia Jones's definition of body art, it becomes less of a leap: "[Body art] provides the possibility for radical engagements that can transform the way we think about meaning and subjectivity (the artist's and our own). ... [It] demonstrates that meaning is an exchange and points to the impossibility of any practice being inherently positive or negative in cultural value (Jones 1998, 14).

Visage is occasionally compared to the better-known work for voice and electronics by Karlheinz Stockhausen, *Gesang der Jünglinge* (Song of the Youth), for manipulated voice and electronics on tape (1956). *Gesang der Jünglinge* was written five years before *Visage*, and in surface terms, the sonic parameters, electronic dramaturgy, and applied technology (see table 12.2) of the two works are very similar. Stockhausen takes a single treble voice, prerecorded in the studio, and then reorganizes and manipulates that recording in a variety of ways. The vocal material is situated in various layers and spatial relationships to the listener within a texture of inorganic sounds that seem to slither beneath or erupt out of the vocal material. If we analyze the two side by side, however, in terms of *how* meaning happens in the works, the differences are significant. The vocal material in *Gesang* is conventional, acoustically and affectively limited, and the body generating it is as yet unencultured or lived in. Its feminine, doughy premasculinity is not that of an individual person's voice but rather a nameless symbol of universalized humanity questioning God's writ.

Stockhausen's path led further into what might now be called performance art. Berberian and Berio kept to concert music. In their work together, they have more in common with body art.

Consider the performative paintings of contemporary painter Yves Klein. In his *Anthropometries* (1961), Klein poured paint on naked women and pressed them, or they pressed themselves, onto canvases. In essence, he engineered a living printing press, resulting in multiple abstract "nudes" without heads. Their "visages," their unique faces, are not included. In a way, Klein engages the classical feminine nude subject in a novel way. Each subject is also an active participant. Yet these women are not named in the work, nor is their agency in the process (such as it is) acknowledged within the creative act. Rather, their participation in the work is reduced to an anonymous imprint; a nameless, headless object; a human paintbrush. Naked women were given the public

Table 12.2

Comparison of *Visage* and *Gesang der Jünglinge*

Visage	*Gesang der Jünglinge*
• No musical or linguistic text or quotations	• Clear referential musical and linguistic text
• Specific (experienced, experiential) body	• An anonymous boy soprano
• Vocal subject has agency	• Vocal subject has no agency
• Process as component of meaning (complex authorship)	• Conventional authorship
• Unconventional engagement with audience	• Easy listening, or conventional receptivity

labor of the painterly act without subjective agency of any kind. This is not to say that the experimental performative works of Stockhausen and Klein should be considered failures but rather that it is important to examine just what is at stake when looking at experimental work.

In 1964, three years after *Anthropometries* and *Visage*, Yoko Ono premiered *Cut Piece* in the Yamaichi Concert Hall in Kyoto. In *Cut Piece*, Ono sits on the concert stage dressed formally with a scissors in her hand. Her "score" (her term) is in the hands of each member of the audience. They are invited to come on stage and cut off a piece of her clothing, which they are permitted to keep. Ono is a vocalist, but she remains silent. The predominant sounds are the footsteps of people approaching (some hesitant and others decisive) and the snipping friction of scissors on cloth. Like the Klein and Stockhausen works, a feminine body is at the center of the performed work. The body is visible and touchable in *Cut Piece*, and the voice within is silent, whereas the opposite is true in *Visage*, there is significant overlap:

1. The specificity of the material body in performance
2. The viscerality of the "everyday" body in tension with the entrained body within a high art context (the concert hall)
3. The agency of the performing subject in the creative process
4. The invitation to and necessity for the audience to situate themselves within the unfolding work
5. The violation of entrained boundaries and the performing body in extremis

These elements take these performances beyond simply experimental or shocking and open the potential for a substantial reorientation of subjectivity and the exchange of meaning within the performative work.

Understanding *Visage* as a visceral performance work that challenges how meaning takes shape from the very process of creation through demands made on the listener, offers a starting point for reevaluating late modernism and early media performance. Recognizing Berberian's active role in her collaborations with Berio is an overdue project, but just as urgent is the recognition of Berio's receptivity and the acts of creation and interpretation, consistent with the "Open Work," in their collaborative process. Taking Berberian's ideas about contemporary vocality seriously, specifically the expressive dichotomy of classical virtuosity and its sonic breakage, may shed new light on the charged reception of her experimental work with Berio. Here is a jumping-off point for the development of a more nuanced historical understanding of late modernism and contemporary vocality that might enrich and refresh classical music making and vocality moving forward.

References

Barthes, Roland. 1977. *Image-Music-Text*. New York: Hill and Wang.

Berio, Luciano, 1961. "Visage" (author's liner), *Electronic Music (LP)*. New York: Turnabout. http://www.lucianoberio.org.

Berio, Luciano, Rossina Dalmonte, and Bálint András Varga. 1985. *Two Interviews*. New York: M. Boyears.

Causton, Richard, 1995. "Berio's *Visage* and the Theatre of Electroacoustic Music." *Tempo* 194:15–21.

Dusman, Linda. 2000. "No Bodies There: Absence and Presence in Acousmatic Performance." In *Music and Gender* (edited by Pirkko Moisala and Beverley Diamond). Urbana : University of Illinois Press, 336–346.

Eco, Umberto. 1962. *Opera aperta*. Milano: Bompiani.

Jones, Amelia. 1998. *Body Art: Performing the Subject*. Minneapolis: University of Minnesota Press.

Jones, Amelia, and Marin Blazevic. 2014. "The Voice of Death, Rupturing the Habitus." *Performance Research* 19 (3) (January: *On Time*): 140–143.

Kristeva, Julia. 1975. *The System and the Speaking Subject*. Lisse: Peter de Ridder Press.

La Barbara, Joan. 1976. "Cathing." In *The Voice Is the Original Instrument*. Vinyl LP). New York: Lovely Music.

Lyotard, Jean-Francois. 1993. "A Few Words to Sing." In *Music/Ideology: Resisting the Aesthetic*, edited by Adam Krims, 15–36. Amsterdam: G+B International.

Muller, Theo. 1997. "'Music Is Not a Solitary Act': Conversation with Luciano Berio." *Tempo* 199 (January): 16–20.

Nordeval, Kristin. 2014. "What We Owe to Cathy: Reflections from Meredith Monk, Joan La Barbara, Rinde Eckert, Susan Botti, Theo Bleckmann and Pamela Z." In *Cathy Berberian: Pioneer of Contemporary Vocality*, edited by Pamela Karantonis, Francesca Placanica, and Pieter Verstraete. Farnham: Ashgate Press. 174–189.

Osmond-Smith, David. 1991. *Berio*. Oxford Studies of Composers 20. Oxford: Oxford University Press.

Osmond-Smith, David. 2004. "The Tenth Oscillator: The Work of Cathy Berberian 1958–1966." *Tempo* 58 (227) (January): 2–13.

Snapper, Juliana. 2014. "All with Her Voice: A Conversation with Carol Plantamura." In *Cathy Berberian: Pioneer of Contemporary Vocality*, edited by Pamela Karantonis, Francesca Placanica, and Pieter Verstraete, 205–212. Farnham: Ashgate Press.

de Swaan, Carrie. 1994. *Cathy Berberian: Muziek is mijn adem (Music Is the Air I Breathe)*. Documentary film. http://www.swaanprodukties.nl/web/index.php?p=3&project=35.

Author Biographies

Taylor Ackley is a performer, composer, and scholar who specializes in aurally based musical practices. Born into a working class family with a remarkable heritage of traditional American music, his work grows directly out of this rich musical expression. While he is first and foremost a folk musician and a scholar of traditional American music, his research also explores aural analysis of twentieth and twenty-first century western art music as well as establishing theoretical foundations for more meaningful conversations between western art and vernacular musics within the academy. He is currently a PhD candidate at Stony Brook University where he studies composition and ethnomusicology.

Marc Battier is an electroacoustic music composer, a distinguished professor at Shenzhen University in charge of computer music, and emeritus professor of musicology at Sorbonne University (Paris). He has taught at the University of California (San Diego and Irvine), Montreal University in Canada, and Aichi University of the Arts in Japan. He is a master of electroacoustic music at DeTao Masters Academy (China) and is a member of the Global Center for Advanced Studies ("where sound meets thought"). He worked at the Institute for Research in Coordination of Acoustics and Music (IRCAM) in Paris. In his younger years, he was assistant to composers such as John Cage, Karlheinz Stockhausen, François Bayle, Joji Yuasa, and others.

He is the founder of EMSAN (Electroacoustic Music Studies Asia Network) and, with Leigh Landy, of the Electroacoustic Music Studies Network (EMS). He is a board member of *Organised Sound* and the *Malaysian Journal of Music*, he has been on the board of *Computer Music Journal* and *Leonardo Music Journal* (MIT Press), and is an honorary editor of the latter. He was a cofounder of the International Computer Music Association.

For his work as a composer, he has received many commissions from France, the United States, China, and Japan, and has composed many works, including several for Asian instruments, often presented in the Central Conservatory of Music (CCOM) festival, Beijing, and music for art films.

Valentina Bertolani is a musicologist working in cultural diplomacy, collective improvisation, and electronic music. She is also interested in cultural policy, listening theory, and tensions between transnational and local cultural networks. She has coedited the book *Live-Electronic Music: Composition, Performance, Study* (2018). She has published chapters in edited volumes and an article in *Music Theory Online*. She received the Deep Listening® certificate from the Deep Listening Institute. She holds a PhD from the University of Calgary (Canada) and master's and bachelor's degrees from the Department of Musicology and Cultural Heritage of the University of Pavia. She recently created Curating Diversity, an online platform that collects data and brings awareness to the challenges that women and minorities face within the music industry in Italy. She has taught at the University of Calgary, the University of Birmingham, and the University of Nottingham.

Kerry L. Hagan is a composer and researcher working in both acoustic and computer media. She develops real-time methods for spatialization and stochastic algorithms for musical practice. Her work endeavors to achieve aesthetic and philosophical aims while taking inspiration from mathematical and natural processes. In this way, each work combines art with science and technology from various domains. She performs regularly with Miller Puckette as *the Higgs whatever* and with John Bowers in the *Bowers-Hagan Duo*.

As a researcher, her interests include real-time algorithmic methods for music composition and sound synthesis, spatialization techniques for 3D sounds, and electronic/electroacoustic musicology. In 2010, she led a group of practitioners to form the Irish Sound, Science and Technology Association, where she served as president until 2015. She also serves on the board of the International Computer Music Association.

She holds a BFA in music composition, with additional studies in conducting, from Carnegie Mellon University (CMU). She also has a BS in electronic and computer engineering from CMU. She received her MA and PhD in music from the University of California, San Diego. She is a Lecturer Above the Bar at the University of Limerick, Ireland, in the Digital Media and Arts Research Centre, where she teaches computer music. She is the principal investigator for the Spatialization and Auditory Display Environment (SpADE) at the University of Limerick.

Yvette Janine Jackson is a composer, sound installation artist, and assistant professor in the Department of Music at Harvard University. She was introduced to electroacoustic music in the 1990s while a student working in the Columbia-Princeton Electronic Music Center as it was transitioning into the Computer Music Center and further developed her practice working as a theatrical sound designer. She combines electroacoustic music, improvisation, and voice to bring attention to social issues and historical events, resulting in the development of narrative soundscape composition, a means of pivoting between academic research and creative practice while exploring culture through sound. Her research on listening and on radio drama as electroacoustic music and her spatial acousmatic music have been presented in Europe and the United States. She holds a BA in music from Columbia University and a PhD in music-integrative studies from the University of California, San Diego.

Leigh Landy holds a research chair at De Montfort University (Leicester, United Kingdom), where he directs the Music, Technology and Innovation—Institute for Sonic Creativity (MTI²). Before that, he directed the Experimental Music program at the Universiteit van Amsterdam, was head of music at Bretton Hall, and head of contemporary arts at Manchester Metropolitan University. His scholarship is divided between creative and musicological work. His compositions, many of which are sample based, include several for video, dance, and theater and have been performed around the globe. He worked extensively with late playwright Heiner Müller, new media artist Michel Jaffrennou, and composer-performer Jos Zwaanenburg, and was composer in residence for the Dutch National Theatre during its first years of existence. He is also artistic director of

Idée Fixe: Experimental Sound and Movement Theatre. Many of his works have been performed around the globe, and he has received commissions from international festivals, radio stations, ensembles, and venues. His publications focus primarily on studies of electroacoustic music. He is editor of *Organised Sound* and author of eight books, including *What's the Matter with Today's Experimental Music?* (1991), *Understanding the Art of Sound Organization* (MIT Press 2007), and *The Music of Sounds* (2012). His more recent publications include the ebook *Compose Your Words* (2014) and the coedited book (with Simon Emmerson) *Expanding the Horizon of Electroacoustic Music Analysis* (2016). He is currently completing the book *On the Music of Sounds and the Music of Things* with John Richards. His analytical writings have appeared in various books and journals. He directs the ElectroAcoustic Resource Site, or EARS, projects (www.ears.dmu.ac.uk and www.ears2.dmu.ac.uk) and is a founding director of the Electroacoustic Music Studies Network (EMS, www.ems-network.org). His personal website can be found at www.llandy.dmu.ac.uk.

Pamela Madsen is a composer, performer, theorist, and curator of new music. From her massive landscape-inspired projects and intimate chamber music creations to her multimedia electroacoustic opera collaborations and immersive deep listening works, she has created a body of work focusing on the integration of image, music, and text, with research on the influence of technology on compositional thought, improvisation, and open form, biomechanisms of vibroacoustics, sound, and the environment. She has a PhD in music composition from the University of California, San Diego, Mellon Foundation awards for her doctoral studies in music theory at Yale University, postdoctoral research at the Institute for Research in Coordination of Acoustics and Music (IRCAM) in Paris, and a Deep Listening® certificate with Pauline Oliveros. Her works have been commissioned and premiered worldwide.

Her works focus on the creation of large-scale, concert-length, transformative multimedia experiences that engage issues of social change. Her large-scale projects include a US embassy/Russian embassy tour with the Moscow Contemporary Music Ensemble for Music Across Borders, National Endowment for the Arts and New Music USA commission for *Oratorio for the Earth: There Will Come Soft Rains* with the Los Angeles Percussion Quartet, Eclipse Quartet, Ashley Bathgate, and Vicki Ray; *Luminous Etudes: Visions of the Black Madonna of Montserrat* with Loadbang and pianists Kathleen Supove and Eleonor Sandresky; *Luminosity: Passions of Marie Curie*, a multimedia opera for musicians from soundscape, Either/OR, and Arctic Research; *Melting Away: Gravity* for orchestra, with photographer Camille Seaman; *Sedna* for Zeitgeist; *Land of the Moon* for the Bugallo-Williams Piano Duo; *Envisioning the Future Project* with visual artist Judy Chicago; and *We Are All Sibyls*, a multimedia installation/opera premiered throughout Los Angeles.

Her intimate chamber music works focusing on spoken text, improvisation, electronics, and music have been commissioned and premiered by such artists as Claire Chase, Jane Rigler, Anne La Berge, Lisa Moore, Sarah Cahill, Ashley Bathgate, Trio Solisti, New York New Music Ensemble, California Ear Unit, Verdehr Trio, Zeitgeist, JACK, Ethel, Lyris, and the Arditti String Quartet, with multimedia collaborations with video artists Quintan Ana Wikswo and Jimena Sarno. Selected as an Alpert Award panelist and Creative Capital artist "on the radar" with awards from the National Endowment for the Arts, New Music USA, and Meet the Composer, and artist fellowship residency awards at MacDowell Colony, UCross, Santa Fe Women's International Studies Center, and American Scandinavian Foundation, she is a frequent guest lecturer, composer-performer-improviser, and invited scholar at universities and festivals worldwide. She is curator of the Annual New Music Festival and World Electro-acoustic Listening Room Project, and director of the New Music Ensemble and InterArts collaborative projects at California State University, Fullerton, where she is professor of music composition and theory.

Miller Puckette obtained a BS in mathematics from the Massachusetts Institute of Technology (MIT) in 1980 and PhD in mathematics from Harvard University in 1986, winning a National Science Foundation graduate fellowship and the Putnam Fellowship. He was a member of MIT's Media Lab from its inception until 1987 and was then a researcher at the Institute for Research in Coordination of Acoustics and Music (IRCAM), founded by composer and conductor Pierre Boulez. At IRCAM, he wrote Max, a widely used computer music software environment, released commercially in 1990 and now available from Cycling74.com.

Puckette joined the music department of the University of California, San Diego, in 1994, where he is now professor. From 2000 to 2011, he was associate director of UCSD's Center for Research in Computing and the Arts (CRCA, now defunct). He is currently developing Pure Data ("Pd"), an open-source real-time multimedia arts programming environment. He has collaborated with many artists and musicians, including Philippe Manoury (whose *Sonus ex Machina* cycle was the first major work to use Max), Rand Steiger, Vibeke Sorensen, Juliana Snapper, and Kerry Hagan. Since 2004, he has performed with the Convolution Brothers. He has received honorary degrees from Université de Mons and Bath Spa University and was awarded the 2008 Society for Electro-Acoustic Music in the United States (SEAMUS) Lifetime Achievement Award.

David Rosenboom is a composer, performer, interdisciplinary artist, author, and educator known as a pioneer in American experimental music. His work explores ideas about the spontaneous evolution of musical forms, languages for improvisation, new techniques in scoring for ensembles, multidisciplinary composition and performance, cross-cultural collaborations, performance art and literature, interactive multimedia and new instrument technologies, generative algorithmic systems, art-science research and philosophy, and extended musical interfacing with the human nervous system. He holds the Richard Seaver Distinguished Chair in Music at the California Institute of the Arts, where he has been dean of the Herb Alpert School of Music since 1990. Recent work highlights include 50-year retrospective performances at the Whitney Museum of American Art, New York (2015); an exhibition of brainwave music at Centre Pompidou-Metz, France (2015–2016); an exhibition of computer music software innovations at Whitechapel Gallery, London (2015–2016); a retrospective of piano music at Tokyo Opera City Recital Hall (2016); the premiere of *Nothingness Is Unstable* at ISSUE Project Room, Brooklyn (2017); electronic music featured by inaGRM at Le Centquatre-Paris (2018); a composer-pianist portrait at the Center for Experiments at Teatro Colón, Buenos Aires (2018); and a spring 2019 tour with performances and presentations in Los Angeles, Rotterdam, Brussels, London, Copenhagen, and Stockholm. Following his Whitney retrospective, he was lauded in the *New York Times* as an "avatar of experimental music." He is a Yamaha Artist. His website is at www.davidrosenboom.com.

Jøran Rudi's first academic training was in the social sciences, followed by a few years as a rock musician in Kjøtt, one of the influential bands that emerged at the end of the 1970s. This brought him in contact with electronic instruments and electroacoustic music, and he traveled to the

United States and studied computer music at New York University. In 1990, he returned to his native Norway and was brought in to be the founding director of the Norwegian Center for Technology in Music and Art (NOTAM) in 1993. From 1993 to 2010, he was responsible for the academic and artistic profiles of the institution, its research and development, mediation, education, administration, and economy. He stepped back to a researcher position at NOTAM in 2010.

His research interests span widely, from educational issues arising from the use of music technology, via studies of artistic genres such as music, music animation, soundscape, and sound art to more conventional musicological work with a historical orientation. As a composer, he has developed a portfolio of works for electronic instruments and/or fixed media, as well as for dance, film, performance art, installation, and multimedia. His most significant artistic contributions are his computer music animations made in the mid- to late 1990s.

Margaret Anne Schedel has had an interdisciplinary career blending classical training in cello and composition, sound/audio data research, and innovative computational arts education, transcending the boundaries of disparate fields to produce integrated work at the nexus of computation and the arts. She has a diverse creative output, with works including the interactive multimedia opera *The King Listens*, virtual-reality experiences, sound art, video game scores, and compositions for a wide variety of classical instruments or custom controllers with interactive audio and video processing. She is internationally recognized for the creation and performance of ferociously interactive media and won the 2019 Pamela Z Innovation Award. Her solo CD *Signal through the Flames* will be released by Parma Records in 2020. She holds a Deep Listening® certificate with Pauline Oliveros and has studied composition with Mara Helmuth, Cort Lippe, and McGregor Boyle and Geoffrey Wright and improvisation with George Lewis and Mark Applebaum. She is a joint author of *Electronic Music* and recently edited an issue of *Organised Sound* on using electroacoustic terminology to describe pre-electric sound. Her work has been supported by the Presser Foundation, Centro Mexicano para la Música y les Artes Sonoras, and Meet the Composer. She has been commissioned by the Princeton Laptop Orchestra, Ictus, reACT, Yarn|Wire, and the Unheard-of//Ensemble. Her research focuses on gesture in music, the sustainability of technology in art, and sonification of data. She coauthored a paper published in *Frontiers of Neuroscience* on using familiar music to sonify the gaits of people with Parkinson's Disease. She serves as a regional editor for *Organised Sound* and is an editor for the open-access journal *Cogent Arts and Humanities*. From 2009 to 2014, she helped run Devotion, a gallery in New York City focused on the intersection of art, science, new media, and design. As an associate professor of music at Stony Brook University, she taught the State University of New York's first Massive Open Online Course (MOOC) for Coursera, and she formerly served as the director of the Consortium for Digital Arts Culture and Technology. She currently serves as the chair of the Art Department and leads the Making Sense of Data Workgroup at the Institute of Advanced Computational Science. She also teaches composition for new media at the Peabody Institute of the Johns Hopkins University. In her spare time, she curates exhibitions focusing on the intersection of art, science, new media, and sound while running www.arts.codes, a platform and artist collective celebrating art with computational underpinnings.

Juliana Snapper is an opera singer, voice researcher, and artist. She received her BM in vocal performance from the Oberlin Conservatory and her MA in critical studies/experimental practices in music at the University of California, San Diego. She is a passionate interpreter of early and contemporary electroacoustic art song and monodrama. She gave the American debut of Philippe Manoury's watershed song cycle *en Echo*, later featured at the Pulitzer Foundation and Ojai Festival Main Stage. She is best known for her original work pushing the operatic voice to its breaking point by singing upside down as the mechanism collapses and singing under (and into) water, techniques she developed into large-scale touring works supported by the Arts Council of Great Britain, the Durfee Foundation, and the Robert Rauschenberg Foundation, among others, and discussed in journals and books. In 2014, the *Huffington Post* named her one of "Fourteen Artists Who Are Transforming the Future of Opera." She is currently based in Izmir, Turkey, where she is on the faculty at Yasar University.

Laura Zattra has used archives in her musicological practice for 20 years to construct histories of works (by John Chowning, Luigi Nono, Agostino Di Scipio, Salvatore Sciarrino, and others), authors (Teresa Rampazzi and Renata Zatti), centers (Centro di Sonologia Computazionale, CSC, in Padova; Institute for Research in Coordination of Acoustics and Music, IRCAM, in Paris; CCRMA in Stanford), collaborations (Fabbriciani-Nono, musical assistants, sound designers, and spectral composers), instruments (the NAGRA, MUSIC programs, and other early software and hardware applied to music), and emerging professions in music (computer music designers and sound designers). In her work, she incorporates philology and archaeology with oral history and ethnography, with an emphasis on science and technology studies.

She is an adjunct professor at Vicenza and Bologna Conservatories of Music and in the Department of Film Music at the Rovigo Music Conservatoire, a research fellow at IRCAM in Paris and IreMus (Sorbonne), and coeditor-in-chief of *Musica/Tecnologia*. She is the founder of the teresarampazzi.it website and is a member of the editorial committee of Projet Analyses (IRCAM, Paris) and *Organised Sound*.

She holds PhDs in musicology from the Sorbonne University and Trento University and is the author of *Live-Electronic Music: Composition, Performance and Study* (with F. Sallis, V. Bertolani, and I. Burle, 2018), *Renata Zatti: Invenzione Musicale* (critical edition, 2012), *Studiare la Computer Music: Definizioni, analisi, fonti* (2011), *Presenza storica di Luigi Nono—Historical presence of Luigi Nono* (with A. I. De Benedictis, 2011), and *Vent'anni di musica elettronica all'università di Padova. Il Centro di sonologia computazionale* (with S. Durante, 2002). She was senior researcher at the University of Padova from 2006 to 2012 and has been research associate at the Analysis of Musical Practices Research Group, IRCAM-CNRS (Paris), since 2012. Her website is at http://lazattra.wordpress.com/.

Index